web journalism://
a new form of citizenship?

web journalism://
a new form of citizenship?

edited by
sean tunney and garrett monaghan

sussex
ACADEMIC
PRESS

Brighton • Portland • Toronto

4 6 8 10 9 7 5 3

First published 2010 in Great Britain by
SUSSEX ACADEMIC PRESS
PO Box 139
Eastbourne BN24 9BP

and in the United States of America by
SUSSEX ACADEMIC PRESS
920 NE 58th Ave   Suite 300
Portland, Oregon 97213-3786

and in Canada by
SUSSEX ACADEMIC PRESS (CANADA)
90 Arnold Avenue, Thornhill, Ontario L4J 1B5

British Library Cataloguing in Publication Data
A CIP catalogue record for this book is available from the British Library.

Library of Congress Cataloging-in-Publication Data
Web journalism : a new form of citizenship? / edited by Sean Tunney and
   Garrett Monaghan.
p. cm.
Includes index.
ISBN 978-1-84519-278-5 (h/c : alk. paper) —
ISBN 978-1-84519-279-2 (p/b : alk. paper)
   1. Citizen journalism. 2. Online journalism. 3. User-generated content.
I. Monaghan, Garrett. II. Tunney, Sean.
PN4784.C615W43 2010
070.4—dc22
                                                        2009023701

Mixed Sources
Product group from well-managed
forests and other controlled sources
www.fsc.org Cert no. SGS-COC-2482
© 1996 Forest Stewardship Council

Text typeset and designed by Sussex Academic Press, Brighton & Eastbourne.
Cover design by Garrett Monaghan.
Printed by TJ International, Padstow, Cornwall.
This book is printed on acid-free paper.

⟨⟨ Contents ⟩⟩

Contents

⦃ *Preface and Acknowledgements* ⦄

At the time of writing the popular face of the Internet — the WWW — is less than two decades old, yet in the developed world it seems difficult to imagine society without its ubiquitous presence. This book came into being in response to a need to explain how one aspect of our media culture, the news, has been dramatically changed by this young phenomenon. The book is also a contribution to the emergence of an exciting new discipline — Internet studies.

Web journalism is the main, but not the only, cultural area considered in this book. A current, popular, supposition is that the traditional flow of information from media to citizen is being reformed into a democratic dialogue between members of a community. Taken as a whole, the chapters in *Web Journalism: A New Form of Citizenship?* bring together key contributors who ask whether the rise of interactive participatory forms of mainstream media, blogging and citizen journalism provide citizens with new opportunities to enter into a dialogue with those who control the flow of news. Even in chapters where citizenship is not obviously under discussion, the underlying questions about transforming the relationship between the traditional professional media and their audience, and the role of the journalist in a democracy are central themes.

Among the most important conduits between the citizen and political and economic institutions are the media. Rapid change in sections of the media is giving rise to fresh and pressing debates about online journalism. As we shall see, Web journalism embraces a number of different practices. In addition to professional journalism, we also examine the process of content production by audiences, which has been referred to variously as online journalism, participatory journalism, open source news, citizen journalism and citizen publishing, as well as blogging. The book stands at a point where it is already possible to look back over the first years of citizen publishing. And it will explore whether citizen journalism has developed in the way that was promised.

Newspaper readership has fallen rapidly over recent years. For instance, Roy Greenslade in the British *Guardian* newspaper carried out a survey of British newspaper sales and found that the monthly year-on-year drop for national dailies was 4.5 percent between December 2007 and December 2008 (Greenslade 2009).[1] The reasons for this decline are numerous, above and beyond competition from the Internet. Some commentators, such as Stuart Allan (2005a), have argued that decreasing public confidence in the credibility and accuracy of reporting is to blame. With the crucial effect of the added impact of reduced advertising, one leading British media commentator, Emily

Bell (2008), believes that parts of the British media industry will struggle to survive in the current economic climate. As Guardian News and Media's director of digital content, Bell has forecast that as many as five national newspapers could fold in the near future, along with local paper and regional radio networks. In the gloomy US press landscape, predictions have been particularly bleak (Pérez-Peña 2009).

As news organizations restructure to develop online media, in a bid to maintain their audiences and advertising, institutional practices are also in a state of transition. One outcome of these shifts is that journalists are under greater economic pressure to sell news. Coupled with the need to perform the new tasks required by a digital media culture, this results in more work pressure on staff, who have less time than they had previously to prepare stories. As Philip Meyer puts it, "journalism is in trouble" (Meyer 2004: 1; see also Hagerty 2005, Merrill Brown Carnegie Corporation Report 2005, Deuze 2007 and Dahlgren 2008).

Prior to this a striking gap had already opened up between what the public perceived newspapers to be doing and what journalists believed they were doing. A decade ago in the US, more than 80 percent of the public believed that newspapers chased sensational stories and over-dramatized them, merely to obtain higher sales. While only 17 percent of US journalists agreed with this view, there was clearly a perception that the codes of ethical journalism were being stretched over a framework of new market values that were less likely to open up new debates and promote a healthy citizenship (Urban 1999).

One way of gaining maximum attention — and thus sales — can be to combine sensation with heavily opinionated copy. An anxiety about the significance of this for democracy is that it potentially creates networks of the like-minded. Indeed, as Stuart Allan puts it, journalism is "even in danger of losing its place at the heart of democratic society" (Allan 2005a: 1). In repeating this we do not wish simply to equate journalism with democracy, as James Carey does in his third axiom — "Journalism is another name for democracy or, better, you cannot have journalism without democracy" (Carey 1996) — an equation that Tim Markham discusses later in this book.

As online news increasingly displaces the traditional formats of print, radio and television, especially for younger audiences, these new avenues of news dissemination call into question the traditional definitions of journalism. In the past journalists, and the organizations they worked for, marshalled information into stories designed to be funnelled in a one-way path from the journalist to the consuming audience. The claims for a new, online journalism is that information will be shared in a communal, pooled process, where the distinction between the journalist and the audience will break down, giving rise to a collective news production dialogue. Some foresee a danger that networks of the like-minded are increasing. How will this affect the news? Some of the central themes that arise include the take-up of online technologies in the newsroom, the concept of gatekeeping and its relationship to the citizen, and the way online news contributes to how audiences adopt, use and integrate news into their daily lives.

In this volume professional journalists and academic theorists, some of whom are also well-known bloggers, explore some of the utopian ideals put forward by early users of the Internet. They consider to what extent journalism has changed its practices to deal with having an online presence and what impact these changes are having on our notions of the media, truth, citizenship and the role of the journalist, and on our understanding of the world around us. The chapters of this book were written before the full extent of the 2008 economic tumult became clear. It was not at all obvious at the time of writing what effect the so-called credit crunch and banking crisis would have on Internet journalism, although there were those prophesying doom (Reeves 2008).

In some quarters there is a tendency to approach Internet journalism as a global phenomenon in a manner that obscures the local differences of practice, economy and political culture. That said, it is outside the scope of this book to provide a comprehensive summary of online journalism in every country, but we have sought to provide a mix of chapters that both deal with some aspects of the longer-established online domains, such as the US and Britain, and also consider other nations beyond the West.

In particular, the differing attitudes to transparency in both US participatory journalism and the mainstream are highlighted and the role of race and accountability in US blogging is examined. By contrast, the public service ethos of the world's largest broadcast news organization, the British Broadcasting Corporation, provides the platform from which its strategy of making user-generated content central is discussed. Alongside this we have included pioneering work that considers the possibilities for participatory journalism to facilitate new forms of citizenship in such diverse environments as China, India and Uganda, and among Palestinians and Israelis.

Following an introduction, the chapters are grouped into thematic sections beginning with a series of chapters that set the scene for what follows, by considering some key ideas and debates. The next section assesses the relationship between professional and citizen journalists. Case studies particularly consider whether citizen journalism is genuinely being incorporated by the mainstream and, if so, whether this is a positive development. They assess whether participatory journalism and blogging are affecting the gatekeeping role of mainstream news organizations. The third section considers the particular role of citizen journalism internationally, before finally considering whether one aspect of Internet journalism is set to undermine, rather than enhance, the rights of citizens. Implicit in a number of these chapters are pointers to careful and rigorous methodologies, which will be of value to those seeking to pursue their own research, particularly students. Thus, this book is directed at undergraduates and postgraduates, professional journalists and others investigating a range of disciplines, such as media and journalism studies, sociology, economics and Internet studies.

The editors would like to thank Matthew Taylor and the contributors for all their work.

Note

1   "That compares with 2% (2007–6), 3.2% (2006–5), 1.7% (2005–4), 3.2% (2004–3) and 3.8% (2003–2). Clearly, therefore, the downward trend is accelerating. I carried out the same survey for the Sunday nationals and the acceleration was even more marked. The decrease between December 2008 and December 2007 was 6.3%, far higher than the declines in the previous five years" (Greenslade 2009).

web journalism://
a new form of citizenship?

⫷ INTRODUCTION ⫸

Web Journalism:
Participation and Incorporation?

GARRETT MONAGHAN AND SEAN TUNNEY

MIGRATION: THE EMERGENCE OF ONLINE JOURNALISM

As some on one side of the digital divide write on our computers and, particularly on the move, other devices, we break off to check our bank statements, track an eBay purchase or reply to emails and MSN messages, update our blogs or post a new message on Facebook or Twitter. Thus we are moving towards both a multiplication and integration not just of different technologies for delivering audio, moving-image and networked computing, but also of social, political and commercial activity. While supply to some extent creates its own demand, the expansion of the everyday into a digital domain is a reciprocal process of technological development, the exploitation of opportunity and social demand — where regulatory frameworks and social and economic control provide the parameters for this process. Although "convergence" has become a widely used term in discussions about the gradual migration of older media forms online (for example, Kolodzy 2006 and Briggs and Burke 2005) it can be argued that, while these traditional forms of print and other media co-exist with new digital platforms, this proliferation also multiplies the facilities for communication rather than this just being a convergence of social, political and commercial activities (see also Hesmondhalgh 2007: 262–3, 274–5).

Many who write about the migration of journalism into a digital form do so through a spectrum of key moments. For example, we can examine peaks of Internet traffic on news sites. Stuart Allan (2005b) suggests that the seminal points in the emergence of online news took place in the second half of the 1990s. Thus the Oklahoma bombing in 1995, the crash of TWA 800 in 1996 and the death of Princess Diana in 1997 were shaping moments. Paul Bradshaw (2008) also created a similar list.

In this model key moments are driven by significant world events. The devastation of the World Trade Center in New York on 11 September 2001 is a quintessential example. As that crisis unfolded, news sites were unable to deal with the sudden increase in demand for up-to-date coverage. The online sites of two British newspapers registered unprecedented levels of activity: telegraph.co.uk received up to 600 hits per second, and guardian.co.uk received a similar surge in traffic. Likewise, in March 2003 the Gulf conflict prompted another increased flow of traffic to UK news sites. At this time guardian.co.uk estimated that 39 percent of its readers were US-based. Similarly, 1.3 million users visited guardian.co.uk on 7 July 2005 in the wake of the London bombings (Plunkett 2005).

While these are socially significant historical moments, the associated traffic jams can also be viewed as a hardware issue. Websites jammed because of insufficient server power, processing speed, bandwidth and so on. Focusing on technological issues such as this offers another historical paradigm to account for the technical and economic history of the hardware and software that have facilitated the emergence of Usenet groups, listservers, blogs, wikis and social media forums. David Carlson (2003) has provided a useful history of many of the technological developments, which it would not be profitable to repeat in this book. Nevertheless, there are some aspects of the history that will serve as a useful starting point for those who have arrived here wishing to consider the debates below within a technological framework. This is not to take a technologically determinist view, however, but to recognize also the social and economic framework within which the technology has operated.

The recent history of online news technology can be considered through perceptible periods of development. The period from the 1970s to the early 1990s saw the emergence of principles that are still central to our experience of computing. The use of central computers that others could link to via a telephone line was developed in the US. This early network (Arpanet) was initially reserved for military purposes but was quickly opened up to the academic community and later to business. For a more detailed history of the early rationale for this technology see Abbate (1999).

As this hardware interconnectivity emerged during the 1970s, new software was developed to exploit the possibilities of the medium. One key development for the dissemination of news was the appearance of bulletin board systems (Carlson 2003). Increasing domestic demand prompted the expansion of business services into the domestic marketplace. The Source and CompuServe emerged as two leading providers of interconnected services. CompuServe facilitated transactions for banking and shopping, as well as providing access to current news and information updates. Although the present network of Internet Service Providers (ISPs) is more complex, the underlying model is still one of streams of connectivity between one and many, many and one, and more recently between many and many. During the 1980s these streams of data became increasingly monitored, market-researched, legislated about and charged for, as cyberspace started to become part of everyday life.

By the start of the 1990s the Internet had become a new province that was being populated by shops, governments, banks, museums, publishers and other institutions. It was also a space where new social spaces began to emerge, in the form of chatrooms and other precursors of social networking sites. In part, this was made possible by further developments in software. The World Wide Web emerged in 1990, but, for many, it was not until the look of a computer screen became more like the graphic interfaces of today that computing became accessible. Significant advances came in 1990, with the arrival of the new, more user-friendly, graphic interface of Windows 3.0 and in 1993 Windows 3.11 — facilitating networking. The first popular web browser Mosaic was also released in 1993 and Netscape Navigator followed in 1994 as a free download.

These new visually friendly interfaces opened the door to personal computing for many more people. Computer networks had originally been developed in the US as military and academic enterprises. Fearful of abuses, US legislation prohibited commercial Internet traffic. However, increasing pressure to allow this led to social and economic assumptions to change, resulting in the US government legislating in favour of commerce and advertising in 1993.

The effect of this on Web journalism can be considered by looking at British national news sites. Although some newspapers were already available as bulletin boards, as millions of people started using the Web, news organizations were persuaded to develop a Web presence. However, the migration of British newspapers online was slower. In November 1994 the *Daily Telegraph* became the first national newspaper with a Web edition, the Electronic Telegraph. One reason the British media were slower to engage with the Internet was the slower rate of growth of home-based online computing in the UK. As this began to take off towards the end of the 1990s, *The Guardian* launched Guardian Unlimited on the World Wide Web in January 1999. By early 2009 this was a major global newspaper site, attracting up to 30 million visitors a month (Oliver 2009). Broadcasters have also taken this path. In December 1997 BBC Online brought BBC News and other aspects of public service broadcasting on to the Web.

Since 2000 the earlier development has been consolidated in a third, and current, phase that has been driven by the increasing development of commercialization applications on the Web. While the concept Web 2.0 provides a useful set of parameters for the current state, there is no significant technical difference between the Web now and when it was first developed. In contrast to Web 2.0, Web 3.0 is a conceptual term that allows thinking about applications, technology and software that are theoretically possible but which have not yet been developed.

The recent phase of fast broadband connections, wireless networks and possibilities for some profit has encouraged more British newspapers such as *The Times* and the *Daily Mail* to launch on the Web. Social networking, wikis, blogging and peer sharing also typify this period. With this, a new vocabulary has also emerged, engendering terms such as "blogosphere" and "folksonomy" (the practice of adding metadata or creating tag clouds). This enables users to personalize their navigation through the unwieldy quantities of information available on the Internet. This can work at an individual or collective level, where what is perceived to be salient is picked out from the background mass of data. At a simple level it might just be a way of organizing holiday snaps in a way that allows others to make quick selections.

Also typical of Web 2.0 usage are Web feeds: for example, Really Simple Syndication (RSS). RSS Web feeds emerged in 1999 using the Netscape browser. They enable the content of a website to reach niche audiences. Websites publish a link that end-users can register with a feed reader or aggregator running in their browser or a separate window. When instructed, the aggregator pulls up the links in its feed list: registering updates such as new blog entries, breaking news headlines, new audio or video postings, which can be read or linked to in the user's window. Most major news sites, blogs and even some public relations services now offer RSS feeds. The feeds allow a wide range of sources to be monitored for news and breaking stories. Examples of feeds include Google News, launched in 2002, followed by Microsoft's Newsbot in July 2004. This gathers news headlines from more than 4,800 sites (Borland 2004). RSS feeds do not just aid news consumers: they are widely regarded as an invaluable tool for journalists.

Automatic news indexes such as Google News use search algorithms to target news stories, where the most recent will move to the top of the list. This can have a significant impact on a mainstream site. For example, *The Scotsman* runs a feed from Associated Press. This is simply unsubbed wire news — something that would be less likely to appear in print in its entirety. The presence of feeds like this or Reuters on the site triggers the search algorithm which, in turn, posts a link back to the site — a link that can be used by the reader. By running the news wire the site will consistently break a story before any journalists will have had the time to rewrite it for the news site.

While RSS feeds are vital to the visibility of blogging sites and search engines and their automatic tools are important sources for pointing visitors to mainstream sites — promoting higher visibility in searches — the numbers of visitors to a mainstream site can also be significantly affected by citizen sites. In 2005 Drudgereport.com was solely responsible for 25 percent of US visitors to British news websites (Thurman 2007). On one story alone telegraph.co.uk had 1 million hits that were driven by the Drudge aggregator. Neil Thurman's valuable analysis of this phenomenon also reveals that British mainstream news website editors have mixed opinions about the relationship between citizen sites and their publications. While there is the obvious benefit of increasing visitor numbers to a site (and this has real material benefits in terms of potential advertising revenue), there is also a sense of the aggregator host benefiting from a freeloading relationship with the mainstream.

"Drudgereport.com and Fark.com have grown large by feeding off the stories their hosts provide. Respectively they receive 150 million (Intermarkets 2005) and 33 million (Fark 2005) page impressions per month and are as or more popular than many of the publications they aggregate content from" (Thurman 2007: 293). Servicing 150 million hits requires substantial bandwidth, which costs money — recouping that, or profiting from those readers, is something editors would like to improve on.

This preceding discussion provides just some of the background to help consider the relationship of citizens to the Internet and online journalism, and it is to this that we must now turn.

CITIZENS AND JOURNALISM

The relationship between the citizen, the state and the public sphere is a basic theoretical consideration in the study of journalism, and this can be traced back to the earliest days of the press. Edmund Burke's assertion in the eighteenth century that the press was a fourth estate of governance may not have the same purchase today as it did when Thomas Carlyle resurrected the idea in the mid-nineteenth century. But it is interesting to understand the relationship that Carlyle proposed between the power to have a voice and governance.

> Printing, which comes necessarily out of writing, I say often, is equivalent to Democracy: invent Writing, Democracy is inevitable. Writing brings Printing; brings universal every-day extempore Printing, as we see at present. Whoever can speak, speaking now to the whole nation, becomes a power, a branch of government, with inalienable weight in law-making, in all acts of authority. It matters not what rank he has, what revenues or garnitures: the requisite thing is, that he have a tongue which others will listen to; this and nothing more is requisite. The nation is governed by all that has tongue in the nation: Democracy is virtually *there*. (Carlyle 1841: 147, italics in the original)

However, not just anyone can speak in Carlyle's society; to have a voice — to be in print or to have your views reported — is only an option for an established elite (Curran 1993). Burke's thinking, which inspired Carlyle, comes from the same period that Habermas (1962) discusses in his idealized conception of a public sphere, where citizens could determine what was of importance and arrive at the best course of action through public debate. Although Habermas's notion of a public sphere is highly contested, it is at the core of theorizing the media and thus an important reference point for discussions about citizen journalism. (Dahlgren and Sparks 1993 provide a comprehensive introduction to these issues.)

However, the notion of a fourth estate suggests that the press was a tool for monitoring and checking the actions of the state as much as for providing news about the world we live in — a conduit between the citizens and the state and, more recently, the corporation. Arguably, Burke's conception of public deliberation is in line with that of Walter Lippmann.

Lippmann (1921, 1927) saw the role of the journalist as being to pass the decisions of the elite on to a public that did not have the time, the inclination or the knowledge to make informed decisions about details of policy. John Dewey (1927) argued a different case. His position promoted the improvement of social institutions: if the public was better educated — not just by schools but also by the quality of a journalism that enlisted the opinion of elites, experts and the general public — then discussions would arise that would promote better and more democratic decisions. This consultation with the many is what makes Dewey attractive to those promoting the concept of citizen journalism as a public voice. (For a fuller account of reclaiming Dewey see Ryfe and Mensing 2008; Gimmler 2001; and Evans 2000.)

THE PRODUCTIVE AUDIENCE

Over recent years a number of theorists have called into question the failure of the term "audience" to take into account the active role taken by consumers who are also becoming producers of content. For example, Silverstone (2006) argues that a sense of shared community is absent from the term "user". Bruns (2008) and Jenkins (2006) respectively propose a conflation of existing terms, suggesting "prosumer" and "produser" (see also Gillmor 2004; and Marshall 2004).

Arguably, the most significant evidence of the consumer as producer came with the emergence of socially networked communities of bloggers that collectively constitute the blogosphere. The blog index website Technorati defines the blogosphere as "[t]he ecosystem of interconnected communities of bloggers and readers at the convergence of journalism and conversation". Blood (2000) traces the emergence of blogs from sites that provided an archive of links to a particular subject that generally the author had a particular interest in, into a diary format where commentary appeared and which now might include graphics and video with links.

While blogs are composed of unfinished (or open-ended) fragments — either of characteristically opinionated, dated entries or conversations in a comments section — they can be understood to be "atomized" in much the same way that Web 2.0 marketeers use that term to refer to content that is broken down into smaller pieces. These atomized fragments can generally be accessed as independent threads or archived entries. However, blogs are also atomized inasmuch as they are dispersed across the time and space that are Web history and the global communications network. While blogging is geographically dispersed and isolated in this way, a blogger has little voice. In practice, blogging becomes a collectivized and collaborative event only through the agency of hyperlinking and the collective actions of networks of bloggers. It is only by being visible on search engines or via RSS feeds that audibility is achieved. Lowrey (2006) also argues that blogging achieves the status of a collective community through the sharing of codes of ethics and conventions. This, in turn, has evolved into a new form of citizen publishing on collective blog sites.

In the early days of the Internet, utopian claims suggested that the spaces for private conversations such as those on the Whole Earth Lectronic Link (WELL) would lead to an interaction between state and citizen, where a new and democratic space for participation in debate and voting would be serviced by the Internet. To some extent this was envisaged as a new public sphere in the Habermasian sense. There is not the space here to examine Habermas in depth — suffice to say that his construction of the public sphere out of spheres of influence that were delineated by issue, place and time is contested, notably by Negt and Kluge (1993), who argue, along with others, that the idea of a unified public is flawed. However, as much as Habermas's notion of the public sphere projects an idealized form, it nevertheless allows us to conceive of a social elite able to discuss important issues and, in turn, lobby for change. Habermas's notion of public place is also dependent on the distinction between public and private. He argues that this distinction broke down when the private became colonized by the institutions of the public world, allowing the traditional hierarchies of order and control to assert themselves. This is something Habermas, rather questionably, likened to a return to feudal society. Blogging has seen similar claims made for its democratizing potential. However, it is arguable that, as blogs increasingly become part of the commercial world, they have also become the subject of a similar "feudalizing" process:

> as the Blogosphere grows in size and influence, the lines between what is a blog and what is a mainstream media site become less clear. Larger blogs are taking on more characteristics of mainstream sites and mainstream sites are incorporating styles and formats from the Blogosphere. (Technorati 2008)

Those who promote the democratizing potential of blogging, such as Dan Gillmor (2008), argue that open access to blogs allows the traditional monological media "to do better journalism" (see also Bowman and Willis 2003; and Regan 2003). Indeed, user-generated content can in itself break or complement news stories (Dahlgren 1996, 2008; Deuze and Dimoudi 2002; Singer 2006b; Thurman 2008). In general, however, blogs respond to stories originating in the mainstream, challenging facts and supplementing the stories, and, at times, reviving them in the mainstream media. This can be considered as a form of agenda-setting (Allan 2006; Lowrey 2006; Reese et al. 2007; Dahlgren 2008).

PLAN OF THE BOOK

This book is divided into four main parts: Setting the Scene; Professional and Citizen Journalists; The Role of Citizen Journalism; and Mainstream Journalism. The first of a series of diverse introductory chapters in **Part I** that consider the changing relationship between mainstream and citizen journalism is by Vincent Campbell, Rachel Gibson, Barrie Gunter and Maria Touri. The authors reflect on the ways they see news blogs and citizen journalism influencing and shaping professional journalism by reconsidering agenda-setting theory. The analysts emphasize that bloggers rarely originate news, with this tending to happen only when citizen journalists have specialist knowledge or privileged access to news events. In other words, citizen journalists' first-level agenda-setting role is limited. However, the writers suggest that bloggers have a sustained influence through what has been described as second-level agenda-setting of mainstream news. They can resuscitate stories that the mainstream media have either ignored or to which they have given a low priority. They can also reframe stories in the mainstream news — either challenging or making transparent assumptions that determine how professional journalism has framed particular news items, which, the writers contend, permits bloggers and citizen journalists to play an important role in helping revitalize mainstream coverage.

Other responses to the blogging revolution taking a similar position advance the idea that blogging has undermined the privileged position occupied by journalists. This has broken down the distinction between the amateur and the professional, undermining the traditional authority of the mainstream media, allowing anyone to be a journalist (Bruns 2005; Lowrey 2006; McNair 2006). As Bowman and Willis put it, journalism's role as "a gatekeeper of news is threatened by not just new technologies and competitors but, potentially, [also by] the audience it serves" (2003: 7). Dahlgren (1996) and, more recently, Singer (2006a) have argued that the sheer volume of raw data available via the Internet is a major factor in the destabilizing of mainstream journalism. The raw data are there for all and thus destabilize the gatekeeping function — allowing audiences to filter the data through their own news values.

In Chapter 2, two renowned figures in the field, Neil Thurman and Alfred Hermida, provide some background to the discussions throughout this book about the distinction between the amateur and the professional. They consider the impact of non-professional journalism on mainstream news, first by usefully delineating and providing a historical analysis of the terms "citizen journalism" and "participatory journalism". The writers consider whether participatory journalism has enabled users to go beyond simple involvement and actually to influence the processes that create, reflect and transmit the culture of, in their case, British national newspaper websites. They note that, while the take-up of participatory journalism among mainstream news sites has increased markedly, if unevenly, there has been relatively little innovation and comparatively few new formats to elicit responses from readers. Yet some of the innovations they consider provide an opportunity for readers to set the agenda, relatively autonomously from the established news sites' control.

Nevertheless Thurman and Hermida judge that, aside from such as aspects as a right of reply being partly realized, participation has been limited. This is due to such factors as the disabling or shortened time limits for participatory comment rejoinders on stories, and the lack of integration between user-generated content and content that is professionally produced. They conclude, similarly to others in this volume, such as the next group of contributors, that mainstream outlets' use of user-generated content has typically been marked by their determination to retain a traditional gatekeeping function — maintaining editorial control over, and extensively moderating, the content.

In Chapter 3 Gary Hudson and Mick Temple strikingly challenge the belief that those providing news blogs are indeed journalists. To mark out journalists from what are termed by others as "citizen journalists", they define journalism as the search for truth, leaving aside the philosophical debates raised by that notion. The writers consider the norms observed by mainstream journalists as important in differentiating them from those who have not operated as professionals. In contrast, they suggest, bloggers need no commitment to balance, objectivity, news-gathering and news analysis.

While Hudson and Temple view the blogosphere as an important new addition to the public sphere, providing for a more participatory role for citizens and challenging elite discourses, they insist that the news agenda is still dominated by mainstream media sources. Rather than user-generated content crowding out mainstream journalism on the blogosphere, the writers suggest that professionals have, by and large, maintained their gatekeeping role. They consider the audience's perception of the mainstream media's reliability and authority, combined with professionals' effective editorial judgement, as key factors in this. Indeed, Hudson and Temple concur that the main way that blogs have had influence has been, as other chapters further consider, as a source for mainstream journalism.

Conversely, in Chapter 4 Tim Markham takes a phenomenological approach to the question of how political meaning should be assigned to blogs. He draws on Bourdieu's field theory to argue that "the democratizing potential of online interaction, and blogging in particular, has been overstated by academic critics, policy makers and media professionals alike" (p. 77 below). Along with many others, Markham argues that most Internet journalism derives from other Web journalism and that the production of this content is thus governed by the internal logic of the Internet rather than by other fields and, in particular, that it continues to be governed by the standard practices of mainstream journalism. Contrary to many claims, he argues that new communications technologies in themselves do not present new democratizing environments *per se*. The mere fact that the audience can interact does not mean that political action beyond the exchange takes place or is necessarily desirable. This is grounded in the claim that the Internet, of itself, does not provide a site of contested political deliberation and is, rather, a field of cultural production.

Furthermore, Markham considers blogging to be best understood as part of a culture of narcissism rather than as a new form of political engagement. He equates this with a "decline of personal responsibility, preoccupation with self-esteem and the broader therapy culture" (p. 86). In doing this, he examines how notions of authority are constructed in the blogosphere. Markham asserts that a blog's influence amounts to the degree to which its community of readers attach importance to its evident symbolic forms, such as "authenticity, common sense, logic, humour, knowledge, intelligence, autonomy and courageousness" (p. 85).

While making these arguments, Markham is mindful of the widely held view that citizen journalism appears to be more representative of its consumers than are the mainstream media. Yet he emphasizes that mere media representation does not necessarily equate with "better" democracy. He concludes that, although some groups may profit from a shift in power relations, unless interactive, participatory journalism and blogging lead "to some form of action, deliberation or contestation outside the confines of this particular arena of cultural production" (p. 90), they do not amount to greater democratization.

Part II, *Professional and Citizen Journalists*, addresses the mainstream media's response to the threat of audiences migrating to independent news and comment sources. Blogging has become part of its output. Blogging by editorial and journalist staff is now a commonplace on the websites of the mainstream media. For instance, in 2008 most UK and US newspapers included blogs by staff journalists, and many provide the opportunity for consumers to blog their comments (Oriella 2008; Pew Center 2008).

In the first of the chapters looking in more detail at the relationship between professional journalists, user-generated content and citizen journalists, another emerging figure in the field, Paul Bradshaw, considers professional journalists who blog. In Chapter 5 he reflects on how they feel blogging has affected their journalism. Based on a survey of 200 journalist bloggers in 30 countries, Bradshaw's research suggests that blogging has significantly disrupted traditional journalism processes. The journalists report having developed a deeper awareness of those they were writing for and broadcasting to, and thereby having created a more personal relationship with their audience. They refer to how they have used reader feedback to their blogs in guiding how they develop stories — exploiting such material for leads and to spot trends. Some highlight the two-way nature of this process, while, for others, the collaboration is more a form of crowdsourcing: seeking material from the public, but still selecting; maintaining much restrictive gatekeeping and editorial control.

Alongside shifts in sourcing, professional journalists report to Bradshaw that their style has changed. They have become more personal and less formal. They also use their blogs to expand on and provide background for their print or broadcast stories. Also, some used their blogs to engage in "news repair", providing updates and changing stories — introducing citizens into the editing process and challenging the notion alluded to earlier in this volume that the inclusion of citizen journalism is often at the expense of accuracy. Others see blogs as merely a distribution tool for journalism first appearing elsewhere.

How much blogging has changed the journalists' mode of operation is dependent on factors such as the type of organization they work for and the type of journalism they engage in, Bradshaw notes. Nevertheless, more recently, the commercial aspect has come more to the forefront, with journalists reporting that their employers' attitude to their blogs has changed from resistance to encouragement, as search engine optimization and links with the audience are seen to be more crucial to commercial survival.

This assimilation of the atomized, non-professional practice of blogging into the corporate body can be understood as a form of incorporation. Some see this as an overwhelmingly positive development. This is reflected in the world's largest broadcast news organization, the BBC. For instance, at its Future of Journalism Conference in 2008, the editor of BBC News blogs, Giles Wilson, claimed that incorporating blogs on its website made the corporation more accountable and transparent.

Kevin Marsh is the former editor of the BBC radio's flagship elite news and current affairs slot the *Today* programme and is now the editor-in-chief of the corporation's College of Journalism. In Chapter 6 he gives an interesting insider's glimpse at how the participation of citizens has been considered within the organization. In considering whether audiences wanted to turn their relationship with the programme from a "lecture" into a "conversation", he refers to the way in which texts such as Gillmor's *We the Media* became a "scary samizdat in BBC newsrooms" (p. 111 below). And he highlights two experiments, among others, where he helped open the *Today* programme up to its audience, both involving citizens in policy-making. In one experiment journalists were involved in a citizens' jury deliberating on new social legislation, which was reported on the programme's website; in the other, the audience was involved in suggesting new laws in Britain. Both instances start to illuminate the complexities of journalist involvement in participatory democracy within a representative parliamentary system.

Einar Thorsen, Stuart Allan and Cynthia Carter also suggest that the BBC's public service ethos has been strengthened by its online operation. Commercial rivals have claimed that the BBC's coverage has encroached on their territory, and this view was given some credence by a British government report conducted by a former chief executive of one of those competitors. Yet, in Chapter 7 the writers focus on the how BBC News Online's election coverage and news provision for children have helped enhance citizenship. Interactivity has become increasingly important for the website of the BBC children's news service *Newsround*. This has also become more of a feature of the adult Web coverage of successive elections since 1997. The chapter describes how the BBC has facilitated public dialogue with its news sites and how citizens have engaged in debate.

In Chapter 8 Simon Gwyn Roberts reflects on how the BBC has helped facilitate discussions concerning identity and politics that are debated in the blogosphere. He considers the impact of the recent rise of the "new identity politics" on Europe by considering the particularity of citizenship in a border community. He looks at the role of the Internet in the debate on the ambiguous identity of citizens in Flintshire, a Welsh border community adjoining north-west England. Anchored around discussions organized by traditional journalism on the BBC website, Roberts assumes the debates offer a form of participatory journalism. He suggests that the blogosphere has given voice to the diversity and fractured loyalties in this community. This is in contrast to the mainstream media, which have provided only a limited platform for the discussion of identity politics, subsequent to powers being devolved to Wales by the British government.

Contrary to the antagonistic dialogue featured elsewhere in this book, where some of those involved perceive themselves to be involved in a life-or-death contest, blog contributors seem aware of the unresolved tensions involved in their disputes on national affiliation and identity. Gwyn Roberts suggests that such online forums provide an effective platform for the narration of different perspectives and experiences as part of an informed debate on notions of citizenship.

Following this, Andy Price, as a practitioner-turned-academic, focuses positively on user-involvement in a commercial environment by considering a hyper-local commercial news site he was previously connected to. Price's implication in Chapter 9 is that the commercial exploitation of user-generated content can be an overwhelmingly benign process, helping to satisfy both democratic and business needs. Predominantly assessing the process from the senior professional's point of view, interviewing a range of senior editorial staff involved in overseeing this innovative award-winning site in the north-east of England, he explores how user-generated blogs on the site have brought the news closer to the community in a cost-effective way. They have led to local issues being discussed in more depth, realizing some of the aspirations of public or civic journalism, Price considers. In addition, editorial staff have found that, while the amateur contributors have had an impact on professional journalism, the bloggers have tended to adopt some of the traits of professional journalists. This has meant that post-moderation has created few "problems" for the professionals at the site, owned by Britain's largest regional newspaper publisher. While emphasizing that any wider application of this approach would have to be undertaken carefully, Price considers that the site has increased citizen participation.

However, it can equally be argued that incorporation has not necessarily led to a more democratic exchange between news organizations and audiences. In a study of the changing newsroom, the Pew Center has drawn attention to the competing values between old and new. Almost half of the editors interviewed believed that while citizen-created content is "an essential ingredient for the website and newspaper of the future", almost as many described citizen-created content as "an interesting, but limited concept in which citizen input is kept to very small stories or to basic informational material". Indeed, only a quarter of the respondents found citizen content "very valuable" (Pew Center 2008). In this model, incorporation becomes more a means to retain the audience or, ideally, to attract new consumers rather than a step towards a greater degree of democracy.

In line with this attitude is the view that the mainstream media tend to constrain audience participation into what Deuze calls a "closed participatory communication" (2003: 207). Dahlgren (2008), Singer and Friend (2007), Thurman and Jones (2005) and Singer (2005) also find that when audiences are not empowered to enter into conversation with the professional journalist bloggers, this reasserts the gatekeeping role over blogging. Thus, traditional journalism continues to deliver news through a controlled and closed system, as opposed to citizen journalism, which is open and continuous (Lowrey 2006; Wall 2005). Another anxiety about the incorporation of blogging is that it promotes opinionated journalism that focuses on the immediate concerns of the author. While incorporation may have the effect of satisfying consumer desires for something different, it may yet turn out to be no more than a stylistic solution, where readers will be no better informed than they were before. That is to say, incorporated blogging will not have served the purpose of improving democracy if readers are content with conjecture and supposition — with the concomitant effect that important citizen journalism, which seeks to confront unsubstantiated claims or to militate for change, will remain at the fringes of the sphere of influence.

Interestingly, some citizen publications have found that by not moderating content they have allowed inaccurate and indecent material to appear on their sites. Thus, they have found the need to adopt similar editorial moderation strategies to the mainstream media — aligning some blogging communities with these traditional gatekeeping practices (Benkler 2006). This in turn has made them attractive partners for mainstream organizations, leading to an amalgam of the institutional and citizen blogs, where news organizations have entered into either loose partnerships or outright buyouts of citizen publications (Lowrey and Latta 2008; MacManus 2008).

Considering this, Chapters 10 to 12 contrast with Chapters 6 to 9 by questioning incorporation. Former senior BBC broadcast producer Janet Jones also views that the BBC regards the use of user-generated content as central to its strategy and potentially forms a powerful reason to support the world's largest broadcaster's public service provision. Yet, in Chapter 10, rather than seeing this as a form of genuine public participation, Jones considers the corporation to be solely crowdsourcing. The BBC has been uncomfortable about fully embracing audiences as producers because of the impact on characteristic aspects of its output — including, she suggests, on impartiality, quality and professionalism. Neither does all the BBC's audience want the corporation to democratize its newsroom; instead they seek reliability and authority. Thus, often voices are "subsumed into the normative practices of the BBC Newsroom and staff" (p. 159), and when experiments in collective editorial control have been attempted, they have petered out quickly. It may be, Jones concludes, that the explosion in democratization of news has happened too quickly and been implemented too crudely. Yet, while considering it naïve to suppose that alternative media sources do not gatekeep, she considers that the corporation faces the danger that, if too many contributions are ignored, contributors will recognize the essentially one-way nature of their conversation and turn away. Alternatively, with the public appetite now whetted, pressures may build up on the BBC to provide more democratic communication, in the context of a younger generation less tolerant of one-way media.

In Chapter 11, Lian Zhu views mainstream journalism's utilization of user-generated content at both the BBC and its commercial rivals in similar terms. She sees that for citizens to become active providers and participants in politics, it is essential to have a free flow of information, extensive cultural diversity and participation of citizens in journalistic production. Yet her research into British mainstream regional TV's use of such content suggests that, despite members of the public receiving training, relatively few news items have been produced by citizen journalists. Instead, content generated by users has been mostly limited to weather pictures and comments on programmes. Mainstream news organizations, Zhu considers, encourage such content to strengthen their relationship with the audience while, again, maintaining their gatekeeping control. Thus, while new technology has allowed people a platform to voice their views, she argues that user-generated content has provided a narrow representation of the public, who are still far from the centre of power.

In his analysis of a very different country and set of media practices, Slovenian academic Igor Vobič comes to a similar conclusion in Chapter 12 about the relationship between mainstream organizations and citizen bloggers in his young nation.

Slovenia provides a valuable opportunity to study the journalistic practices and structures of a country still in transition from its particular Communist past, when it was part of Yugoslavia, yet independent of the Soviet bloc, through the break-up of Yugoslavia in 1991 to its present-day membership of the EU. The media landscape in Slovenia is in a state of flux, as many old media companies emerge into the capitalist market, which makes it particularly interesting to research. However, some of this research has painted a damning picture of the industry. Martine Robinson Beachboard and John Beachboard (2009) set out to map the way journalists perceived the differences before and after Communism. Their findings demonstrate a journalistic environment that is not supportive of democratic journalism. The country's new constitution and its Mass Media Act support freedom of expression, and there are two codes of ethics: the Code of Practice for Slovenian Journalists (2002) and RTV Slovenia's in-house code of ethics (2000) (Milosavljevič n.d.). However, Robinson Beachboard and Beachboard find that, despite this legislation and ethical codes, journalists are deterred from investigative journalism because they fear reprisals, lack job security and are under pressure to orientate their work solely around maximizing profits. This has even given rise to ethical corruption, where "commercial pressure on many media companies to make a profit has reportedly trickled into the newsroom, leading to biased editorial policies and an increase in publication of advertorials, or paid advertising disguised as editorial content" (Press Freedom 2000, cited by Robinson Beachboard and Beachboard 2009: 13).

In another rather damning report Sandra Bašić-Hrvatin and Lenart Kucić (2004) also describe the state of journalism in Slovenia. They claim that:

> only a few journalists sincerely care for their education, read widely or have a good overview of international and domestic developments. Similarly, few of them are willing to dig deeper into their subjects and few have the feeling that their reporting based on references to "official sources," or their comfortable cohabitation with the political or commercial power centers, or their stenographic coverage of Parliament's sessions or press conferences are flawed in any way. (2004: 488)

They add:

> Few journalists are willing to participate in projects not directly related to personal advantage, while solidarity with fellow journalists and awareness about the primary interests that journalists should represent are very low. (2004: 488)

These conclusions are further borne out by more recent findings. Kovačič and Erjavec (2008) have examined commercial television's claims to be promoting citizen journalism. Like Lian Zhu, the authors found a market-driven pretence of citizen journalism that is merely an exploitation of the term "citizen journalism" and the exploitation of an opportunity for profit via new media technologies. Rather than seeing citizens generating content, the authors find producers and editors who, while acting as gatekeepers, consciously reduce audience participation to a culture of denunciation. Contributors are encouraged to provide photographic evidence of public officials participating in alleged offences or irregularities. The authors see this practice as emerging out of old Communist patterns of social responsibility that are now being used for purely commercial gain.

Vobič has worked as an international news reporter in Slovenia television and now teaches journalism at the University of Ljubljana. Here he examines Slovenian mainstream media organizations to consider how participatory journalism affects the gatekeeping roles of journalists and others in the newsroom. Vobič surveys the online sites of the "big three" Slovenian quality daily newspapers, that of the mass-circulation free title and those of the public service broadcaster and largest commercial TV stations, and he interviews the editors of these sites. In a similar way to other researchers in this area, he also finds that, although blogging has been somewhat normalized as part of the mainstream Slovenian media scene, there is, for the most part, merely an "illusion of interactivity". He challenges a technologically determinist view, contending that, while it has become technically possible to have dialogical communication, the mainstream media's distinct ambivalence to this has ensured that the journalist's traditional gatekeeping role has also stayed intact here. While there is a level of interactivity, it is

relatively modest, predominantly one-way and often guided by commercial imperatives.

One further concern of critics of citizen journalism and blogging has to do with
anonymity. In Chapter 13 Serena Carpenter considers this question by comparing how
transparent citizen journalists and professional online newspaper journalists are. That
is, she considers how much both sets of journalists disclose to their readers, in order to
promote openness in their relationship with their audience. Carpenter compares the
transparency of a sample representing the 50 states of the US. She considers the willingness of both groups to use anonymous sources, provide background information on
themselves and their sources and offer contact opportunities.

Promoting transparency is seen as helping link journalists to the community.
Rather than focusing on any dangers of political vetting by employers if professional
journalists are encouraged to provide biographical material, Carpenter considers that
by exposing themselves, journalists make themselves more accountable. Such transparency is said to encourage readers' involvement in the news process. Also she notes
that the credibility of journalism is bolstered by making sources more transparent.
Carpenter discovers that citizen journalists are typically less transparent in their use of
sources but are, in fact, less opaque about their own background. They are also more
likely than the professionals to engage in open dialogue with their readers.

Nonetheless, the criticism of anonymity in citizen journalism and blogging
persists. Some studies have attributed anti-social online behaviour to anonymity. It is
felt that "[u]sers may not care if they hurt other users because they have little sense that
others are 'real,' little expectation that their bad behaviour has consequences for them,
and little expectation that they will ever have to interact with the other person in the
future" (Davis 2002: 1).

Part III, _The Role of Citizen Journalism_, investigates issues relating to participatory journalism. In Chapter 14, Aaron Barlow and Annie Seaton assume a loose
definition of such journalism and its overlap with blogging to focus on the use of race
in masking identity and accountability in the US. In a piece that is set to provoke
debate, they consider the place of race in the election of President Barack Obama, before
particularly considering the role of avatars. They suggest the use of avatars is emblematic of the place of race in Internet journalism and the "perceived licence to step beyond
historical context that, in some minds, the Internet provides" (p. 217 below).
Moreover, they suggest that to pull away the mask and identify oneself as "other" can
lead to a backlash. They further explore the ALL CAPS phenomenon in this context.
Finally, they reflect on the role of misrepresentation of the self and sources in Internet
journalism in the reporting of President Obama's election.

There are differences between the way online journalism has emerged in the UK,
in Europe, in the US and in other parts of the world: differences in political structure
and in the economics of investment in technology. After three centuries of economic
domination by Europe and the US, our socio-economic world is in turmoil as new
economies from the East become superpowers, while the global banking system experiences crisis. While such considerations are beyond the parameters of this book, we
wish to consider what is happening to citizen journalism beyond the West.

Much of the discussion about the political potential of the Internet, citizen journalism and blogging and many debates that explore concepts of citizenship tend to be seen through the prism of democracy. However, not all of the chapters here deal with the media in representative democratic regimes: for example, those on China. Thus, for the purposes of this book we subsume many of the competing definitions of citizenship into a minimalist notion of those who are governed. (See Ellison 1997 and Turner 1990 for a further discussion of definitions.) In doing this, we hope to embed the fundamental principles of the civil, political and social citizen offered by Marshall (1949) and the notion of the citizen who is the subject of the law of their community proposed by Pocock (1995). Nevertheless, it is only recently that the Western concept of citizenship has had any purchase for discussions of Asiatic relationships between the individual and the state. (For a more comprehensive discussion of this, see Turner and Hamilton 1994.)

As Gunther and Mugham have demonstrated, mass communications media are "central to the dynamics of the relationship between governors and the governed in all types of political regime" (2000: 3). While this may imply a passive citizen, citizenship is also an activity. But, as Hamelink (2000) and other have pointed out, "in most conceptions of democracy only a limited interpretation of people's participation is foreseen" (2000: 165). Even though blogs represent an important revolution in the ability of citizens to communicate their thoughts, it may be unlikely that more participation will be achieved than at present. Nevertheless, they may provide politicians with significant indicators of public opinion. As Perlmutter put it, "blogs are both different from and similar to familiar methods of political campaigning and influence" (2008: 188), indeed, as a tool to lobby for change, blogs may turn out to have little actual impact on the broader political issues, and marginal groups may achieve no more voice than before.

Even in countries that are formally representative democracies, such as Israel, times of conflict may change the potential impact of blogging as a force for greater democracy. In Chapter 15 Dmitry Epstein and Dor Reich assess how bloggers have considered the Israel–Palestine conflict through the controversial analysis of peace journalism. Peace journalism, most simply, is that which, rather than prioritizing objectivity above all else, consciously "seeks to constructively help the resolution of conflict" (Spencer 2005: 169) by identifying usually silenced voices and "highlighting peace initiatives and action that would prevent conflicts from escalating" (p. 231 below).

Reflecting on assumptions from peace journalism theorists that market pressure leads mainstream journalism to accentuate conflict, Epstein and Reich consider whether the absence of such pressure has led bloggers to produce material that is considered closer to peace journalism. They analyse the bloggers' posts, applying peace journalism as a normative analytical framework, where the mention of conflict, rather than resolution, identifies the discourse as not peace journalism.

They find their assumptions that there would be a richer and deeper discussion of the conflict on the blogosphere confounded. Instead there is a "surprisingly hostile" discourse. Rather than focusing on structural inequality in the Middle East, as peace journalism's originator, Johan Galtung (1990: 297), has done, they offer a possible explanation by emphasizing that bloggers, like journalists, are products of cultures that are not oriented to peace.

In another survey of the impact of citizen journalism, Ryan Bowman considers its role in Uganda (Chapter 16). It would be impossible in a publication of this scale to offer any kind of comprehensive account of new media journalism in Africa. Even the universalizing concept of Africa fails to take into account the divide between the north, Saharan and sub-Saharan Africa — 53 countries, each of which has its own economic and social structure. Even this statement fails to take into account the complexities of tribal socio-economic geography. As recently as 2004 it was clear that sub-Saharan Africa was only just beginning to develop online news (Stanbridge and Ljunggren 2004). The nature of expansion is also significantly different in Africa from that of developed countries. There is little in the way of a telecoms infrastructure on which to build. Thus, much of the focus is on infrastructure development rather than content regulation, and most countries see the Internet as crucial to their future development (Croen and Mapes 2008).

In addition to newspapers, radio has been an important means of disseminating news. The most rapid take-up of new technologies has been mobile phones. This may lead to greater levels of investment in African telecoms infrastructure as foreign operators take up investment opportunities in this rapidly growing market. In addition, "[g]overnments' ability to raise much-needed capital through mobile license fees is also providing a substantial boost to many countries' telecoms expenditure funds" (Karake-Shalhoub and Al Qasimi 2006: 83).

Like Igor Vobič previously, Ryan Bowman examines the practices of journalism in a newly emerging state that was previously not a liberal democratic regime. In Chapter 16 he gives one African perspective on the changing role of the Internet and new media on news, citizenship and democratic participation in that continent. Considering Uganda, he chronicles how innovations in news and participatory political communication have sprouted outside the mainstream journalism providers on the Internet. While the two main newspapers sites have essentially replicated their print editions, it is a blogging site operated by ex-journalists spreading political gossip that would never be published by mainstream news providers which has "captured the imagination", he contends. While not branding this "citizen journalism", he identifies this as an example of nascent democratic expression made more possible by new technology, in a country where government interference in the media has been extensive.

Yet, in a country where Internet usage is mainly confined to the urban elite, Bowman identifies the forum where more participatory political communication has operated as the newly available radio, where open-access talk shows have opened the possibility for free expression for Uganda's predominantly rural population. Moreover, what is also striking here are the parallels with China, which we will consider in a moment, in the use of text messaging. Bowman chronicles how texting has become a powerful tool in mass communication and campaigning, and, in the case study examined, to affect journalism and news agenda setting. While Rena Bivens and Chen Li outline a little later in this volume how censorship has forced campaigners concerned about their environment to spread news and campaign information by text, Bowman identifies how economic forces have driven their Ugandan counterparts to use mobiles and also engage in smart mob tactics with some success. (For a fuller account of smart mobs see Rheingold 2002.)

Worldwide, bloggers increasingly face imprisonment for their work. The Committee to Protect Journalists recorded that more online journalists than print, radio or television journalists were in jail for the first time in 2008. Of all media workers in jail worldwide, 45 percent were bloggers. One reason suggested for this is that, unlike those journalists who have the relative protection of large media organizations, "when the knock comes on the door they are alone and vulnerable" (Committee to Protect Journalists 2008).

China, the most populous country in the world, now also has more Internet users than any other. There were 253 million in June 2008, although the Internet penetration rate was slightly lower than the world average, at 21 percent. The top ten Internet applications were: online music, online news, instant messaging, online video, search engine, email, online game, blog/personal space, forum/BBS and online shopping. Some 42 percent of users also had personal Web space or blogs (China Internet Network Information Center 2008; for a brief overview of the emergence of modern journalism in China, see Lee 2005).

During the 1990s China moved much of its newspaper business away from state funding towards a capitalist commercial model that has depended on advertising. Since the late 1990s Chinese commercial news sites such as Sina.com.cn and Sohu.com.cn have started to attract large audiences. These sites offer real-time domestic and international news, as well as politically driven chatrooms. These Chinese commercial news sites are restricted in their ability to engage in investigative reporting, forcing "them to become news aggregators, "pasting" news from officially approved outlets" (Chan, Lee and Pan 2006: 930). However, there is evidence of an increasing desire on the part of Chinese journalists to engage in investigative reporting, and more examples of this have begun to appear (De Burgh 2003).

One theme this book considers is whether new technologies and Web journalism have facilitated new forms of citizenship, as part of a transition in the case of China to what has been described as "liberalized authoritarianism". In Goldsmith and Wu's (2006) significant book on regulation of the Internet, a key theme is the Chinese government's powerful control — aided by US multinationals — over its population's use of the Web, with little liberalization. An important way this operates, the authors argue, is that the government has encouraged the burgeoning Chinese chatrooms that promote the political consciousness it supports, as opposed to outlawed concepts such as democracy. The main example given of this is the Qiangguo Forum (Strong Country Forum). This, the authors suggest, was created by the Chinese Communist Party paper the *People's Daily* and is linked to anti-American Chinese nationalism, tacitly endorsed by the government. Moreover, the US professors liken such forums' manipulation to the government-sanctioned anger of the Cultural Revolution (see Goldsmith and Wu 2006: 87–104).

In her challenging study presented in Chapter 17, Qian Gong looks at the forum from an entirely different perspective. She speaks to the forum's participants and to its originator to explore its reformist function in opening up the possibility for debate and encouraging a limited form of participatory citizenship, while recognizing its nationalist origins. In particular, a remarkable interview with the forum's creator reveals its role in testing how far the government, chastened by the experience of the Cultural Revolution, has been prepared to go in opening up discussions where "people could talk . . . from the bottom of their heart" (p. 268). Gong focuses on discussions in the forum on the area of income inequality — particularly controversial for a regime that wants to encourage entrepreneurs and a mushrooming middle class, while seeking to legitimize its authority, with its party's ostensibly egalitarian historic ideology.

Gong considers forum participants to be operating as citizen journalists, whose contributions are regarded by other contributors as more trustworthy than information provided by the Chinese state media. Rather than simply endorsing the government, posters have exhibited an implicitly critical attitude to the political system, she concludes. While the forum has provided a sounding board to consider the competing interests of different social classes, Gong suggests it has also operated as a participatory conduit between those involved and the government and the party, where reformist demands have sometimes been acted on by officials.

In Chapter 18 Rena Bivens and Chen Li survey a wider range of Chinese new media to look at citizenship and democracy separately. They argue that, while there is little democratic dialogue — despite the seeming potential the Internet affords — new media are aiding the development of citizenship "at least when people have reacted to very specific, local issues that have provoked a widespread emotional response" (p. 276). To consider this, the writers look at how Chinese citizens have circumvented censorship on Internet forums and used other new media to protest at local decisions made by the authorities. They consider case studies involving community campaigns highlighting planning and environmental concerns — of paramount importance in a country that has experienced such a massive expansion of industrialization and building development.

They argue that such protests are necessarily limited and non-confrontational — avoiding seeking to undermine the Chinese state's legitimacy. Yet by using innovative tactics such as "walks" organized by flash mob-style mobile text-based communication, citizens have again had some notable successes in shifting local government policy in specific cases, while becoming empowered, to an extent. Some of those involved have operated as citizen journalists, the writers argue, using the Internet, for example, to highlight battles against property developers and campaigns against a chemical plant being built. Despite the dangers — one such citizen was killed by an official after chronicling local misconduct — in other cases such journalism has chronicled the campaigns, leading again to concessions by local authorities. While being cautious about the broader applicability of their research, the authors thus point to the participatory and challenging opportunities of new media at least at a local level, notwithstanding the Chinese administration's endeavours at control.

Part IV, *Mainstream Journalism*, concludes the volume. The evolution of journalism in India, the world's other emerging superpower, offers another unique history. In the first of three chapters focusing on mainstream journalism itself, Saayan Chattopadhyay (Chapter 19) assesses Indian journalism. In the second half of the twentieth century journalism in India was very closely linked to the anti-colonial and nation-building ideologies of the newly independent state. Independence from Britain in 1947 left a legacy of a private press and a government-controlled broadcasting system, as well as a democratic practice, even though India is highly segregated along class and caste lines. At this time,

> most journalists in India saw their task following a developmental agenda set by an activist state. For its part, the government subsidised news agencies, newspapers and magazines by providing them with cheap newsprint and public-sector advertising, thus indirectly affecting even the privately owned and diverse press. However, despite such interference by the government, the relative autonomy of the private print media significantly contributed to the evolution of multi-party democracy in India. It helped create and then sustain a public sphere within which a democratic discourse could flourish. (Thussu 2005: 128)

More recently, over the past decade India has become very successful in providing services, such as software production, to a global marketplace. But indigenous access to computing still lags far behind the West and other emerging economies such as China. Indeed, "web reading is quite rare in India and it is mostly confined to a tiny percentage of newspaper readers in the metropolitan cities" (Vilanilam 2005: 168).

In Chapter 19 Saayan Chattopadhyay considers how mainstream journalism has excluded "voices from below" in the seemingly participatory Internet environment of this developing country as it emerges into an economic powerhouse. He focuses on how the digital divide has developed in India and reflects on the corporatization of mainstream Web journalism, as part of the particular neo-liberal development of the post-colonial economy. This he sees as potentially giving the opportunity for democratization, but within the constrictions of an overwhelmingly commercialized system, initially confined to a narrow elite. As consumption and participation have expanded beyond this, elite commercialized Web journalism in India has targeted the huge, but largely apolitical, youth market with soft news, he contends. Any political activity flowing from this, Chattopadhyay insists, has been confined to an upper-class elite and restricted to the Internet, providing what he rather dismisses as "clicktivism". The rural masses have been ignored by Internet content, as the infrastructure has not developed to translate Web journalism into India's regional languages. Thus social and economic inequality, also reflected in language barriers, has made participation and dialogic communication very difficult. (For a detailed examination of government policies regarding the development of Internet use in India and China, see Dossani 2007; Franda 2001; and 2002.)

Following from this, providing a different emphasis from Hudson and Temple and Markham, Chattopadhyay asserts that it is perhaps only with the deprofessionalizing of journalistic practices that news content can be produced "without the hegemonic restrictions of a nation-state, global market economy or ideologically motivated editorial policy" (p. 297). He considers that the nature of Web journalism gives the opportunity for a wider pluralism and for the role of contradictions to be explored more fully than with traditional unidirectional mainstream news. Chattopadhyay sees a role for professional journalists if they are unshackled from some of the norms of objective journalism. And he notes that both in the mainstream and, particularly, independent sites in India there is the opportunity for democratic participatory journalism. Yet, challenging technological determinism, he suggests that, without wider access to skills to operate the new tools of communication, this potential remains untapped.

Alfred Hermida was a BBC journalist and an online news pioneer before becoming an academic. In analyzing the BBC, he rather positively considers, in Chapter 20, the extensive use of blogging by mainstream journalists within the organization. He sees this as a way of providing a particular form of accountability and transparency, turning the relationship between producers and citizens into more of a conversation. While other mainstream media organizations have encouraged staff to blog, the BBC, he argues, has specific reasons to open itself up in this way, with particular results.

The corporation has faced long-standing criticism of its elite paternalism and a contingent contemporary need to build renewed trust in itself. This followed the Hutton inquiry, a British judicial investigation that threw the BBC into crisis after it was controversially accused of failings in its reporting of government claims concerning Iraqi weapons of mass destruction. Facing that backdrop, Hermida endorses the suggestion that the BBC blogs' informal and conversational tone has opened up to readers some of the dilemmas facing BBC editors and journalists in their day-to-day decision-making. However, the one-way assumptions of BBC staff, rooted in elitist broadcasting traditions, as well as the popularity of some of the blogs, have meant that journalists have been reluctant to keep up with responses and to foster a more free-flowing dialogue with their audience.

In contrast, in the final chapter (21), which significantly challenges some libertarian assumptions of Web journalism analysis, a veteran reporter and analyst argues that one new aspect of Internet journalism is set to undermine citizenship rights. Former senior BBC political journalist Nicholas Jones argues that online television threatens to undermine a key foundation of the operation of representative democracy in Britain — balanced broadcast news coverage. He argues that the delicate ecology of media coverage of British politics, based on relatively impartial broadcasting balancing a politically partisan press, is being undermined. Long-standing British broadcast regulations, which have sought to provide fair allocation of airtime for political parties — and through their rigid application at election times have provided for some coverage of minority parties — are now under threat.

Jones implies that this threat, rather than being technologically determined, is the result of a concerted attempt by the self-regulatory body that oversees press ethics to seek oversight in this new arena. This initiative by the Press Complaints Commission was encouraged by the reluctance of the state-funded regulator for British communications, Ofcom, to regulate in this area, he contends. Moreover, following a US presidential election that again highlighted the role of politically funded advertising, such moves have already opened the door to television-style attack advertising in

Britain, which is further set to marketize the democratic process in forthcoming general elections.

References

Abbate, J. (1999) *Inventing the Internet*. Cambridge, MA: MIT Press.

Allan, S. (ed.) (2005a) *Journalism: Critical Issues*. Maidenhead: Open University Press.

Allan, S. (2005b) "News on the Web: The Emerging Forms and Practices of Online Journalism". In *Journalism: Critical Issues*. Maidenhead. Open University Press, pp. 67–81.

Allan, S. (2006) *Online News*. Maidenhead: Open University Press.

Bašić-Hrvatin, S., and Lenart Kučić, L. J. (2004) "Report on Slovenia". In B. Petković (ed.), *Media Ownership and its Impact on Media Independence and Pluralism*. Ljubljana: SEENPM and Peace Institute, pp. 464–92.

Bell, E. (2008) Cited by L. Oliver, "Media Industry on 'Brink of Carnage', Says Guardian Digital Chief". Retrieved 12 December from: http://www.journalism.co.uk/2/articles/532538.php.

Benkler, Y. (2006) "The Wealth of Networks: How Social Production Transforms Markets and Freedom". Retrieved 16 January 2007 from: http://www.jus.uio.no/sisu/the_wealth_of_networks.yochai_benkler/portrait.pdf.

Blood, R. (2000) "Weblogs: A History and Perspective. Rebecca's Pocket". Retrieved 8 July 2007 from: http://www.rebeccablood.net/essays/weblog_history.html.

Borland, J. (2004) "Microsoft 'Newsbot' Apes Google News". *Zdnet*. Retrieved 15 November 2008 from: http://news.zdnet.co.uk/internet/0,1000000097,39161696,00.htm.

Bowman, S., and Willis, C. (2003) *We Media: How Audiences are Shaping the Future of News and Information*. The American Press Institute. Retrieved 16 January 2007 from: http://www.hypergene.net/wemedia/download/we_media.pdf.

Bradshaw, P. (2008) "Are These The Biggest Moments in Journalism Blogging History?" Retrieved 2 December 2008 from: http://onlinejournalismblog.com/2008/11/20/are-these-the-biggest-moments-in-journalism-blogging-history/.

Briggs, A., and Burke, P. (2005) *A Social History of the Media from Gutenberg to the Internet*. 2nd edn. Cambridge: Polity.

Brown, M. (2005) "Abandoning the News. Carnegie Corporation Report". Retrieved 12 December 2008 from: http://www.carnegie.org/reporter/10/news/.

Bruns, A. (2005) *Gatewatching: Collaborative Online News Production*. New York: Peter Lang.

Bruns, A. (2008) *Blogs, Wikipedia, Second Life and Beyond: From Production to Produsage*. New York: Peter Lang.

Carey, J. (1996) "Where Journalism Education Went Wrong". Retrieved 8 November 2008 from: http://frank.mtsu.edu/~masscomm/seig96/carey/carey.htm.

Carlson, D. (2003) "The History of Online Journalism". In K. Kawamoto (ed.), *Digital Journalism: Emerging Media and the Changing Horizons of Journalism*. Oxford: Rowman & Littlefield Publishers, pp. 31–56.

Carlyle, T. (1841) *On Heroes, Hero-Worship and the Heroic in History. Six Lectures: Reported, with Emendations and Additions*. Repr. New York: John Wiley.

Chan, J. M., Lee, F. L. F., and Pan, Z. (2006) "Online News Meets Established Journalism: How China's Journalists Evaluate the Credibility of News Websites", *New Media and Society*, 8 (6), pp. 925–47.

China Internet Network Information Center (2008) *Statistical Survey Report on Internet Development in China*. Abridged edn. Retrieved 15 December 2008 from: http://www.cnnic.cn/uploadfiles/pdf/2008/8/15/145744.pdf.

Committee to Protect Journalists (2008) *2008 Prison Census: Online and in Jail*. Retrieved 4 December 2008 from: http://www.cpj.org/imprisoned/cpjs-2008-census-online-journalists-now-jailed-mor.php.

Croen, E., Kim, J., and Mapes, K. (2008) "Internet Filtering in Sub-Saharan Africa". In R. Deibert, J. Palfrey, R. Rohozinski, and J. Zittrain (eds), *Access Denied: The Practice and Policy of Global Internet Filtering*. Cambridge, MA: MIT Press, pp. 213–25.

Curran, J. (1993) "Rethinking the Media as a Public Sphere". In P. Dahlgren, and C. Sparks (ed.), *Communication and Citizenship: Journalism and the Public Sphere*. London: Routledge, pp. 27–56.

Dahlgren, P. (1996) "Media Logic in Cyberspace: Repositioning Journalism and its Publics", *Journalism at the Crossroads*, 3 (3), pp. 59–72.

Dahlgren, P. (2009) *Media and Political Engagement: Citizens, Democracy and Communication*. New York: Cambridge University Press.

Dahlgren, P., and Sparks, C. (1993) *Communication and Citizenship: Journalism and the Public Sphere*. London: Routledge.

Davis, J., (2002) "The Experience of 'Bad' Behavior in Online Social Spaces: A Survey of Online Users". Retrieved 14 August 2008 from: http://research.microsoft.com/scg/papers/Bad%20Behavior%20survey.pdf.

De Burgh, H. (2003) "Kings without Crowns? The Re-Emergence of Investigative Journalism in China", *Media, Culture and Society*, 25 (6), pp. 801–20.

Deuze, M. (2003) "The Web and its Journalisms: Considering the Consequences of Different Types of News Media Online", *New Media & Society*, 5 (2), pp. 203–30.

Deuze, M. (2007) *Media Work*. Cambridge: Polity Press.

Deuze, M., Bruns, A., and Neuberger, C. (2007) "Preparing for an Age of Participatory News", *Journalism Practice*, 1 (3), pp. 322–38.

Deuze, M., and Dimoudi, C. (2002) "Online Journalists in the Netherlands: Towards a Profile of a New Profession", *Journalism*, 3 (1), pp. 103–18.

Dewey, J. (1927/1991) *The Public and Its Problems*. Athens, OH: Ohio University Press.

Dossani, R. (2007) *India Arriving: How This Economic Powerhouse Is Redefining Global Business*. New York: American Management Association.

Ellison, N. (1997) "Towards a New Social Politics: Citizenship and Reflexivity in Late Modernity", *Sociology*, 31 (4), pp. 697–717.

Evans, K. G. (2000) "Reclaiming John Dewey: Democracy, Inquiry, Pragmatism, and Public Management", *Administration and Society*, 32 (3), pp. 308–28.

Franda, M. (2001) *Launching into Cyberspace: Internet Development and Politics in Five World Regions*. Boulder, CO: Lynne Rienner Publishers, Inc.

Franda, M. (2002) *China and India Online: Information Technology, Politics and Diplomacy in the World's Two Largest Nations*. Lanham, MD: Rowman & Littlefield.

Galtung, J. (1990) "Cultural Violence", *Journal of Peace Research*, 27 (3), pp. 291–305.

Gillmor, D. (2004). *We the Media: Grassroots Journalism by the People, for the People*. Sebastopol, CA: O'Reilly.

Technorati (2008) "State of the Blogosphere / 2008. Technorati Report". Retrieved 28 December 2008 from: http://technorati.com/blogging/state-of-the-blogosphere/.

Gimmler, A. (2001) "Deliberative Democracy, the Public Sphere and the Internet", *Philosophy & Social Criticism*, 27 (4), pp. 21–39.

Goldsmith, J., and Wu, T. (2006) *Who Controls the Internet: Illusions of a Borderless World*. New York: Oxford University Press.

Greenslade, R. (2009) "Sales Decline is Accelerating". *The Guardian*, 9 January 2009. Retrieved from: http://www.guardian.co.uk/media/greenslade/2009/jan/09/abcs-national-newspapers.

Gunther, R., and Mugham, A. (eds) (2000) *Democracy and the Media*. Cambridge: Cambridge University Press.

Habermas, J. (1962) *The Structural Transformation of the Public Sphere: An Inquiry into a Category of Bourgeois Society*. Trans. T. Burger with F. Lawrence. Cambridge, MA: MIT Press.

Hagerty, B. (2005) "Nightmare Scenario", *British Journalism Review*, 16 (2), pp. 3–6. Retrieved 10 November 2008 from: http://www.bjr.org.uk/data/2005/no2_editorial.

Hamelink, C. J. (2000) *The Ethics of Cyberspace*. London: Sage.

Hesmondhalgh, D. (2007) *The Cultural Industries*. London: Sage.

Jenkins, H. (2006) *Convergence Culture: Where Old and New Media Collide*. New York: New York University Press.

Karake-Shalhoub, Z., and Al Qasimi L. (2006) *The Diffusion of e-Commerce in Developing Economies: A Resource-based Approach*. Cheltenham: Edward Elgar.

Kiss, J. (2008) "ABCe: US Election Build-Up Helps UK Newspaper Sites To Record Traffic". Retrieved 20 November 2008 from: http://www.guardian.co.uk/media/2008/nov/20/abcs-pressandpublishing.

Kolodzy, J. (2006) *Convergence Journalism: Writing and Reporting across the News Media*. Lanham, MD: Rowman & Littlefield.

Kovačič, M. P., and Erjavec, K. (2008) "Mobi Journalism in Slovenia: Is This Really Citizen Journalism?", *Journalism Studies*, 9 (6), pp. 874–90.

Lee, C. (2005) "The Conception of Chinese Journalists: Ideological Convergence and Contestation". In H. De Burgh (ed.), *Making Journalists*. London: Routledge, pp. 107–26.

Li, K. (2009) "US Newspaper Crisis Deepens", *Financial Times*, 26 March 2009.

Lippmann, W. (1921) *Public Opinion*. London: Allen and Unwin.

Lippmann, W. (1927) *The Phantom Public*. New York: Macmillan; repr. New Brunswick, NJ: Transaction Publishers.

Lowrey, W. (2006) "Mapping the Journalism–Blogging Relationship", *Journalism*, 7 (4), pp. 477–500.

Lowrey, W., and Latta, J. (2008) "The Routines of Blogging". In C. Paterson, and D. Domingo (eds), *Making Online News: The Ethnography of New Media Production*. New York: Peter Lang.

MacManus, R. (2008) "Mixed Messages in the Blogging Landscape". Retrieved 20 September 2008 from: http://www.readwriteweb.com/archives/mixed_messages_blogging.php.

McNair, B. (2006) *Cultural Chaos: Journalism, News and Power in a Globalised World*. London: Routledge.

Marshall, P. D. (2004) *New Media Cultures*. London: Hodder Arnold.

Marshall, T. H. (1949) *Citizenship and Social Class*. Cambridge: Cambridge University Press.

Meyer, P. (2004) *The Vanishing Newspaper: Saving Journalism in the Information Age*. Columbia, MI: University of Missouri Press.

Milosavljevič, M. (n.d.) "Media Landscape – Slovenia". European Journalism Centre, Retrieved from: http://www.ejc.net/media_landscape/article/slovenia/.

Negt, O., and Kluge, A. (1993) *Public Sphere and Experience: Toward an Analysis of the Bourgeois and Proletarian Public Sphere*. Minneapolis: University of Minnesota Press. [Originally published as *Öffentlichkeit und Erfahrung: Zur Organisationsanalyse von bürgerlicher und proletarischer Öffentlichkeit*, Frankfurt: Suhrkamp Verlag, 1972.]

Oliver, L. (2009) "January ABCes: Guardian Edges 30m Unique Users; All Sites Record Growth". Retrieved 28 February 2009 from: http://www.journalism.co.uk/2/articles/533621.php.

Oriella PR Network (2008) "European Digital Journalism Study: How the Digital Age has Affected Journalism — and the Impact for PR". Retrieved 14 September 2008 from: http://www.europeandigitaljournalism.com/downloads/EDJS_June08_27.pdf.

Pérez-Peña, R. (2009) "As Cities Go From Two Papers to One, Talk of Zero". Retrieved 26 May 2009 from: http://www.nytimes.com/2009/03/12/business/media/12papers.html?_r=5.

Perlmutter, D. D. (2008) *Blogwars: The New Political Battleground*. Oxford: Oxford University Press.

Pew Center's Project for Excellence in Journalism (2008) "The Changing Newsroom". Retrieved 12 September 2008 from: http://journalism.org/node/11961.

Plunkett, J. (2005) "Record Numbers Visit Guardian Unlimited", *The Guardian*, 8 July 2005. Retrieved from: http://www.guardian.co.uk/technology/2005/jul/08/media.newmedia.

Pocock, J. G. A. (1995/1998) "The Ideal of Citizenship since Classical Times". In G. Schafir (ed.), *Citizenship Debates: A Reader*. Minneapolis: University of Minnesota Press.

Reese, S. D., Rutigliano, L., Hyun, K., and Jeong, J. (2007) "Mapping the Blogosphere: Professional and Citizen-Based Media in the Global News Arena". *Journalism*, 8 (3), pp. 235–61.

Reeves, I. (2008) "Will the Internet Survive the Economic Meltdown?", *The Independent*, 6 October 2008. Retrieved 10 November 2008 from: http://www.independent.co.uk/news/media/online/will-the-internet-survive-the-economic-meltdown-952287.html.

Regan, T. (2003) "Weblogs Threaten and Inform Traditional Journalism", *Nieman Reports*, 57 (3), pp. 68–9.

Rheingold, H. (2002) *Smart Mobs: The Next Social Revolution*. New York: Basic Books.

Robinson Beachboard, M., and Beachboard, J. C. (2009) "Newspapers in Slovenia: (Re)Constructing Print Journalism on the Fault Lines of History". Paper presented at the annual meeting of the International Communication Association, Sheraton New York, New York City. Retrieved from: http://www.allacademic.com/meta/p14351_index.html.

Ryfe, D., and Mensing, D. (2008) "Participatory Journalism and the Transformation of News". Paper presented at the annual meeting of the Association for Education in Journalism and Mass Communication, Marriott Downtown, Chicago, IL. Retrieved from: http://www.allacademic.com/meta/p271585_index.html.

Silverstone, R. (2006) *Media and Morality: On the Rise of the Mediapolis*. London: Polity.

Singer, J. B. (2005) "The Political J-Blogger: Normalising a New Media Form to Fit Old Norms and Practices", *Journalism*, 6 (2), pp. 173–98.

Singer, J. B. (2006a) "The Socially Responsible Existentialist: A Normative Emphasis for Journalists in a New Media Environment", *Journalism Studies*, 7 (1), pp. 2–18.

Singer, J. B. (2006b) "Stepping Back from the Gate: Online Newspaper Editors and the Co-Production of Content in Campaign 2005", *Journalism & Mass Communication Quarterly*, 83 (2), pp. 265–80.

Singer, J. B., and Friend, C. (2007) *Online Journalism Ethics: Traditions and Transitions*. New York: Sharpe.

Spencer, G. (2005) *The Media and Peace: From Vietnam to the War on Terror*. Basingstoke: Palgrave Macmillan.

Stanbridge, R., and Ljunggren, M. (2004) *African Media and ICT4D: Documentary Evidence. A Baseline Study on the State of Media Reporting on ICT and Information Society Issues in Africa*. Economic Commission for Africa.

Technorati (2008) "State of the Blogosphere / 2008. Technorati Report". Retrieved 28 December 2008 from: http://technorati.com/blogging/state-of-the-blogosphere/.

Thurman, N. (2007) "A Transatlantic Study of News Websites and their International Readers", *Journalism*, 8 (3), pp. 285–307.

Thurman, N. (2008) "Forums for Citizen Journalists? Adoption of User Generated Content Initiatives by Online News Media", *New Media & Society*, 10 (1), pp. 139–57.

Thurman, N., and Jones, S. (2005) "From Nexus to Newslog: Online Journalism from the Grassroots". In R. Keeble (ed.), *Print Journalism: A Critical Introduction*. London: Routledge, pp. 251–65.

Thussu, D. K. (2005) "Adapting to Globalisation: The Changing Contours of Journalism in India". In H. De Burgh (ed.), *Making Journalists: Diverse Models, Global Issues*. London: Routledge, pp. 127–41.

Turner, B. S. (1990) "Outline of a Theory of Citizenship", *Sociology*, 24 (2), pp. 189–217.

Turner, B. S., and Hamilton, P. (eds) (1994) *Citizenship: Critical Concepts*. London: Routledge.

Urban, C. D. (1999) "Examining Our Credibility: Perspectives of the Public and the Press". Journalism Credibility Project, American Society of Newspaper Editors.

Vilanilam, J. V. (2005) *Mass Communication in India. A Sociological Perspective*. Beverly Hills, CA: Sage.

Wall, M. (2005) "Blogs of War: Weblogs as News", *Journalism*, 6 (2), pp. 153–72.

Wilson, G. (2008) "Report Back from the BBC Future of Journalism Conference". Retrieved 1 December 2008 from: http://onlinejournalismblog.com/2008/12/01/bbc-future-of-journalism-day-1-some-reflections/.

⟨⟨ PART ⟩⟩
I
Setting the Scene

⑊ CHAPTER ⑊
1

News Blogs, Mainstream News and News Agencies

VINCENT CAMPBELL, RACHEL GIBSON,
BARRIE GUNTER AND MARIA TOURI

Chapter 1 examines the extent to which news blogs are shaping the mainstream news media's agenda.[1] It then examines a series of case studies in which blogs are alleged to have played a leading role in news production and assess how far their success can be explained through the lens of agenda-setting. Based on our analysis, we propose a new classificatory scheme for blogs that seeks to clarify the circumstances under which they can successfully influence the mainstream news media.

To consider the role of news blogs in news production, we focus specifically on their capacity to set the agenda in relation to the mainstream news media. While there have been a number of high-profile cases where blogs appear to have had a major role in bringing new issues to the news agenda or in shaping the coverage of an existing issue, an important question that such cases raise is how far they are simply exceptional. Alternatively, could they be seen as signalling an emerging and increasingly prominent role for blogs in news reporting? In order to explore this question this chapter examines news blogs in the light of agenda-setting theory. In particular, we ask how blogs can be understood in terms of theories of first- and second-order agenda-setting. We formulate a series of propositions regarding the circumstances that appear to be associated with blogs' effectiveness in this regard. We then examine a series of cases in which blogs played a prominent role in shaping the news agenda, taking into account our expectations, to establish how far agenda-setting can explain such success. It is based on this that we propose our new classificatory scheme.

Vincent Campbell, Rachel Gibson, Barrie Gunter and Maria Touri

THE RISE AND RISE OF THE BLOGOSPHERE

The explosion in the number of "weblogs" (now commonly truncated to "blogs") in recent years is a well-documented phenomenon. Close to 90 million existed by mid-2007, according to Technorati, the online monitor of blogs (2007). And 120,000 more sites were being created worldwide every day (*The Guardian* 2007: 31). Advances in the "user-friendliness" of blogging software during the late 1990s and particularly the launch of blogger.com in 1999 did much to promote this growth, moving the practice from a small, highly IT-literate elite to the domain of "everyman". This shift in the locus and ease of blog production also changed its nature and practice. Initially, blogs were rather simple creatures, consisting of a set of annotated hyperlinks and little else. So the site of Jorn Barger, who is said to have coined the phrase "weblog" in 1997, in reference to his own site, robotwisdom, contained little more than a list or log of the Web pages he found interesting (Du and Wagner 2006).

Taking this definition as a starting point, observers have gone on to argue that the first weblog actually pre-dates Barger. It instead belongs to the Web founder, Tim Berners-Lee, who, in 1991, listed new websites on a dynamic Web page at CERN (Auty 2005; Winer 1999). Before the turn of the millennium, however, it was clear that blogging had taken on a new form, as "filter"-type blogs were rapidly superseded by a newer "free-style" mode that centred on individual self-expression and personal journal keeping (Blood 2000).

This proliferation and re-fashioning of the so-called blogosphere has meant that to produce a definitive description of a blog, or the practice of blogging, has become like trying to hit a moving target. Certain features do appear to recur among the descriptions provided by leading writers in the field, however. Paquet (2003), for instance, itemizes a range of central characteristics or traits that identify a blog. These include personal editorship by the owner/creator, the inclusion of hyperlinks, regular updates, free public access and maintenance of a postings archive.

Along similar lines, Coleman defines a blog as "a web page that serves as a publicly accessible personal journal (or log) for an individual . . . [that is] updated daily, providing an ongoing account of the beliefs, discoveries and personality of the author" (2005: 274). Drezner and Farrell (2004b) similarly emphasize the commentary and links components of blogs, along with periodic updating and entries being presented in reverse chronological order.

The importance of chronology or timing in blogs is underscored by Hopkins and Matheson in their study of the New Zealand election blogs that they describe as "online diaries" or "webpages which are regularly updated, with the most recent material appearing at the top, usually date-stamped" (2005: 94). Lawson-Borders and Kirk also describe them as "online diaries" in which "information is electronically posted, updated frequently, and presented in reverse chronological order", with the added dimension (compared to print media) that they allow responses from readers (2005: 548). Of course, there are some areas of disagreement that arise, such as whether the presence of a blogroll or a "trackback" facility is required, or whether multiple authors can write a blog. Furukawa et al. (2006), for instance, note that "one blog is updated by one user". Parallel to this increasing focus on identifying what unites blogs have been continuing attempts to categorize them. Krishnamurthy (2002) offered a four-category schema that divided blogs according to two criteria — their individual vs. community orientation and topical vs. personal focus. This follows Blood's (2000) basic distinction between the more topical filter blogs and the highly personalized journal-style blogs. Additionally, the typology included space for highly personalized, community-based blogs (friends/social networks group blog) and more topical community blogs. Actual examples of these latter types proved somewhat thin on the ground, however.

Subsequent work by Herring et al. (2005) confirmed that filter and particularly personalized journal-style blogs predominate in their empirical analysis of randomly selected blogs from a blog tracking site. Nevertheless, they also proposed a new category of "k-logs": corporate and project-specific blogs. More recently the list has been expanded yet further to include a range of more topically oriented blogs such as warblogs, campaign blogs (run by politicians, their supporters and opponents), legal blogs (discussing developments in law and legislation), science and technology blogs, disseminating information to user communities, and, of course, news blogs, focusing largely on politics and current affairs (Gordon-Murnane 2006).

THE DEVELOPMENT OF NEWS BLOGS

News blogs, defined as "Web logs dedicated to the dissemination of news" (MacDougall 2005: 575), were first reported as part of a breaking news story in the *Charlotte Observer*'s coverage of Hurricane Bonnie in 1998[2] (Singer 2005). The events of 11 September 2001, however, probably did most to raise the profile of blogging in relation to news reporting. The dramatic quality and unprecedented scale of the disaster fuelled public hunger for regular updates, and the mainstream media struggled to cope. The Internet provided an alternative platform for reportage by those caught up in the events, offering a more direct and immediate channel of communication to those seeking information about the tragedy.

Arguably the next key landmark for news blogs was the US presidential election of 2004, which saw an explosion in the practice, with candidates and journalists, as well as a number of amateur independents, introducing blogs to their home pages and official news sites (Lawson-Borders and Kirk 2005).

The election also provided the setting for one of the most talked-about blogging news "coups" to date: what has gone down in the annals as the "Rathergate Affair", which led to the early retirement of one of America's most revered broadcasters, CBS anchorman Dan Rather. In this case, bloggers effectively challenged the authenticity of particular documents that Rather had presented on air that "proved" President Bush had lied about his service in the National Guard. A subsequent internal inquiry by the news organization, corroborated by the opinions of a number of "expert" bloggers, confirmed that the documents were fraudulent. This led to the dismissal of several CBS newsroom employees, including the story's producer.

This apparent growing influence of blogs in shaping the news agenda has, not surprisingly, encouraged academics to characterize and assess their place within wider journalistic practices and processes of news production, dissemination and consumption. These efforts have generally taken one of five basic approaches: (1) a series of detailed case studies of high-profile news events featuring blogs such as the Rather incident (Allan 2006; Thelwall and Stuart 2007; Kivikuru 2006); (2) in-depth accounts of various individual news blogs (Matheson 2004); (3) analysis of a sample of news blogs within traditional news organizations (Singer 2005; Robinson 2006); (4) attempts to theorize and categorize news blogs *vis-à-vis* one another (MacDougall 2005) or in relation to online journalism more generally (Deuze 2003); and finally (5) attempts to place news blogs in the wider democratic sphere and assess their implications for increasing public knowledge and citizen involvement in politics (Coleman 2005).

While these analyses have yielded somewhat different insights into the function and significance of news blogs, a common theme running through them, either implicitly or explicitly, is the need to interpret them in the context of the mainstream news media. In particular, most accounts seem to point toward news blogs being dependent on mainstream news media for their notoriety and contents.

Thus, although protagonists might see news blogging as a new style of journalism bringing power to the people and new issues to the fore, many of the most influential early blogs were produced by professional journalists or political insiders seeking to free themselves from the editorial shackles of mainstream newsrooms or the central party HQ. Indeed, in terms of content, as Thelwall and Stuart revealed in their analysis of blog coverage of several major crisis events in 2005, postings focused largely on mainstream news media reports (2007: 538).

While there has been much discussion of the inter-dependence of blogs and the established news media, to date there has been a lack of systematic empirical or theoretical attempts to unpick exactly how this relationship works. That is what we attempt to do here. We detail the relationship between blogs and the mainstream news media in a more formalized way. In particular, we are interested in the extent to which blogs can be seen to provide an agenda-setting function and act as news producers in their own right. Thus, before going on to consider the evidence for blogs as agenda-setters, we first revisit the origins and meaning of agenda-setting.

THE AGENDA-SETTING THEORY

We will employ agenda-setting theory to interpret existing findings on blogs' impact on news production and how the media agenda is shaped. This will be used to provide an early inference of the extent to which blogs are challenging the status of mainstream news journalism.

There has been much debate about agenda-setting that has centred on conceptual issues concerning how to define the term 'agenda', the meaning of agenda-setting and the different levels at which it can potentially be measured (Edelstein 1993; Kosicki

1993; Rogers, Dearing and Bregman 1993). Some writers have also helpfully differentiated different sub-areas of agenda-setting (Rogers, Dearing and Bregman 1993).

In their original analysis McCombs and Shaw (1972) were concerned primarily with the public agenda. They examined to what extent the news media covered the issues the public considered important. Then there is policy agenda. This entails the study of which issues are of current significance to governments, public bodies or elected officials (Rogers and Dearing 1988). There is, then, an important question about the extent to which the policy agenda becomes a media agenda. Finally, there are studies of the media agenda, which involve the investigation of the selection of news stories for coverage and the kinds of emphasis they receive. In many studies there are attempts to link the media agenda directly to the public agenda. However, some research is concerned also, or exclusively, with elucidating the different factors that can underpin the media agenda.

Originally, agenda-setting focused on links between the media agenda and the public agenda. In their seminal study McCombs and Shaw analysed how the media, through their coverage of topics or stories, could effectively tell the public what to think about (1972). But they later considered how news content could also tell people *how* to think about particular objects of coverage (McCombs 1992; McCombs and Shaw 1993). Thus, the news media could raise the salience of an issue and this could then become translated into a public perception of the current importance of that issue.

Selection and salience are therefore fundamental in the agenda-setting process, underlining also the way the news *frames* a story (McCombs and Shaw 1993). This additional level of agenda-setting is encapsulated in the so-called "two-level agenda-setting". In the domain of traditional agenda-setting effects or first-level agenda-setting, the media agenda is defined by a set of objects. These objects have a variety of characteristics and traits, which are then emphasized selectively in what can be described as a second-level agenda-setting process. This distinction is useful in considering the role and impact of blogs.

In our discussion of blogs we are concerned with how the (news) media agenda interacts with the "blog agenda". This could have a cascading effect on the public agenda, whereby the blog agenda is assumed initially to influence the mainstream news media agenda, which, in turn, impacts on public perceptions of news issues. Another possibility we examine is the direct impact of the "blog agenda" on the public agenda, by-passing the mainstream news media.

Based on the key components of the agenda-setting process, the following sections reflect an attempt to re-conceptualize existing theoretical and empirical evidence of the role and status of the blogosphere in the news making process. Hence, through the theoretical formulation of three roles, named here as the news originator, resuscitator or re-framer, we seek to evaluate the prominence of blogs as influential news sources and offer some insight into their role in the future of newspapers and print journalism in its entirety.

Vincent Campbell, Rachel Gibson, Barrie Gunter and Maria Touri

BLOGS AND FIRST-LEVEL AGENDA-SETTING: THE NEWS ORIGINATOR

As news-related blogs have proliferated, and it has become increasing evident that journalists and citizens are using them, various writers have developed theories assuming that their influence on mainstream journalism is far-reaching.

The suggested impact falls within the notion of first-level agenda-setting, with blogs functioning as originators of the objects covered by mainstream media. Relevant to this concept, Brosius and Weinman (1996) approached agenda-setting through the prism of the two-step flow model, in which opinion leaders mediate between journalists and the public. They linked the two-step flow to agenda-setting research, arguing that agenda-setting is a process in which influential individuals "collect, diffuse, filter, and promote the flow of information". This could ultimately be the correct description of journalistically focused blogs, which can change the agenda-setting question from what issues the media tell people to think about to what issues bloggers tell the media they want to think about.

Along similar lines, Drezner and Farrell (2004b) have suggested that if a critical number of elite blogs raise a particular story, it can attract the interest of mainstream media outlets. If the mainstream media therefore construct focal points through which political actors must operate, the blogosphere has the capacity to construct focal points through which mainstream media operate. If blogs generate a consensus about a particular issue, this acts as a barometer of interest and opinion on the issue. The media will be affected by that consensus in the same way that the media affect the mass public.

In addition, Branum (2001) identified the blogging phenomenon as a form of hybrid between interpersonal and mass communication, in which case the blogging community could define the parameters of discussion on those issues that the mainstream media avoid, setting the agenda for their readership on certain topics.

Effectively, the potential role of blogs as originators of the news agenda could revolutionize the journalistic process as a whole, creating scope for so-called "citizen journalism". However, the above are mostly theoretically based observations elaborated with limited or no empirical data. A key reason for this might be that the opportunities for blogs to originate news seem to be limited to circumstances in which mainstream news media's capacity to cover a news story is compromised in one way or another. Moments when blogs have become originators of news have been often linked to circumstances such as the limits in mainstream media's communication capacity (as for US online news providers in the immediate wake of 9/11), the speed and location of the new event (as in the Asian tsunami of 2004) or the difficulty and danger of getting to important event locations. The wars in Afghanistan and, particularly, Iraq have provided some of the best-known examples of circumstances that have provided a niche for blogs to become news originators, not least a variety of "soldier blogs" or "milblogs", but also blogs from locals caught up in the conflict.

Among the best-known war-related blogs was Where is Raed?, produced by the "Baghdad blogger", who called himself Salam Pax. Pax's blog accounts of daily life during the war gave a degree of eyewitness detail that Western journalists, embedded or otherwise, simply were not able to provide at the time. Interestingly, Pax's blog was intended as a personal diary for a friend in Jordan and not as an explicit attempt to influence news and/or public agendas. Similarly, many soldier blogs were also started for reasons other than to influence news and public discourses: for instance, that of US GI Colby Buzzell (Kline and Burstein 2005). What made these blogs stand out was, at least in part, that they were picked up by mainstream news media outlets extensively monitoring the web, alongside their more conventional newsgathering techniques.

Given the degree of dependence of news blog authorship and content on the mainstream media organizations, it is unrealistic to consider the blogger as the originator, except when the mainstream media's capacity to cover issues and events is limited or non-existent. However, if we examine evidence concerning the status of blog authors and content through the agenda-setting prism, this can ultimately lead to the formation of two additional potential roles of the blogosphere: as the resuscitator and as the re-framer.

BLOGS AND INTER-MEDIA AGENDA-SETTING: THE NEWS RESUSCITATOR

Perhaps a more realistic approach to the role of blogs as mainstream media agenda setters can be obtained through the further unfolding of the agenda-setting theory and the pattern of news coverage that defines the media agenda in the first place. McCombs (2005) referred to the norms and traditions of journalism, the interactions among news organizations and interactions of journalists with sources and their agendas as "inter-media agenda-setting" — in other words, the influence of the news media on each other (McCombs 2005: 548–9).

The role that blogs play in inter-media agenda-setting could be verified through evidence that media elites — editors, publishers, reporters and columnists — are regular consumers of blogs. *New York Times* columnist Paul Krugman gave a lengthy interview to one blog, in which he discussed the blogs that he read on a daily basis (Drezner and Farrell 2004a: 14). Other opinion columnists, including Michael Barone, Walter Shapiro and Fareed Zakaria, have indicated that blogs form a part of their routine information-gathering activities. Prominent political reporters and editors at *The New York Times*, *The Washington Post*, *Los Angeles Times*, ABC News, *The New Yorker*, *Newsweek* and *Time* have also made similar statements (Smolkin 2004; Packer 2004).

In line with McCombs, who argues that it is the popularity and wide use of blogs among journalists themselves that could yield an agenda-setting role on the media agenda (2005: 549), the empirical evidence from online authors points towards an inter-media agenda-setting role. In this case, the potential impact of blogs on the mainstream agenda could be assessed as the power of journalists (and other prominent bloggers) to re-build the media agenda and, free from the constraints of journalistic professionalism, return to and *resuscitate* past news items. A key ingredient of this function lies in the expertise that journalist-bloggers can provide on substantive issues. As Drezner and Farrell argue, general interest journalists have limited specialized knowledge. They suggested that "blogs can serve as repository of 'local knowledge' for relevant policy issues or current event histories" that mainstream media reporters can use when the issue in question emerges as a news topic again (Drezner and Farrell 2004a: 16).

In addition, established theoretical assumptions and empirical evidence encourage the view that news blogs can be located within the inter-media agenda-setting process. From a theory-driven perspective Bennett (2003) conceived of new media technologies being utilized extensively for political activism through outlets he called "micro media" (such as pressure group websites and political discussion forums). He saw mainstream news media outlets as "macro media", providing the primary sites of mainstream political reporting and discussion. Bennett considered blogs as sitting somewhere in between these, as "middle media", sometimes bridging the gap between the mainstream and alternative/underground media (Bennett 2003). This was a process that resembles the interaction among journalists, sources and other external news agenda-setters, defined by McCombs as inter-media agenda-setting.

The resuscitation role of blogs has been illustrated by the part they have played in the coverage of major political scandals. In one well-documented case blogs kept alive a story that finally resulted in the resignation of the prominent US political figure Senator Trent Lott as Senate majority leader. In a speech to celebrate the hundredth birthday of Senator Strom Thurmond, Lott endorsed racist sentiments attributed to Thurmond to an audience that included journalists from the major news media. Only one newsroom (ABC News) picked up the story, however, and even then gave it only passing coverage.

The story might have been forgotten but for the fact that it was subsequently followed up by ABC News' own blog, The Note. This gave rise to much "blog chatter". The chatter reached a climax, further helped by additional postings by The Note. Within a matter of a few days the mainstream news media picked up the story again, after Lott himself had issued a public apology for his remarks. Even President George W. Bush was drawn into the story and expressed disappointment about Lott's comments. The story reached such a pitch that Lott was forced to resign. This outcome was trumpeted as a significant "result" for blogging that placed centrally on the news agenda a story that the major news media had initially chosen to ignore.

On a general basis, it emerges that, in the context of current affairs journalism in particular, blogs have become increasingly normal form of communication (e.g. Kerbal and Bloom 2005), with any potential impact of news blogs on the mainstream media agenda being filtered through journalists' use and consumption. This normalization process was among the findings of Singer's study (2005), which provided evidence of the dominance of experienced journalists in the production and dissemination of blog content. The study examined ten national news blogs in the USA and ten regional/local blogs published within mainstream media news outlets, in an attempt to derive some general principles of their status as journalism. Looking quantitatively at political news blogs in particular, Singer examined the existence and extent of journalists' opinions, of "user-generated content" (such as reader comments, or readers being able to post new articles) and the extent of links (Singer 2005: 182).

The findings suggested to Singer that, within the mainstream media, blogs are undergoing a "normalizing" process (Singer 2005: 192), in which it is mostly journalists that retain control of the news medium and incorporate blogs into established practices. Combined with the fact that four-fifths of the examined sites contained links and around three-quarters of these were to mainstream media outlets (Singer 2005: 187), Singer's findings demonstrated a strong interconnection between political news blogs and journalists. This can reflect blogs' position in the inter-media agenda-setting circle as a platform where news items can be re-accessed and re-assessed by journalists themselves before they reappear on the mainstream news agenda. In effect, the increasing normalization of news blogs within the structure of mainstream media renders their role as resuscitators a more realistic approach than that of originators.

BLOGS AND SECOND-LEVEL AGENDA-SETTING: THE NEWS RE-FRAMER

A key constituent in the emerging role of blogs as resuscitators is the status of the author, with journalists and elite bloggers being the key players in this intermediate agenda-setting function. The suggestion made here is that looking at the type of content provided by blogs, yet independent of the author, could give rise to an additional function that blogs have in the agenda-setting process. In this case, the content that news blogs traditionally disseminate can generate a direct impact on public perceptions and become the focus of public attention.

In relation to the impact of blogs on the public agenda, a central assumption that has emerged is that the introduction of myriad online news sources and channels has resulted in a highly fragmented audience and the generation of multiple personal agendas (McCombs 2005). In this landscape blogs are seen as highly individualized news sources composed by a selection of links, online news and information. They turn into personal agendas, leading to the public agenda becoming fragmented and public attention becoming dispersed. From this standpoint blogs could define the issues the public thinks about through a first-level agenda-setting process. This phenomenon could imply an indirect impact on mainstream media agenda as well. As Branum (2001) argued, the public agenda fragmentation could result in the mainstream media's power declining. However, such an impact is debatable, considering that readership on the Web and in the blogosphere is highly concentrated, with many of the popular news sites and/or blogs being subsidiaries of established traditional media.

Data released on 17 January 2007 by media measurement company Nielsen//NetRatings showed an increased readership, particularly among the visitors to blog sites affiliated with the largest US Internet newspapers, rising to 3.8 million in December 2006 from 1.2 million a year earlier (Reuters 2007). This suggests that the mainstream media are central to blogosphere audience preferences. Thus, there could be a potential blog influence on the public agenda, seen from the perspective of second-level agenda-setting. This would operate as a consequence of the distinctive content disseminated by blogs, rather than from the selection of the actual news items discussed. In this case, blogs can influence the public's understanding of the news through the promotion of alternative frames of reference for news items already in the mainstream media agenda.

One prominent case that illustrates the way blogs can act to re-frame a story was the "Rathergate" affair, mentioned earlier. First, a blogger questioned the documents' authenticity. Then other bloggers, many of whom had relevant expertise in such matters, quickly backed this up with evidence and insights. The blog chatter was picked up by *The Washington Post*, which immediately gave the story more weight and credibility. CBS eventually bowed to the pressure from expert critics in the blogosphere, backed up by other mainstream news coverage.

Thus, as commentary and analysis have become predominant, bloggers have not only revisited and resuscitated news items but re-framed them as well, re-distributing focal points for public attention. Blogs could then be seen as integral parts of the journalistic and newsmaking process, not necessarily as a domain for original news reporting but as sources of opinion, analysis and discussion, contributing to the development of a more open and interactive form of journalism.

Evidence of this distinctive content provided by blogs in relation to current news items emerges from a number of studies that have attempted to explore the nature of blogs. An analysis conducted by Matheson (2004) of *The Guardian* weblog looked at aspects of "layout, style, voice, textual coherence and forms of hypertext reference . . . by implicitly contrasting these with the textual practice of Anglo-American print news" (Matheson 2004: 447–8). Matheson assessed the blog's content as responding to news media "along three dimensions: the establishment of a different interpersonal relation, of a different authority and of a journalism focused upon connection rather than fact" (Matheson 2004: 453). Although, as Matheson suggested, "the weblog is grounded in traditional notions of the role of the journalist" (2004: 460), the information output it provides tends to complement rather than replace traditional media's news. The nature of this output could then operate to influence the level of salience of items placed on the media agenda, leading to a second-level agenda-setting effect on public perceptions.

Along similar lines, Robinson's study (2006) of 130 blogs published within mainstream news media outlets in the USA identified seven different forms of news blog. These included:

> a reporter's notebook of news tidbits and incidentals; a straight column or opinion for the Web; a question-and-answer format by editors; a readership forum; a confessional diary written by the reporter about his or her beat; a round-up of news summaries that promote the publication; and a rumour-mill blog that the report uses as an off-the-record account. (Robinson 2006: 69–70)

These forms are also indicative of an attempt to comment on, evaluate and even re-frame existing news, which Robinson describes as the emergence of a postmodern "nonlinear and interactive" form of journalism. This involves breaking the boundaries of conventional news reporting, through features such as first-person narration, contradictions, speculation and so on (Robinson 2006: 80). Moreover, studies that have looked at the position of blogs within wider news media coverage of specific events, especially large-scale crises, have also shown that "news" blogs essentially provide distinctive kinds of content that relate to, comment on, interrogate and analyse information already on mainstream media news (Thelwall and Stuart 2007; Kivikuru 2006).

The reliance of blogs on mainstream news media, and the distinctive types of information they disseminate, is therefore suggestive of news blogs' attempt to perform a "news repair" through commentary, opinion and criticism of the news items already in the media agenda. The re-framing process involved in these blog activities could offer new focal points for the public's attention regarding news events promoted by the mainstream media agenda.

The idea of the blogs' role within the context of second-level agenda-setting could be reinforced through research findings from the study of non-mainstream media blogs. In particular, Wall (2005) conducted a content analysis of non-mainstream blogs during the Iraq War in 2003, focusing explicitly on the nature of the news content in blogs produced by a variety of sources. Looking at the narrative style of reporting in the examined blogs, she described blog news as "personal, opinionated [and] one-sided", promoting a personal outlook that is a key characteristic of how they frame (or re-frame) the news. It was also suggested that blogs presented stories in an open, incomplete and fragmented form, giving audiences the possibility to follow links that could transfer them to different views. Moreover, there was no indication of the writers taking a more neutral stance and tailoring their messages to appeal to the greater audience, while they were also not afraid to offend others or include information about themselves (Wall 2005: 162). Wall also suggested the emergence of a postmodern journalism; this highlighted the key differences between the content provided by the mainstream media and blogs. It created the scope to locate news blogs in the agenda-setting process as potential initiators of public agenda effects, triggered through the re-framing of the mainstream media agenda.

THE NATURE OF LINKS BETWEEN BLOGS AND THE NEWS MAINSTREAM

The three approaches discussed in the preceding sections have sought to offer a more systematic organization of the existing knowledge of blogs as components of the production and dissemination of news and of the routes through which their influential power could be evaluated. The evidence used in this analysis, regarding the alleged influence of news blogs on the mainstream news agenda, has depended mostly on case studies associated with specific news stories. These stories have tended to comprise challenges and alternative views on stories released in the mainstream, stories initiated as exclusives by bloggers themselves, or stories that have been dropped by the mainstream media and then rejuvenated by bloggers (Allan 2006). Although some high-profile stories have served to underline the significant impact that independent bloggers can have on the biggest news media, it is less clear whether this remains an unusual occurrence or whether it is becoming more normative. What we also need to know, however, is whether news blogs have become a part of the normative news environment and represent sources with which mainstream news organizations maintain regular links. Or is news agenda-setting via blogs still an unusual phenomenon?

One exploratory attempt to shed light on this question was undertaken by the authors in a project funded by the Nuffield Foundation that investigated the online information flow links between the news websites of mainstream news organizations (broadcast and print) in the UK, sites operated by independent bloggers and sites operated by professional journalists who worked for major media organizations (Gunter, Gibson, Campbell, Touri and Ackland 2009). These sites were designated as "seed" sites (initiating nodes from which the broader complex network of links could be mapped). The research utilized web crawler software that could measure the volume of communication links between different web sites and the direction in which information flowed between them over pre-designated time periods (see Ackland and Gibson 2004; Ackland 2005; Ackland, O'Neil, Standish and Buchhorn 2006).

This research was an exploratory study that was conducted to test a methodology for examining links between independent news bloggers and the news mainstream. It was conducted entirely within the online world, on a limited time-scale and with UK seed site samples. The authors' eventual aim is to expand this work to a larger and international scale.

The analysis began with the selection of three seed sets of mainstream news media sites, blogs associated with major news media and operated by professional journalists affiliated to major news organizations, and independent news bloggers who had no affiliation with major news organizations. An initial set of 18 mainstream news media sites was selected on the basis of online traffic data. A further set of 20 independent news blogs was also selected on the same basis.

Online website mapping software was used to conduct an initial crawl of the mainstream news media sites. This analysis found that each of these seed sets linked to thousands on other sites, among which were a number of blogs produced by journalists who worked for major news organizations. To create more manageable sets of data, the seed sets were reduced to the top five sites in each category. URLs were page grouped to reduce the overall numbers of sites further. Further crawls were then run with all three seed sets. These revealed that mainstream news media sites and blogs operated by professional journalists associated with major news organizations occupied larger networks (3,000+ sites each) than did the independent news blogs (2,500 sites).

The networks were further reduced to more manageable sizes by excluding less well-connected sites. This analysis revealed that independent news blogs linked mostly to other sites within their own category and relatively rarely to sites of mainstream news organizations or blogs run by professional journalists who worked for major newspapers or news broadcasters. The blogs of professional journalists affiliated to major news organizations, in contrast, linked evenly to independent news bloggers, the sites of major news organizations and to the sites of other affiliated professional journalists, as well as to a catch-all miscellaneous "Other" category.

The sites of major news organizations exhibited most links to "Other" sites (for example, operated by government departments, political parties, politicians, regulators, commercial organizations and other institutional websites), followed by links to independent news bloggers.

In general, it emerged that independent news bloggers appeared to work harder to establish links to other sites of all kinds, while the sites of mainstream news media had many other sites linking to them, indicating that they had authority as news sources. Independent news bloggers linked out to other independent bloggers more than they did to mainstream news media or the blogs operated by affiliated professional journalists. The blogs of affiliated professional journalists were linked to mainly by "Other" sites and by independent news bloggers, and linked out mostly to the sites of major news media and to selected independent bloggers. The sites of the major news media were linked to mostly by "Other" and by independent bloggers, with little evidence of links out emerging.

The evidence that emerged from this initial study indicated that independent news bloggers and mainstream news organizations are connected. At least within the context of the wider Web, the mainstream news media appear to be the more dominant and authoritative voices of online news. Within the smaller online sphere of news producers, however, online communication linkage patterns show the major news media are more likely to direct their readers to information posted in the independent blogosphere than the latter are to link into the mainstream sources (either news sites or blogs). As such, the findings of this preliminary empirical study lend some support to the idea of an independent news blogosphere as a somewhat separate if not equal source of news content to the mainstream media. While news blogs may receive a lot of attention and potentially traffic from the likes of *The Guardian*, *The Times* and the BBC, they occupy their own densely populated networks and display a preference for linking to one another over and above the bigger news-producing sites. These early data suggest that the notion of blogs generating a "buzz" and an alternative agenda outside of the domain of regular news reporting is a credible way of interpreting their influence.

CONCLUSIONS

Many of the conceptual considerations of the impact of blogs on news are normatively concentrated on the question of whether blogs are significantly altering the nature of news and journalism. Much hyperbole exists on both sides — from those relishing the perceived undermining of mainstream news media and their failings to those concerned about the undermining of the professional processes and standards of "proper" journalism by the activities of untrained and unthinking amateurs. Trying to test such positions requires placing these positions in a conceptual framework within which to evaluate some of the high-profile examples of blogs' impact on the news. The conceptual framework of agenda-setting is useful in this regard in providing different levels of potential influence, and this chapter has suggested three potential agenda-setting roles of blogs. Despite the claims of blog proponents, first-level agenda-setting, in which blogs act as *originators* of news, is limited to circumstances when mainstream media are compromised in their ability to cover issues and events. In such situations, in addition, those that take advantage often have such specialist knowledge or access to events, so that when the news agenda inevitably moves on (and when mainstream news media catch up), they lose their currency as a primary news source.

However, opportunities for more sustained influence through second-level agenda-setting of mainstream news agendas are evident in at least two ways. Bloggers can act as *resuscitators*, for instance, following up stories that mainstream media fail to follow up or accord low priority, and can give a story enough new impetus to remerge on the mainstream news agenda. Bloggers can also act as *re-framers*, interrogating, challenging and making transparent elements contributing to mainstream media framing of news events. The challenges these kinds of influence have created for some mainstream news organizations have seen blogs sometimes dubbed as parasitic. But while these are certainly examples of symbiosis between blogs and news, there is no reason to presume that the relationship is necessarily detrimental to mainstream news. For newspapers, in particular, the possibility that blogs are not necessarily parasitic but commensal (of neutral impact) — or even mutualist (that the relation between themselves and blogs could be of mutual benefit to both) — is evident in the way that blogs, as both a news-gathering tool and a format of content delivery, are gradually being incorporated into and normalized by mainstream news organizations. Exploratory research has yielded empirical data within the world of online news to show that independent news bloggers display links with mainstream news organizations, but that information seems to flow in much larger volumes from the major news media to bloggers than the other way around (Gunter, Gibson, Campbell, Touri and Ackland 2009). This evidence does not deny the possibility of bloggers setting or influencing major news agendas, but indicates that it has not yet emerged as a normative phenomenon.

To conclude, the examination of blog coverage of certain news items through the prism of agenda-setting theory leads to two main observations. First, the distinct content and approach of blogs to news events are perhaps the key element of any influence they might exert on the media and/or the public agenda. Second, while by resuscitating and re-framing the news, blogs could challenge media organizations and newspapers in particular, this process appears to remain in the hands of major news operators. The instrumental role of blogs in providing more in-depth, interactive and accessible news is clearly being recognized by journalists, who have seized the opportunity to give audiences more reasons to read, draw more attention to newspapers' websites and help maintain trusted brands. So long as journalists recognize and respond to the reality created by the Internet as a whole, blogs can prove a means of revitalizing newspapers.

Notes

1   This chapter is based on a paper presented at the Future of Newspapers conference 12–13 September 2008, Centre for Journalism Studies, Cardiff, Wales, UK.
2   The *Charlotte Observer's* coverage is archived at: http://web.archive.org/web/20010417195542/www.charlotte.com/special/bonnie/0828dispatches.htm.

References

Ackland, R. (2005) "Mapping the U.S. Political Blogosphere: Are Conservative Bloggers More Prominent?" Paper presented to BlogTalk Downunder, Sydney, 19–22 May 2005. Retrieved from: http://voson.anu.edu.au/papers/polblogs.pdf.

Ackland, R., and Gibson, R. (2004) "Mapping Political Party Networks on the WWW". Paper presented at the Australian Electronic Governance Conference, University of Melbourne, 14–15 April 2004. Retrieved from: http://voson.anu.edu.au/papers/political_networks.pdf.

Ackland, R., O'Neil, M., Standish, R., and Buchhorn, M. (2006) "VOSON: A Web Services Approach for Facilitating Research into Online Networks". Paper presented at the Second International Conference on e-Social Science, University of Manchester, 28–30 June 2006. Retrieved from: http://voson.anu.edu.au/papers/ncess-conf06-full-paper-final.pdf.

Allan, S. (2006) *Online News*. Maidenhead: Open University Press.

Armstrong, J., and Moulitsas Zuniga, M. (2006) *Crashing the Gate: Netroots, Grassroots, and the Rise of People-Powered Politics*. White River Junction, VT: Chelsea Green.

Auty, C. (2005) "UK Elected Representatives and Their Weblogs: First Impressions." *Aslib Proceedings*, 57 (4), pp. 338–55.

Bennett, W. L. (2003) "Communicating Global Activism: Strengths and Vulnerabilities of Networked Politics", *Information, Communication and Society*, 6 (2), pp. 143–68.

Blood, R. (2000) "Weblogs: A History and Perspective". www.rebeccablood.net/essays/weblog_history.html.

Bowman, S., and Willis, C. (2003) *We Media: How Audiences Are Shaping the Future of News and Information*. The Media Center at the American Press Institute. Retrieved from: http://www.hypergene.net/wemedia/.

Branum, J. (2001) "The Blogging Phenomenon: An Overview and Theoretical Consideration", Final Term Paper for Theories of Mass Communication, Southwest Texas State University, Dr. Sandy Rao. Retrieved from: http://www.ajy.net/jmb/blogphenomenon.htm.

Brosius, H., and Wiemann, G. (1996) "Who Sets the Agenda? Agenda Setting As Two-Step Flow", *Communication Research*, 23 (5), pp. 561–80.

Coleman, S. (2005) "Blogs and the New Politics of Listening", *Political Quarterly*, 76 (2), pp. 273–80.

Deuze, M. (2003) "The Web and its Journalisms: Considering the Consequences of Different Types of Newsmedia Online", *New Media and Society*, 5 (2), pp. 203–30.

Drezner, D. W., and Farrell, H. (2004a) "The Power and Politics of Blogs". Paper presented at the annual conference of the American Political Science Association, Chicago, 2–5 September.

Drezner, D. W., and Farrell, H. (2004b) "Web of Influence" *Foreign Policy* (November/December 2004). Retrieved from: http://www.foreignpolicy.com/ story/cms. php?story_id=2707&popup_delayed=1.

Du, Helen S., and Wagner, C. (2006) "Weblog Success: Exploring the Role of Technology", *International Journal of Human-Computer Studies,* 64, pp. 789–98.

Edelstein, A. S. (1993) "Thinking about the Criterion Variable in Agenda-Setting Research", *Journal of Communication*, 43 (2), pp. 85–99.

Furukawa, T., Matsuzawa, T., Matsuo, Y., Uchiyama, K., and Takeda, M. (2006) "Analysis of User Relations and Reading Activity in Weblogs", *Electronics and Communications in Japan*, Part 1, 89 (12), pp. 88–96.

Gordon-Murnane, L. (2006) "Politics and Tech Tools: Blogs, Aggregators and Tracking Tools", *Information Today*. Retrieved from: http://www.infotoday.com/searcher/oct06/Gordon-Murnane.shtml.

Griffiths, M. (2004) "e-Citizens: Blogging as Democratic Practice", *Electronic Journal of e-Government*, 2. Retrieved from: http://www.ejeg.com/volume-2/volume2-issue3/v2-i3-art2-griffiths.pdf.

Gunter, B. (2006) "Who Do Online News Consumers Trust?", *Library and Information Update*, 5 (9), pp. 40–41.

Gunter, B., Gibson, R., Campbell, V., Touri, M., and Ackland, R. (2009) *Blogging and the Impact of Citizen Journalism.* Report to the Nuffield Foundation, Department of Media and Communication, University of Leicester.

Herring, S. C., Scheidt, L. A., Wright, E., and Bonus, S. (2005) "Weblogs as a Bridging Genre", *Information Technology and People*, 18 (2), pp. 142–71.

Hopkins, K., and Matheson, D. (2005) "Blogging the New Zealand Election: The Impact of New Media Practices on the Old Game", *Political Science*, 57 (2), pp. 93–105.

Hurwitz, R. (2003) "Who Needs Politics? Who Needs People? The Ironies of Democracy in Cyberspace". In H. Jenkins, and D. Thorburn (eds), *Democracy and New Media*. Cambridge, MA: MIT Press, pp. 101–12.

Kerbel, M. R., and Bloom, J. D. (2005) "Blog for America and Civic Involvement", *Harvard International Journal of Press/Politics*, 10 (4), pp. 3–27.

Kivikuru, U. (2006) "Tsunami Communication in Finland: Revealing Tensions in the Sender–Receiver Relationship", *European Journal of Communication*, 21 (4), pp. 499–520.

Kline, D., and Burstein, D. (2005) *Blog! How the Newest Media Revolution is Changing Politics, Business, and Culture*. New York: CDS Books.

Kosicki, G. (1993) "Problems and Opportunities in Agenda-Setting Research", *Journal of Communication*, 43 (2), pp. 100–127.

Krishnamurthy, S. (2002) "The Multidimensionality of Blog Conversations: The Virtual Enactment of Sept 11". Paper presented at Internet Research 3.0, Maastricht, October 2002.

Lasica, J. D. (2001a) "Blogging as a Form of Journalism", *Online Journalism Review*, 24 May 2001. Retrieved from: http://www.ojr.org/ojr/workplace/1017958873.php.

Lasica, J. D. (2001b) "Weblogs: A New Source of News", *Online Journalism Review*, 31 May 2001. Retrieved from: http://www.ojr.org/ojr/workplace/1017958782.php.

Lasica, J. D. (2001c) "How The Net Is Shaping Journalism Ethics". Retrieved from: http://www.well-com/-jd/newsethics.html.

Lasica, J. D. (2002) "When Bloggers Commit Journalism", *Online Journalism Review*. Retrieved from: http://www.ojr.org/ojr/workplace/1032910520.php.

Lasica, J. D. (2003) "Blogs and Journalism Need Each Other; 'The Transparency of Blogging Has Contributed to News Organizations Becoming a Bit More Accessible and Interactive . . .'", *Nieman Reports*, 57 (3), pp. 70–74.

Lawson-Borders, G., and Kirk, R. (2005) "Blogs in Campaign Communication", *American Behavioral Scientist*, 49 (4), pp. 548–59.

Lee, J. K., and Jeong, J. (2006) "The WMD Coverage of Blogs and Mainstream Media: A Comparison of Two Media Types". Paper presented at the AEJMC Convention, San Francisco, 2–5 August, 2006. Retrieved 15 September 2006 from: www.blog.basturea.com/archives/2006/07/17/aejmc-2006-papers.

Ludtke, M. (ed.) (2005) "Citizen Journalism", *Nieman Reports*, 59 (4), pp. 5–33.

MacDougall, R. (2005) "Identity, Electronic Ethos, and Blogs: A Technologic Analysis of Symbolic Exchange on the New News Medium", *American Behavioural Scientist*, 49 (4), pp. 575–99.

Matheson, D. (2004) "Weblogs and the Epistemology of the News: Some Trends in Online Journalism", *New Media and Society*, 6 (4), pp. 443–68.

McCombs, M. E. (1992) "Explorers and Surveyors: Expanding Strategies for Agenda-Setting Research", *Journalism Quarterly*, 69, pp. 813–24.

McCombs, M. E. (2005) "A Look at Agenda-Setting: Past, Present and Future", *Journalism Studies*, 6, pp. 543–57.

McCombs, M. E., and Shaw, D. L. (1972) "The Agenda-Setting Function of Mass Media", *Public Opinion Quarterly*, 36, pp. 176–85.

McCombs, M. E., and Shaw, D. L. (1993) "The Evolution of Agenda-Setting Research: Twenty-Five Years in the Marketplace of Ideas", *Journal of Communication*, 43 (2), pp. 58–67.

McIntosh, S. (2005) "Blogs: Has Their Time Finally Come — Or Gone?" *Global Media and Communication*, 1 (3), pp. 385–8.

McNair, B. (2006) *Cultural Chaos: Journalism, News and Power in a Globalised World*. London: Routledge.

Packer, G. (2004) "The Revolution Will Not Be Blogged", *Mother Jones*, 29 (3), pp. 28–32.

Paquet, S. (2003) "Socio-Technological Approaches to Facilitating Knowledge Sharing Across Disciplines". Ph.D. diss., Université de Montréal.

Reuters UK (2007) "Web Newspaper Blog Traffic Triples In Dec-Study". Retrieved 17 January 2007 from: http://uk.reuters.com/article/governmentFilingsNews/idUKN1733423820070117.

Robinson, S. (2006) "The Mission of the J-Blog: Recapturing Journalistic Authority Online", *Journalism*, 7 (1), pp. 65–83.

Rogers, E. M., and Dearing, J. W. (1988) "Agenda-Setting Research: Where Has It Been, Where Is It Going?" In J. A. Anderson (ed.), *Communication Yearbook*, 11, pp. 555–94. Newbury Park, CA: Sage.

Rogers, E. M., Dearing, J. W., and Bregman, D. (1993) "The Anatomy of Agenda-Setting Research", *Journal of Communication*, 43 (2), pp. 68–84.

Rosen, J. (2005) "Bloggers vs Journalists Is Over". Retrieved 21 January 2005 from: http://journalism.nyu.edu/pubzone/weblogs/pressthink/2005/01/21/berk_essy.html.

Singer, J. B. (2003) "Who Are These Guys?: The Online Challenge to the Notion of Journalistic Professionalism", *Journalism*, 4 (2), pp. 139–63.

Singer, J. B. (2005) "The Political J-Blogger: 'Normalising' a New Media Form to Fit Old Norms and Practices", *Journalism*, 6 (2), pp. 173–98.

Smolkin, R. (2004) "The Expanding Blogosphere", *American Journalism Review*, 26 (3), pp. 38–43.

Stanyer, J. (2006) "Online Campaign Communication and the Phenomenon of Blogging: An Analysis of Web Logs during the 2005 British General Election Campaign", *Aslib Proceedings*, 58 (5), pp. 404–15.

Tewksbury, D. (2003) "What Do Americans Really Want to Know? Tracking the Behavior of News Readers on the Internet", *Journal of Communication*, 53 (4), pp. 694–710.

Thelwall, M., and Stuart, D. (2007) "RUOK? Blogging Communication Technologies during Crises", *Journal of Computer-Mediated Communication*, 12 (2), pp. 523–48.

Wall, M. (2005) "'Blogs of War': Weblogs as News", *Journalism*, 6 (2), pp. 153–72.

Winer, D. (1999) "The History of Weblogs". Retrieved from: http://oldweblogscomblog.scripting.com/historyOfWeblogs.

⦃ CHAPTER ⦄
2

Gotcha: How Newsroom Norms are Shaping Participatory Journalism Online

NEIL THURMAN AND ALFRED HERMIDA

For some time commentators (see Saffo 1992; Matheson 2004; Gillmor 2004) have welcomed the Internet as a medium that promotes active participation rather than passive consumption and, as a result, has the potential to help create a more democratic and representative public sphere. In 2006 *Time* magazine named "You" as their Person of the Year, in recognition of what it called "community and collaboration on a scale never seen before . . . the many wresting power from the few". The Web, they said, is the "tool that makes this possible" (Grossman 2006). Jon Pareles (2006) went as far as to say that user-generated content was the "paramount cultural buzz phrase of 2006".

Although Pareles may have been right to identify the importance of user-generated content in discourse *about* the media, we must not forget that only a small minority of citizens actually use the technologies that facilitate media participation. The 2007 Oxford Internet Survey (Dutton and Helsper 2007) showed that just 16 percent of current Internet users in the UK had tried to set up a website or blog, or posted messages on discussion boards. Because 33 percent of Britons do not classify themselves as Internet users at all, the true extent of participation is even lower — at just over 10 percent — with participation rates amongst retired people and women lower still. On the other hand, the number of Internet users posting photos did increase by 10 percent between 2005 and 2007 (Dutton and Helsper 2007), showing that, to a limited extent, the culture of participation is growing.[1]

In the context of the hype surrounding user-generated content and the growing numbers who are creating and publishing certain types of content online, this chapter will focus on two issues. These are, first, the opportunities that exist for users to participate with mainstream online news websites in the UK and, second, the effect such participation is having on journalistic processes. The news media are an important object of study because of the active role they play "in the creation and manipulation of reality" (Nicholson and Anderson 2005) for the "readers" they "serve".

A key question we aim to address is whether the Internet in general, and participatory journalism in particular, can give greater agency to its users to influence the processes that create, reflect and transmit culture via the news media. We have chosen to focus on the mainstream media because — despite the success of "pure-play"[2] sites such as YouTube, Google, Wikipedia and eBay in categories such as entertainment, e-mail and search, reference material and e-commerce — news and current affairs are still dominated by sites with print or broadcast parentage. In fact, the twelve news and current affairs websites with the most monthly users are all owned by established news providers (Thurman 2007).[3]

Although established corporations dominate the provision of online news, the alternative media have had considerable influence on practices in the mainstream, particularly in the area of reader participation. Sites such as OhMyNews.com and the "many news-related weblogs maintained by people who are not journalists" (Matheson 2004) have helped prompt editors and executives to adopt the formats for participation developed by Internet pioneers and popularized by such citizen journalism endeavours.

Defining "Citizen" and "Participatory" Journalisms

The terms "citizen journalism" and "participatory journalism" are often used interchangeably when referring to the "act of a citizen, or group of citizens, playing an active role in the process of collecting, reporting, analysing and disseminating news and information" (Bowman and Willis 2003). But there is an important distinction to be made between genuinely independent "citizen journalism" endeavours and opportunities citizens have to participate with existing, institutional news publishers. The media used to consider any form of engagement with their public to be "citizen journalism". For example, organizing a "citizen panel" to question a US senator was described as an "exercise in 'citizen journalism'" by *The Boston Globe*, which helped organize such an event in 1995 (Rezendes and Ford 1995). The term has also been used to refer to professional journalism done with civic virtue, as in this example from Canada's *Globe and Mail* in 1998:

> Be sensitive to and studious of the values that your community has declared to itself, and to the agenda that it has set itself . . . Then get to work to tell stories of how life is being lived against that framework of values . . . Then you'll be doing citizen journalism. (Watson 1998)

Only after the turn of the millennium did we start to see the term "citizen journalism" used in the way most people understand it today: citizens reporting without recourse to institutional journalism — the "peer-to-peer journalism" that Howard Rheingold has referred to (Hanluain 2003). The growth of blogging helped cement the association between "citizen journalism" and independence from the mainstream. An example of this is a 2004 report from CNN.com on the removal from office of Ed Schock, a two-term Republican congressman from Virginia, which referred to how "investigative reporting from a blogger showed the growing political power of citizen journalism" (Sifry 2004).

The phrase "participatory journalism" has a similarly mixed history. In the 1970s and 1980s it referred to journalists participating in the events, and working alongside the people they were reporting, rather than any opportunities citizens had to participate with the processes of journalism. This example, from *The Washington Post*, is typical, involving a reporter trying his hand as a stand-up comic:

> "I was kind of thinking of doing maybe a little routine myself." I shrugged my shoulders and smiled with self-deprecating modesty. I looked over at him to check his reaction. I continued, "You know, as part of the article, I might see how a performer feels on stage. It's kind of . . . participatory journalism." (Levine 1977)

In the 1990s, with the rise of dotcoms, "participatory journalism" began to take on other meanings, used to refer both to professionally run sites that actively sought user-generated content and to independent electronic publishing endeavours. Examples of the former included Slashdot, the "quintessential example of participatory journalism", according to the *Orange County Weekly* in 1999, which described the editorial model it was deploying: "Rather than passively opening their mouths and letting the pros shovel in stories, the readers at Slashdot provide the news themselves by sending in tips on stories and commenting on issues in the discussion forums that follow each story" (Hilty 1999). *The Northwest Voice* was another example, described by its founder as "an example of what's being called participatory journalism, where we look to the community to tell us what's going on" (Kridler 2004). Blogs were considered to be participatory journalism too. A 2004 CNN.com article quoted Dan Gillmor: "Gillmor touts the blog movement as a primary sign of this new participatory journalism" (Boese 2004).

Samantha Henig (2005) picked up on this definition problem back in 2005 in the *Columbia Journalism Review*:

> The problem here is an unclear definition of what the *New York Times* called "participatory journalism, or civic or citizen journalism". For starters, pick a name! As we see it, there are two separate things going on here. And, leapin' lizards, at least two separate names at our disposal. First, there's the move of established newspapers and news sites to solicit and publish material, such as photos or personal accounts, from their readers — that we'd like to call "participatory journalism". Then there's the creation of blogs and unedited news sites that allow users to write and post their own content. That one we'll call "citizen journalism".

We have followed Henig's suggestion, so the subject of this chapter is "participatory journalism", in our terms: the technical, editorial and managerial process that allow readers' contributions to be elicited, processed and published at professional publications.

Table 2.1 User-generated content initiatives at British newspaper websites, May 2008 (developed from: Thurman 2008 and Hermida and Thurman 2008)

	Format	Description
1	'Blogs'	Allow journalists to publish short articles — or 'posts'— which are presented in reverse chronological order. Most allow readers to comment on the entries. 'Blogs' are explicitly authored by one or more individuals, often associated with a set of interests or opinions, and can include links to external websites.
2	'Comments on stories'	Readers can submit their views on a story, usually from a form at the bottom of an article.
3	'Have your says'	Resembling 'Messageboards' but with significant differences. These are areas where journalists post topical questions to which readers send written replies. A selection is made, edited, and published by journalists, with the submissions either fully or reactively moderated. 'Have your says' usually remain open for a limited number of days.
4	'Messageboards'	Areas that allow readers to engage in threaded online conversations or debates on topics often initiated by readers. They are usually reactively moderated. They are structured so that users can reply to any of the posts rather than just the original one. The discussions usually remain open for weeks or months.
5	'Polls'	Topical questions where readers are asked to make a multiple choice or binary response. They provide instant and quantifiable feedback to readers but offer very limited interaction: restricted to 'yes' or 'no' answers, or a multiple-choice response.
6	'Q&As'	Interviews with journalists and/or invited guests, with questions submitted by readers. By their very nature, 'Q&As' are moderated. But since they are usually webcast in audio or video, or transcribed, as live, they offer a sense of interactivity and immediacy.
7	'Reader blogs'	Allow readers to create a blog and have it hosted on a news organization's website.
8	'Your media'	Galleries of photographs, video, and other media submitted by readers and vetted by journalists.
9	'Your story'	Sections where readers are asked to send in stories that matter to them. These then are selected and edited by journalists for publication on the website.

THE EVOLUTION OF FORMATS FOR PARTICIPATION

As our definition suggests, technical processes are required in order that user-generated content can be elicited, processed and published at professional news sites. This section outlines what those technical formats are and describes how they have evolved over time. As Table 2.1 shows, we have identified nine generic formats used to encourage contributions from the public at mainstream news websites. This taxonomy of formats was first formulated as a result of a survey in April 2005 (Thurman 2008). It was further developed after a second survey in November 2006 (Hermida and Thurman 2008). For this chapter we have again reviewed the range of formats deployed on mainstream news sites.

The evolution of formats between April 2005 and May 2008 shows that there has been relatively little innovation, and this at a time when discussion about participatory media and the related concept of "Web 2.0" has grown dramatically.[4] The only new formats that became established between the first and the second survey were "Reader blogs", "Your story" and "Your media".[5] No new formats appeared between the second and the third survey.

This lack of innovation is not entirely surprising given the slow rate of change in the news industry. The traditional model of newspaper consumption survived for more than 300 years until the advent of the World Wide Web. In another news medium, radio, FM technology was unchallenged for sixty-one years until the disruptive technology of digital radio was licensed for use in the USA in 2002 (Thurman 2005). Partly as a result of this stasis, "newspaper routines have not changed significantly since 1990" (Sylvie and Witherspoon 2002).

With such little change, proprietors have put scant investment into research and development, an important source of innovations in other industries. The economic imperative, another source of innovation, has not been powerful either. Meyer (2004) likens owning a newspaper in the twentieth century to "having the power to levy a sales tax", evidenced by his assertion that "a monopoly newspaper in a medium-size market could command a margin of 20 to 40 per cent", compared with average profit margins of "6 to 7 per cent" found in typical retail products. "Newspapers have been slow to adapt," he says "because their culture is the victim of that history of easy money."

DIFFUSION OF USER-GENERATED CONTENT INITIATIVES

Although mainstream news sites have been relatively reluctant to innovate with new formats during the period studied, we have seen greater changes in how they have adopted these formats. Back in 2005, only one of the national news sites surveyed — Guardian.co.uk — hosted real blogs (those with comments enabled), and one national newspaper website — Independent.co.uk — had no formats for readers to contribute at all. Compare this with the distribution thirty-eight months later, when the number of "blogs"[6] at national newspaper websites had increased from seven to 207, and the number of publications allowing 'Comments on stories' had increased from one to eight.

This growth was partly a result of editors' and executives' fear of being marginalized by user media, as this quote from the then editor of Telegraph.co.uk illustrates: "[T]he idea of becoming a forum for debate was an area that newspapers had to get into, otherwise they'd get left behind." But it was also due to a shift in attitudes which saw managers such as Peter Bale start to appreciate "the extra flexibility that the dialogue with readers" had given to the publication for which he was responsible, TimesOnline.co.uk (Hermida and Thurman 2008).

Our third survey — conducted in May and June 2008 — showed some interesting changes in mainstream publications' adoption of participatory journalism. The picture was mixed, with some expanding their provision, others remaining stable and some even scaling back.

SCALING BACK

Some publications that were relatively advanced in November 2006, after a period of rapid adoption, have experienced a period of stability and have not expanded their provision of user-generated content initiatives. In other cases, initiatives that were launched on the back of the citizen media phenomenon have been quietly dropped. Take, for example, theSun.co.uk which, in November 2006, hosted twelve blogs, a format that Thurman (2008) considers to be "the best-known form of invitation that writers use to initiate conversations with readers online". At the end of May 2008 there was no trace of "Arthur's Blog"[7] or "Street Chic Blog", "Trevor Kavanagh's Blog" ("the blog politicians fear") or any of the other "blogs" hosted back in November 2006.[8] The four blogs that were recorded in our May 2008 survey were different in character, and used to report on specific events — the French Open, a *Sun* reporter's trip to the North Pole[9] and the television series *The Apprentice* — rather than as an ongoing platform for debate. Here the term "blog" is being used as a journalistic device to help differentiate types of news content. In this regard blogs are not, as they have the potential to be, about initiating a conversation with the audience but rather just another way of presenting copy. The editor of theSun.co.uk in an interview (2004) expressed this view of blogs as no different from traditional journalistic practice:

> What's the difference between a blog and a column . . . [or] a colour piece as we used to call it? We used to do "24 hours in the life of a nurse" and that's the same thing. I'm not against them I just don't understand why they are called anything different. (Pete Picton, quoted in Thurman 2008)

CONTINUED GROWTH

Although there has been some scaling back, there was considerable growth in the provision of user-generated content initiatives between November 2006 and May 2008. For example, in our 2006 survey one British national newspaper — *The Independent* — again had no formats for reader participation. This period of self-imposed isolation between 2005 and 2006 was prompted by an earlier, negative, experience with participatory journalism. The editor of its website, Martin King, explained the problem, describing the users on its, now defunct, message boards as:

> a bunch of bigots who were shouting from one side of the room to the other and back again without even bothering to listen to what the other side of the room were saying. If someone did try to put a reasonable, balanced view, it was an exception. (Quoted in Thurman 2008)

By the summer of 2006 Independent Digital's New Media Strategies director, Richard Withey, was acknowledging that user media were a "phenomenon you can't ignore" and saying that "the whole idea of the newspaper proprietor and his editors telling people what was going on in the world and the world neatly reading that . . . that self-perpetuating oligarchy has been broken down very rapidly" (quoted in Hermida and Thurman 2008). By May 2008 the newspaper had launched eighteen blogs, allowing comments on selected stories, running the occasional "Q & A" and publishing some readers' photos.

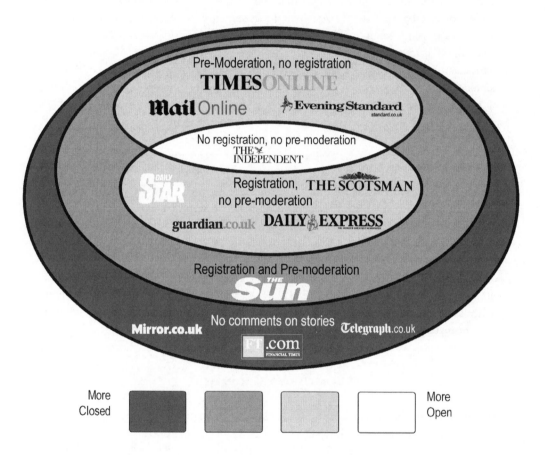

Figure 2.1 Moderation of "Comments on stories" at British newspaper websites, May 2008

Further, as shown in Figure 2.1, they have gone from being the most closed of the news sites studied to being the most open and unique in publishing "Comments on stories" without registration[10] or pre-moderation.[11] Along with *The Independent*, other publications have substantially increased their provision of user-generated content initiatives. The Express.co.uk hosts nineteen blogs (up from one in the previous survey), allows "Comments on stories" and provides "Reader blogs" and "Message boards". FT.com too has launched "Blogs" since the last survey — twelve in their case.

We must, however, be wary of judging this "expansion" of participatory journalism on numbers alone. Qualitative factors are as important, if not more so. And in that regard the situation is more mixed. Take, for example, the eight blogs hosted by Dailystar.co.uk. In May 2008 three had no posts at all, and one had just a single post (dating from 23 August 2007). In fact, only three of the eight bloggers had posted anything in the eight months up to the date of our survey. Although Dailystar.co.uk was by far the worst example of a failure to engage with its readers, some blogs at FT.com,[12] Independent.co.uk and Mirror.co.uk were also infrequently updated.

Part of the problem is fitting blogging into the demands of a typical journalist's routine, as this comment from the then editor of FT.com, Tracy Corrigan, illustrates:

> Maybe we would do more blogs if we had lots of people who had time to write but I think it is difficult to get journalists to commit to doing very long-term blogs when they are doing full-time jobs as well . . . you might have time to do a daily blog [on magazines] but not here. (Quoted in Thurman 2008)

The deployment of "Comments on stories" is similarly problematic when analysed qualitatively. Although the feature is built into the content management system used at Dailystar.co.uk and Express.co.uk, it is barely used. Take, for example, the "News/Showbiz" page of Express.co.uk on a typical day.[13] Of the thirty-four stories that appeared on that page, readers were able to leave comments on just thirteen. This feature had only been used on eight stories, with the average number of comments low — at just under seven. The situation was even worse at Dailystar.co.uk, where just a single story on the "News > Full news" page had "Comments on stories" enabled — "Am I Your Fantasy?", by Vanessa Feltz. Part of the problem is that these Northern & Shell titles do not deliver on their promise of participation. On the Express.co.uk website a link encouraging "Comments on stories" is displayed on *all* stories, even where the facility is disabled. This frustrates users and may help explain the low participation rate. Here we are seeing tokenism displayed in the deployment of participatory functionality. Without sufficient resources or an engaged management, user-generated content initiatives are liable to wither on the vine, becoming little more than a figleaf to cover the traditional "we write, you read" dogma of modern journalism (Deuze, quoted in Hermida and Thurman 2008).

INSTITUTIONALIZING FORUMS FOR DEBATE

Part of the reason that sites such as Independent.co.uk, Mirror.co.uk, Dailystar.co.uk, FT.com and Express.co.uk have struggled, to a greater or lesser extent, to keep the "Blogs" they launched up-to-date is that the burden of maintenance falls mainly on the shoulders of individual journalists. At Independent.co.uk only their "Open House" blog is a group endeavour. In contrast at Guardian.co.uk only two of their twenty-eight blogs are individual efforts.[14] The rest are themed ("news", "arts&entertainment", "travelog", "games" etc.) and have several contributors, making these "Blogs" more dynamic than would be possible if they were the responsibility of a single writer. There are also group "Blogs" at FT.com, TimesOnline.co.uk and Telegraph.co.uk.

Group "Blogs" are a smart commercial move for another reason. They lessen the likelihood that a journalist will create a successful "brand" and jump ship. This danger was raised, in a slightly different way, by the then editorial director of TimesOnline.co.uk, Peter Bale, who explained that "*Times* and *Sunday Times* correspondents were offered blogs as an attempt to 'give them a piece of property on the Internet themselves, within our site'" (quoted in Hermida and Thurman 2008), and thus remove the temptation to set up their own blogs outside their employer's sphere of control. This movement of "Blogs" from the personal to the institutional can also be seen as part of the normalization of user-generated content, as it becomes embedded in the culture of mainstream journalism. This development allays concerns that some professional journalists have had about the personal voice of "Blogs" and the way they challenged the strongly established tradition that most reporting is done anonymously, as this anecdote concerning the then editor of Telegraph.co.uk illustrates:

> Burton, also a visiting lecturer at the University of Westminster, recounted telling journalism students of his who were learning to write features that "the message is the only thing that is important. No one knows you, no one cares about you. The reader wants information", and spoke to them of the "traditional journalist who is a fly on the wall and will be delivering information" — very different in concept from the tone of most blogs, and a reason why he said, "blogs worry me". (Thurman 2008)

USER-GENERATED CONTENT DEVELOPS

Up to 2008 there has been relatively little innovation in the formats used to encourage contributions from the public at mainstream news websites. Although these formats have been more widely adopted over this period, providing more opportunities for readers to get their voices heard, contributions are, in the main, still limited to short textual "comments" on subjects or stories determined by professional editors.[15] There is little in the way of longer-form contributions or opportunities for readers to decide what they write about. Where opportunities to set the agenda do exist (for example, in message boards),[16] they often seem to be part of what Bowman and Willis (2003) have described as "closed-off annex[es] where readers can talk and discuss, as long as the media companies don't have to be involved". Attempts to create genuinely open spaces with adequate bridges to sites' professionally produced content are few and far between. Two formats stand out, which we call "Your Story" and "Reader Blogs".[17]

"YOUR STORY"

TimesOnline.co.uk's "Your World" travel site was a typical example of the "Your Story" format and was identified in our November 2006 survey. Readers could write about their travel experiences and geo-tag their story, a link to which would appear on a zoomable world map. By the standards of participatory journalism, contributors were given a relatively generous 500-word limit. At that time, alongside Scotsman.com's "My Story" feature,[18] it was a rare example of participatory journalism where readers could set the agenda, choosing to write about any place on earth.

Our survey, in May 2008, revealed that both of these initiatives had been dropped. There was no sign of the Scotsman.com's "My Story" format, despite the enthusiasm expressed in 2006 by its then General Manager, Alistair Brown, who said "we've got quite big plans in that area". Back then, Scotsman.com intended to develop original user-generated content around a theme — Scottish heritage — in order to help to attract and retain certain types of advertiser. Brown explained that the idea was "to create a kind of honey pot of ex-pats where we could get whisky brands and some of the airlines [to advertise] . . . we've tried to build products that will attract those audiences". However, even then doubts were creeping in, owing to *The Scotsman*'s takeover by another publisher. "The jury is still out, we're still looking at it . . . because of the Johnson Press involvement now, we've got wider requirements to look at in terms of how that will shape up moving forward" (Brown, personal communication 2006).

Over the course of the research for this chapter, TimesOnline.co.uk's "Your World" went from being only occasionally live to being permanently offline. While it could be accessed, it was clear that the site was not being updated, with the most recent readers' contributions being four months old. *The Times* had taken a different approach to the development of their "Your Story" format, securing a "seven-figure" sum from BMW to cover initial development, promotion and running costs. Indeed, it appears they only ever intended the feature to run for twelve months, rather than make it a sustainable participatory journalism feature on their site (Simpson 2006).

Despite these failures, there is some cause for optimism that such novel forms of user-generated content can succeed in the mainstream media and allow readers the opportunity to set the agenda. One such example can be found at Guardian.co.uk. Their "Been there" site is also based on travel stories, but, unlike at TimesOnline.co.uk, there are no restrictions on story length, and users can edit and update other submissions. Furthermore, readers can aggregate other readers' tips to create travel guides, hence performing a real editorial role for the first time. Here user-generated content goes beyond simply publishing material from users and instead emphasizes the sharing and remixing of content. However, we must not forget that this feature is outside what most journalists would consider to be "news", in the softer area of lifestyle, and so is perhaps a more acceptable area for publications to cede control to.[19]

"READER BLOGS"

"Reader blogs" have been progressively adopted since they were launched by theSun.co.uk in October 2006 (Schofield 2006). As of May 2008, "Reader blogs" were also hosted at the websites of the *Daily Star* and *The Telegraph*. Like the "Your Story" format, they represent a relatively open form of participatory journalism. They allow readers to set the agenda by initiating conversations, rather than responding to institutional content, and publishing contributions — once users are registered — without pre-moderation. In contrast to "Message boards", "Reader blogs" *can* be better integrated with mainstream content. This is certainly the case at Telegraph.co.uk, where their "Reader Blogs" (called "My Telegraph") are given the same prominence as professionally staffed sections such as "Arts", "Education" or "Science", and blog posts from readers are routinely promoted, for example in a sidebar of the main "news home" page.[20]

"Reader blogs" touch on a much wider range of topics than the "Your Story" features discussed earlier, including: "Current affairs", "Economics", "Education", "EU" and "Politics".[21] Telegraph.co.uk's "Reader blogs" have drawn criticism in some quarters, accused, for instance, by Sean Dodson (2008) in *The Guardian*, of publishing "distasteful" copy and providing a home for "unsavoury characters . . . including . . . anti-abortionists, europhobes and members of an anti-feminist 'men's movement'".[22] Dodson comments that Telegraph.co.uk is "providing the platform for others [i.e., its readers] to start the debate", whereas, he continues, "on most comment sites, bloggers sanctioned by the newspaper group typically do so". Dodson repeats the point later in his article, considering debate on Guardian.co.uk's "Comment is Free" site as being centred around articles that are "always written by a 'commissioned' blogger", in his words, the "gatekeepers". This "sanctioned" model is, by implication, his preferred approach and is in line with a general tendency for established news sites to want to control the conversation they have with readers. TimesOnline.co.uk, too, has talked about wanting to use plenty of user-generated content, but only if it is "the right user-generated content. . . [that] fit[s] with our brands" (quoted in Hermida and Thurman 2008).

MODERATION AND CONTROL

Dodson's attitude, and his reference to readers as "others", is typical of the ways in which many journalists and editors have viewed user-generated content since it became a feature of mainstream news websites. Historically, mainstream news websites have edited or pre-moderated readers' submissions — they did so in 80 percent of cases back in April 2005 (Thurman 2008). In this sense the media have sought to retain a traditional gatekeeping role, with journalists acting as message filters. The reasons editors took this approach included a desire to "avoid duplication, keep the standards of spelling and grammar high, select material that was newsworthy with broad appeal, and ensure balance and decency" (Thurman 2008). This gatekeeping mode remained largely unchanged between April 2005 and November 2006, as more and more news sites offered opportunities for participation (see Hermida and Thurman 2008). More recently, the picture has become more complex, with evidence of a loosening of moderation practices at some publications and a tightening at others, as news sites compete for readers and struggle to manage the user-generated content they are receiving.

As part of their June 2008 relaunch of "Comment is Free" — the Guardian.co.uk's blogging / comment platform — the time limit for commenting was reduced to forty-eight hours, "mainly", it was said, "to try and keep conversations as topical and relevant as possible" (Henry 2008). Another likely reason was to limit the number of comments and hence the costs of moderation.

The Guardian.co.uk's then Director of Digital Publishing, Simon Waldman, anticipated the implementation of such "traffic-calming techniques" in 2006 as a result of his experience with a World Cup football blog, where the volume of comments was "almost too much" (quoted in Hermida and Thurman 2008). TimesOnline.co.uk has also had concerns that "the volume of comments being posted [at least 3,000 per day] . . . outstrips(s) [its] ability to handle them". For this reason it has outsourced moderation to an external company — eModeration — which employs moderators in Europe, the Americas and Australia (Baker 2008).

In contrast, a more relaxed attitude to moderation is now in evidence at the websites of three national newspapers — *The Independent*, the *Financial Times* and the *Daily Mirror*. As of June 2008 all published readers' comments to their blogs without registration or pre-moderation. The shift away from moderation might well be a result of the increase in opportunities readers have to participate. With more choice, news websites may be finding that readers are less likely to participate if barriers to participation — such as registration — exist, or if they don't get the immediate, positive feedback that instant publication gives.

CONCLUSIONS

How far has participatory journalism in the UK delivered on the expectations of its proponents to allow "widespread engagement with the public" and foster a more democratic form of public service journalism (Greenslade 2008)? The evidence is mixed. As we have shown, national newspaper websites did considerably increase their provision of user-generated content initiatives between April 2005 and June 2008: the number of publications hosting "Blogs" and "Comments on stories" increased eleven and eight times respectively. There was also a smaller increase in the provision of formats — "Message boards", "Reader blogs" and "Your story" — allowing readers to initiate discussions rather than simply responding to the institutional news agenda.

However, in order to determine the true nature and extent of participation, it is necessary to look beyond the presence of these technical modes of interactivity to the ways in which they are implemented and managed. From this perspective, participation is being limited by a combination of factors including:

- out-of-date "Blogs" that do not provide new material for readers to comment on
- the widespread disabling of "Comment on stories" functionality
- the shortening of time-limits for readers to comment on stories or "Blog" posts
- the closing of certain user-generated content initiatives altogether

- the corralling of user-generated content into defined areas of sites with a lack of promotion and integration with professionally-produced content
- the use of participatory journalism terminology — such as "Blogs" — as a branding device without the accompanying functionality for participation
- editorial attitudes and moderation practices that seek to normalize user-generated content so that it is "right", "fits the brand" or matches institutional ideas of "taste".

These broad generalizations having been made, we must also acknowledge that a wide range of practices exist, both across the industry as a whole and within individual publications. For example, although Telegraph.co.uk does not allow "Comments on stories", it does host a vigorous "Reader blogs" platform, the content of which is well integrated with its professionally produced output. And although some of Independent.co.uk's "Blogs" are infrequently updated, readers are able to comment on "Blog" posts and some news stories without the hurdle of initial registration or the delays that accompany pre-moderation.

These variations in provision are, in part, consistent with Thurman's (2008) findings that "local conditions" have a "considerable influence on the range and character of the [user-generated content] initiatives adopted", with costs, quality standards, the legal environment and the management and professional preparedness of journalists all playing a part. As the numbers wishing to contribute to mainstream news websites increase, so does the costs of moderating user-generated content so that it meets newspapers' expectations. When these costs exceed the budgets available, restricting opportunities for participation often becomes the preferred strategy.

This desire for control is partly due to legitimate fears that, without such processes in place, some of the obscene, defamatory and libellous content that news websites receive will be published. It also stems from journalists' and editors' long-held belief that they know what their readers want — and the associated traditions of selection and editing. These journalistic norms have played an important part in the implementation and regulation of participatory journalism in the mainstream. They betray the innate conservatism of newsroom culture — a culture forged during a long period of technological and financial stability and one that has now come to a sudden end.

The new technological and financial realities that newspapers face have yet to transform such ingrained cultural practices. But they are chipping away at the edges. Significantly, readers are now routinely given the "right to reply", although this "right" is still often only granted to submissions that are within certain bounds of "taste". The notion that participatory journalism is more than a right to reply, but could encompass agenda-setting, include the full spectrum of public discourse and compete with professional journalism is still widely taboo in the profession.

For some, if newspapers are to survive, this taboo must be broken and journalists have to stop "acting as secular priests" (Greenslade 2008). For others, such as Lee Siegel (2008), there is a danger that such a move will "keep the most creative, intelligent, and original voices from being heard". Newspaper websites in the UK have progressively allowed more and more material from the "laity" to appear on their pages. However, this process has been tortuous, as publications have reacted to the "poor" quality of some contributions by periodically raising the bar to entry or closing the gate altogether. Whether they will take the next step and start to relinquish their gatekeeping role in favour of a more collective, collaborative approach will, in part, depend on the success of pilot projects such as "My Telegraph" and Guardian.co.uk's "Been there". Moreover, it will also be dependent on whether the lay participants in these experiments deliver on the responsibilities that come with their newfound freedom.

Notes

1　Although the 2007 Oxford Internet Survey showed that posting pictures or photos on the Internet grew in popularity between 2005 and 2007, other forms of creativity and production online became less popular: the numbers of current Internet users who maintained a "personal website" fell by 3 per cent over the same period.

2　The Internet Encyclopaedia (Flicker 2004) defines a firm as "pure-play" if "its only distribution channel is the Internet or the wireless Web".

3　As classified by Nielsen//NetRatings. Data from April 2005 (US Internet users only).

4　In April 2005, "Web 2.0" was mentioned just 25 times in the English language news sources catalogued by the LexisNexis 'Business and News' database. By April 2008, that number had increased by more than 100 times to 2,531. Over the same time period, mentions of "user-generated content" increased nearly 75 times from 9 to 671.

5　The "Your media" and "Your story" formats were deployed sporadically by news sites in April 2005. It was not until November 2006 that their use was sufficiently established for them to appear as generic formats in their own right.

6　Thurman (2008) considers that "blogs represent the best-known form of invitation that writers use to initiate conversations with readers online".

7　Arthur Edwards MBE, the Sun's royal photographer.

8　These "blogs" were blogs in name only. None allowed that most fundamental requirement of the form — readers' comments — let alone the other function that the blogging community has come to expect: "the blogroll, permalinks . . . trackback and syndication". In this case, as with early blogs at the BBC and other mainstream news providers, blogs failed "to conform to some of the social conventions of the blog" (Thurman and Jones 2005).

9　"The Arctic blog".

10　Users must provide basic personal information (such as their name and email address) in order that they can submit content.

11　A process by which user-generated content is checked by internal or external moderators and is either rejected, published with changes or published unchanged.

12　At the time of our survey, four months had passed since FT.com's "Energy Filter" blog had been updated.

13　2.26 p.m. on 7 May 2008.

14　"Ask Jack" (a computer/technology blog by Jack Schofield) and "Greenslade" (media commentary by Roy Greenslade).

15　Limits, where they exist, are between 60 and 300 words.

16　"Message boards" are hosted by the websites of the *Daily Star*, the *Daily Mirror*, the *Financial Times*, *The Guardian*, the *Daily Telegraph* and the *Evening Standard* (survey: May 2008).

17　"Reader blogs" are hosted at the websites of *The Sun*, the *Daily Star* and the *Daily Telegraph* (survey: May 2008).

18 "My Story" gave Scotsman.com readers the opportunity to write about their Scottish heritage. As with TimesOnline's "Your World", there was a 500-word limit, and submissions were pre-selected and edited before publication.

19 Dailymail.co.uk also hosts a "Your Story" feature, again based on holiday content. Called "Your Holiday", it too has a 500-word limit on textual contributions. Readers can also upload photos and video and contributions are tagged by destination and holiday type. Submissions pass through a moderation process that can take up to a week.

20 Although promoted by the *Telegraph* on its website, no content from its "Reader blogs" appeared in the print edition on a typical day (11 June 2008).

21 These topics are taken from the "tag cloud" that appeared on the http://my.telegraph.co.uk/ front page at 1.37 p.m. on 11 June 2008. In this case the tag cloud depicts the occurrences of tags added by users to describe the content of the pages they have created or amended within the My Telegraph site. Tags are usually single words, and in tag clouds they are typically listed alphabetically, with the more commonly used tags shown in a larger font.

22 *The Guardian*'s own forums for user-generated content also reflect a wide range of opinion, including views that would not normally appear in the paper. Examples include comments on an article about a visit made by Condoleezza Rice to the Middle East (Tisdall 2007) in which readers referred to the US Secretary of State as an Aunt Jemima", a racially loaded term, seeking to characterize Rice as a "faithful slave" (see McElya 2007).

References

Baker, S. (2008) "Have Your Say, Three Thousand Times a Day", *The Times*, 23 February. Retrieved 19 June 2008 from: http://www.timesonline.co.uk/tol/life_and_style/court_and_social/article3418858.ece.

Boese, C. (2004) "Will Cyber Journalists Turn the Tables on Big Media?" CNN.com, 15 September. Retrieved 6 June 2008 from: http://edition.cnn.com/2004/TECH/09/15/cyber.journalist/index.html.

Bowman, S., and Willis, C. (2003) "We Media: How Audiences Are Shaping the Future of News And Information". *The Media Center,* 21 September. Retrieved 5 June 2008 from: http://www.hypergene.net/wemedia/weblog.php.

Dodson, S. (2008) "Platform for Free Speech . . . Or Hate?", *The Guardian*, 19 May. Retrieved 11 June 2008 from: http://www.guardian.co.uk/media/2008/may/19/pressandpublishing.telegraphmediagroup.

Dutton, W. H., and Helsper, E. (2007) "Oxford Internet Survey 2007 Report: The Internet in Britain", *Oxford Internet Institute*. Retrieved 3 June 2008 from: http://www.oii.ox.ac.uk/research/oxis/OxIS2007_Report.pdf.

Flicker, M. H. (2004) "Securities Trading on the Internet", *The Internet Encyclopedia*. Hoboken, NJ: Wiley, vol. 3, p. 284.

Gillmor, D. (2004) *We the Media: Grassroots Journalism by the People, for the People*. Sebastopol, CA: O'Reilly.

Greenslade, R. (2008) "Move Over: Journalists Will Have to Share Their Space", *Sydney Morning Herald*, 1 May. Retrieved 20 June 2008 from Nexis UK database.

Grossman, L. (2006) "Time's Person of the Year: You", *Time,* 13 December. Retrieved 9 June 2008 from: http://www.time.com/time/magazine/article/0,9171,1569514,00.html.

Hanluain, D. O. (2003) "Forget F-Stops: These Cameras Have Area Codes", *New York Times*, 3 July. Retrieved 20 June 2008 from Nexis UK database.

Henig, S. (2005) "Citizens, Participants and Reporters", *Columbia Journalism Review*, 8 July.

Retrieved 6 June 2008 from: http://www.cjr.org/politics/citizens_participants_ and_repo.php.

Henry, G. (2008) "Welcome to the New Comment is Free", Guardian.co.uk, 4 June. Retrieved 5 June 2008 from: http://www.guardian.co.uk/commentisfree/2008/jun/04/1.

Hermida, A., and Thurman, N. (2008) "A Clash of Cultures: The Integration of User-Generated Content within Professional Journalistic Frameworks at British Newspaper Websites", *Journalism Practice*, 2 (3).

Hilty, W. (1999) "News for Nerds", *Orange County Weekly*, 12 November. Retrieved 20 June 2008 from Nexis UK database.

Kridler, K. (2004) "Maryland Launches $1M Program to Cultivate New Media Outlets", *The Daily Record* (Baltimore, MD), 26 October. Retrieved 19 June 2008 from Nexis UK database.

Levine, A. (1977) "Knocking Them Dead: The Reporter Tries Out on Amateur Night", *Washington Post* magazine, 14 August. Retrieved 17 June 2008 from Nexis UK database.

Matheson, D. (2004) "Weblogs and the Epistemology of the News: Some Trends in Online Journalism", *New Media and Society*, 6 (4), pp. 443–68.

McElya, M. (2007) *Clinging to Mammy: The Faithful Slave in Twentieth-Century America*. Cambridge, MA: Harvard University Press.

Meyer, P. (2004) *The Vanishing Newspaper*. Columbia, MI: University of Missouri Press.

Nicholson, L., and Anderson, A. R. (2005) "News and Nuances of the Entrepreneurial Myth and Metaphor: Linguistic Games in Entrepreneurial Sense-Making and Sense-Giving", *Entrepreneurship Theory and Practice*, 29 (2), pp. 153–72.

Pareles, J. (2006) "2006, Brought to You by You", *New York Times*, 10 December. Retrieved 3 June 2008 from: http://www.nytimes.com/2006/12/10/arts/music/10pare.html.

Rezendes, M., and Ford, R. (1995) "Gramm's Vision of Streamlining is Put to a Test", *The Boston Globe*, 28 November. Retrieved 16 June 2008 from Nexis UK database.

Saffo, P. (1992) "Consumers and Interactive New Media: A Hierarchy of Desires", Saffo.com. Retrieved 3 June 2008 from: http://www.saffo.com/essays/consumers.php.

Schofield, J. (2006) "*The Sun* Beats *The Guardian* at Reader Blogs", *The Guardian*, 25 October. Retrieved 11 June 2008 from: http://blogs.guardian.co.uk/technology/2006/10/25/ the_sun_beats_the_guardian_at_reader_blogs.html.

Siegel, L. (2008) *Against the Machine: Being Human in the Age of the Electronic Mob*. New York: Spiegel and Grau.

Sifry, D. L. (2004) "Daily Blog Roundup: Thursday, September 2, 2004", CNN.com, 3 September. Retrieved 6 June 2008 from: http://edition.cnn.com/2004/ALLPOLITICS /09/03/thursday.blog.roundup/index.html.

Simpson, R. (2006) "*The Times* Readers to Contribute to BMW Travel Promo", *New Media Age*, 21 December. Retrieved 27 June 2008 from Nexis UK database.

Sylvie, G., and Witherspoon, P. D. (2002) *Time, Change, and the American Newspaper*. Mahwah, NJ: Lawrence Erlbaum Associates.

Thurman, N. (2005) "From Blogrolls and Wikis to Big Business: Going Online". In R. Keeble (ed.), *Print Journalism: A Critical Introduction*. London: Routledge.

Thurman, N. (2007) "The Globalisation of Journalism Online: A Transatlantic Study of News Websites and Their International Readers", *Journalism: Theory, Practice and Criticism*, 8 (3), pp. 285–307.

Thurman, N. (2008) "Forums for Citizen Journalists? Adoption of User Generated Content Initiatives by Online News Media", *New Media and Society*, 10 (1), pp. 139–57.

Thurman, N., and Jones, S. (2005) "From Nexus to Newslog: Online Journalism from the Grassroots". In R. Keeble (ed.), *Print Journalism: A Critical Introduction*. London: Routledge.

Tisdall, S. (2007) "Duff Diplomacy", *The Guardian*, 5 November. Retrieved 16 June 2008 from: http://www.guardian.co.uk/commentisfree/2007/nov/05/duffdiplomacy.

Watson, P. (1998) "The Journalist as Storyteller Sure, Contemporary Media Are Tainted by Commerce, But Much of What's Wrong, Two Veteran Newsmen Say, Is That Media Have Forgotten That the Business Is Really about Telling Stories. TRIVIA PURSUIT: How Showbiz Values Are Corrupting the News", *The Globe and Mail*, 17 October. Retrieved 26 June 2008 from Nexis UK database.

⦊ CHAPTER ⦊
3

We Are Not All Journalists Now

GARY HUDSON AND MICK TEMPLE

This chapter disputes the widespread belief that technological developments have made us "all journalists now". While accepting that blogging and independent online news sites challenge both established perceptions of journalism and supposedly authoritative journalistic accounts of the world, we argue that they have clear differences from established journalistic norms, most notably in their commitment to the "truth". We agree that blogs are a valuable addition to the public sphere and potentially offer the opportunity of a more bottom-up and participatory democracy. However, the rise of blogs on established news sites and the increasing use of user-generated content on those sites suggest a colonization of the blogosphere by mainstream journalism. To a large extent, the professionals have maintained their gatekeeping role in the new environment and have become the arbiters, ethical guides and role models for the many amateurs using the new technology. While we conclude that anyone who commits to the professional norms we outline has the right to call themselves a "journalist", regardless of their organizational status or the platform on which they deliver authoritative content, the crude generalization that all bloggers are "journalists" cannot (and should not) be supported. Journalism is too important to cheapen in this way.

THE WEB 2.0 REVOLUTION

Web 2.0 has been one of the buzz phrases of the twenty-first century, with everyone from the popular press to cutting-edge technology magazines "talking about a revolution we're supposedly in the midst of" (Carton 2007), although there is still considerable disagreement about exactly what "Web 2.0" means (see O'Reilly 2005). A broad definition would refer to the interactivity now available through developments such as blogs, wikis and podcasts. However, for Carton a number of key elements define the changes in how we use and think about the Web and that, essentially, Web 2.0 is:

> about moving from a one-to-many publishing model to a many-to-many one . . . [it's] about connections between people, between sites, between the Web and mobile worlds, between buyers and sellers . . . about allowing people to manipulate data, not just retrieve data. All of a sudden, we're actually in there with the data, moving it around, playing with it, and interacting with it in real time. (Carton 2007)

For the purposes of this chapter the crucial aspect of the "Web 2.0 revolution" is that technological developments such as blogging have led to a widespread belief that "we are all journalists now" (for example, Gillmor 2004; Weisberg 2005; Jarvis 2006; Geist 2006; Gant 2007). Clearly, the digital revolution means almost anyone can write an opinion piece or produce a video report and put it on a website. These are great ways to spread opinion and information, but they should not be confused with journalism. The reaction of "traditional" journalists to such claims has been, unsurprisingly, hostile. Especially when the professional status of the occupation is disputed (as it is with journalism), those claiming membership of the profession "typically claim certain levels of technical performance and community orientation" and label those who fall short of such standards as "charlatans" (Singer 2003: 139–140). For professional journalists the profession can be fulfilled only "by people with particular talents, judgement or education" (Allison 1986: 15).

We would dispute such attempts to limit the concept of "the journalist". The arguments in this chapter are *not* an attempt to limit entry into the hallowed halls of journalism or to insist that only those working for certain types of publication can be seen as journalists. As both teachers and practitioners, we welcome the explosion of media outlets, which offer huge opportunities to disseminate one's work. They also, undeniably, offer a route into professional journalism for anyone with some talent. But that does not mean that every blog, every piece of "user-generated content", every letter to the editor, qualifies the contributor to call himself or herself a journalist.

Despite the belief (even as early as 2003) that the argument as to whether blogging was or was not journalism was an "increasingly stale debate" (Lasica 2003: 73), the debate has become even more febrile as the "blogosphere" has exponentially expanded to challenge journalistic authority (see Singer 2007; Carlson 2007). As we argue below, the debate is not an irrelevance because a special status is attached to "journalism" (McNair 1998), and it therefore matters that the term is not used indiscriminately.

WHAT IS A JOURNALIST?

As Lowrey acknowledges, journalism is a "porous occupation" (2006: 485), but the lazy assumption that "we are all journalists now" is an insult to an already undervalued profession; even some established journalists are sniffy about the "profession". Rod Liddle, former editor of BBC Radio 4's *Today* programme, arguably the most influential news and current affairs output in the British media, believes that the basic principles of journalism could be mastered by "most sentient beings . . . in a couple of hours" (Liddle 2007). Maybe this has been the case in Liddle's world, where waving a newly acquired degree from either Oxford or Cambridge University in the direction of the BBC was enough to secure a job for life. But today's journalism professionals have to master an impressive range of skills. Liddle's comments show that the late Nicholas Tomalin's famous view that the only qualities needed for journalistic success are a "ratlike cunning, a plausible manner and a little literary ability" (cited in Randall 2000: 1) is still shared by some "professional journalists".

Although the focus within the dominant discourse tends to be on the mainstream media sectors, while alternative media such as blogs are effectively ignored (Keeble 2006), the lack of "professional boundaries" and the absence of standard career paths for journalists means there is no "definitively recognised divide" between who is or isn't a journalist (Carlson 2007: 265). So, in this multi-media world, what is journalism — and what is not journalism? The question might also be asked "does it matter?" Is it, as noted, already a "stale debate"? We're with Brian McNair, who argues that it matters because:

> the sociological significance of journalistic communication arises largely from the audience's expectations of a distinctive form and content and from their agreement that when these distinguishing characteristics are present the resulting communication enjoys a special status over others which are not journalistic. (1998: 4)

However, the absence of a "definitively recognised divide" makes definition difficult. There are also as many definitions of "journalism" as there are introductory books on the subject — and there are hundreds of those. McNair offers one typical definition of journalism: "any *authored* text, in written, audio or visual form, which *claims* to be (i.e., is presented to its audience as) a *truthful* statement about, or record of, some *hitherto unknown* (new) feature of the *actual, social* world" (1998: 4; emphasis in original).

Of course, this definition (like any other) probably raises more questions than it answers. And the rise of commentary, "new journalism", "gonzo journalism" and "drama-documentary" — which all offer challenges to notions of "truth" — poses problems. However, McNair's formulation does indicate three key factors (in our opinion) in any definition of journalism; truth (which by implication and for our purposes encompasses "accuracy"), newness and authorship. Journalists are generally assumed to share "professional practices of objectivity, balance and news analysis" (Lowrey 2006: 481–2), although one can immediately think of a number of mainstream journalism areas (such as British tabloid newspapers and Fox TV News) that arguably subvert these values. The notion of "objectivity" in reporting is also arguably a particularly North American newspaper concept that may be a contributory factor to the rather anodyne (not to say, boring) content of many US newspapers.

Despite such caveats, we maintain that the central element of "journalism" is the search for truth. It is imperative that, whatever the spin put on "facts" by different media outlets, that readers, listeners and viewers know that what is being produced is essentially truthful. Journalists, whatever their outlet, must strive for this. In a post-modern world subjectivity and relativity reign, producing undeniable problems for notions of, for example, objectivity. But a commitment to truth (and ignoring for the purposes of this chapter the philosophical and epistemological problems of the concept) is a central journalistic value (Singer 2007: 83).

Blogging, it is claimed, has challenged or even ended journalism's "reign of sover-eignty" (Rosen 2005). Coleman argues that blogs have become key sources of information for those "who prefer to trust their own judgement rather than depend upon the spin, censorship and narrow agenda of the usual sources" (2005: 276), but such sites are not seen as being as reliable as "traditional sources" (in Singer 2007: 80). Not only has the notion of "original authorship" been "seriously compromised" in today's Internet culture, but truth and trust have become the "whipping boys" of the Web 2.0 revolution (Keen 2007: 20–23). In short, blogs tend to lack the essential central characteristics of truth and accuracy. This is not to say bloggers don't value "truth" — but their perception of the concept is different. The "wisdom of crowds" (Surowiecki 2004) — that is, the idea that the aggregated views and knowledge of large groups of people are more likely to produce "truth" — is a fundamental principle of the blogging communities and the rationale behind wikis such as Wikipedia. However, it does make it difficult for the individual to judge the veracity of any one site in the way they can judge, for example, the veracity of information in *The New York Times*.

Certainly, the process of "newsgathering" is "routine for journalists, rare for blog-gers" (Lowrey 2006: 480): most bloggers are not paid for their work and therefore lack the financial incentive "for the grittier, less glamorous aspects of news work, such as tracking down sources" (Lowrey 2006: 483). Bloggers tend to value immediacy and comment as opposed to accuracy (Weintraub 2003), which traditional news sources value for a number of reasons, including their reputation and as a protection against legal action (Lowrey 2006: 484). But many of the differences between "bloggers" and "journalists" are ones of degree. Efforts to delineate bloggers and journalists therefore tend to argue that the organization of production is the "most fundamental distinc-tion" with differences in, for example, content, processes, tone and values being "symptoms of this underlying structural difference" (Lowrey 2006: 480).

However, Deuze (2003: 211) argues that online comment and discussion sites and "group weblogs" belong to "a professional domain of journalism", as the function of such sites is the same as the "main purpose of journalism according to its dominant liberal-progressive definition": namely, providing citizens with "the information they need to be free and self-governing". This is stretching the concept of journalism to extremes; we would not call a letter-writer to the local paper a journalist, and what, essentially, is the difference between the letter-writer and a contributor to a group blog? Interactivity and the more rapid dissemination of information may be one answer, although interactivity *per se* is not new: talk radio and television phone-ins have long been features of more traditional media.

While Lasica (2003: 73) admits that "not by a long shot" can all blogging be called journalism, Weisberg (2005) argues forcefully that the answer to the question "who is a journalist?" is now "anybody who wants to be". This belief was given a substantial boost by a California appellate court decision which argued that online journalists, no matter what their provenance, are indistinguishable from journalists working for traditional print and broadcast media and are entitled to the same legal protections. The court's argument that there was no reliable test that would distinguish between "legitimate" and "illegitimate" news or journalists means, in effect, that anyone gathering, selecting and preparing information about current events "for purposes of publication to a mass audience" is a journalist (see Geist 2006). This legal debate may be of specific relevance to American journalists because in the USA journalists have distinct legal rights, unlike in the UK, where for most practical purposes journalists are subject to the same laws as other citizens.

There is no doubt that blogging and online journalism challenge established traditional perceptions of journalism, and have implications "for the way in which media production processes are focused, how news organizations are managed, and how a journalistic culture operates (in relationship with audiences and technologies)" (Deuze 2003: 216). But the lazy assumption that just because someone presents an opinion they are a journalist is given a scathing rebuke by Patrick Burns, the BBC's West Midlands political editor:

> The notion that "we're all journalists now" is part of what I see as the crass illusion that the new electronic technologies can deliver instant gratification. If we can all be Tiger Woods on the electronic golf course or pilot a "Triple Seven" just like that, why can't everyone also become an expert communicator or commentator? No need to understand boring old stuff like the law; the place of the media in a supposedly free society; respect for privacy alongside our mission to investigate and expose: all this is just so much old hat, like the idea that Tiger ever has to go through the grind of practising his swing over and over again. (Burns 2008)

Nick Pollard, former head of Sky News, agrees that technological advance should not be mistaken for journalism: "All it does is allow you to get stuff on air quicker, perhaps in better quality and cheaper . . . you still have to have people who understand what the story is [and] put it in context" (Pollard 2008). As we shall see, such views are instrumental in the colonization of the blogosphere by mainstream journalists. Journalists have always sought first-hand accounts (in the form of interviews) and pictures ("pick-ups") from the public. Now they also seek video and first-person narrative in the form of video diaries and blogs.

JOURNALISM, BLOGGING AND THE PUBLIC SPHERE

Traditional ways of public access to the media have, undeniably, operated to exclude views seen as unrepresentative, unacceptable or not fitting broad organizational requirements. The Web has changed this. It is clear that never before have so many people been able to communicate their views to a potential audience of millions: despite this potential, the audience for most blogs is tiny. Andy Warhol's proposition that everyone will be famous for fifteen minutes has been modified by the idea that anyone can be "famous for fifteen people", a phrase coined in 1991 by Momus, a Scottish punk techno artist, talking about the fragmentation of the music industry.

Even developments designed to enhance an alternative public sphere, such as community broadcasting, have often replicated traditional patterns of exclusion. Indeed, it has been argued that the normative ideal of an open and accessible public sphere conflicts with a "necessary strategy" of exclusion by community broadcasters to ensure "access and participation are fairly distributed" (Van Vuuren 2006: 381–2).

As Yeatman points out, "democratic discourse that is oriented in terms of a centric public sphere is truly anachronistic" (1994: 113). The public sphere needs to be reconceptualized in order to reflect more accurately what Dahlgren (1995) has called the "mediated public sphere", which consists of many (and multi-dimensional) public spheres. The blogosphere — importantly, largely unmediated — is undeniably a significant new element in the public sphere. Technological developments offer a chance for a more participatory public sphere; one in which public opinion really can contribute to the debate, unmediated by professional gatekeepers or media that claim (almost always spuriously) to represent "public opinion" (see Lewis et al. 2005). The top-down perspective of most traditional media is demonstrated by British research that found a majority of the public agreeing with the statement that "much of the news is not relevant to me" (Hargreaves and Thomas 2002: 80). Blogs could be seen (rather romantically, perhaps) as "the public's journalism", offering an alternative to the traditional news media (Haas 2005). For some, such developments mean that the "rigid distinctions of the past" need to be broken down. The resultant "networked journalism" would embrace everything from citizen journalism to wikis to "mainstream professional" journalism, changing the way journalists relate to society and becoming an "essential part of news production" (Beckett 2008: 4–6). In short, "networked journalism" encompasses an enhancement of journalism's social role.

Central to the idea of a re-conceptualized public sphere is the abandonment of elite perceptions of what is or is not permissible in "civilized" debate (Temple 2006: 270). Working-class opinion on, for example, immigration, capital punishment or race is often assumed to be the result of false consciousness emanating from media (especially tabloid newspaper) manipulation (Watson 2003: 107–8). As well as expanding entry into the public sphere, blogs perform the very useful function of challenging elite perceptions of what is legitimate discourse in the public sphere. It is not intended here to deal with the intricacies of discussions on the public sphere, or to recount Jürgen Habermas's original exposition (1989) of the notion, from the birth of the public sphere to his belief in its effective murder by the same forces that created it. (For a lucid and accessible introduction to Habermas and later developments, see Dahlgren 1995.) As a starting point we can consider the public sphere as "that realm of social life where the exchange of information and views on questions of common concern can take place so that public opinion can be formed" (Dahlgren 1995: 7).

This space or realm, however constituted, idealized or theorized, is essential for democracy — a space where people in their role as citizens can access discussion on issues of common concern. So it is vital that issues of public interest are discussed there, but also that what the public thinks illuminates and informs that public sphere. The public sphere needs to be more than an "informational forum" — it also needs to be a "deliberative forum" (see Harrison 2006: 109). But for Habermas the public sphere has become a mechanism by which powerful and dominant groups in society — capitalist organizations and governments — manufacture consensus through the mass media.

The public sphere of today is so dominated by the mass media that it now makes more sense to talk of a "mediated public sphere" (Dahlgren 1995). In this mediated public sphere, it is argued, the citizen is replaced by the consumer; news has moved from its primary role of constituting public opinion among active citizens to being predominantly driven by commercial considerations (Street 2001: 42). Critics see declining levels of participation in "traditional" methods of politics as a sign of a crisis in the public sphere, caused largely by a crisis of legitimacy for news in its role in "the social construction of public life" (Jones 2005: 28). In traditional broadcast news, for example: "the principal role for the citizen is not as a participant but as a viewer. Indeed, definitions of 'good citizenship' often involve watching the news, whereby spectatorship becomes a form of civic duty" (Lewis et al. 2005: 16).

New technology potentially provides a more participatory role for citizens, offering the possibility of a revived and bottom-up public sphere that will challenge elite agenda-setting and allow the views of the public to be more widely represented:

> the breakdown of what were once formidable barriers to entry into the field of journalism is good news for democracy . . . thousands [sic] of bloggers ranting from their soapboxes mean that our political culture encompasses bracing debate about everything people disagree about. (Weisberg 2005)

That may be true, but it does not follow that "anyone who thinks he's [*sic*] a journalist is a journalist" (2005). Nor does it mean that our opposition to the indiscriminate use of the title is an attempt at exclusion. We broadly agree with Gillmor that "some grassroots journalists will become professionals" and that this will result, beneficially, in "more voices and more options" (Gillmor 2004: 4).

The commercialization of the media is seen as responsible for the "effective elimination" of Habermas's original notion of a "rational critical public sphere" (Street 2001: 42). For many critics, while the Internet offers the opportunity for a revitalization of the public sphere, elite opinion still dominates (Savigny 2002). Bloggers potentially offer the public alternative sources of information. Clearly a less elite-driven news agenda — one driven from the bottom-up rather than top-down and representing many different interests — offers the opportunity for effective engagement with political issues by far more participants. For example, the build-up by political pressure groups to the 1999 World Trade Organization talks bypassed the traditional media, and the scale of the consequent protests ensured massive media attention for a hitherto sidelined and not insignificant body of public opinion.

In consequence, some observers believe that technological advances are undermining the claims of top-down or dominance models. McNair has argued that as a result of the impact of new technology we are all now living in an "environment of communicative turbulence" (2005: 151), in which the proliferation of outlets and information means we must move away from old models of control. Elites still desire to control the media and the democratic process, but this exercise of control is "increasingly interrupted and disrupted by unpredictable eruptions and bifurcations arising from the impact of economic, political, ideological and technological factors" on the communication process (McNair 2006: 3). For McNair, the traditional and Marxist-influenced "control paradigm" — exemplified in the propaganda model of Herman and Chomsky (1988) — is now unsustainable. In short, "chaos" rather than "control" best describes the current journalistic environment. McNair advances a number of reasons for the "emerging chaos" in political communication, including his argument that new media technologies have provided a more crowded and unpredictable media environment and challenged the hegemony of mainstream and traditional news in the public sphere (McNair 2006: 37–49). Present-day elites face a "political environment of substantially greater volatility and uncertainty than was faced by previous generations of governing elite" (McNair 2005: 157).

Campbell (2007: 13) finds "significant points of contention" with McNair, in particular disputing his claim that, in the fight to control the news agenda, "subordinate social actors" (i.e., bloggers) have as much chance of succeeding "as their better-resourced opponents" (McNair 2006: 65). Campbell argues that most of the seminal examples of claims for Internet journalism influencing the big players are "demonstrably reactive rather than proactive": the online Drudge report's famous outing of Bill Clinton's dalliance with Monica Lewinsky was achieved by obtaining information that the magazine *Newsweek* had "decided not to publish" (2006: 7). Campbell points out that the "persistent importance of mainstream media news outlets on the internet" does not suggest a significant growth of bottom-up journalism. In support of Campbell's scepticism, something of significance appears to be happening: the blogosphere is rapidly becoming colonized by the traditional media who initially ignored its existence.

THE MEDIATED PUBLIC SPHERE — COLONIZING THE BLOGOSPHERE?

There is no disputing the benefits that new technology can bring to established news outlets: indeed, bloggers could be seen as complementary to the "work of the professional journalism establishment" (Lasica 2003: 72). As the BBC's former media correspondent Nick Higham acknowledges: "News has to find ways of re-presenting itself, reconfiguring itself, redefining itself in ways that are going to be meaningful to people who have new and different technologies" (Higham 2008).

But Higham indicates a problem for a revitalized public sphere. He maintains that the democratization of the media — the fact that anyone can get access to the Internet — strengthens the position of journalists, particularly with organizations such as the BBC that have a reputation for trustworthiness.

> The Internet is a huge great rumour factory, and it produces all kinds of fascinating stuff, but
> . . . you've no way of knowing what you can believe and what you can't believe. Our job is to

say: "This much we know and you can believe this much." If you then want to go off and swap gossip with someone online or blog or whatever, that's fine, but bear in mind that what you're seeing there may not be reliable. It may be hearsay. It may be half-truth. So there's a very important role for us, for the BBC and for other news organisations which have built their promise to the audience and promise to the readership on trustworthiness and reliability. (Higham 2008)

For Nick Higham there is a potential mismatch when news providers offer a forum for hosting blogs. He believes there needs to be a clear separation between an authoritative news station and something that provides a forum for comment and exchange of views — just as there is on radio between a news bulletin and a phone-in. User-generated content — for example, blogs, wikis, posts on discussion forums and, more importantly, audio and video — allows the public to become more active participants within mainstream media, but the reliability of the information the public gives is often difficult to judge (Chin 2006). In addition, the traditional media still act as gatekeepers of user-generated content. For example, Sky News' series in March 2007 of reports "Inside Iraq", consisting of films by "ordinary" Iraqi citizens, demonstrates that new technology can provide an avenue into the mainstream public sphere — but this is a process in which Sky still act as a "gatekeeper".

Technology, via an increased number of channels, offers the opportunity for access to television; *Current TV* in the UK features programmes "made by you". Tim Burke, an experienced BBC journalist and the community content editor for the corporation's local TV experiment in 2005–6, says:

I'm not the gatekeeper. I'm the butler. I'll answer the door for you and not shut it in your face. I'll invite you in and show you round and make you comfortable. People like seeing people like themselves on the telly, but for most of the audience TV was not made by people like them. It was made by people like me. My job now is to make it with them and help them make it. (Burke 2008)

Such developments are welcomed, but it is apparent that access is still controlled by the professionals. Although they agree that the structures of established media control are generally reflected in the online world, Curran and Seaton have argued the possibility of a more discursive and deliberative public sphere as, while "alternative voices tend not to be heard in the main square of the electronic public sphere . . . they tend to get heard in some online backstreets" (2003: 270).

Emily Bell (2006), director of digital content at the British Guardian News and Media, argues that the events of July 2005, when 52 people were killed and more than 700 injured in attacks on London's transport systems, signalled a "paradigm shift" in the way the media report breaking news stories. It was the first domestic news story where "the most significant coverage came from people on the scene . . . rather than established news outlets". Bell's assertion of a "paradigm shift" looked less authoritative less than two years later, however, when only one passenger took mobile phone photographs of a rail crash at Grayrigg in Cumbria in February 2007. That passenger was Caroline Thomson, a BBC employee, and therefore a media professional (BBC News Online 2007). Similarly, Gillmor points to 9/11 as a significant turning point in media history, in that "the first draft of history" was no longer the sole prerogative of the professionals. The audience was helping to write that draft "adding first-person accounts and nuance to what the professionals were doing" (Jardin 2004).

However, this is surely what the public have always done: the audience now may be more pro-active, but essentially the relationship remains the same. First-person accounts have long been a feature of the fabled "first draft of history" and, no matter how well written the blog, it still requires journalists to add context to personal accounts and, just as importantly, add an imprimatur of authority to such accounts. But for Gillmor, blogs have joined the "journalism ecosystem" in a symbiotic, rather than competitive, relationship with "professional journalism" (in Jardin 2004).

Lasica offers a compromise for those who reject the bald label of "journalism" for developments such as blogging: "Call it participatory journalism, or journalism from the edges . . . it refers to individuals playing an active role in the process of collecting, reporting, sorting, analysing and disseminating news and information — a task once reserved almost exclusively to the news media" (Lasica 2003: 71).

Bell (2006), noting that "a trusted local paper is a brilliant aggregator", sees a network of local and regional contributors providing the "backbone of daily coverage" where there are "not enough reporting resources" — but our trust in local newspapers is something that has been built up on generations of painstakingly accurate news coverage by professionally trained journalists. New technology offers the unscrupulous the opportunity for fraud (for example, manipulating pictures, manufacturing fake press releases and creating bogus websites), and it would take very little for our faith in established local news sources to be seriously dented.

Blogs and alternative news sites are notoriously unreliable. Lies, rumour and supposition pose as truth, and our inability to weigh up the merits of such sources ensures that traditional news providers have tended to flourish in the new media. For example, in the UK, we know the provenance and the ideological bias of the BBC's website and those of newspapers such as the *Guardian*, *Sun* and *Telegraph*, enabling us to weigh up, relatively accurately, the news we find there. Online versions of such established media are seen as particularly credible by the public (Johnson and Kaye 2002). Indeed, there is compelling evidence that blogs have been moulded by journalists to fit and "in some ways, augment, traditional professional norms and practices": in other words, blogs are being "normalized by journalists much as other aspects of the Internet have been" (Singer 2005: 174).

Guardian Unlimited claims that, rather than try to control its content, more than any other newspaper website it has opened up its portal to its users: "They can now take part in political debate, send in pictures, offer running sports commentaries, discuss books, culture, travel, food, environmental issues — and generally participate with other *Guardian* readers" (Editorial 2006).

Other *Guardian* sites offer readers the chance to recommend "favourite hotels, restaurants bars and clubs" (2006). Their 'Comment is Free' site offers the chance for readers' contributions to sit alongside those of professional journalists, academics and commentators. Such developments have the appearance of a chatroom for the socially conscious middle classes — they are not journalism as we define it. As the *Guardian* says: "We wanted to create an extension of the paper — where serious matters could be discussed in a reasonably serious way by intelligent people." However, there is strict editorial control, and material that is deemed "unacceptable" is deleted and "in some cases, the commentator banned from the site" (2006). Similarly, the majority of reader participation on other newspaper websites is "edited or pre-moderated" (Thurman 2008: 142).

Alternative media "set out to privilege the powerless and the marginal", offering an alternative to a mainstream media, which generally privileges the powerful (Harcup 2003: 371). Even most "alternative" print media, while making great play of their openness — "the great thing is you don't have to be able to 'write' to write for the *Salford Star* . . . it's open and accessible to everyone" — also still act as gatekeepers, checking submissions for "facts and libel" and helping to "structure pieces before publication" (Kingston 2006: 61). In the same way, evidence indicates that, while online independent news sites can offer a "radical way of sharing and selecting news", despite their commitment to "open publishing" and a relatively "non-hierarchical relationship" with their users and contributors, the traditional top-down editorial control appears to take place (Platon and Deuze 2003: 351–2).

There is a clear technological argument that anyone with access to the means of distributing media is in the same position as a traditional broadcaster. That is not the same as being able to command an audience and earning the trust of viewers and listeners. Indeed, there is evidence that, worldwide, most blogs are short-lived and that the "blogging phenomenon" is now in decline (Allen-Mills 2007). That is except, of course, for the blogs of established media professionals — for example, the BBC's political editor Nick Robinson's *Newslog* — which have successfully replicated the feel and spirit of blogging within established news websites. It is also the case that the main way in which blogs have "exercised their influence" is through links with, and citations in, established media: while blogs have broken a "small number of big news stories", the significance of such stories was felt only after "mainstream news media followed them up" (Nip 2006: 227–8). More damagingly for those who argue the influence of bloggers, US research shows the large majority of blogs read by media professionals are those "written by journalists with close ties to mainstream media outlets" (2006). It appears that the mainstream mass media retain, to a large extent, their traditional gatekeeping role.

CONCLUSION

Despite the belief that the forums that debate the question of "what is journalism" are controlled by communities (for example, the journalism academic community) with a vested interest in a limited definition (Lowrey 2006: 485), we have no wish to limit access to "the profession". Indeed, such a wish would be ludicrous in today's world. The blogger, the online pundit, the producer of an online community newsletter *can* call themselves journalists, but unless they are committed to writing new and accurate material they have no right to do so.

There are clear differences between most blogs and most traditional journalism. On a purely practical level, most bloggers don't get paid and are not bound by the pressure of deadlines. More importantly, they need have no commitment to objectivity, balance, newsgathering, news analysis or accuracy (see Singer 2005: 176). They also tend to have a cavalier approach to legal restraints. In the view of *Guardian* journalist Michael White, they don't have to worry about the legal implications of what they say because they're "not worth suing" (BBC *Newsnight* 2007).

However, blogs (especially when unmediated) are a valuable addition to the public sphere, ensuring a greater plurality of voices. Significantly, they offer the chance of a more bottom-up and participatory democracy. At their best, blogs challenge received opinion and supposedly "authoritative" journalistic accounts of the world (Lowrey 2006: 489). They can also inform mainstream journalism, and it is here — despite the claims of many in the blogging community — that they have had and are likely to continue to have their greatest impact. It remains the case that the most likely way for blogs to come to the attention of a wide audience is through the established mass media.

Trends suggest a colonization of the blogosphere by mainstream journalism. It is not only that the number of blogs by professional print and broadcast journalists has dramatically increased in the last few years and proved popular with the online community. Broadcast news programmes and newspapers also invite picture content and online comment from viewers by advertising web addresses and offering instruction on how to upload still and video pictures. With the prospect of a wider audience, and sometimes payment for the more significant images, users are encouraged to deliver material to established news organizations rather than alternative, often amateur, outlets. The professionals are no longer the only people who have access to the means of distributing news. But they have largely retained their gatekeeping role and, in the process, have become the arbiters, ethical guides and role models for the many amateurs using the new technology.

Journalists have to be authoritative content providers for the multiplicity of delivery platforms available for news and factual information. They have to deliver compelling information to engage audiences. They have to collect, check and order facts. They weigh up arguments. They make judgements. *And they tell stories* — stories that have to be trusted by their audience. These are the factors that make a "journalist", and anyone who commits to such professional standards does have the right to call him- or herself a "journalist", regardless of their organizational status or the platform on which they deliver authoritative content.

Journalists are certainly all content providers in a converged multimedia age. It doesn't follow that all content providers are journalists. They never have been, and they never will be.

References

Allen-Mills, T. (2007) "Lost for Words Online as Blog Craze Falters", *The Sunday Times*, 25 March.

Allison, M. (1986) "A Literature Review of Approaches to the Professionalism of Journalists", *Journal of Mass Media Ethics*, 1 (2).

Beckett, C. (2008) *SuperMedia: Saving Journalism So It Can Save the World*. Oxford: Blackwell.

Bell, E. (2006) "The Media Have Yet to Harness the Power of Citizen Journalism", *The Guardian*, 8 July.

Burke, T. (2008) Personal communication with authors.

Burns, P. (2008) Personal communication with authors.

Campbell, V. (2007) "Political Communication and the 'Chaos Paradigm'". Paper presented at the Political Studies Association's Annual Conference, Swansea University, 1–3 April.

Carlson, M. (2007) "Blogs and Journalistic Authority: The Role of Blogs in US Election Day 2004", *Journalism Studies*, 8 (2).

Carton, S. (2007) "Web 2.0: What Is It Really?", 5 March, www.clickz.com.

Chin, P. (2006) "The Value of User-Generated Content", *Intranet Journal*, 3 July, www.intranetjournal.com.

Coleman, S. (2005) "Blogs and the New Politics of Listening", *Political Quarterly*, 76 (2).

Curran, J., and Seaton, J. (2003) *Power without Responsibility: The Press, Broadcasting, and New Media in Britain*, London: Routledge.

Dahlgren, P. (1995) *Television and the Public Sphere: Citizenship, Democracy and the Media*. London: Sage.

Deuze, M. (2003) "The Web and Its Journalism: Considering the Consequences of Different Types of Newsmedia Online", *New Media and Society*, 5 (2).

Gant, S. (2007) *We're All Journalists Now: The Transformation of the Press and Reshaping of the Law in the Internet Age*. New York: Free Press.

Geist, M. (2006) "We Are All Journalists Now", 5 June. www.michaelgeist.ca.

Gillmor, D. (2004) *We the Media: Grassroots Journalism by the People, for the People*. www.authorama.com/we-the-media-1.html.

Guardian Unlimited (2006) "The Digital Challenge", editorial, 25 October.

Haas, T. (2005) "From 'Public Journalism' to 'the Public's Journalism'? Rhetoric and Reality in the Discourse on Weblogs", *Journalism Studies*, 6 (3).

Habermas, J. (1989) *The Structural Transformation of the Public Sphere*. Cambridge: Polity.

Harcup, T. (2003) "The Unspoken — Said: The Journalism of Alternative Media", *Journalism*, 4 (3).

Hargreaves, I., and Thomas, J. (2002) *New News, Old News*. London: ITC/BSC.

Harrison, J. (2006) *News*. London: Routledge.

Herman, E. S., and Chomsky, N. (1988) *Manufacturing Consent: The Political Economy of the Mass Media*. New York: Pantheon Books.

Higham, N. (2008) Personal communication with authors.

Jardin, X. (2004) "We're All Journalists Now", *Wired News*, 11 August. www.wired.com/news.

Jarvis, J. (2006) "The Bloggers and Journalists Are Comrades-at-Keyboards", *Media Guardian*, 21 August.

Johnson, T. J., and Kaye, B. K. (2002) "Webelievability: A Path Model Examining How Convenience and Reliance Predict Online Credibility", *Journalism and Mass Communication Quarterly*, 79 (3).

Jones, J. (2005) *Entertaining Politics*. Oxford: Rowman & Littlefield.

Keeble, R. (2006) "What is Journalism? Reflections and Provocations", *State of Nature*, September/October. www.stateofnature.org.

Keen, A. (2007) *The Cult of the Amateur: How Today's Internet is Killing Our Culture and Assaulting Our Economy*. London: Nicholas Brealey.

Kingston, S. (2006) "Voices of the People", *British Journalism Review*, 17 (4).

Lasica, J. D. (2003) "Blogs and Journalism Need Each Other", *Nieman Reports*, 57 (3).

Lewis, J., Inthorn, S., and Wahl-Jorgensen, K. (2005) *Citizens or Consumers? What the Media Tell*

Us about Political Participation. Maidenhead: Open University Press.

Liddle, R. (2007) "Chairman Tony's Gone Pol Potty Over University Admissions", *Sunday Times,* 18 March.

Lowrey, W. (2006) "Mapping the Journalism-Blogging Relationship", *Journalism,* 7 (4).

McNair, B. (1998) *The Sociology of Journalism.* London: Arnold.

McNair, B. (2005) "The Emerging Chaos of Global News Culture". In S. Allan (ed.), *Journalism: Critical Issues.* Maidenhead: Open University Press.

McNair, B. (2006) *Cultural Chaos: Journalism, News and Power in a Globalised World.* London: Routledge.

Nip, J. Y. M. (2006) "Exploring the Second Phase of Public Journalism", *Journalism Studies,* 7 (2).

O'Reilly, T. (2005) "What is Web 2.0? Design Patterns and Business Models for the Next Generation of Software", 30 September. www.oreillynet.com.

Platon, S., and Deuze, M. (2003) "Indymedia Journalism: A Radical Way of Making, Selecting and Sharing News?", *Journalism,* 4 (3).

Pollard N. (2008) Personal communication with authors.

Randall, D. (2000) *The Universal Journalist.* London: Pluto.

Rosen, J. (2005) "Bloggers vs. Journalists Is Over", *PressThink,* 15 January. www.journalism.nyu.edu/pubzone/weblogs/pressthink.

Savigny, H. (2002) "Public Opinion, Political Communication and the Internet", *Politics,* 22 (1).

Singer, J. B. (2003) "Who Are These Guys? The Online Challenge to the Notion of Journalistic Professionalism", *Journalism,* 4 (2).

Singer, J. B. (2005) "The Political J-Blogger: 'Normalising' a New Media to Fit Old Norms and Practices", *Journalism,* 6 (2), pp. 173–98.

Singer, J. B. (2007) "Contested Autonomy: Professional and Popular Claims on Journalistic Norms", *Journalism Studies,* 8 (1).

Street, J. (2001) *Mass Media, Politics and Democracy.* Basingstoke: Palgrave Macmillan.

Surowiecki, J. (2004) *The Wisdom of Crowds: Why the Many are Smarter than the Few.* New York: Anchor.

Temple, M. (2006) "Dumbing Down Is Good for You", *British Politics,* 1 (2).

Thurman, N. (2008) "Forum for Citizen Journalists? Adoption of User Generated Content Initiatives by Online News Media", *New Media and Society,* 10 (1).

Van Vuuren, K. (2006) "Community Broadcasting and the Enclosure of the Public Sphere", *Media, Culture and Society,* 28 (3).

Watson, J. (2003) *Media Communication: An Introduction to Theory and Process.* Basingstoke: Palgrave Macmillan.

Weintraub, D. (2003) "Scuttlebut and Speculation Fill a Political Weblog", *Nieman Reports,* 57 (3).

Weisberg, J. (2005) "Who is a Journalist?", *Slate,* 9 March. www.slate.com.

Yeatman, A. (1994) *Postmodern Revisionings of the Political.* New York: Routledge.

CHAPTER 4

The Case against the Democratic Influence of the Internet on Journalism

TIM MARKHAM

The past decade has seen myriad claims of the democratizing potential of the Internet in general, and in particular of the possibility for mass, non-professional, online media production.[1] The thrust of these claims ranges from the enhanced opportunities for citizenship (Coleman 2005) and the dismantling of elite gatekeeping structures and hierarchies (Delli Carpini and Williams 2001; Lievrouw and Livingstone 2006) to the egalitarianism of horizontal networks (Bentivegna 2002) and improved oversight of mainstream politics and media (Drezner and Farrell 2004; Cornfeld 2005; Regan 2004). Democratization is, needless to say, a highly contested term. It will be used here to designate not the advance of normative principles of equality, freedom or justice, but simply agency to effect change in the public realm. The definition of publicness is also very debatable; here it refers to any arena in which issues of shared concern are contested and negotiated (Couldry et al. 2007: 6–7) — it is not limited to traditional political institutions or Habermas's rational public sphere.

In this chapter I argue that the democratizing potential of online interaction, and blogging in particular, has been overstated by academic critics, policy makers and media professionals alike. This will involve suggesting different ways of theorizing online media production, although it will also draw at least tangentially on three very different pieces of research: a large-scale UK project investigating the relationship between people's sense (or absence) of media and public connection (Couldry et al. 2007), a qualitative analysis of symbolic economies of professional identity amongst UK and US journalists (Markham 2007) and an exploratory survey of a selection of opinion blogs. Blogging is conceived methodologically in Bourdieusian terms as a field of cultural production, characterized by field positions differentiated according to forms and volumes of symbolic capital and by the collective misrecognition (although there is also evidence of reflexivity) among bloggers and media analysts of the "rules of the game"; in particular, regarding what constitutes authority in the blogosphere. It is suggested that blogging may be connected phenomenologically (rather than politically) to the "culture of narcissism" thesis. And the implications in terms of field autonomy of an increasingly self-referencing blogosphere are considered.

Any argument that posits blogging as a democratizing influence on journalism risks committing the fallacy of casting in political terms what is instead a cultural phenomenon. The mainstreaming of this form of cultural production (which, given research into the endurance of the digital divide, must be regarded as a limited universalization) should be seen not as a natural political good but simply as a horizontal proliferation. Hierarchical proliferation of news production, although it by definition entails a defence of elitism, can be defended on the grounds that it is only by the maintenance of a restricted space of production that certain cultural forms are possible. This is not to suggest that hierarchical structures in journalism should be treated as sacred. Instead, the necessity of hierarchy as a general principle should be defended, while the specific forms that hierarchization takes should be made transparent and contested. This means that, rather than depicting blogging as a force opposing cultural consecration — that is, the collective valorization of particular symbolic forms according to mainstream or institutional principles of differentiation — and the subsequent reproduction of unequal power relations in journalism, we should accept the necessity of rarefied spaces of journalistic production and instead turn our attention to exposing the strategies and criteria by which these positions are defined and occupied.

The chapter also makes a broader claim about the democratic limits of online practices of citizenship: in short, interaction in itself is of no political value if that interaction, in the words of one interviewee, "doesn't go anywhere". Further, there is evidence of a significant minority that is "already turned away" (Couldry et al. 2007) from both media and public engagement, and the Internet cannot, and should not, be expected to correct disconnection and broader alienation. (These claims run parallel to the arguments against policies of social inclusion which fail to answer either of the questions of "inclusion in what?" and "for what purpose?"). Arguments for the democratizing influence of blogging on journalism rely on a questionable premise of personalized authenticity, by which authority is perceived to consist in the genuineness with which a claim is made, rather than according to some external frame of reference, and wrongly presume that political efficacy logically follows from freedom of expression. Our attentions — as both academics and bloggers — would be more effectively directed at the mechanisms that sustain the hierarchies and dominant symbolic forms of journalism today (rather than opposing such structures outright) and at the political forces — rather than cultural or media phenomena — that undermine democratic engagement.

THEORIZING ONLINE MEDIA PRODUCTION WITH BOURDIEU

One of the principal weaknesses in the claim that the Internet is a democratizing influence on journalism is the assumption that the Internet is a political arena. I argue below that the Internet *should* be seen as political in the sense that it can be partly character-ized as a field of struggle, rather than a neutral space of communication providing the basis for collaborative engagement. This, however, is distinct from depicting the Internet as a political field as such — i.e., one whose essence, if not reality, is in conflict with and negotiation over issues of shared concern. Rather, in Bourdieusian terms, it is best defined as a field of cultural production,[2] which subsists in the metafield of power but is distinct from the field of politics and operates relatively, if weakly, autonomously. This means that online interaction proceeds to a significant extent according to the Internet's internal rules of engagement, driven by an emerging etiquette. However, those external principles affecting the Internet (the broader cultural context, the regulatory structure of the news media, market economics and so on) must also be taken into account. This is not to suggest that only traditional arenas should count as "political" — countless viable alternative political spaces, from community media activism to online organizing and campaigning networks, have been identified (see, for instance, Downing 2001; Kahn and Kellner 2004). But what these arenas share is a common dominant set of principles of "vision and division" — the key differentiating factors by which value is ascribed to symbolic capital. Such principles are associated with normative and historical factors, including public and social insti-tutions, and embedded modes of practice internalized and instinctively recognized as political. These discursively instituted modes of interaction and communication are not intrinsically legitimate but achieve a contingent stability as political practice through repeated enactment and historicity: namely, contestation, campaigning and mobiliza-tion over civil, economic and potentially cultural rights. There is nothing naturally superior about these: indeed, from the Bourdieusian perspective, it is presumed that the internalization and naturalization of such norms proceeds alongside a systematic misrecognition of other, more insidious, economies of power.

To characterize the Internet as a field of cultural production, then, is not to say it is a degraded political sphere, as much as it is not in itself a new and improved poli-tics. While practices of citizenship do, of course, take place online, there is nothing about new communication technologies that is naturally democratizing: they operate according to a set of principles that are distinct from the field of politics and should be understood on their own terms. That is, the elements that constitute the lifeworld [3] of the Internet — discourse, identity, norms of practice, anticipation, creativity, profes-sionalism, amateurism, instinct and so on — are determined fundamentally differently from those of other lifeworlds in which the centrality (if not specific form) of political norms such as citizenship, democratization, coercion, justice, domination and so on has long been established. This is in itself problematic, but the point is that such critical problematization is both possible and widely practised; the practically universalized dominant principles of politics are routinely challenged and picked apart. However, to conceive of the Internet in such terms is to forgo the critical assessment of its own prin-ciples of differentiation. This is not to suggest that the blogosphere is internally coherent and strongly autonomous from other fields, but as a distinct subfield of cultural production it should be thought of as structured according to adaptable, durable logics that are different from those of adjacent and intersecting fields. And given the sheer speed with which such principles and norms have become effectively natural and universal, it seems particularly important that we understand the contingent generative structures of this quasi-autonomous lifeworld. To import criteria from other fields with their own internal logics is to neglect the logics of determination of symbolic value in online communication — logics that are doubtless contingent on specific social, historical and political conditions of possibility.

What does it mean, then, to characterize the Internet as a field of cultural production related to, but also partially autonomous from, other fields? First, like any field, the Internet should be thought of as simultaneously structured and structuring: there is no virtual world characterized by competing but unresolved theories of its existence. Rather, there is a symbolic world (like others) manifesting a particular determination of a range of possible worlds. It is for this reason that we should not see any field of cultural production as being comprehensible *only* in its own terms, *or* as essentially arbitrary in relation to the economic and social contexts in which it subsists. (And by structuring, online media production should be conceived as having determining functions beyond the field of its genesis — including in what I have identified here as the public arena.) From a practical point of view, this means that we can certainly interpret changes in journalistic practice and consumption in political terms, without extrapolating either that there is a corresponding determination on the political field or that new structures of journalism themselves have a political teleology, or final end, goal or purpose. These new structures are particular expressions of generative logics: this means that their political determination is reasonable without being predictable and that their determining effects will sometimes, haphazardly, include practices of democratization, without such determinations "completing" those structures.

By way of an (admittedly imperfect) analogy, let us consider Bourdieu's critique of opinion polling as a democratizing force in politics. The problem with claims made on the basis of polling, for Bourdieu, is that they misrepresent as political that which should be regarded as cultural. In short, the value of an opinion poll is contingent on a culturally dominant principle of differentiation — popularity — and as such it should not be conflated with political, and specifically democratizing, criteria (Bourdieu 1994). To reiterate, this is not to suggest the superiority of (traditional) criteria for ascribing political symbolic value, nor to suggest that politics exists in a vacuum. But importing exogenous principles of domination undermines in the same blow both the iniquities and the benefits of a field historically operating with a significant degree of autonomy. Further, those criteria do not have the same meaning when applied in different contexts (Matheson 2004), and their normalization in another field may proceed only through the misrecognition of specific political conditionalities. For example, the idea that the multiplication of sources of information online represents a democratization of knowledge conflates the criteria of freedom and choice. Likewise, ascribing value according to popularity — as is the norm for the majority of search engines — can lead to the conflation of competitive success and political mandate. (It has also been argued that the personalizability of search engines indicates the increasing prevalence of a discourse of individualization; see Carlson 2007b.) Further, the proliferation of media producers online may be interpreted as culturally empowering, but to assert that this is a politically democratizing function is to make commitments to specific interpretations of representation and self-determination — which are by no means uncontested within the realm of political debate. The danger is that, if such specific values are normalized, then their exogenous origins will go increasingly unrecognized, along with the normative commitments that they may entail. I would suggest that such culturally determined criteria may include a politics of competitive individualism — not that this is necessarily indefensible, but that the colonization by this logic of other fields may contribute to its decontestation and dominance in political and other spheres of interaction.

FOUCAULT, HABERMAS AND THE DEFENCE OF HIERARCHY

A second and related way of theorizing the massification of media production is to characterize it, after Foucault, as the incitement of discourse. For Foucault power operates not (only) through negative injunction — explicit constraints on freedom of speech, say, or restrictive social norms — but through 'positive', stimulatory mechanisms. Psychiatry, for instance, wields coercive power not by broadly prohibiting behaviour but by encouraging individuals to talk — leading to sense being made of behaviour in terms of a discourse that categorizes, rationalizes and pathologizes. Likewise, from a Foucaultian perspective, increasingly prevalent representations of sexuality in the media (in women's magazines, for instance) should be interpreted not as liberating but as discursive production which acts as a form of discipline by inciting structured internal monologues in individuals. Instead of regarding media production as the realization of some latent or natural desire for self-expression made possible by new communication technologies, this approach sees the "will to blog" as the product of cultural, economic and political forces. These might include a culture of narcissism, consumerist production of desire or the technological genesis of cultural practices — although in each case there are allegations of determinism to answer. At the more conspiratorial end of Foucaultian thinking, this may amount to interpreting any apparently unstructured proliferation of expression as evidence of new regimes of discipline, especially the instigation of internal discourses that regulate the individual. The blogosphere thus represents neither a democratized public sphere providing the preconditions for unfettered rational discourse nor a top-down imposition of power by political or corporate elites, but the inculturation of norms whose coercive political effects are masked by their appearance as will and instinct, and whose durability is masked by their being re-presented as new norms.

The appearance of novelty is associated with a cultural form that is under-determined (that is, relatively freer from structural determination), masking the common determining structures that have given rise equally to media forms new and old. (The same logic might be argued to apply to "citizen journalism" or public participation in mainstream news production; see, for instance, Deuze, Bruns and Neuberger 2007.) Brian McNair (2003) usefully distinguishes between the control and chaos paradigms of media politics, although by characterizing chaos as a lack of (authoritarian) control

81

there is an implicit equating of chaos and freedom in his model. While a norm of unruliness as central to a healthy democracy is certainly defensible, the Foucaultian position emphasizes the ongoing need to identify patterns of political determination in seeming disorder. After Giddens (1984), individuals do not act with voluntaristic agency; nor are they mere structural effects. Behaviour is structured by rules, resources, relationships and authority, yet the ongoing existence of these is predicated on their production and reproduction in social interaction. Accordingly, changing practices do lead to changes in rules, but these should be seen as re-structuration rather than de-structuration. New practices indicate not an absence of determination but a different determination, which in this context boils down to asking what determines identity, orientation, behaviour and action in an arena such as the blogosphere, and who benefits from its mainstreaming.

To characterize the Internet as not naturally democratizing does not then equate to seeing it as an ideological state apparatus, whose political functions of controlling citizens and reproducing hierarchies precede its use as a means of address, reception and interaction. The restructuration that journalism has been through over the past ten years does not represent an inexorable path towards increased coercion operating largely unnoticed. Restructuration does involve changes (and continuities) at the macro level, while the microscopic "intimate structuration" to which Foucaultian theory lends itself does not reside only in the realm of the intangible. The task of the theorist is to illuminate the conditions of possibility, constraints and contingencies misinterpreted as unremarkable and unintended consequences of newly emerging restructured symbolic economies. This is entirely consistent with recognizing that the Internet does provide an arena in which large numbers of individuals can communicate, notwithstanding the enduring caveat of the digital divide, much discussed elsewhere (see, for instance, Norris 2000; Norris 2001; Lievrouw and Livingstone 2003; and Rice and Haythornthwaite 2006).

But relative freedom of communication is not in itself a sufficient criterion of democratization. Even if we characterize the Internet *pace* Habermas primarily as a field of communication, we are not bound to the narrow premise that communication is foremost a matter of deliberation towards an agreed end-point. In short, if we take a Bourdieusian rather than a Habermasian perspective, the Internet should be characterized at least partly as a field of struggle or *practical strategy*. "Strategy" here does not refer to the political potential of the Internet in terms of its efficacy in furthering the interests of political ideologies and movements. Rather, it refers to the political determination of the terms of communication, as well as authority, authenticity and so on: communication should be regarded as a structured set of embodied practices oriented towards some kind of gain beyond that which the communicative act announces. Interaction between bloggers and their peers and readers then may serve to obscure an underlying symbolic economy in which competition for misrecognized forms of capital proceeds; I consider below the possibility that systematically misrecognized authority and authenticity underpin struggles over status.

If this seems over-conspiratorial, and if the mere fact of expression or interaction is to be rejected as a sufficient condition of democratization, then the Habermasian alternative — a structured discourse with established rules of engagement and means of ascribing merit — will need to be defended or developed (Bohman 2007). This means defending a system of media production that is variously describable as elitist, institutional and bourgeois: that is, professional journalism. And while journalism's role as a democratic force in late capitalist societies depends on a code of practice, enshrining a set of ethical principles adherence to which is accountable to peers or external regulatory bodies, it is demonstrable that the implementation of and reflection on those ethics are themselves effective means by which journalism's gatekeeping structures and internal hierarchies are preserved. In short, journalists' ethical practice, and the way they talk about the ethical dimension of journalism, has the effect of mystifying what it takes to be a good (and ethical) journalist (Matheson 2003). This is anti-democratic in the sense that this process serves as a barrier against entry into the journalistic field — and there is no shortage of evidence that the demographic failing to break into professional journalism over-represents minorities, women and people of low socio-economic status (see, for instance, Sutton Trust 2006; Chambers et al. 2004).

As such, the deprofessionalization of journalism for which new communication technologies are in part responsible might be welcomed as a good thing. Sociologists since Johnson (1972) have argued that professional identities and norms have more to do with the universalization of professional ideologies and the power relations they concretize than safeguards of best professional practice (see also Deuze 2005). However, in line with the point made about restructuration above, deprofessionalization should be seen as replacing one set of criteria with another, rather than as simply doing away with dominant criteria. Like other fields of cultural production, this new journalism — however restructured — would be expected to run between two poles: broadly speaking, elitist and mass culture. What Bourdieu terms the pole of unrestricted cultural production is associated with specific criteria for ascribing value — in particular popularity, although analysis of print journalism suggests other plausible examples of valorized symbolic capital operating at this pole including authenticity (see below), moralism and underdog status (see also Conboy 2006). My own research (2007) indicates that the elite pole is associated with traditional journalistic values such as autonomy, integrity and objectivity, although there are further largely misrecognized values, including cynicism and ambivalence towards power at work. Importantly, while it is true that the criteria associated with the pole of restricted production are peer-defined and serve the interests of established professional journalists, it is also only at this pole that certain forms of cultural production are possible. To be sure, this reasoning is more germane to a field such as scientific research, in which scientific peer review can be more easily seen as serving a properly democratic function of safeguarding the quality of knowledge defensibly regarded as being in the public interest. (However, Bourdieu also notes that even in the scientific field there are misrecognized economies at work that mask the strategizing that underpins competition between scientists, namely the "interest in disinterest" in financial gain.) It is more problematic to apply this logic to journalism, but at least in the case of investigative journalism the reasoning is sound: it is a journalistic practice possible only at the pole of restricted production and which, despite its insitutionalization and elitism, may serve a democratic function

— say, holding power to account in a way that only a well-funded journalist, with experience of mixing in elite circles, and with ample time, could be expected to do (Lowrey 2006).[4]

JOURNALISTIC AUTHORITY AND THE CONTINGENCY OF AUTHENTICITY

One of the most interesting developments is how quickly new norms of practice, identity and appearance have become established, and a political-phenomenological approach can attempt to discern the processes of decontestation, naturalization and embodiment by which normalization proceeds. This is by no means methodologically uncomplicated, as it often means seeking to establish contingency where none is directly observable, but it does mean that we can ask on what grounds a particular piece of media content is perceived in certain definable contexts or among specific audiences as culturally valuable, or why a particular media producer is regarded as authoritative.

Weber's embodiment thesis is useful in this regard. Writing about the clergy, Weber argued that institutional religious practice is perceived (by peers and public alike) not as the successful performance of the acquired requisite skills of this field but rather as an expression of personal character. Authority, then, consists not in the enactment of valorized practices but in their embodiment. Likewise, a journalist's authority would be expected to be perceived by colleagues and audience in terms of personality or innate instinct, rather than the nature of skills executed or work produced (Markham 2007). But this talent, enacted and interpreted as deontological or moral obligation, can be "denaturalized" or unpacked. For instance, in (supposed) contrast to elite journalists, it seems bloggers are frequently valorized (this is apparent especially in comments made by readers) for their common sense and plain-speaking, presumably in opposition to the inauthenticity of the official language of politicians and the mainstream media (see also Robinson 2006). Theorists from Durkheim to Goffman have demonstrated the complex and conflicted configurations of decontestations, (re)significations and embedded practices on which any recognizable form of common sense is predicated, even if the more functionalist accounts of discursive hegemony are avoided. (Both Gramsci and Chomsky, for example, hold that the primary function of cultural forms is the reproduction of hierarchy, and any other functions of culture are essentially incidental; see Herman 1998.) It remains valid to claim that common sense is a determination of specific social and political forces rather than something deontological. This is not to suggest that Internet media producers cannot speak sensibly, but rather that what counts as sensible is not universal but an alignment with the positions, orientations and trajectories of specific audiences or publics. This may not go further than the classic observation that people tend to read the newspaper that confirms their existing prejudices, but it does bear out the importance of decoupling common sense and democratization. It is certainly possible that wide recognition of a blogger's tendency to "talk sense" equates to better media representation of the interests of media consumers than is offered by "traditional" journalists, but it is also worth stressing that the relationship between media representation and democratic representation is highly contestable (Butsch 2007).

An exploratory qualitative analysis of attributions of value across a month's output in ten opinion blogs was undertaken to investigate this seeming personalization of values in attributions by and about opinion bloggers.[5] It concluded, tentatively, that authority is constituted through a variety of valorized symbolic forms, including authenticity, common sense, logic, humour, knowledge, intelligence, autonomy and courageousness. This would suggest that it is difficult to maintain an artificial distinction between the substance of an Internet journalist's output from the style and context of its expression. And it is especially notable that authority and authenticity appear to be significantly conflated (see also Livingstone 1998). This, again, is not to suggest that media producers of every ilk are innately manipulative. But it is also important to take account of research that has looked at exactly how the authentic journalistic voice is constituted and received across various genres. Some of this goes on at the level of the Durkheimian non-conscious,[6] and a Bourdieusian approach building on this would look at the conditions of possibility of the experienced natural fit between the phenomenal object and subject (that is, what preconditions exist for it to feel natural for a journalist or blogger to write about a particular phenomenon in a certain way) and between the producer and her audience. It also goes on very much at the conscious level in journalistic training: there are widely acknowledged techniques — Conboy (2006) identifies informality, complicity, metaphors and humour, among others — by which a journalist can encode a voice that appears without artifice to a specific audience.

While not automatically at odds with this, it bears emphasizing that authenticity of voice is also a crucial strategy for getting ahead in the journalistic (or blogging) game. It has rapidly become unremarkable practice — not in all blogs, needless to say, but certainly in the majority of those examined here — to include details (sometimes relevant, sometimes not) of the blogger's tastes, mood and other aspects of an apparent internal monologue among external observations, which tend to take a fairly standard print journalistic form (Wall 2005). This can defensibly be construed as a performance of authenticity or as a claim, not necessarily conscious, to authority through endearment. Interestingly, and against Weber's account of how individuals come to be seen as authoritative embodiments of the skills they enact, it is arguable that bloggers (also) accrue reputability through articulations of character unrelated to the external phenomena that form their analytic object — or even, in the case of three blogs studied here, through a self-effacing disavowal of authority. Of course, personal asides are a key aspect of blogging discourse and provide respite from the strictures of traditional journalistic narrative. However, the dominance of such principles of differentiation as attribute norms risks substituting the performance of blogging (and interactions between bloggers) for its engagement with objects outside the blogosphere. It is this elevation of the personal, or more precisely a highly mutually referential group of individuals valued according to perceived personal character, which weighs against the collective addressing of issues of shared concern, which I have here set out as a necessary component of democratization. Personal sympathy and charisma have long been important factors of journalistic success in particular contexts; it is possible that their domination as criteria for judging journalistic worth, however, points towards a nascent culture of narcissism, narrowly defined, in shared blogging practices.

CULTURES OF NARCISSISM?

Christine Rosen has over the past decade sought to update Christopher Lasch's "culture of narcissism" thesis (Lasch 1978) and to apply it to contemporary trends in education and parenting (Rosen 2005) and, most recently, social networking sites (Rosen 2007). In large part these are normative critiques of neo-liberal individualism, targeting especially the decline of personal responsibility, preoccupation with self-esteem and the broader therapy culture that Lasch saw as responses to the pervasive sense of insecurity experienced by increasingly atomized individuals. Writing about MySpace user profiles, Rosen describes "an overwhelmingly dull sea of monotonous uniqueness, of conventional individuality, of distinctive sameness" (Rosen 2007: 24; see also Liu 2008), sensing behind the relentless drive towards cultural signification and projection of identity an impossibility of same.

As regards blogging, it is tempting to use similarly normative allegations of self-indulgence and egoism to demonstrate, perhaps a little glibly, that present cultures of blogging are not compatible with democratic collectivism. A potentially more productive extension of Rosen's argument is to link the idea of incitement to discourse mentioned above to a drive to relentless signification where Internet users are always already alienated from the signifiers available to them. There is not space to develop this argument fully here, but it will suffice for present purposes to stress that if narcissism is a useful device for interpreting cultures of practice in Web journalism, it is not in its more rhetorical deployment but rather in a phenomenological sense. By this way of thinking, individual subjects seek identity in part through seeing themselves as others do — i.e., as objects. However, if the subject who engages with the world is in fact a homogenized collection of generic signifiers of subjectivity, then the already alienated self who enacts these significations cannot attain identity with the self as reflected back by the social world. If Rosen's argument is transposable from social networking sites to online deprofessionalized journalistic practices, then blogging represents a futile attempt at full subjectivity based on homogenized cultural forms; the self being reflected back by other journalists similarly comprises the arbitrary and alienating. And instead of simply demonstrating the existential impossibility of full subjectivity (and if it is impossible on phenomenological grounds, why would we expect the Internet to provide the solution?), subjectification as it specifically proceeds online instead can be seen to suffer, counter-intuitively, from under-mediation (see also Couldry 2008). In reality, it's all too easy to project one's subjectivity and to see oneself as reflected back by the Internet: it's right there on the screen. But this represents a short-circuited subjectivity lacking mediation by other subjects. This is not to lionize an insupportable ideal of "real" or "face-to-face" interaction: the above Bourdieusian characterization of communication as politically complicit shows that no form of interaction is unproblematic, but each can be understood in terms of its own symbolic world.

Phenomenologically, subjective identity cannot be an aim in itself; it arises only though mediation by other subjects and through acting in public spaces and, conservative as this may sound, institutions. Rosen's interpretation of MySpace illustrates the degraded subjectivity that can result from the prioritization of the projection of identity over interaction. Similarly, while blogging undeniably encourages a great deal of interaction, the dominance of the personal as criteria for recognizing cultural value in the blogosphere, where the value of the personal is not pre-given but contingent on the projection of systematically recognizable and hence homogenous signifiers of authenticity, likewise short-circuits the mediation of subjectivity. Such mediation does, of course, occur, and there is no sense in denying the extent of interactivity online — although there is some evidence that interactivity between journalists and their audience is overstated (Domingo 2008) and that blogging is more of a monologue than a dialogue (Wilhelm 2000). Where it does occur, *public* interaction, meaning that whose primary function is the contestation and negotiation of issues of shared concern, proceeds independently of any mooted collectivist teleology of the Internet, not because of it.

THE OBJECTIVITY DILEMMA

Knowledge about public issues has long been regarded as central to democratic politics and, more broadly, to self-determination. It was noted earlier that Foucault's problematization of the knowledge/power connection has specific implications for media disseminated online — namely that it can be argued to have a rationalizing effect on media content and online identity, which, in turn, are claimed to have political effects. There is another concern, however, regarding the quality of information available rather than the politically complicit, structurally incited will to produce online content. This is not the place for a critique of the reliability of information published online — there is no shortage of such assessments, after all — but there is a point to be made about how changes in the mode of production of journalistic content may impact on the democratic process. Nick Davies notes in his book *Flat Earth News* (2008) that only 12 percent of the news articles he analysed contained evidence of original research — and he concludes that the main reason for this is that journalists increasingly research stories online. (This is contestable, though, and several scholars have pointed to the countervailing potential for "citizen" journalists' use of alternative sources; see, for example, Deuze et al. 2007; Rauch 2007.) The upshot is that the information available to news consumers is increasingly filtered through secondary and tertiary sources, and this has potentially significant implications, beyond the immediate point that reliability is not enhanced as one would expect from a multiplication of sources, since that multiplication takes the form of an echo effect rather than substantively different origins of information and interpretation.

One such implication leads us back to the Bourdieusian field model. If sources of news come increasingly from within the online arena, and the resulting news is recycled and reinterpreted, then there is a case for claiming that its internal logic rather

87

than those of other fields increasingly governs the Internet as a field of cultural production. Different fields have varying levels of autonomy from other fields, and all — including the Internet as much as any other — are increasingly subject to market demands. A highly autonomous field has the advantage of preserving its specialist modes of production (as in investigative journalism, above), but its "rules of the game" — inevitably tied to the reproduction of hierarchies of power — are less susceptible to challenge. The journalistic field has historically been typified by gatekeeping structures, the mystification of journalistic practice and an acculturated professional ideology, all of which have the effect of preserving both the internal structures of the field and the broader social positioning of journalists. However, routine exposure to other fields has meant that the dominance of these internal logics has been tempered by the constant demonstration that, elsewhere, they are not regarded as natural or inevitable. In short, the recognition that things are done differently elsewhere means that the complete internalization of the rules of the journalistic game is effectively impossible. This tempering, though, comes through interaction with sources from different fields. Diminished exposure to external actors would be expected to lead to greater decontestation of the contingent norms of online journalism. This is not an argument that applies to the Internet in general, since to posit it as a space insulated from the "real" world is self-evidently indefensible. However, in journalistic terms, it is feasible that the circularity of interactions between journalists, bloggers and sources (who are frequently other journalists and bloggers) would lead to a more internally coherent and autonomous journalistic lifeworld, which would in turn serve as a more effective means of reproducing both the positive (restricted production) and negative (political relations internalized and forgotten as political) aspects of cultures of media production.

Of course, this argument appears to validate the primary source (or, in other words, considers this abstraction as real to a degree). The implication is that for knowledge to be democratizing it has to be reliable, and reliability here is cast in strongly objectivist terms. It has been noted elsewhere that not only is objectivism an unachievable aim for journalists, but it is used (consciously or otherwise) strategically by journalists competing with each other and cultural producers from other fields (Matheson 2003). This instrumentalist characterization of the journalist — as an intrepid hunter of facts — needs to be set alongside its centrality to cultural capital. It is also worth stressing that a journalist's engagement with online sources need not be set in opposition to a face-to-face interview or characterized as a degraded form of communication. However, without wishing to exaggerate the phenomenological experience of witnessing an event at first hand, it is valid to set out a theoretical position consistent with the above characterization of fields of cultural production as neither arbitrary nor simply objectively determined. This means interpreting events in the field as reasonable — which is to say explicable but not predictable from outside the field — rather than as having meaning only within the field as a discrete world. This in turn leads to the proposition that, while a multiplicity of perspectives is an essential component of the democratization of knowledge, it is important that these be regarded as different interpretations of the same external event or phenomena, rather than merely as different cultural manifestations within a discrete symbolic world which cannot be critically assessed from without. If Davies is correct, the disconnection of journalists from primary sources could feasibly amount to a wider dislocation between the online journalistic world and the material context in which it subsists.

CONCLUSION: HOW SHOULD WE ASCRIBE POLITICAL MEANING TO BLOGS?

The symbolic value of online media production is by no means easy to define; individuals similarly oriented towards recognizing certain cultural forms and people as valuable ascribe it collectively. This circularity means that, instead of looking for the origins of value in the media form itself or in its audience, we should look instead at the generative criteria that precede both production and reception. These can be thought of as being locatable according to two axes: one roughly characterized by popularity, the other by "volume" of symbolic capital recognized or consecrated in given contexts. This boils down to a familiar distinction between types of cultural value — namely, between that whose value is predicated on broad popularity and that whose perceived value exceeds its limited popularity, because of its association with elite, alternative or niche interests. The cultural value of most media content is, of course, determined by a combination of these two principles. What is important in the context of this chapter is to emphasize that neither criterion is naturally compatible or antithetical to democratization. I suggested earlier that size of audience does not itself entail democratization, or at least that it assumes a democratic model defined according to freedom of choice of consumption. Similarly, a blog popular with a narrow elite audience is not necessarily anti-democratic, as by the logic set out above it is possible that only in such an elite space of production are certain cultural forms possible, including those having democratizing effects, however defined.

There is not space here to develop a precise means of measuring the cultural value of a blog, but it is worth emphasizing that different methodologies carry distinct political commitments and implications. For instance, the claim that expression of opinion is intrinsically politically valuable would suggest that no broader cultural value needs to be measured — this does logically follow, but represents either a narcissistic perspective or a merely formal political definition of political deliberation (much like Hegel's identification of the inadequacy of formal citizenship in the absence of substantive engagement and recognition in political life) in which the act of expressing or participating is prioritized over questions of content and context. A common gauge of a blog's success is its uptake by media practitioners in the traditional field of political–cultural production — that is, politicians, think-tanks and media commentators (Carlson 2007a). However, this entails the perseverance of traditional journalism's gatekeeping and hierarchical structures (Singer 2005), which thus rules out the possibility of reforming the undemocratic tendencies of institutionalized journalism. There is no reason to think that these traditional structures would be opened up or challenged by having new forms of media production feeding in: indeed, there is every reason to

89

believe that existing structures, complicit as they are in reproducing hierarchies, are easily capable of assimilating new online discourses and, after Foucault, neutralizing and rationalizing them (Domingo 2008; Robinson 2006; Robinson 2007; Singer 2005). It does not follow that deprofessionalized media production feeding in to existing political structures will lead to their democratization.

Likewise, if the democratizing effect of the blogosphere is judged by the level of interaction it generates, this needs to be balanced against the argument that interaction itself is not in any sense democratizing unless it leads to some form of action, deliberation or contestation outside the confines of this particular arena of cultural production. This is certainly in line with one of the tangential conclusions of the Public Connection research project.[7] It found that, against the democratic potential of media interactivity championed by the BBC and others, for a significant number of media consumers interaction makes little difference to their sense of connection to or disconnection from any sort of public world, unless there is a sense that such interaction leads to influence or change in some form of public world beyond the arena of information exchange. In line with the digital divide arguments made by many scholars over the past decade, this research found that new media forms tend to be taken up for political purposes only by those who are already politically engaged (see also Levine and Lopez 2004). If an important aspect of democratization is encouraging participation, then these (admittedly limited) data suggest that the Internet will not lead those who are already turned away from public issues to engage politically online, whether through responding to existing online political content — which for our purposes was defined as referring to any issues of shared concern, however conceived — or producing their own.

Furthermore, the evidence suggests that we should not even necessarily *want* the Internet to encourage participation. This is not because, after Walter Lippmann (1925), citizens invariably engage haphazardly and on the basis of insufficient knowledge, and journalism should not be expected to educate people and thus correct the democratic deficit. Rather, our data indicated that, for a significant minority, disconnection is not experienced as problematic: some are happily turned away from any sort of mediated public world — and there is nothing the Internet can or should do about it.

Ultimately, the question of the cultural value of a particular piece of online journalism is secondary to what such a measurement can tell us about the dominant principles of differentiation in a given cultural field, which, in turn, have only an indirect relation to broader democratic and anti-democratic forces. We should start from the principle that in order to understand the "meaning" of a blog we have to take into account all those who have an interest in ascribing value. That is, as well as taking seriously (and distinctly) the value ascribed to online journalism by professional journalists, political actors, online activists, consumers both active and passive, it is important to acknowledge that these groups are themselves engaged in a struggle in which the stakes are the capacity to define dominant criteria of control. The upshot is that we should not only be open to different interpretations of online content made by professional journalists and non-professional bloggers, for instance; we should see such differences as structured, and not necessarily overt, claims for power. Such struggles *may* have democratizing effects or lead to new spaces of citizenship, but there is no reason to assume that they will.

Methodologically, it should be possible roughly to measure the cultural purchase of particular forms of online journalism: my initial research suggests that this should be done not by aggregating page impressions, responses or uptake in traditional media, but through qualitative analysis. This means in particular looking at the manner in which blog content is picked up on, with narratively or discursively normalized references to a blogger's status or views, their decontesting appearance in expressions of common sense, humour or throwaway comments, and references out of context revealing far more than a response from a recognized authority. Evidence of such cultural purchase does not simply mean that views expressed in online media production are gaining influence — or by extension, that this could be seen as democratic insofar as it represents wider, or at least different, representation. It could also be interpreted as signifying simply that power has moved from one site of media production to another. This is not in itself democratic; it represents a shift from one prevailing form of authority (Robinson 2007; Thurman 2008) — roughly speaking, professional and institutional — to another deprofessionalized one, which I have characterized here as being contingent on projected authenticity. And while different groups may benefit from a new configuration of power relations, there is no reason to invest the shift itself with a teleology of democratizing reform. Moreover, shifting centres of power in journalism, as well as the decentring of power, do not inevitably change what Bourdieu terms the game itself. New forms of cultural production emerge, as do distinct principles or economies for attributing value to cultural production. Such emergences may coincide with democratizing trends, but there are no reasons, beyond the strategic or complicit, to locate the teleology of such trends in these new forms.

Notes

1   This chapter will focus mainly on the democratizing potential of non-professional "opinion" bloggers, as distinct from blogs maintained by professional journalists, linklogs and personal online journals (i.e., those lacking external observations).

2   Bourdieu (1993: 115) defines the field of cultural production thus: "The field of production and circulation of symbolic goods is defined as the system of objective relations among different instances, functionally defined by their role in the division of labour of production, reproduction and diffusion of symbolic goods." More generally, it can be characterized as that space inhabited by individuals and groups who have a stake in producing, disseminating, legitimating and valorizing information.

3   'Lifeworld' (*Lebenswelt*) is used in the Husserlian sense of a taken-for-granted stream of everyday routines, interactions and events that constitute individual and social experience, rather than Habermas's concept of shared understandings and values that develop over time through face-to-face communication in a social group.

4   There are several counter-examples where bloggers have carried out significant investigative journalism, most notably in the reports leading up to the resignation of US Republican Senate Majority Leader Trent Lott.

5   The following sites were surveyed in May 2008 and coded using NVivo: Guido Fawkes (http://www.order-order.com/); Oliver Kamm (www.oliverkamm.typepad.com); Chicken

Yoghurt (www.chickyog.blogspot.com); Bloggerheads (www.bloggerheads.com); Samizdata (www.samizdata.net/blog/); Normblog (normblog.typepad.com); Harry's Place (hurryupharry.bloghouse.net); Slugger O'Toole (www.sluggerotoole.com); Conservative Commentary (concom.blogspot.com/); What You Can Get Away With (http://www.nickbarlow.com/blog/).

6   For Durkheim, the social must be explained not by the conceptions of its participants, but by the structural causes which elude awareness but which necessitate the phenomena observed by the social scientist. For Bourdieu (1977) all observed behaviour (including participants' conscious reflections) should be seen, after Bachelard, as "particular instances of the possible" — i.e., as specific expressions of common generative structures that are the key objects of social analysis.

7   Media Consumption and the Future of Public Connection, funded by the Economic and Social Research Council and the Arts and Humanities Research Council's Cultures of Consumption programme, grant number RES-143-25-0011.

References

Bentivegna, S. (2002) "Politics and New Media". In L. Lievrouw and S. Livinsgtone (eds), *Handbook of New Media.* London: Sage, pp. 50–61.

Bohman, J. (2007) "Political Communication and the Epistemic Value of Diversity: Deliberation and Legitimation in Media Societies", *Communication Theory,* 17, pp. 348–55.

Bourdieu, P. (1977) *Outline of a Theory of Practice.* Cambridge: Cambridge University Press.

Bourdieu, P. (1994) "L'emprise du journalisme", *Actes de la Recherche en Sciences Sociales,* 101–2, pp. 3–9.

Bourdieu, P. (1993) *The Field of Cultural Production: Essays on Art and Literature.* Cambridge: Polity.

Butsch, R. (2007) "Introduction". In R. Butsch (ed.), *Media and Public Spheres.* London: Palgrave Macmillan.

Carlson, M. (2007a) "Blogs and Journalistic Authority: The Role of Blogs in US Election Day 2004 Coverage", *Journalism Studies,* 8 (2) pp. 264–79.

Carlson, M. (2007b) "Order versus Access: News Search Engines and the Challenge to Traditional Journalistic Roles", *Media Culture & Society,* 29 (6), pp. 1014–30.

Chambers, D., Steiner, L., and Fleming, C. (2004) *Women and Journalism.* London: Routledge.

Coleman, S. (2005) "The Lonely Citizen: Indirect Representation in an Age of Networks", *Political Communication,* 22 (2), pp. 197–214.

Conboy, M. (2006) *Tabloid Britain: Constructing a Community through Language.* London: Routledge.

Cornfeld, M. (2005) "Buzz, Blogs and Beyond: The Internet and the National Discourse in the Fall of 2004". Retrieved 26 April 2006 from: http://www.pewInternet.org/PPF/p/1088/pipcomments.asp.

Couldry, N. (2008) "Mediatization or Mediation? Alternative Understandings of the Emergent Space of Digital Storytelling", *New Media & Society,* 10 (3), pp. 373–91.

Couldry, N., Livingstone, S., and Markham, T. (2007) *Media Consumption and Public Engagement: Beyond the Presumption of Attention.* Basingstoke: Palgrave Macmillan.

Davies, N. (2008) *Flat Earth News.* London: Chatto & Windus.

Delli Carpini, M., and Williams, B. (2001) "Let Us Infotain You". In L. Bennett, and R. Entman (eds), *Mediated Politics.* Cambridge: Cambridge University Press.

Deuze, M. (2005) "What is Journalism?", *Journalism,* 6 (4), pp. 442–64.

Deuze, M., Bruns, A., and Neuberger, C. (2007) "Preparing for an Age of Participatory News", *Journalism Practice*, 1 (3), pp. 322–38.

Domingo, D. (2008) "Interactivity in the Daily Routines of Online Newsrooms: Dealing with an Uncomfortable Myth", *Journal of Computer-Mediated Communication*, 13, pp. 680–704.

Downing, J. (2001) *Radical Media: Rebellious Communication and Social Movements.* Thousand Oaks, CA: Sage.

Drezner, D., and Farrell, H. (2004) "Web of Influence", *Foreign Policy*, 145, pp. 32–40.

Giddens, A. (1984) *The Constitution of Society: Outline of the Theory of Structuration.* Cambridge: Polity.

Herman, E. (1998) "The Propaganda Model Revisited". In R. W. McChesney, E. Wood, and J. Foster (eds), *Capitalism and the Information Age: The Political Economy of the Global Communication Revolution.* New York: Monthly Review Press.

Johnson, T. J. (1972) *Professions and Power.* London: Macmillan.

Kahn, R., and Kellner, D. (2004) "New Media and Internet Activism: From the 'Battle of Seattle' to Blogging", *New Media & Society*, 6 (1), pp. 87–95.

Lasch, C. (1978) *The Culture of Narcissism: American Life in an Age of Diminishing Expectations.* 1st edn. New York: Norton.

Levine, P., and Lopez, M. (2004) *Young People and Political Campaigning on the Internet.* University of Maryland: CIRCLE.

Lievrouw, L., and Livinsgtone, S. (2006) "Introduction". In L. Lievrouw and S. Livinsgtone (eds), *Handbook of New Media.* London: Sage, pp. 1–14.

Lippmann, W. (1925) *The Phantom Public.* New York: Harcourt Brace.

Liu, H. (2008) "Social Network Profiles as Taste Performances", *Journal of Computer-Mediated Communication*, 13, pp. 252–75.

Livingstone, S. (1998) *Making Sense of Television: The Psychology of Audience Interpretation.* 2nd edn. Oxford: Butterworth-Heinemann.

Lowrey, W. (2006) "Mapping the Journalism–Blogging Relationship", *Journalism*, 7 (4), pp. 477–500.

Markham, T. (2007) "Bourdieusian Political Theory and Social Science: The Field of War Correspondence 1990–2003". Unpublished D.Phil. thesis, University of Oxford.

Matheson, D. (2003) "Scowling at their Notebooks: How British Journalists Understand their Writing", *Journalism*, 4 (2), pp. 165–83.

Matheson, D. (2004) "Weblogs and the Epistemology of the News: Some Trends in Online Journalism", *New Media & Society*, 6 (4), pp. 443–68.

McNair, B. (2003) "From Control to Chaos: Towards a New Sociology of Journalism". *Media Culture and Society*, 25 (4), pp. 547–55.

Norris, P. (2000) *A Virtuous Circle.* Cambridge: Cambridge University Press.

Norris, P. (2001) *Digital Divide.* Cambridge: Cambridge University Press.

Rauch, J. (2007) "Activists as Interpretative Communities: Rituals of Consumption and Interaction in an Alternative Media Audience", *Media Culture & Society*, 29 (6), pp. 994–1013.

Regan, T. (2004) "Weblogs Threaten and Inform Traditional Journalism", *Nieman Reports*, 57 (3), pp. 68–70.

Rice, R., and Haythornthwaite, C. (2006) "Perspectives on Internet Use: Access, Involvement and Interaction". In L. Lievrouw and S. Livinsgtone (eds), *Handbook of New Media.* London: Sage, pp. 92–113.

Robinson, S. (2006) "The Mission of the J-Blog: Recapturing Journalistic Authority Online", *Journalism*, 7 (1), pp. 65–83.

Robinson, S. (2007) "'Someone's Gotta Be in Control Here': The Institutionalisation of Online News and the Creation of a Shared Journalistic Authority", *Journalism Practice*, 1 (3), pp. 305–21.

Rosen, C. (2005) "The Overpraised American", *Policy Review*, 133, pp. 27–42.

Rosen, C. (2007) "Virtual Friendship and the New Narcissism", *The New Atlantis*, pp. 15–31.

Singer, J. B. (2005) "The Political J-Blogger: Normalising a New Media Form to Fit Old Norms and Practices", *Journalism*, 6 (2), pp. 173–98.

Sutton Trust (2006) *The Educational Backgrounds of Leading Journalists*. London: Sutton Trust.

Thurman, N. (2008) "Forums for Citizen Journalists? Adoption of User Generated Content Initiatives by Online News Media", *New Media & Society*, 10 (1), pp. 139–57.

Wall, M. (2005) "'Blogs of War': Weblogs as News", *Journalism*, 6 (2), pp. 153–72.

Weber, M., Roth, G., Wittich, C., and Fischoff, E. (1978) *Economy and Society: An Outline of Interpretive Sociology*. Berkeley, CA: University of California Press.

Wilhelm, A. (2000) *Democracy in the Digital Age*. New York: Routledge.

PART II

II

*Professional and
Citizen Journalists*

5

Blogging Journalists: The Writing on the Wall

PAUL BRADSHAW

How Blogging Has Changed How Journalists See News Processes

Blogs have become part of the editorial furniture. After a period of resistance, they have been co-opted by news organizations to the point where a news website without a blog is seen as unusual. As of 2008, 70 percent of US newspapers (PEJ 2008), 85 percent of UK news organizations and 44 percent of European news organizations (Oriella PR Network 2008) were offering journalist-authored blogs. All the signals from editors and management suggested these figures would continue to rise.

Previous studies have focused on how newsroom cultures have reacted to the rise of the online newsroom (Boczkowski 2004; Friend and Singer 2007; Paterson and Domingo 2008) and how news organization blogs themselves have adopted the format (Singer 2005; Robinson 2006). Much has been written of the potential of blogs for journalism as a whole (Gillmor 2004; Wall 2005; Beckett 2008), but few have looked at how journalists themselves have considered how blogging has affected their work process.

Based on a survey of 200 professional journalists with blogs in thirty countries, this chapter seeks to explore those perceptions and identify areas for further research. The findings suggest that, in generating ideas and leads, in gathering information, in news production and post-publication, and most of all in the relationship with the audience, the networked, iterative and conversational nature of the blog format is changing how many journalists see their work. However, this transformation is by no means universal, and there are notable variations between industries and sectors.

In this chapter blogging refers specifically to blogs produced by professional journalists who work either for a news organization or freelance. Although blogs have existed for over a decade, in their short history the format has undergone a number of generic developments. They began as lists of links to similar sites, developed to become more diary-like, with accompanying cults of personality (Blood 2000), and have been more recently adopted by news organizations. These have started blogs by their own journalists, employed bloggers on their staff, teamed up with blogging and citizen journalism operations (Gant 2007), or targeted them for takeovers (The Outlook 2007; MacManus 2008). It might be argued that this has in turn affected the generic qualities of blogs. And, more recently, there have been suggestions that blogging as a whole has lost its relational focus as it has become more professionalized (MacManus 2008). It has also been claimed that successful bloggers have curbed their creativity in order to appeal to a wider audience (Lowrey and Latta in Paterson and Domingo 2008). It is also the case that much of the personal material that was previously published on blogs is now being published on "lifestreaming" and "microblogging" platforms such as Twitter (Perez 2008). Of particular interest to this research is what has happened to journalistic processes in this meeting of cultures — particularly as some theorists have argued that journalism is in a process of adapting in the face of technological, social and economic changes (Lowrey 2006; Wall 2005; Robinson 2006).

Lowrey (2006) sees blogging as an occupation, noting that bloggers see themselves as part of a community that shares values, rituals and language, organizes conferences and explores codes of ethics. As Singer notes (2005), professional journalists who blog have had to negotiate this occupational culture alongside their own — and these cultures differ in important ways. Blogs, for example, are typically opinionated, while journalism aspires to objectivity. Blogs treat the audience as a co-creator, while traditional journalism treats them as a passive recipient. And whereas blog journalism is incomplete and fragmented, traditional journalism is structured and closed (Lowrey 2006; Wall 2005: 162). Ultimately, Lowrey argues, it is "the organisation of production [that] is the most fundamental distinction between journalism and blogging" (2006: 480), and it is with this that this chapter is primarily concerned.

METHODOLOGY

To consider whether journalists feel blogging has affected their working processes, an online survey was distributed in June and July 2008. A self-completing survey method was chosen, owing to its efficiency, scalability and global reach (Robson 2002). A diverse range of public and internal distribution channels was used in an attempt to attract a variety of respondents. The survey employed both open and closed questions to draw a large response, allowing respondents to answer in their own terms (Bryman 2001).

Respondents came from all sectors of the news industry. Almost half of respondents worked in the newspaper industry, and a third were online-only or freelance. Television, radio and magazine journalists accounted for the lowest proportions. Half of respondents worked in the US or Canada and a further fifth in the UK, with the remainder coming from mainland Europe, South America, Australia, Africa, Asia and the Middle East.

The journalists reported on a wide range of sectors, and most covered more than one. Local journalism made up the largest proportion (43 percent), but media and technology correspondents also featured heavily. Along with a number of well-represented areas such as business, politics, lifestyle and culture, there was a "long tail" of small numbers of respondents covering "other" areas, ranging from education and health to travel and the environment.

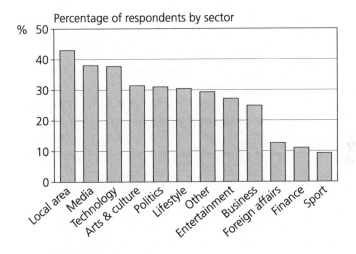

Figure 5.1 Percentage of respondents by sector

In analysing the data, I have attempted to take these factors into account and to use the differences between industries and sectors as a valid finding in itself, rather than focus on the figures coming from the entire sample. It is important to note that generalizing from this study should be done with caution, given the diversity of nationality, industry, sector and blogging experience of respondents. The study is intended to highlight a number of areas that warrant further research.

The study takes as its structure the three elements identified by Quinn and Lamble (2007) as constituting the basic parts of the journalistic process: generating ideas, gathering information and production. It also looks at the relationship with the audience and at post-publication, both of which are frequently identified as areas undergoing change as a result of networked technologies such as blogging (Gillmor 2004; Bruns 2005; Beckett 2008).

BLOGS AND NEWS IDEAS: "THE CANARY IN THE MINE"

For blogging journalists, blogs have disrupted the traditional processes of journalism in a number of ways. Respondents spoke of having a clearer perception of audience needs and interests as a result of comments and visitor statistics, which, in turn, have fed into their selection of topics and angles they cover. In some cases journalists now post ideas on their blogs, and reader feedback helps guide how they develop the story, which is often changed by this process. Some saw the editorial role as a mediator reduced as their agenda-setting influence diminished. This is understandable. The editorial role in determining who the reader is, and what that reader wants, becomes undermined, arguably, when writers, through their blogs, have a closer and more immediate access to that information. In some cases reader feedback resulted in stories being covered that would have otherwise fallen through Tuchman's "news net" (Tuchman 1978).

At the same time there was a framing of blogging and the blogosphere in old media terms. Many respondents considered that the most important change brought by blogs was an increased need for speed. They focused on spotting trends early, or following the "chatter", suggesting that the "herd instinct" of mainstream media remains. Blogs are sometimes "the canaries in the coal mine" (Respondent 69, US, Online). Some respondents also spoke of using blogs in the same way as they had previously relied on the trade press for leads, expertise and case studies.

It is clear that the often highlighted (McNair 1998; Allan 2004; Deuze 2008) reliance of journalists on public relations firms, pressure groups and diary events has also been affected. Respondents considered their range of contacts and the sources of ideas for potential stories had broadened. Some spoke of thinking in terms of multimedia or interactivity, in turn opening new approaches to some ideas and leads. Many mentioned getting story leads from comments on the blog or through private communication initiated via the blog. Others noted the ease of accessing contacts through other blogs. This represents an important challenge to traditional theories of news processes that rely on routinization, predictability, and an "understanding that society is bureaucratically structured [which] furnishes the reporter with a 'map of relevant knowers' for newsworthy topics" (Allan 2004: 62). For some reporters that map is being redrawn along networked lines: the "relevant knowers" are so defined no longer by their position in hierarchical organizations but by positions as key nodes in online networks.

BLOGS AND STORY RESEARCH: "WE SWAPPED INFO"

When journalists move on to gathering information for a story, publishing a blog broadens the range of easily accessible sources. In some cases publicizing news ideas on that blog, as mentioned above, means readers are increasingly researching stories before, or alongside, journalists. And once they begin to pursue a story, journalists are using the blog format as a way to "put the call out" for information and sources while they work.

Although for journalists to ask members of the public for information on a story is nothing new, the nature of the relationship appears to be different, in that it is a two-way, ongoing process:

> On hot-button stories where our readers are asking a lot of questions, we post updates every time we make a phone call. For example, [a company] declared bankruptcy and the new owner wouldn't take the previous owner's gift cards. Our readers were peeved and hounding us to do something. The corporate folks weren't saying anything so we didn't have any new information to report. Because we didn't have any new info, we didn't write anything in the paper. But on our blog, we would post updates at least daily to tell people when we left a message and if we had heard back yet. We eventually scored an interview with the new CEO and posted it in its entirety on our site. Another reporter saw it and called us. We swapped info. Our readers also post links to other stories on the topic from other news orgs. (Respondent 63, US, newspapers)

In some examples this collaboration becomes a form of crowd-sourcing, with readers asked to help undertake part of the story research. Many journalists post links to original material and ongoing updates. But for some, the pressure to publish has meant more reliance on rumours, and less rigorous research, with the onus placed on blog readers to clarify and fact-check.

On a practical level, the actual process of newsgathering is also changing as a result of the demands of the blog. Journalists report being more likely to gather multimedia material such as images, video and audio to post on the blog — or, in the case of broadcast journalists, to gather more material than they used to, as there is now a platform for material that wouldn't otherwise make it to broadcast. "It ensures avoiding that trap of TV reporting", noted one: "one sequence, two interviews and we have a story without digging deeper" (Respondent 156, Belgium, TV).

BLOGS AND NEWS PRODUCTION: "I THINK IN HYPERLINKS, EVEN WHEN WORKING IN PRINT"

But it was in their writing style that most respondents had noticed a change in their news production. Their style had become looser, more personal and less formal — echoing the findings of Wall (2005). For some, this fed back into their work in mainstream news, particularly for broadcast journalists whose work previously involved less writing.

The requirement for immediacy was clearly a factor in this, with respondents noting that they worked more quickly, breaking stories on their blogs before following up both online and in print or broadcast news. Journalists also reported writing shorter, more tightly edited pieces — not just for blogs but also for print and broadcast.

Conversely, the Web provided a space for expanding in ways that print and broadcast did not allow. "Stories that otherwise would have been footnotes in print can be explored more fully on the blog", noted one (Respondent 33, US, newspapers). Perhaps the most significant change was in the way that blogs provided a platform for stories or detail that would otherwise not make the print or broadcast version at all. Respondents talked of augmenting coverage that "would otherwise fall through the cracks". There were pieces that were interesting but wouldn't merit space in the paper, or that used elements that didn't "necessarily fit into the rigid lengths of radio pieces". Technology also gave journalists the opportunity to link elsewhere when time or space constraints meant they were unable to report in full — to some extent fulfilling Jeff Jarvis's rule (2007) of "Cover what you do best and link to the rest".

POST-PUBLICATION: "YOU'VE GOT TO BE READY FOR THAT CONVERSATION"

In the post-publication or post-broadcast phase of journalism, blogging has introduced a more iterative and ongoing format. Some journalists phrased this in terms of old paradigms — items have "more legs" — while others identified how the previous process of "moving on" to the next big story and forgetting about the old one applies less.

The ability to enter into correspondence with users, to fix errors and post updates was frequently identified as changing journalistic work. This turns on its head Lowrey's suggestion that bloggers "often emphasise immediacy and opinion at the expense of accuracy" (2006) and that journalism would protect itself by focusing on editing (see also Hudson and Temple in this volume). Responses suggest that, conversely, journalists are relying on commenters to contribute to the editing process.

The lack of print or broadcast deadlines means that journalists could, and did, add or correct information that wasn't available or was incorrect when going to press or air, while the permanence of the Web meant stories were always 'live':

> The audience remains able to comment on the content, and regularly provides information which updates it. The reporter then has the opportunity to revisit the subject, creating a great "off diary" print story (loved by news editors everywhere), crediting the information to the online contact, therefore cross promoting platforms, sparking more online conversation, generating more comment, updates and on and on and on. (Respondent 126, UK, newspapers)

> Well, you never finish, do you? You write something that may or may not spark a conversation and you've got to be ready for that conversation even if it happens months later. Besides, I find that more and more of what we do online is writing parts of the picture, not the whole and unvarnished truth. (Respondent 147, Norway, freelance)

This importance of distribution is an emerging but particularly important change. While the print and broadcast news industries have long-established distribution infrastructures and conventions, online news does not. It might be argued that "[e]veryone is a paperboy/girl now" (Bradshaw 2008). Supporting this, journalists spoke of forwarding links to bloggers, posting updates on the microblogging/texting service Twitter and syndicating through RSS. For others, the blog itself was seen primarily as a distribution tool for stories that appeared on the main news website, or in the print or broadcast editions.

But this is a two-way process. And the most common theme mentioned by respondents with regard to post-publication was the rise of "[f]eedback, quick, straight, unforgiving. Miss a story or its real meanings and you're screwed" (Respondent 14, Romania, TV). Unlike "letters to the editor", the real-time and more intimate feedback of blog comments has a real effect on the ongoing story. Respondents spoke of changing lines, stories and sometimes trashing complete stories due to comments. For some, this represented unnecessary extra work, with the quality and relevance of comments varying enormously. But, for many, sifting through comments has led to new stories, angles and, particularly, follow-ups.

BLOGGING AND THE AUDIENCE RELATIONSHIP: "THE BEST STORIES ARE A RESULT OF INCREDIBLE CONVERSATIONS"

Of all areas covered by the survey, the relationship with the audience was by far the most affected. Over half of respondents reckoned it had changed either "enormously" or "completely". In particular, journalists felt they had developed a more personal relationship with the reader, who was no longer an anonymous figure. As a consequence, journalists felt more pressure to be both accountable to their readers and less "arrogant". There was a need to make themselves understood, to explain their decisions in the face of increased and more personal feedback from a community they felt part of.

Interactivity and "conversation" were frequently mentioned:

I cover more than thirty countries: the reaction of people who live in a place I visit tells me a lot about the issues I am writing about. My blog seems to generate arguments which at least help me understand a story more. (Respondent 156, Belgium, TV)

For some, this has led to a newfound sense of respect for readers — and for others it has meant a realization that readers were "total idiots" (Respondent 54, US, newspapers) or had a poorer comprehension than they had assumed. Journalists also identified a change in how they saw other bloggers, subscribing to more blogs and commenting or participating in discussion more often.

Respondents also considered that blogging had commercial and bureaucratic advantages. Some saved time by answering comments in public rather than dealing with the same question via private emails. Others mentioned that they could maintain a relationship with audiences between publication dates via their blogs or attract work from employers.

DISCUSSION AND CONCLUSION: "THE WRITING ON THE WALL"

Blogging has grown and developed considerably in the years since the studies of journalism blogs by Singer (2005) and Robinson (2006). Indeed, three-quarters of respondents had only started blogging since that research was published. Respondents frequently highlighted how their employers' attitude to blogs had been transformed. From resisting them, they were now encouraging their wholesale adoption.

103

Commercial considerations have played an important role in this shift. These ranged from search engine optimization (blogs help improve the rankings of news websites on search engines such as Google) to "bringing readers back more often". They were "a cheap way of getting lots of content online . . . resulting [in] ad impressions" (Respondent 113, UK, freelance), a perceived opportunity to make money and a form of protection against the threat from citizen media and the declining state of the news industry itself.

> They went from [being] forbidden to encouraged in a year. Why? They saw the writing on the wall. We're moving from [a] newspaper and Internet firm to an Internet and newspaper firm. (Respondent 38, US, newspapers)

Journalists in the survey admitted to "news repair" (Robinson 2006) or normalization (Lowrey 2006; Singer 2005; Wall 2005; Hermida 2008), as they have sought to reassert and redefine their own work against those of independent operators. But they widely acknowledged the role of their audience in identifying, researching, verifying and correcting the news. The evidence also supports Robinson's contention that "The notion of who is a source — and what they can say — has evolved online" (2006: 74). This sometimes means that the blog is used as a place to publish rumours and unverified information, with the aim of readers contributing to its verification.

Friend and Singer list a number of advantages that journalist-bloggers identify in the blog format, including "the ability to share information that does not fit in the limited news hole of the traditional media format, to incorporate more voices in their reporting, to get potentially valuable feedback from the public, and even to counteract media corporatization" (2007: 136). Matheson (2004) adds speed, depth and informality — to these can be added new ways of pursuing stories, access to a broader field of knowledge, and therefore ideas, a multimedia-interactive mindset, and ongoing, fragmented "postmodern" (Wall 2005) reporting.

How much journalists felt blogging had changed their work was clearly related to the work that they did. Journalists who worked outside the institutional constraints, legacies and cultures of print or broadcast media — i.e., freelance journalists or those who worked for online-only organizations — were more likely to say that their work as a journalist had been transformed "enormously" or "completely". In contrast, no one permanently employed by the television or radio industries felt that blogging had "completely" changed any aspect of their work. Career progression is also an important factor. Blogs act as portfolios and networking tools for freelancers, while blog literacy and multimedia skills have become professionally important for employees in a converging industry. Many respondents, however, expressed frustration at employers who did not allow for the extra time required to blog, or who did not understand or undervalued the format.

Just as responses differed by industry, journalists covering certain sectors differed in how much they felt their work processes had changed. Sport journalists consistently reported less change in their processes than journalists covering other sectors. In contrast, media and technology journalists, finance and arts and culture journalists were more likely to say that blogging had changed their processes "enormously" or "completely". And journalists covering foreign affairs reported a particularly strong effect on how both ideas were generated and they related to their audience.

The journalists' feedback certainly appears to support Lowrey's prediction that the journalism community "may try to redefine blogging as a journalistic tool, and bloggers as amateur journalists . . . (rather than as a unique occupation)" (2006: 493). It also affirms his contention that increasing use of non-elite sources may repair vulnerabilities in journalism. In addition, the research supports his prediction that "news organizations will try to repair these vulnerabilities on the cheap by encouraging journalists to monitor blogs, tap the specialized expertise of the blogosphere, and track stories that have staying power with audiences" (2006: 494).

Although many respondents mentioned how blogging affected their routines in print and broadcast production, further research is needed into how much "crossover" there is, and how much of this effect is restricted to the blog itself. Related to this are questions considering why journalists blog in the first place. For instance, are they typically younger and less powerful? It is also important to make a distinction between journalists' perceptions of how their processes have changed and the content they actually produce. As Matheson points out, while many journalists "are enthusiastic about the potential to rearticulate practice in the new forms that are available online, the texts that these same journalists produce do not show strong evidence of this" (2004: 444).

Finally, these are still early stages in the adoption and evolution of the blog format, with a third of respondents having only started blogging in the past year. In the same way as many non-professional bloggers have developed and changed their approach to blogging over the past few years (MacManus 2008; Perez 2008), journalists can be expected to change and develop as they gain similar experience and the cultures surrounding blogs change. Continual research will be needed to track this change, as the industry faces one of the biggest transformations in its history.

References

Allan, S. (2004) *News Culture*. Buckingham: Open University Press.

Beckett, C. (2008) *SuperMedia*. Oxford: Blackwell.

Blood, R. (2000) "Weblogs: A History and Perspective", *Rebecca's Pocket*, 7 September 2000. Retrieved from: http://www.rebeccablood.net/essays/weblog_history.html.

Boczkowski, P. (2004) *Digitizing the News*. Cambridge, MA: MIT Press.

Bradshaw, P. (2008) "Ten Changes in 10 Years for Journalists", *Press Gazette*, 20 February 2008. Retrieved from: http://www.pressgazette.co.uk/story.asp?sectioncode=6&storycode =40263.

Bruns, A. (2005) *Gatewatching: Collaborative Online News Production*. New York: Peter Lang.

Bryman, A. (2001) *Social Research Methods*. Oxford: Oxford University Press.

Deuze, M. (2008) "Understanding Journalism as Newswork: How It Changes, and How It Remains the Same", *Westminster Papers in Communication and Culture*, 5 (2), pp. 4–23.

Friend, C., and Singer, J. (2007) *Online Journalism Ethics*. Armonk NY: M. E. Sharpe.

Gant, S. (2007) *We're All Journalists Now*. New York: Free Press.

Gillmor, D. (2004). *We the Media: Grassroots Journalism by the People, for the People*. Sebastopol, CA: O'Reilly.

Hampton, M. (2008) "The 'Objectivity' Ideal and its Limitations in 20th-Century British Journalism", *Journalism Studies*, 9 (4), pp. 477–93.

Hermida, A. (2008) "The BBC Goes Blogging: Is 'Auntie' Finally Listening?" 9th Annual International Symposium on Online Journalism, University of Texas, 2008. Retrieved from http://online.journalism.utexas.edu/2008/papers/Hermida.pdf.

Jarvis, J. (2007) "New Rule: Cover What You Do Best. Link to the Rest", *Buzzmachine*, 22 February. Retrieved from: http://www.buzzmachine.com/2007/02/22/new-rule-cover-what-you-do-best-link-to-the-rest/.

Lowrey, W. (2006) "Mapping the Blogging–Journalism Relationship", *Journalism: Theory, Practice and Criticism*, 7.

Lowrey, W., and Latta, J. (2008) "The Routines of Blogging". In C. Paterson, and D. Domingo (eds) *Making Online News*, New York: Peter Lang.

MacManus, R. (2008) "Mixed Messages in the Blogging Landscape", ReadWriteWeb, 27 July. Retrieved from: http://www.readwriteweb.com/archives/mixed_messages_blogging.php.

Matheson, D. (2004) "Weblogs and the Epistemology of the News", *New Media & Society*, 6.

McNair, B. (1998) *The Sociology of Journalism*. New York/London: Arnold.

Oriella PR Network (2008) "European Digital Journalism Survey 2008". Retrieved from: http://www.europeandigitaljournalism.com/downloads/EDJS_June08_27.pdf.

Outlook, The (2007) "Blogs: The Next Takeover Target?", 23 October. Retrieved from: http://outlook.standardandpoors.com/NASApp/NetAdvantage/i/displayIndustryFocusEditorial.do?&context=IndustryFocus&docId=12491873.

Paterson, C., and Domingo D. (eds) (2008) *Making Online News*, New York: Peter Lang.

PEJ (2008) "The Changing Newsroom — The Influence of the Web". Retrieved from: http://journalism.org/node/11961.

Perez, S. (2008) "The Future of Blogging Revealed", ReadWriteWeb, 4 August. Retrieved from: http://www.readwriteweb.com/archives/the_future_of_blogging_reveale.php.

Quinn, S., and Lamble, S. (2007). *Online Newsgathering*. Oxford: Focal.

Robinson, S. (2006) "The Mission of the J-Blog: Recapturing Journalistic Authority Online", *Journalism: Theory, Practice and Criticism*, 7.

Robson, C. (2002) *Real World Research*. Oxford: Blackwell.

Singer, J. (2005) "The Political J-Blogger: Normalising a New Media Form to Fit Old Norms and Practices", *Journalism: Theory, Practice and Criticism*, 6, pp. 173–98.

Thompson, B. (2003) "Is Google Too Powerful?" BBC News, 21 February. Retrieved from: http://news.bbc.co.uk/1/hi/technology/2786761.stm.

Tuchman, G. (1978) *Making the News: A Study in the Construction of Reality*. New York: The Free Press.

Wall, M. (2005) "'Blogs of War': Weblogs as News", *Journalism: Theory, Practice and Criticism*, 6.

Yun, G. W., and Trumbo, C. W. (2000) "Comparative Response to a Survey Executed by Post, E-mail, and Web Form", *Journal of Computer-Mediated Communication*, 6 (1), Retrieved from: http://jcmc.indiana.edu/vol6/issue1/yun.html.

⦃ CHAPTER ⦄
6

"An Essential Service in the Life of a Nation"

KEVIN MARSH

"An essential service in the life of the nation". That quote is from a BBC executive in the relatively innocent 1960s — when it was taken for granted that journalism was a trade on the up, full of hope and promise, its role as broker between citizen and power assured. It's an unironic, unhyperbolic reference to the new BBC news and speech station, Radio 4.

In the 2000s you don't have to look far to find news executives and journalists musing on the end of their trade . . . or at least, the end of its comforting familiarities. Here's one example, more or less at random, from Geneva Overholser, Director of the School of Journalism at the University of Southern California's Annenberg School for Communication: "The long-building plaint is now undeniable: journalism as we know it is over" (Overholser 2005).

There's no doubt the two-centuries-old business model in which we journalists paid our way by scribbling on the back of adverts, collecting pence from citizens who wanted to read it, has collapsed. As journalists, we find that grim. But, as citizens, we sometimes seem to like the idea that journalism is in trouble; the Web has stripped the old trade of its sovereignty and handed to us citizens the means to build our own agorai, invite attention to our civic needs in our way and with our voices. We are liberated from the dictates of a trade that's spent the last two decades retreating from servicing our basic civic needs, systematically shredding its right to mediate our public discourse, losing our trust as fast as it loses our attention.

But here's something to think about. Are we sure that a public sphere in which the proportion of our civic discourse hosted by traditional journalism falls and that hosted on a demotic, disaggregated Web will support our acts of citizenship better — or at all? Sure, we citizens can build our own personal agorai. But to be of any civic use, a useful public sphere, anything other than a kind of burbling vanity, agorai need to be crowded; and with interested people of different minds. Anything else is a vacuum or a mob.

Geneva Overholser goes on to warn: "A critical element of our democracy is threatened, for no self-governing people can long continue without a press that is not only free but also meets the basic needs of the citizenry." And for a press — you could read "journalism as we know it" here — to serve those needs, it must first exist. The critical threat is that it won't.

A few years ago — it seems like more — people like myself who were at the heart of journalism "as we know it" were reading the signs, and writers like Dan Gillmor with something like resignation. Gillmor considered that "the 'former audience' . . . has . . . turned its endless ideas into such unexpected, and in some cases superb, forms of journalism". And, in implicit condemnation of the persistent failings of "Big Journalism" and in exhortation to realize Web journalism's opportunities, he went on: "The net should be the ally of thought and nuance, not a booster shot for knee-jerk reaction. An informed citizenry cannot sit still for more of the same" (Gillmor 2004: 238).

Later, Joe Trippi — the man who persuaded US Democratic presidential contender Howard Dean to put his trust in the Web in the 2004 primaries — predicted "the overthrow of everything" in the failed relationship between the media and politics. The Web was, he wrote, "the last place where democracy stood a chance" (Trippi 2004). But Geneva Overholser warns well. For all journalism's delinquency, depression and demi-demise ("as we know it", at least), citizens should stifle the farewell cheer. Even in this new, adespotic, networked, online universe, "journalism as we know it" (carried out by the big news organizations with our money and on our behalf) remains vastly more able to support our lives as citizens, to enable us to realize our citizenship than any alternative . . . except the handful of Web journalism projects that has embraced many of the distinguishing features of "journalism as we know it".

Here are a few reasons why:

- Numbers. Journalism "as we know it" consistently convenes citizens in the numbers and diversity necessary for meaningful, collective discourse around the most important acts of citizenship. And in a democracy numbers — very big numbers — are, if not everything, then very nearly everything.
- Professionalism. Although journalism is not a profession — journalism is a trade anyone can practise, not a profession to which aspirants are admitted — it professionalizes the collection, verification and prioritization of accounts of the world; it professionalizes our debates through focused interlocutors and assures continuous engagement with power — even if vicariously — as well as access to elite and expert voices as a matter of course rather than chance.
- Weight and presence in the public sphere, by longevity and consuetude if not by virtue. That weight enables traditional journalism continually to challenge power and to demand its attention.
- Resilience and adaptability. Traditional journalism now looks distinctly untra-

ditional in both multimedia newsgathering and distribution and a transformation in attitudes. One British tabloid, the ultra-traditional right-wing *Daily
Mail*, used to go to extraordinary lengths to avoid admitting error or printing
corrections; now, although it still has trouble separating news from comment,
it has opened all its journalism to the scrutiny of its readers.

And traditional journalism's ability knowingly to adapt both transitively and intran-
sitively — something an anonym like a wise crowdlet cannot do — has changed the
trajectories of some of our certainties. Whereas we were once sure that citizens on the
Web would transform journalism, there is now a degree of consensus that transformed
journalism is changing what Web journalism means and how we use our media to
realize our citizenship.

Professor Jay Rosen, of New York University, as one of the chief thinkers of the
public journalism movement in the 1980s and 1990s, was among the first to argue that
without a public purpose the American press had no future. He was also in the vanguard
of thinkers predicting journalism's loss of sovereignty to "the people formerly known
as the audience".

For some time now Rosen (2005, 2006) has been describing the transformation of
journalism from traditional to future as a migration across the digital divide: "Like
reluctant migrants everywhere, the people in the news tribe have to decide what to take
with them. When to leave. Where to land. They have to figure out what is essential to
their way of life. They have to ask if what they know is portable" (Rosen 2006).

Migration, note: what he doesn't assume is that journalists will become asylum
seekers in Webland:

> the press is shared territory. It has pro and amateur zones . . . It belongs equally to the amateur
> and the pro. Online the two zones connect, and flow together. It still works vertically: press
> to public. It also works horizontally: peer to peer. Part of it is a closed system — and closed
> systems are good at enforcing editorial controls — the other part is an open system. (Rosen
> 2008)

In Britain, too. Charlie Beckett runs a politics/media thinktank — POLIS — at the
London School of Economics. In a recent book he argued that journalism's emerging
shape was "networked journalism" (Beckett 2008) — a form of the trade rooted in journalism's traditional strengths supplemented by citizen networks: "The whole point of
the networked model is that you do not surrender the journalistic judgement, the journalistic values and the journalistic nous that enables you to filter out information, to
edit and prioritize stories and to package information in a way that can be consumed".[1]

Martin Moore is Director of the Media Standards Trust — a UK charity whose aim
to is improve British journalism: his vision for the future of news organizations also
draws on the best of their past: "Their role should be as much about collecting information, verifying that information and then providing the tools for the public to assess
that information, to investigate it, to compare it. And I think only by empowering
them to do that will journalism reinvent itself."[2]

Migration to a pro/am shared territory, networked journalism around the trade's core values, journalism reinventing itself. This consensus is saying clearly and loudly: our civic discourses need the attributes and capacities of traditional journalism to validate them.

This consensus lines up completely with my own experience as editor — between 2002 and 2006 — of one of the biggest beasts in the UK media jungle: BBC Radio 4's *Today* programme. On the face of it, *Today* is no more than BBC radio's biggest breakfast time news programme. But in its fifty years on air it has become what broadcasting historian David Hendy's describes as: "an organ of the British constitution" (Hendy 2007: 319). This unique place in Britain's civic ecology derives not just from the size of its audience: some 6 million Britons listen each week.

It's also because of the make-up of that audience. The programme is:

> required listening for politicians, journalists and other opinion formers . . . largely through a virtuous cycle of cause and effect . . . [*Today*] succeeded, day after day, in having "big hitters" among the government and the opposition as its guests, thus signalling to others with a role in running the country that here was the one programme on which they, too, should appear. (Hendy 2007: 318)

So much so that an appearance on *Today* was the inevitable starting point of the publicity grids of the insanely over-controlled government information operation under the then Prime Minister's press secretary, Alastair Campbell. For better or worse, ministers preferred to float and test policies in a *Today* grilling heard by millions of citizens rather than to a deserted House of Commons — some saw that as a usurping of the scrutiny function of MPs. More than once, the Speaker of the House of Commons — the officer elected by MPs to protect the rights of the House — rebuked ministers for telling the citizens and voters listening to *Today* what, according to Parliament's rules, they should have told first to legislators.

But *Today*'s place in Britons' lives as citizens also derives from the explicit, publicly articulated and accountable civic purpose both of the programme and its parent organization, the BBC — the national broadcaster which, while publicly funded, is independent of government. And which also dominates the news market.

Public funding through a licence — effectively a tax on TV ownership — entails a compact between broadcaster and citizen, a compact most comprehensively expressed in the BBC's Editorial Guidelines, a body of case law rooted in five values: truth and accuracy, impartiality, independence, the public interest and accountability. These values and guidelines are an essential component in the relatively high level of trust Britons have in the BBC — a level of trust that is an essential precursor of any realistic civic or public purpose.

It derives, too, from citizens expectations of its daily, professionalized testing of power that has a permanence and continuity and which mirrors the adversariality that is the default mode of British public life — not without cost. One presenter earned the title of "the politician's chief irritant" (Hendy 2007: 319); another was accused of "poisoning the well of democracy" with his persistent, sceptical questioning (Culf

1995) — although that charge was levelled by a minister who was later jailed for perjury. This within the context of routinely convening citizens in large numbers, diversity of discourse and consistency of access to expert and elite voices.

These were the known quantities when I took over as editor in December 2002. What was a not such a known quantity was the audience's growing desire to turn their relationship with *Today* from a one-to-many lecture into, in part at least, a conversation, just as the theorists were describing and predicting.

Two features in particular: one was the extraordinary number of well-argued emails that arrived daily at the programme. Something like 200 a day — more than 50,000 a year — sent in spite of the knowledge that they would not be published. The other was the accidental popularity of the message board on the *Today* website. Launched in 2001, it was notoriously unfriendly and difficult to use. Yet it was calculated in 2006 that listeners had begun over 18,000 threads in five years, with some threads attracting up to 3,000 posts.

The question was not whether we should attend to these voices. It was how: how to do it in a way that enhanced our listeners' civic possibilities but did not degrade *Today*'s self-evident service to the public discourse. There were plenty of helpful suggestions — suggestions of the kind that crystallized by 2003–4 in texts such as Chris Willis and Shayne Bowman's *We Media* and Dan Gillmor's *We the Media*. These and similar texts became scary samizdat in BBC newsrooms, while inside the BBC, a handful of senior and influential figures including Richard Sambrook, then Director of News, urged change. But there was an unknown variable. No one — least of all me — was clear what would happen if we were to convene citizen listeners in large numbers not just to participate in producing journalism or to enrich the public discourse but to carry their citizenship to the next stage and use the power of *Today* to command the attention of authority and actually change things.

So that's what we decided to test. Between 2003 and 2006 we launched a number of experiments calculated to test some of the ways in which we could open the programme to its citizen audience; including "Guest Editors", listeners reports, listener-led interviews and mining emails and the message board for agendas and expertise.

Two experiments in particular stood out — largely because of the way in which they adumbrated attitudes towards boundaries within and between our public spheres. One offered *Today*'s citizen listeners the opportunity to make law, not just talk about it or join a campaign. The other offered a group of citizens the opportunity to deliberate at length on one aspect of the government's agenda and to take its solutions direct to the government minister responsible.

The first of these, a poll called "Listeners' Law", replaced the traditional "Man and Woman of the Year" poll over Christmas and New Year 2003. We invited listeners to submit their suggestions for a new law they'd like to introduce. From these initial submissions a panel drew up a shortlist of five, which listeners then voted on in a phone poll. We undertook to have the winning proposal expertly drafted and presented to parliament as a Private Members bill by the Labour MP for Ealing, Stephen Pound. Because of the conventions of British lawmaking, the chances of it becoming law were low — but chance there was, and, at the very least, it took commanding the attention of power to a different level.

Listeners sent some 10,000 ideas, all passionately argued, many lengthily so, but about half of them — according to a review by the Law Commission — proposed laws already on the statute book. There were five short-listed proposals: a ban on smoking in workplaces, bars and restaurants; a limit on the number of terms a Prime Minister could serve, plus compulsory voting in General Elections; allowing the use of all organs for transplant after death, subject to opt-out; a ban on Christmas advertising and street decorations before 1st December; and a law to authorize homeowners to use any means to defend their home from intruders. Twenty-six thousand listeners voted, almost 40 percent of them for the winner, the homeowner's "defence by any means" law.

The impact on the poll on the public discourse as articulated in the press was significant: the right-of-centre tabloid the *Daily Express*, stated: "The government cannot ignore the fact that this issue is the single matter of over-riding concern to many of us. Yet that is exactly what it seems to be doing . . . The law must be reformed so that it gives them clear rights of protection."

In the right-wing *Daily Mail* a columnist opined: "The *Today* poll graphically highlights the mounting frustration of the British public, of all classes and races, with the way this country is being governed . . . If the *Today* programme brings that mood to the notice of our political leaders, it will have performed a far better service than could be achieved through all its other worthy features." But there were those who saw it differently. The columnist Simon Jenkins wrote in *The Times*: "Not content with usurping the scrutiny function of the House of Commons, it now purports to legislate" (Jenkins 2004).

Of course, the point of "Listeners' Law" was not to legislate . . . any more than *Today*'s daily testing of power on behalf of citizens was designed to usurp the scrutiny function of the House of Commons. Its purpose was to see whether a link could be fashioned between citizens, legislators and legislation through the medium of journalism.

In the event, the controversial proposal fell to parliamentary procedure — it proved almost impossible to draft a watertight Bill and absolutely impossible to produce one that could command a majority of legislators. Later in 2004, a Conservative member of the House of Commons introduced an almost identical bill while at the same time denouncing the efforts of "Listeners' Law", which he called an "endeavour to interfere in the course of legislation in a manner that many of us on both sides of the House regard as wholly unacceptable". He added: "I do not believe that it is the business of the public service broadcaster of this country to engage in the drafting of a piece of legislation".

It was a powerful illustration that for some legislators and journalists, the boundary — drawn, it is true, by no more than convention — between civic discourse and political action "allowed" citizens to notice, debate, discuss and campaign . . . but not take the results and demands of their discourse into the legislative chamber itself. The tens of thousands convened for "Listeners' Law" were insufficient, insignificant even, measured alongside the tens of millions who elect British legislators.

The later experiment, in 2005, took on a different civic challenge: could journalism in the form of *Today* become the "ally of thought and nuance" (Dan Gillmor's term)? The assembly of a Citizens' Jury was billed as "an experiment to find out if citizens can solve the problems that politicians can't". An independent oversight panel and academic guidance ensured a rigorous process.

The jury comprised twenty-four residents from Reading — a town in the Thames valley — chosen at random but to reflect the community's demographic make-up. Their task was to deliberate on what was called "the respect agenda" ahead of a government White Paper — a form of legislative consultation paper designed to signal the government's intentions.

There was no undertaking that the juries' views and solutions would be implemented, but local politicians and the government minister responsible had agreed to meet the jury to discuss their findings.

The jury's weekly deliberations — two sessions of about two and a half hours — defined what they saw as the problems and took evidence from experts whom they cross-examined. Some of the juries' deliberations were reported on air and on the *Today* website, but generating material for broadcast was not the priority.

In the event, the jury produced over a dozen nuanced recommendations on which local and national politicians could act, should they choose to do so. They ranged far beyond the narrow agenda being contemplated by the government; they considered questions of young people's poverty, homelessness, vulnerability, health services, civic rights and responsibilities and the role of charities.

The *Today* reporter overseeing the experiment, Polly Billington, reported their deliberations on the programme's website:

> Listening to them struggle with big issues, clash over solutions and gently find a compromise, change their minds one way and then back again, the jurors became much more than lab rats. They changed, perhaps inevitably, as they studied different policies, scrutinized different analyses and came into contact with views different from their own. (Billington 2005)

It was, she said, conducted "without rancour, faction or bitterness. It might have lacked the kind of 'balanced' political perspective we broadcasters work hard to produce on air, but it felt honest and people's views were heard respectfully. That in itself is an object lesson for politicians and the media alike perhaps" (Billington 2005).

CONCLUSIONS?

It certainly achieved nuanced thinking, and it demonstrated a way in which convened citizens with the weight and presence of journalism could demand the attention of their democratic representatives; the deliberations, evidence, cross-examinations were all carried in full at greater length and in greater detail than could be included in a traditional news broadcast.

But it's difficult to see this as a process that could be scaled up without it either collapsing under its own weight or its outputs becoming reduced to a few simple de-

nuanced "knee-jerk" concepts around which sharp arguments could be assembled — something not very different from the outputs of "journalism as we know it".

As Polly Billington reported:

> People who support this kind of initiative as a form of reinvigorating democracy, sometimes suggest that the "empowerment" felt by the people on the jury is a justification in itself. But that would be wrong. If this is a "talking cure" for the problems for democracy I doubt it will work; you can't re-engage people two dozen at a time. (Billington 2005)

Both experiments had flaws. But they told us much, too, about employing the power — both rhetorical and civic — of journalism "as we know it" to offer citizens a richer discourse that has a real potential to solve common problems. They raised, without answering, what seem to me the two most difficult questions: how, if not by a form of journalism that has huge convening ability and which demands power's attention, can we give our discourse as citizens the potential to change things? And how can we scale rich, nuanced civic discourse to produce meaningful outcomes on which we can all act?

There is no debate that journalism "as we know it" — as some of us citizens have come to disdain and ignore it — is over — financially, civically, existentially. There's no real debate, either, that Web journalism, or more accurately citizens practising Web journalism, is one of the things that has broken it and one of the things that can help mend it. If that mending happens in broadly the way the consensus assumes, our public sphere and therefore our lives as citizens will at least be safe. It may even be extended — though don't count on it.

In any event, we'd better hope that something — if only the essential elements — of journalism "as we know it" remains. Over a couple of centuries or more, our lives as citizens and journalism "as we know it" came to make a mutual fit. Off the peg, sure — rarely, if ever, bespoke and never better than the best we could do at the time, but a fit nonetheless and one that time tested and which was more comfortable than not. Journalism "as we know it", with all its failings, proved a good fit for all the reasons discussed in this article but mostly because it did what we citizens couldn't or didn't want to — not every day, anyway: routinely keeping a presence in our civic lives and in power's face.

We citizens shouldn't assume we can create such a fit with new forms of journalism on the Web . . . except where journalism "as we know it" adapts itself to the Web or the Web to it. It will take time to re-draw some of the boundaries — between citizen and legislation, for example — as our experiments on *Today* showed. But in that re-drawing, elements of journalism "as we know it" are the *sine qua non*. Without it, Web journalism — as in millions of self-published citizens — is little more than background radiation of our civic universe.

Notes

1 BBC WAC Oral History Project: Clare Lawson Dick, former Controller of the BBC Home Service/Radio 4, 1967.

2   Interview with author for *Analysis*, on BBC Radio 4, 3 July 2008.

3   Interview with author for *Analysis*, on BBC Radio 4, 3 July 2008.

4   Available at: http://www.bbc.co.uk/guidelines/editorialguidelines/.

5   Historian Peter Hennessy wrote in his book *The Secret State* that the absence of *Today* from the air is a test that the commander of a nuclear submarine should use to determine whether a nuclear attack on Britain had been successful and retaliation should begin.

6   Hansard: 30 Apr 2004: Column 1147.

7   Hansard: 30 Apr 2004: Column 1147.

8   The then British Prime Minister, Tony Blair, said that the issue of "respect" kept coming up on the doorstep during the 2005 general election campaign and that it would be a key theme for his third term in government, a term he did not complete.

References

Beckett, C. (2008) *SuperMedia: Saving Journalism So It Can Save the World*. Oxford: Blackwell.

Billington, P. (2005) Retrieved from: http://www.bbc.co.uk/radio4/today/reports/politics /citizenjury_reading_20050908.shtml.

Culf, A. (1995) "BBC Chief Backs 'Effective' Humphrys", *The Guardian,* 29 March.

Gillmor, D. (2004) *We the Media: Grassroots Journalism by the People, for the People.* Sebastopol, CA: O'Reilly.

Hendy, D. (2007) *Life on Air: A History of Radio 4*. Oxford: Oxford University Press.

Jenkins, S. (2004) "How the BBC Made Democracy Just a Show", *The Times*, 2 January.

Overholser, G. (2005) "On Behalf of Journalism: A Manifesto for Change". The Annenberg Foundation Trust. Retrieved from: http://www.annenbergpublicpolicycenter.org/Overholser/20061011_JournStudy.pdf.

Rosen, J. (2005) Retrieved from: http://journalism.nyu.edu/pubzone/weblogs/pressthink/2005/04/27/mig_nwsp.html.

Rosen, J. (2006) Retrieved from: http://journalism.nyu.edu/pubzone/weblogs/pressthink/2008/06/26/pdf.html.

Rosen, J. (2008) Retrieved from: http://journalism.nyu.edu/pubzone/weblogs/pressthink/2008/06/26/pdf.html.

Trippi, J. (2004) *The Revolution Will Not Be Televised: Democracy, the Internet and the Overthrow of Everything*. New York: HarperCollins. Also available at: http://joetrippi.com/blog/?page_id=1379.

{{ **CHAPTER** }}

7

Citizenship and Public Service: The Case of BBC News Online

ENAIR THORSEN, STUART ALLAN AND CYNTHIA CARTER

Since its launch at a press conference held in an Internet café in London on 4 November 1997, BBC News Online has been playing a key role in helping to take the "core values" of the corporation's "brand" forward into the digital era. "The BBC reinvented itself once, when television was invented, and now we feel we have got to do it again," stated Edward Briffa, the controller of BBC Online and Interactive. "It is not that radio and television are going to diminish, but it is that people's time is going to be taken up, in increasing amounts, with this third opportunity" (cited in *The Scotsman*, 17 December 1997). Important here was the need to demonstrate how it could forge a new relationship with British citizens and, subsequently, the licence-fee payers. "It's very exciting indeed," BBC News Online editor, Mike Smartt, remarked shortly after the launch. "This medium is now our third broadcast service alongside radio and TV, and we believe it could take over as the main way people receive BBC journalism in the UK and around the world" (cited in *PR Week*, 21 November 1997).[1]

This chapter maps the launch of BBC News Online and how the corporation has re-inflected its public service ethos in the online domain. It begins by examining the development of BBC News Online until its first major independent review, the Graf Report, published in 2004, to highlight the way in which the public value of the corporation's Web provision has been assessed within the larger and increasingly globalized mediascape. Against this backdrop, the chapter proceeds to investigate two areas of particular importance to the BBC in its articulation of citizenship: the Children's BBC *Newsround* website, which aims to engage young people with news and current affairs, and its *ad hoc* national election sites, which seek to provide informational resources for citizens at election time. Central to both of these examples, we will show, are important debates about interactivity. Of particular relevance, where citizenship is concerned, is the extent to which the BBC's traditional top-down model of information distribution has been called into question by Web users demanding a greater sense of civic engagement and democratic value from the corporation.

ESTABLISHING BBC NEWS ONLINE

The design of BBC News Online's Web pages at the time of its launch in November 1997 may have looked "bleak and amateurish from the vantage point of today", admitted Bob Eggington (2007) recently, but the "site got off to a cracking start". Eggington, the first head of the service, recalled that members of staff were facing a "nightmare" of a challenge from the outset. "The price of building the content production system at such speed was six months of technical instability," he remembered. "The bloody thing kept crashing." It took a dedicated team, willing to experiment with new ideas, to ensure that logistical problems were soon resolved.

Originally, the BBC was granted a one-year trial for an online news service by the British government Department for Culture, Media and Sport, which was then ratified a year later (Barrett 2007: n.p). BBC News Online represented a significant initiative within the corporation's strategy to reaffirm its public service ethos in a multi-channel universe — and thereby be better placed to challenge commercial rivals such as CNN, MSNBC, EuroNews and News Corp. "We are this autumn only at the starting block," stated Tony Hall, chief executive of BBC News, the day before the launch. "My ambition is, first, to ensure that we preserve and build a public service in news for the next generation. And, second, to ensure that BBC News develops as a global player" (cited in *The Guardian*, 3 November 1997). Widely perceived to be late on to the scene, arriving long after both British and international competitors had established their online presence, the initiative nevertheless represented a bold move. "Our basic aim is to extend our public service remit on to the Web," Bob Eggington, the director of project, said at the time. "The design is simple and it is easy to use." The decision to proceed was justified, in his view, "because that's where young people are going[.] We have to be there because the Web audience is increasing by 10 per cent every month" (cited in *The Times*, 5 November 1997).

Despite its late official arrival on the scene, the BBC quickly established itself as the leading British content site on the Internet. By March 1998 BBC News Online recorded 8.17 million page impressions and by June that year BBC Online offered 140,000 pages of content, of which about 61,000 consisted of news. While the move online was aimed at extending the BBC's public service to the Web, it was not until the corporation's submission to the licence fee review panel in March 1999 that the remit of BBC Online was articulated in clear policy terms. The core objectives were stated as being:

- The provision of news and information.
- The role of trusted guide to the Internet, helping users to enjoy its full potential.

- The development of communities of interest, based around BBC content.
- The opportunity for viewers and listeners to provide feedback on programmes and services.
- The provision of a range of educational sites and services.
- Local and regional content. (Graf 2004: 69)

During the licence fee review in 1999 there were significant external pressures to turn BBC Online (including news and sport) into a commercial operation by accepting advertising. Two of the key drivers behind this move were a finding that many of the visitors to the site connected from abroad and did not contribute through the licence fee, as well as the commercial proposition to float BBC Online as a business on the stock market. Other ideas, such as sponsorship, subscription fees and direct government funding, were also considered and largely rejected as they "could change fundamentally the purpose and nature of the BBC's public services, both broadcast and online" (Davies et al. 1999: 68).

Such commercial pressures persisted, however, and were further fuelled by a sense that the BBC's investment into new media was to the detriment of the commercial sector and indeed overstepping the original objectives that had granted them government approval in the first place. This criticism ultimately helped precipitate the first major independent review into the BBC's online services, commissioned by Tessa Jowell, the then government Culture Secretary, in 2003 and published in 2004. The review centred on a public consultation exercise conducted by former Trinity Mirror chief executive Philip Graf. The extent to which Graf qualified as an impartial adjudicator was open to question in the eyes of some commentators, given his previous position with an organization that was in direct competition with the BBC. He had also been involved in lobbying with the Newspaper Society over concerns about BBC Online websites competing with local newspapers. In any case, Graf described BBC Online as "one of the leading providers of online news and current affairs content" and, as such, "entirely consistent with the BBC's broader purposes". He pointed out that there "is clearly great public affection and appreciation of BBC Online" and that the service acted as an important guide to the Internet for those who required one.

The Graf Report reaffirmed news and current affairs as a strategic priority for BBC Online, while retaining the inextricable link to citizenship and democracy. Specifically, the report stated that BBC News Online:

should continue to provide fair, independent (national and local) news and current affairs coverage, ensuring citizens have the necessary knowledge to make informed choices and decisions and supporting the UK's democratic processes and institutions. The public value of this type of service will continue to grow, as more people use the Internet as a — or even the — primary source of their news and basic information. (Graf 2004: 75)

Regarding the question of whether the BBC's websites were damaging commercial interests, Graf believed that it could neither be proved nor disproved. "It was difficult to find evidence to prove one way or another," he maintained, "but logic says there's a reasonable chance that the BBC Online can lessen competition in certain areas." In any case, his report called for the BBC to redefine the remit and objectives for its online services "around public purposes" — coverage of news, current affairs, education and information of value to the citizen were to be prioritized. Moreover, the report declared that a small number of websites were not "sufficiently distinctive from commercial alternatives or adequately associated with public service purposes, to be justified by the remit". In response, Ashley Highfield, the BBC's director of New Media and Technology, promptly confirmed that five websites would be closed on "the grounds that their market impact might be greater than their public value".

In the next section, our attention turns to the emergence of a Web presence for the BBC television programme *Newsround*. Often heralded as the world's first daily news bulletin for children, it has proven to be a much-loved institution for successive generations since it first appeared on television screens in 1972.

NEWSROUND ON THE WEB — CITIZENS IN THE MAKING

Children's BBC *Newsround* launched its interactive website on 22 October 2001.[2] Tim Levell, online editor, welcomed young people to the site, declaring it to be one of the "first in the world to provide stories for children every day of the year".[3] In the months leading to the launch, *Newsround* had been offering a rudimentary online news provision consisting of stories taken from its CEEFAX service (the BBC's teletext information service). *Newsround*'s team of television reporters, who posted stories whenever the opportunity arose alongside their other responsibilities, prepared this material. Graphics were scarce, and there was no scope for citizen feedback. All in all, it was an experimental effort of sorts, intended to hold the space until a more substantive strategy could be forged.

The 2001 launch, therefore, signalled a bold initiative to extend a fully fledged Web strategy for *Newsround*. By now its website had evolved to include its own dedicated news team, consisting of sixteen reporters, editors and technicians. Two schoolteachers complemented their efforts by helping to develop the site's citizenship and media literacy resources in line with the national curriculum. News content was updated more often than the television bulletin throughout the day, and it offered a much wider range and depth of content. The online team was situated as part of BBC News Online and CBBC, which meant that it was located in a different building from the *Newsround* television team.[4] Later, in 2003, both teams were moved into new offices so that resources and operations — including editorial responsibilities — could be merged.[5]

Newround's relationship with its audience has become steadily more sophisticated since the launch of the interactive website. The heightened emphasis placed on interactivity went some way to addressing criticisms made by commentators sceptical about whether *Newsround* was succeeding in its efforts to engage children critically with the world around them (children sometimes being described as "citizens in the making" at the time: see Buckingham 2000). The interactive structure of the site meant that its news agenda could be more responsive to children's needs, not least by facilitating their responses to news content. Spaces were opening up for young people to challenge what they were being told and to offer alternative views or perspectives in light of their own experiences. This dimension has been especially pronounced on the site's "In the News" message board, where participants can choose to construct their own discussion strings around specific news stories. In this way *Newsround*'s reporting is monitored and debated, often passionately so. Children have made the most of this unique forum to share their views about current affairs and how they are being reported.

The current provision has been developed in accordance with long-standing public service principles. Since the introduction of the television bulletin in 1972, former *Newsround* editor Ian Prince (2008) points out, the BBC's central aim has been to create the best children's news service in the UK. Over the years this ambition has been strengthened, in his view, through the establishment of clear and consistent news values that endeavour to ensure audience trust, by sustaining a commitment to understanding the audience, by expanding the number of platforms available when the audience wants it and through the production of high quality journalism that is both accessible and interactive, so as to give children a space in which to see themselves reflected and have their voices heard.[6] On the thirty-fifth anniversary of *Newsround* in 2007, current editor Sinéad Rocks (2007) declared that the increasingly interactive character of *Newsround* has been central to maintaining the BBC's long-standing public service obligation to fostering children's sense of social engagement and inclusion. In her words:

> The central premise remains the same. We aim to help children make sense of the world around them and give them the chance to have their say on what is going on. Technology has helped in the case of the latter. We get hundreds of emails from our audience every day and have more than a quarter of a million Press Packers: members of our online journalism club. They don't get a badge for joining but they do get the chance to report on issues that matter to them. You could say that *Newsround* pioneered UGC long before everyone else saw its benefits. (Rocks 2007)

Across CBBC, interactivity is seen to be increasingly important way to engage children with both its television programming and online resources. As the BBC's recent *Statements of Programme Policy 2007–2008* report states: "Interactivity underpins the service, and the CBBC online and interactive television services offer a rich array of related in-depth content." Moreover, it adds: "CBBC combines its linear programming with interactive digital content that encourages children to participate or to deepen their experience of a programme or topic."[7]

Interactivity and fostering children's citizenship are thus regarded as being inextricably linked. In a section of the report entitled "Sustaining Citizenship and Civil Society", the corporation reaffirms its responsibility for providing a dedicated, interactive children's news service that "introduces children to issues facing the world in which they live and helps them to understand the issues better". Likewise, Ofcom's 2007 report "The Future of Children's Television Programming" concludes that young people (and their parents) value children's news and associated websites, "particularly at times of crisis, conflict and danger", precisely because they are able explain what is happening in a way that is both understandable and reassuring. Given that *Newsround* is now the only provider of children's news in the UK, this makes its television bulletin and linked website especially vital resources for children in their development as young citizens.[8]

BBC NEWS ONLINE AND CITIZENS AT ELECTION TIME

While the *Newsround* website represented a clear commitment from the BBC to inter-activity for citizens in the making, BBC News Online's election sites have been a key aspect of the corporation's aim at creating "democratic value" and "civic engagement" for adult citizens. In the past ten years the BBC has published three websites dedicated to UK general elections — in 1997 as a pilot site a few months prior to the official launch of BBC News Online, and in 2001 and 2005 as a special section of BBC News Online. News reports and election information were centre-stage for each of these sites, although it was the opportunities for interactivity and dialogue that were the real inno-vations.

Despite the political parties not making much of an attempt at engaging with voters on their sites in 1997, the BBC often requested feedback both on their website and on specific election issues. The BBC published a small selection of this feedback in a section entitled You Say!, which would in 2001 become Talking Point and in 2005 Have Your Say. Interactive features included an early attempt at recreating Peter Snow's Swingometer (a BBC graphic device illustrating party electoral swings) and some more basic calculation forms to predict outcomes based on percentage of overall vote, as well as a quiz based game entitled "Have you got what it takes to be an MP?" The BBC also invited people to submit questions, which were then put to politicians and published in a Forum section. Young adults were encouraged to take part in the mock General Election taking place in the week leading up to the actual poll on the Newsround Election '97 website. Many of the features were not fully developed or were indicative of innovative forms of use being held back by technological limitations.

By the 2001 UK General Election, the Internet was starting to have a more signif-icant impact on campaigning, and even the BBC announced (in their *Guidance for all BBC Programme Makers during the General Election Campaign*) that "this will be the first full Online election". The BBC's Vote 2001 site again provided several animated inter-active features, and two key sections for civic engagement. The first of these, entitled Talking Point, allowed citizens to post comments on a range of pre-defined issues and questions. This section can essentially be seen as an attempt at facilitating debate between ordinary members of the electorate, and was the precursor to the Have Your Say section during the 2005 election. The second feature, entitled Forum, was vastly improved from the Election '97 equivalent. Essentially an extension of the Talking Point feature, the Forum section allowed citizens to submit questions to the BBC, a selection of which would then be put to politicians by one of their correspondents. The BBC this time also commissioned ICM Research to conduct regular online surveys of a 2,000-strong voter panel, aimed to be representative of the UK adult population and not just Internet users. The feature was dubbed Online 1,000 and contained a new issue every month, and every week in the three weeks leading up to the election. Again there was also an opportunity for children to get involved — this time they were invited to suggest political policies on the *Newsround* feature "If U were Prime Minister", which according to Coleman (2001: 683) received several thousand posts.

Following their early attempt in 1997 and more successful execution in 2001, the BBC again created a dedicated section for their election coverage in 2005 — this time entitled Election 2005. As in previous years, BBC News Online featured several sections to complement its traditional news coverage, designed to give citizens a more in-depth knowledge of election issues. Compared to the election sites of 1997 and 2001, the BBC in 2005 significantly improved the opportunities for ordinary citizens to post their comments to and influence debates. The Talking Point feature was rebranded Have Your Say and contained fifty-three topics across sixty-eight pages, with a small minority of news and feature articles also containing comments posted by citizens. These pages combined attracted 7,684 comments. The UK voters' panel, created in collaboration with the BBC Breakfast television programme, was seemingly an evolution of the Online 1,000 feature from the 2001 election. However, this panel consisted of only twenty voters, who had been asked in advance to contribute their views "in text and in video, using 3G mobile phones" throughout the election. There were nine different debate topics, with an average of six panellists publishing a response on each occasion. Citizens could discuss each of these entries, and the section attracted some 524 comments. The *Newsround* website also had a special Election 2005 section, offering children opportunities to engage in discussion with other children on a dedicated election chat board or to send a message to the Prime Minister on another one, to vote on which issues they believe matter the most (more than 1,800 children participated) as well as a range of online election guides, polls and quizzes to interact with and test their political knowledge.

New for this year was the BBC News Online's election blog, entitled Election Monitor, which announced on the main page that it aimed at "bringing you first-hand reports from around the country from our team of correspondents, as well as the best of the newspapers, choice morsels from the web, and your e-mails". The blog followed a by now traditional reverse chronological order, identifying the author of blog entries with name and title next to their picture, and providing a space for people to post their comments. It finished on 276 posts (in addition to the main holding page), of which 189 received one or more comments from members of the public, totalling 783 comments across all blog posts.

The level of interactivity and opportunities for citizens to engage in debate on the Election 2005 site demonstrates that the BBC clearly recognizes its role in facilitating spaces for public dialogue. Indeed, it maintains, "news judgements at election time are made within a framework of democratic debate" (BBC Producers' Guidelines 2005). Moreover, in relation to new media services, the *BBC Statements of Programme Policy for 2005/2006* devotes an entire section to "democratic value":

In line with the new remit, our news and information service will be aimed primarily at creating democratic value and civic engagement, complementing the BBC's broadcast news coverage across all subject areas. (BBC 2005: 40)

Justifying the interactive features in terms of public service, the Editor of BBC Interactivity, Vicky Taylor, argued that it is "much better if you're getting your audience telling you what they think than just the officials or people in power . . . it's a form of democracy — more people get their chance to have their say about something" (Taylor 2007).

While the Internet may not be perceived as having had a significant impact on the election outcome, the BBC has certainly had a considerable impact on citizens' online activities. On average, 550,000 people visited the Election 2005 site each day of the campaign, although this only represented 10 percent of all BBC News Online users (Ward 2006: 17). On election day, 5 May, the number of unique visitors to the election site tripled to 1.5 million, with the figure doubling on 6 May, when the results were published (Ward 2006: 17). During the 2005 campaign BBC News Online accounted for 78 percent of all Internet news traffic, about one in five of the total election news audience (Ward 2006: 10). Blogging, which had featured noticeably in the US presidential election the year before, attracted only 0.5 percent of the online audience during the election (Ward 2006: 11).

CONCLUSION

BBC News Online has come a long way since the heady days of technological experimentation in the early 1990s — having not only established itself as "the third broadcast medium" but also as an essential part of the British democratic fabric. To date, the BBC has successfully defended its online operations from commercial pressures and managed to establish a dynamic public service model for the Web — one that is being emulated around the globe. The public value of such an offering, as we have sought to highlight in the discussion above, is particularly noticeable in relation to citizenship.

The BBC's online offering complements both "citizens in the making" and adult citizens alike, through innovative strategies in providing news and information that are seen to be both relevant and responsive to citizen interests. Indeed the conclusion of the BBC Trust's service review of bbc.co.uk, published in May 2008, stated that the website "is especially strong in promoting the Citizenship and civil society, Nations and regions, Education and learning, and Global purposes" (BBC Trust 2008: 12). The future is uncertain, of course, as the types of criticisms first rehearsed in the Graf Report continue to resonate in current policy debates. Certain commercial providers are insistent that, while the BBC may have led the first decade of online news provision, the future will be shaped much more strongly by the competitive ethos of the global market-place. Precisely what counts as "public service" — and thus "citizenship" — in this regard may very well be dramatically recast in the years to come.

Notes

1　From 1926, when it was agreed to set up the BBC as a new corporation by Royal Charter, competing conceptions of the appropriate aims and objectives of a public service remit have recurrently highlighted the importance of citizenship. John Reith, as first managing director, was determined that the BBC should serve the whole nation — a commitment that soon found expression as an overarching mission to "inform, educate and entertain". Interestingly, by 2005, this mission was extended during the Charter review to address five criteria by which the success of the corporation should be judged — the first and most important of which was "sustaining citizenship and civil society" (Department for Culture Media and Sports 2005: 5). While this move was seen as important in protecting the BBC's standing in an increasingly commercial media landscape, its reassertion in online contexts represents a significant benchmark for a number of media organisations across Europe and the rest of the world (many of which have been modelled on corresponding formulations of citizenship *vis-à-vis* public service).

2　*Newsround*'s website address is http://news.bbc.co.uk/cbbcnews/default.stm.

3　See http://news.bbc.co.uk/cbbcnews/hi/sci_tech/newsid_1614000/1614357.stm for this story.

4　Levell was the first online editor (2001–2), followed by Tim Masters (2002–3).

5　Personal interview, with Ian Prince, former editor of *Newsround* from 1999–2006, 9 July 2008.

6　Personal interview with Ian Prince, 9 July 2008.

7　The current BBC Statements of Programme Policy document may be found at http://www.bbc.co.uk/info/statements2007/pdf/BBC_SoPPs_200708.pdf.

8　Channel Four discontinued its weekly schools news programme *First Edition* in 2002 and Nickelodeon ceased production of *Nick News* in 2003.

References

Barrett, C. (2007) "Revolution Not Evolution: The Birth of bbc.co.uk". BBC Internet blog [Article originally appeared in *Ariel*, reproduced in the blog by Alan Connor]. Retrieved 4 December 2007 from: http://www.bbc.co.uk/blogs/bbcinternet/2007/12/revolution _not_evolution.html.

Buckingham, D. (2000) *The Making of Citizens: Young People, News and Politics*. London: Routledge.

BBC (2005) *BBC Statements of Programme Policy for 2005/2006*. London: BBC.

BBC (2007) *BBC Statements of Programme Policy for 2007*. London: BBC.

BBC Trust (2008) *Service Review: bbc.co.uk*. London: BBC Trust.

Coleman, S. (2001) "Online Campaigning", *Parliamentary Affairs*, 54, pp. 679–88.

Davies, G., Black, H., Budd, A., Evans, R., Gordon, J., Lipsey, D., Neuberger, J., and Newton, T. (1999) *The Future Funding of the BBC: Report of the Independent Review Panel*. London: Department for Culture, Media and Sport.

Department for Culture Media and Sport (2005) *Review of the BBC's Royal Charter: A Strong BBC, Independent of Government*. London: Department for Culture, Media and Sport.

Eggington, B. (2007) "In the Front Line, Online", *Press Gazette*, 13 November.

Graf, P. (2004) *Report of the Independent Review of BBC Online*. London: Department for Culture, Media and Sport.

Levell, T. (2001) "Welcome to Our Website!" Retrieved from: http://news.bbc.co.uk/cbbcnews /hi/sci_tech/newsid_1614000/1614357.stm.

Ofcom (2007) "The Future of Children's Television Programming". Retrieved from: http://www.ofcom.org.uk/consult/condocs/kidstv/.

Prince, I. (2008) Personal interview, 9 July.

Rocks, S. (2007) "After 35 Years, Newsround is as Vital as Ever, Says Sinead Rocks", *Broadcast*, 27 November. Retrieved from: http://www.broadcastnow.co.uk/opinion_and_blogs/hot_topic/hot_topic_newsround.html.

Taylor, V. (2007) Personal interview, 27 March.

Ward, S. (2006) "What's the Story . . .? Online News Consumption in the 2005 UK Election" [Unpublished]. Oxford: Oxford Internet Institute.

{{ CHAPTER }}
8

Shut Out but Switched On: Web Forums, Border Identities and the Evolving Narrative of Post-Devolution Wales

SIMON GWYN ROBERTS

The continuing trend towards political devolution in "supranational" states across Europe is generating a range of unresolved issues in terms of individual engagement with the process. The media's role in addressing, interpreting and articulating often complex and diverse issues of identity politics is becoming increasingly important as devolution takes root. This is of particular relevance to areas historically marginalized by the dominant national narrative of the newly devolved entity. Wales was granted limited self-governing powers (through the Welsh Assembly government) by the UK government after a closely contested referendum in 1997. There is a growing sense that this devolution has heightened some of the unresolved political and cultural tensions within marginal areas of the country, particularly those adjacent to the English border, and that this demands a response via, and within, the wider media. This chapter will explore the role of participative Web discussions in considering citizenship and identity politics in one such marginalized region.

The administrative region of Flintshire, in north-east Wales, is perhaps the most notable example of this tension, with the highest percentage of English-born residents and few Welsh-speakers. Its geographical position, bordering populous urban areas of north-west England and far removed from the centres of Welsh cultural and political life, has given rise to an unusually nebulous cultural identity and a marked reluctance to engage with the newly devolved Welsh political system. In 2003 only 25 percent of the electorate in the Alyn and Deeside constituency voted in the Welsh Assembly Government elections.

Inevitably, the lack of engagement with Welsh politics in Flintshire raises questions about the role of the media in the democratic process. The issue has received some attention at a national level: polls found that "very substantial" proportions of the Welsh population consumed little or no news about the 2003 Assembly elections (Thomas, Jewell and Cushion 2004). The Welsh Assembly has been forthright in its plea to broadcasters to "reflect devolution" and "give Welsh people access to Welsh governance" through their programming. But, since devolution, the mainstream media's role in providing a platform for discussion of identity politics and democratic engagement, in an area where this has increasing significance, has been limited. Nor has it succeeded in creating a sense of cohesiveness or inclusiveness among Flintshire residents, who are among the most detached from Cardiff-based Assembly politics.

Barlow, Mitchell and O'Malley (2005) highlight concerns that the media fail to represent adequately the diversity of Wales, leading to a sense of cultural deficit. This sense of cultural deficit is rarely, if ever, related to intensively anglicized areas of Wales such as Flintshire. Yet it remains pertinent to residents' relationship with the media. Instead, Internet forums have almost entirely replaced the traditional media as a vehicle for interactive debate of post-devolution politics in the area, with the examples from online discussions explored in this chapter illustrating a strong awareness of both identity politics in general and the specific civic engagement deficit affecting Flintshire. In particular, the scope of the BBC's long-standing public service remit to increase social cohesion by facilitating community dialogue has been lent new impetus by Web technology. Regional websites and their associated discussion forums reveal a potential for meaningful citizen engagement with post-devolution identity politics in a region where that has a wider political significance.

WELSH CULTURAL AND POLITICAL GEOGRAPHY

Wales as a whole has long been characterized by a fragmented political and cultural geography. In the words of Smith (1999): "Wales is a singular noun but a plural experience." Several attempts have been made to encapsulate that fragmentation — the best-known being Denis Balsom's "Three Wales Model" (1985). Balsom argued that Welsh voting patterns, alongside related issues of media usage and language, could best be illustrated by dividing the county into three broad units. The "Bro Gymraeg" represents the Welsh-speaking, culturally distinct areas of north-west and west Wales, characterized by widespread support for Plaid Cymru, the nationalist party. "Welsh Wales" consists of the industrialized south Wales valleys and West Glamorgan (largely socialist, primarily Welsh-identifying but English-speaking), with "British Wales" comprizing the rest (north-east Wales, Pembrokeshire and areas adjacent to the English border). In "British Wales", argued Balsom, voters' primary loyalty is to the British state, and residents prioritize their British identity over their Welsh one. This has traditionally resulted in electoral competition between the main British parties, with a meaningful Conservative presence and low levels of support for Plaid Cymru.

Post-devolution critiques of Balsom's model have challenged its continuing validity. Critics argue that Welsh people across almost all geographical regions of the nation now express high levels of affiliation to Wales, and that Welsh identity is buoyant and more widespread than Balsom's model suggests (Coupland, Bishop and Garrett 2006). Moreover, research by Jones and Scully (2004) found that British identity in Wales has weakened since devolution, with a corresponding rise in Welsh people claiming an exclusively Welsh identity.

These findings, however, obscure two further issues. First, people in border regions may construct their identities in ways not always preferred or envisaged by politicians (Williams 2005a). Second, Balsom's "British Wales" itself masks substantial cultural and political differences. The "problematic", often mixed, identities typically found within border areas such as Flintshire have been compounded by devolution and the related increasing adherence to national identities that, as Jones and Scully's research suggests, do not necessarily identify with traditional notions of "Britishness". This puts the border areas of the "British Wales" region identified by Balsom into a difficult position following devolution, illustrated by the emerging democratic deficit. As Horsman and Marshall (1995) argue, there has always been a tension between the fixed, durable and inflexible requirements of national boundaries and the unstable, transient and flexible requirements of people. Prior to devolution, the border between England and Wales was largely symbolic. Since devolution, the border has assumed a renewed political significance. This has far-reaching implications for residents who may not identify with the principles of devolution — and whose identity may not comfortably accommodate the new political paradigm.

Flintshire is where "British Wales" reaches its apotheosis, particularly the industrialized eastern fringe along the English border. The unitary authority (hereafter "county") of Flintshire is situated in the north-east of Wales, bordering the Dee estuary and the English county of Cheshire. The current county of Flintshire was created following a local government reorganization. From 1284 until 1974 it had existed as Flintshire, although with slightly different boundaries from the present county. The specific socio-cultural reasons for the area's post-devolution marginalization from the rest of Wales revolve around a combination of two factors. First is its geographical location, particularly its proximity and links to the large culturally coherent urban areas of north-west England. Second is its extensive history of immigration during the first half of the twentieth century following the establishment of the Shotton steelworks in the east of the county. The area became a virtually contiguous urban area, overwhelmingly anglicized from the outset, leading to an inevitable blurring of socio-cultural boundaries. As a result, Flintshire has a more ambiguous, less cohesive identity than both the rest of Wales and neighbouring parts of north-west England.

BRITISH IDENTITY POST-DEVOLUTION

Examining "problematic" national identities has featured prominently in both political and academic debates in recent years. This is partly because, as Kiely, McCrone, Bechhofer and Stewart (2000) point out, in contexts where national identity is not taken for granted the complex process of identity construction becomes more clearly apparent. Indeed, McCrone, Stewart, Kiely and Bechhofer (1998) argue that the British Isles are a good place to study the impact of what they call the "new identity politics" because there is something inherently problematic and contested about British identity. As a supranational form of identity, Britishness has always had to contend with older national forms (English, Scottish and Welsh).

Within this context, border communities in the UK occupy an intriguing position post-devolution. For Williams (2005a), borders are the places that facilitate the identification of difference — and of congruence. Gill (2005) argues that border communities experience a public/private split in their identities. Publicly, a border community is ascribed an ambiguous national identity by surrounding national communities. Privately, and among fellow community members, they unambiguously assert national identity. But it is also worth noting that some of the most common identity rules (typically birth-place, ancestry, upbringing, accent and name) tend to be disregarded by the residents of some border areas in the UK. The study by Kiely et al. (2000) of the residents of Berwick upon Tweed, on the English–Scottish border, found that residents had developed alternative identity rules of their own: "People in the town turned out to be claiming, attributing, rejecting, accepting and side-stepping national identity, in ways that we had seldom or never previously encountered." In Flintshire this might also be expected, given the confused markers most residents use to support national identity claims. For instance, many Flintshire residents were born just across the border in Chester but have never lived in England. They therefore immediately send out mixed markers, although claiming a hybrid "Berwickesque" identity as a means of solving these contradictions seems relatively uncommon.

The ambiguity of Flintshire's position post-devolution also seems pertinent to the wider debate about citizenship and political engagement in Wales but has received little academic attention. Williams (2005b) points to the fact that much contemporary writing on "post-colonialism" celebrates the fractured identity of those on the "edge" and gives a voice to those on the margins of the nation. In a Welsh context, he suggests, this might mean paying greater attention to the geographical borderland as well as the affective borderland. The fact that some communities in this area feel (to paraphrase Gilroy's 1987 work on the black British experience) external to and estranged from the imagined community is highlighted by a letter from St David's High School in Saltney, eastern Flintshire. It was a sentiment notable enough to be quoted in *The Economist*: "Our local community sees itself socially and culturally as English, living yards from a border which to them does not effectively exist" (Anon 1998).

MAINSTREAM MEDIA WEAKNESS AND THE PUBLIC RESPONSE

The extent to which the press meets its democratic responsibilities has traditionally tended to be assessed in terms of its success in providing a politically active and informed public sphere, with newspapers having a particular symbolic importance in terms of informing a shared national consciousness (Anderson 1983; Habermas 1989;

McNair 2000). Inevitably, the nature of public debate in Wales is adversely affected by the well-documented and much-lamented lack of a pan-Wales national newspaper and the consequent predominance of English media consumption over that produced in Wales (Thomas 2006). This weakness is amplified by Flintshire's local print press, which again reflects the area's particular geographical and cultural circumstances. Local and regional newspapers have Flintshire editions, but there is no newspaper aimed specifically at the county.

Instead, Internet forums have almost entirely replaced traditional media as a vehicle for interactive debate of post-devolution politics in the area. The recent use of partici-patory journalism in Flintshire is revealing for its role in the creation of an engaged online community, formulating its response to the new and evolving political para-digm. Some have argued that the Internet, as a potential vehicle for active citizenship, has revitalized local democracy and that a reinvigorated public sphere has a particular resonance for Wales (Barlow et al. 2005; Mackay and Powell 1998). The technology offers the possibility of transcending the limitations of physical infrastructure (poor north–south transport links) commonly held to contribute to the "fragmented culture" of Wales. While such expectations may have been tempered elsewhere, following the early burst of enthusiasm for the Web's democratic potential, it still seems pertinent to argue that Web-based communication offers a more suitable platform for the kind of evolving debate necessary in Wales post-devolution.

As access to the Internet started to expand across Wales from 2002 onwards (Richards 2007), albeit with the usual heavily skewed demographic profile, the BBC's regional websites (in this case North-East Wales) began to host a range of interesting debates. These illustrated a strong awareness of both identity politics in general and the specific civic engagement deficit affecting Flintshire. Notably, the lack of engage-ment with devolved politics served to sharpen the debate and provide a focal point for discussion. Wahl-Jorgensen (2007) points out that the editorial gatekeeping process governing newspaper letters pages — that most traditional of democratic forums — inevitably privileges some voices while silencing others. By contrast, Web forums avoid the problems associated with newspaper letters pages by lessening or removing edito-rial control and influence over the agenda. The result is an "unbounded" and immediate space for interaction, the "cultural terrain of cyberspace", which has the potential to capture the features of dialogue more robustly than the print medium and collapses spatial boundaries (Bohman 2004; Everard 2000).

Despite continuing access problems, Web forums represent the only possibility of a true "shared text" in Flintshire, because of the previously cited issues surrounding media access and choice. However, recent developments have seen the media fragment in unexpected ways. Notably, the BBC website serving the area has changed editorial direction. There has been a renewed focus on "local issues" and a move away from wider political discussion, even if that discussion is conducted specifically from the local perspective.

The wider debate on identity politics, however, has continued unabated, via a series of participatory, independent blogs, around the best of which there has developed a tendency among interested parties to coalesce and contribute. Lasica (2003) highlights the dynamism of this form. When journalism becomes a process, not a static product, audiences discard their traditional role as passive consumers of news and become empowered partners with a shared stake in the end result. Blogs, argues Lasica, offer one way to promote that kind of interactivity.

COMMUNITY AND DEMOCRACY

There is a reductive tendency to polarize professional and Web-based journalism. However, it can be argued that the mobilization of new spaces such as those created by BBC journalists contradicts this. The public are mobilized by professional journalists online in a way that extends the public sphere beyond the boundaries policed by the traditional news media.

This chapter analyses two discussions. The first, which received by far the most contributions and continued to attract comments for several months, was entitled: 'Identity Debate: Welsh or British?' It attracted 173 online responses and was later archived by the BBC as a debate that "people still want to view". The second discussion concerned the use by the Royal Mail (the UK's postal service) of "English" postcodes for north-east Wales. It attracted a further seventy responses.

Reese, Rutigliano, Hyun and Jeong (2007) argue that the impact of blogs of this kind is enhanced by anchoring their discussions to the stream of information, opinion and analysis produced by traditional media — which is something the BBC clearly has the potential to do, largely because its public service remit increasingly emphasises audience interactivity via Web technology. Indeed, this structure ultimately "has great potential in meeting the normative expectations we have of the public sphere" (Reese et al. 2007: 235–61). The formation of a two-tiered public sphere pre-dated the Web (Dahlgren and Sparks 1991). But it now allows for an alternative participatory media, with stronger links to the experiences of the everyday lives of its members, and has a growing capacity to transmit its version of political reality to the mainstream, dominant media. The vibrancy of the dialogue, anchored to traditional journalism, indicates obvious potential for political and cultural expression.

Online communities tend to attract assertive and engaged individuals, owing to the media's "opt-in" nature, and opinion groups form around certain ideological positions. While cynics might argue that the "weak link in conversational democracy is loud-mouths, bores and fanatics" (Peters 1999: 106), the debates on the Flintshire Web forums rarely exhibited such features. Rather, contributors were well informed, aware that the area presents a range of difficult and unresolved tensions. They made frequent references to Flintshire's ambiguous and mixed identity and often attempted to provide solutions to the "problem". Robinson (2006: 65–83) optimistically points out that, by letting readers and sources decide on and craft the frame of the blog (as the BBC editorial team did), their constructed version of truth will merge with the professional journalists' varied definition of meaning. And, with this, there comes a corresponding evolution in "the existing order of community and democracy".

Those opposed to the "imposition" of a Welsh identity on an anglicized area tended to approach the issues pragmatically, highlighting the historic and geographical reasons for the area's anglicized population. Contributors frequently referred to the fact that they felt industrial parts of Flintshire (known as "Deeside") to be a neglected corner of Wales, far removed from traditional Welsh identity "markers". This is arguably the key issue — and one that has received little academic attention. Williams (2005b) argues that most Welsh intellectuals have been reluctant to face up to the implications of Wales's "fuzzy borders", concerned only to advance the political and cultural claims of the Welsh nation. Some contributors to the forums were critical of what they felt were "post-devolution" moves towards a kind of civic bilingualism in the area, typically focusing on the use of "symbolic Welsh" in public buildings: "Few of the Deeside communities speak or understand any Welsh. To impose a phoney Welsh identity on these places and their people is ridiculous and offensive."

Another comment anecdotally confirmed the habit of "tuning out" of Welsh broadcasting:

> Since this is a BBC website, it is apt to mention that all one needs to do is to examine the direction of television aerials in the area to get a picture of people's self-identity. Almost all point towards Winter Hill [BBC North-West England] rather than Moel y Parc [BBC Wales], a fact ignored by the BBC!

One contributor went further still, rejecting the very notion of estuarine Flintshire (Deeside) as being part of Wales: "Just 30 years ago, addresses for Connah's Quay [a Flintshire town] all ended in 'Chester' as it was considered a natural satellite town of the city. Calling Deeside a 'Welsh town' can only be done with an enormous stretch of the imagination."

In the debates analysed there was, however, some evidence of an acceptance of "civic" definitions of nationality. The issue of alternative, inclusive definitions of civic Welsh identity has received some consideration in the wider literature, although not necessarily as it applies to intensively anglicized urban border areas. Williams (2005b) optimistically suggests that the preoccupation with cultural identity has gradually been relaxed from seeing identity in the singular (Welsh, English, Irish) to being prepared to view identity as hybridized (Anglo-Welsh, Chinese-Welsh) and has moved on to embrace concepts of multiple identity. Indeed, Williams argues for a post-national Wales as a means of constructing a national identity, embracing those who tend to be marginalized in the dominant national narrative. He observes that the diversity of the country tends to be ignored as it attempts to define itself post-devolution. Flintshire residents, inextricably linked to urban north-west England, are likely to be overlooked in such a narrative. Their characteristics do not fit those of the imagined nation.

A post-national Wales would, in Williams's deliberately utopian vision, be a partially autonomous Wales, where that autonomy has a liberating effect for all citizens — and not just those who subscribe to conventional views of what the characteristics of that nation-state should be. It would favour inclusivity and cultural diversity over homogeneity. One contributor wrote:

> Do I consider myself to be Welsh or British? Welsh first, British second. English? No, thank you. I was born in Lancashire, but have lived in Wales since five years of age. Wales provided my father with employment, provided me with an education, a job for life and a home. I learned Welsh as an adult and became aware of the rich vitality of Welsh culture. Britain is a multicultural cake and Wales provides the icing.

Another group of respondents felt Welsh but also felt under-represented by the Assembly, choosing to focus their comments on the divisions within Wales and the perceived disconnect between north and south. Indeed, the distance between Flintshire and Cardiff, both physical and cultural, was a common theme for contributors on all sides of the argument — reinforcing Thomas's observation (2005) that an element of distrust of devolution, related to geography, remains a feature of Welsh life.

> North east Wales is home. North west Wales is great to visit. I feel a great sense of North Walian identity but don't feel that we are seen as Welsh by the seats of government. The Welsh Blood Service only covers the south and that's how I feel Wales is perceived by the rest of Britain.

> It's a shame there is a huge divide between the north and south: totally different people.

> We are inextricably linked to Chester, more than we are to distant Cardiff.

Several contributors highlighted the strong economic and social links between estuarine Flintshire and Chester: there were frequent references to the fact that Chester's western suburbs straddle the Welsh border.

> The CH postcodes of Flintshire reflect the long standing connection between the estuarine communities and Chester. There is no equivalent traditional, socio-economic or historical link with Mold, Wrexham or Llangollen.

A small number of contributors attempted to crystallize the issues surrounding the "mixed identity markers" sent out by many Flintshire residents — suggesting that many do recognize and feel disadvantaged by their position, although none attempted to mobilize a specific Flintshire identity as a way of dealing with the issue, transcending both English and Welsh national identities.

> If people don't feel Welsh closer to the border then it is mostly because of the attitudes of a minority of Welsh-speakers who believe that to be Welsh you have to speak Welsh. Wales is a broad church and a diverse place. I will stand up to anyone who questions my right to be Welsh, even though I don't speak much of the language and live near to the border.

There were also significant contributions from those strongly supportive of devolution, the Welsh language and Welsh identity. Given the low levels of participation in Assembly politics, and the popular image of the county in the rest of Wales, this is

133

perhaps surprising — although the "opt-in" nature of Web debate encourages the most engaged to participate.

CONCLUSION: SETTING THE AGENDA?

Devolution continues to have profound implications for Flintshire. Its geographical location, socio-cultural history and consequent ambiguous identity put residents in an awkward position when responding to the new political paradigm and the resultant upsurge in both Welsh and English identity, even when it is merely symbolic. There is a significant democratic deficit in Flintshire. Residents are increasingly affected by the decisions of the Welsh Assembly, yet they show little sign of engagement. In Flintshire these issues are compounded by a weak sense of local identity that has implications in terms of broader civic engagement on a local level. If the ambiguities and complexities that render Welsh devolution problematic are to be addressed, the media has a fundamental role to play. If they are not addressed, those citizens marginalized by the national narrative will not embrace the project.

Yet, in Flintshire any idealistic public sphere role of the mainstream press is unavoidably compromised by wider economic realities, quite apart from the technological limitations of the conventional media struggling to frame an evolving political dialogue of this kind. Whether blogs or online forums have the potential to set a wider agenda is perhaps the key point in terms of the relationship with the conventional news media and mainstream politics. Drezner and Farrell (2004) argue that if a critical number of high-profile blogs raise a particular story, it can attract the interest of mainstream media outlets. If the mainstream media therefore address and frame critical issues, which political actors feel obliged to address, new media can perhaps construct focal points through which the mainstream media choose to operate.

A significant critical mass needs to develop around blogs of this kind if they are to succeed in attracting the attention of the mainstream media. The local BBC websites in the UK are in the process of achieving a dominant position within this market, backed by the corporation's resources, reputation and reach. Although this monolithic dominance runs counter to the original ethos of blogging, it does offer more potential to shape debate as Web journalism matures. The regulated nature of British public service broadcasting, exemplified by the BBC, is underpinned by a belief in the social impact of media and its facility for the creation of social bonds among the audience via shared experiences. The BBC has actively sought to increase social cohesion by facilitating community discussion; regional Web forums represent a technology-driven development of this long-established founding principle.

Online communities are not entirely virtual: they are grounded in social, cultural and geographical contexts. At their best, these public forums elevate the wider debate by drawing on a lived experience of marginality, or at least a perceived experience of it, to seek democratic solutions to the situation in which they find themselves. While it would be something of an exaggeration to describe this as a form of cyber-democracy, online forums are arguably the most effective platform for the narration of different experiences and perspectives, and effective examples are Europe-wide. In Italy, for example, a blog founded by Romanian migrants evolved into a functioning political party, which won the support of numerous other diasporic websites (Trandafoiu 2008). This is particularly pertinent in the current climate, when some of the early optimism associated with the public sphere potential of new media has faded. If the modern public sphere is one to which "the people" have unprecedented access, the political dimension of all our lives is thus being transformed by the co-evolution of the Internet and society (McNair 2000; Castells 2001). Web forums, particularly those with the public service reach of the BBC, are ideally placed to form a new platform for the discussion of post-devolution identity politics in the area. Such participatory platforms cannot represent a new public sphere until they become truly universal, but the vibrancy of the dialogue and the interactive and immediate nature of the media point to an interesting future for informed public debate about identity in areas, such as Flintshire, where the topic has political significance.

References

Anderson, B. (1983) *Imagined Communities*. London: Verso.

Anon. (1998) "Patriot Games", *The Economist*, 16 July.

Balsom, D. (1985) "The Three Wales Model". In J. Osmond (ed.), *The National Question Again: Welsh Political Identity in the 1980s*. Llandysul: Gomer.

Barlow, D., Mitchell, P., and O'Malley, T. (2005) *The Media in Wales: Voices of a Small Nation*. Cardiff: University of Wales Press.

Bohman, J. (2004) "Expanding Dialogue: The Internet, the Public Sphere and Prospects for Transnational Democracy". In N. Crossley, and J.M. Roberts (eds.), *After Habermas: New Perspectives On the Public Sphere*. Oxford: Blackwell, pp. 131–56.

Castells, M. (2001) *The Internet Galaxy*. Oxford: Oxford University Press.

Coupland, N., Bishop, H., and Garrett, P. (2006) "One Wales? Reassessing Diversity in Welsh Ethnolinguistic Identification", *Contemporary Wales*, 18 (1), pp. 1–27.

Dahlgren, P., and Sparks, C. (1991) *Communication and Citizenship: Journalism and the Public Sphere*. London: Routledge.

Drezner, D., and Farrell, H. (2004) "The Power and Politics of Blogs". Paper presented at the American Political Science Association Conference, July 2004. Retrieved from: http://www.utsc.utoronto.ca/~farrell/blogpaperfinal.pdf.

Everard, J. (2000) *Virtual States: The Internet and the Boundaries of the Nation-State*. London: Routledge.

Gill, F. (2005) "Public and Private: National Identities in a Scottish Borders Community", *Nations and Nationalism*, 11 (1), pp. 83–97.

Gilroy, P. (1987) *There Ain't No Black in the Union Jack: The Cultural Politics of Race and Nation*. London: Routledge.

Habermas, J. (1989) *The Structural Transformation of the Public Sphere*. Cambridge: Polity.

Horsman, M., and Marshall, A. (1995) *After the Nation-State: Citizens, Tribalism and the New World Disorder*. London: HarperCollins.

Jones, R. W., and Scully, R. (2004) "Devolution in Wales: What Does the Public Think?", *Economic and Social Research Council Research Programme on Devolution and Constitutional Change*, Briefing 7.

Kiely, R., McCrone, D., Bechhofer, F., and Stewart, R. (2000) "Debateable Land: National and

Local Identity in a Border Town", *Sociological Research Online*, 5 (2), paras 1.1–6.2. Retrieved from: http://www.socresonline.org.uk/5/2/kiely.html.

Lasica, J. (2003) "Blogs and Journalism Need Each Other", *Nieman Reports*, autumn 2003, pp. 70–75.

Mackay, H., and Powell, T. (1998) "Connecting Wales: The Internet and National Identity". In B. Loader (ed.), *Cyberspace Divide: Equality, Agency and Policy in the Information Society*. London: Routledge, pp. 203–16.

McCrone, D., Stewart, R., Kiely, R., and Bechhofer, F. (1998) "Who Are We? Problematising National Identity", *The Sociological Review*, 46 (4), pp. 629–52.

McCrone, D. (1997) "Unmasking Britannia: The Rise and Fall of British National Identity", *Nations and Nationalism*, 3 (4), pp. 579–96.

McNair, B. (2000) *Journalism and Democracy: An Evaluation of the Political Public Sphere*. London: Routledge.

Peters, J. (1999) "Public Journalism and Democratic Theory: Four Challenges". In T. Glasser (ed.), *The Idea of Public Journalism*. New York: Guilford Press, pp. 99–117.

Reese, S., Rutigliano, L., Hyun, K., and Jeong, J. (2007) "Mapping the Blogosphere: Professional and Citizen-Based Media in the Global News Arena", *Journalism*, 8 (3), pp. 235–61.

Richards, S. (2007) *Internet Inequality in Wales: Update 2006*. Cardiff: Welsh Consumer Council.

Robinson, S. (2006) "The Mission of the J-Blog: Recapturing Journalistic Authority Online", *Journalism*, 7 (1), pp. 65–83.

Smith, D. (1999) *Wales: A Question for History*. Bridgend: Seren.

Thomas, A. (2005) "Awaiting the Quiet Revolution". In J. Aaron, and C. Williams (eds.), *Postcolonial Wales*. Cardiff: University of Wales Press.

Thomas, J., Jewell, J., and Cushion, S. (2004) "Stirring Up Apathy? Political Disengagement and the Media in the 2003 Welsh Assembly Elections", *Journal of Public Affairs*, 4 (4), pp. 355–63.

Thomas, J. (2006) "The Regional and Local Media in Wales". In B. Franklin (ed.), *Local Journalism and Local Media*. London: Routledge.

Trandafoiu, R. (2008) "European Micro-Politics: Romanian Work Diasporas Online". Unpublished paper, Edge Hill University, Ormskirk.

Wahl-Jorgensen, K. (2007) *Journalists and the Public*. New Jersey: Hampton Press.

Williams, C. (2005a) "Borders and Identities in a Globalising Age". In D. Cunliffe, R. Thompson, and C. Williams (eds), *E-dentity: Borders and Identities in the Internet Age*. Pontypridd: University of Glamorgan.

Williams, C. (2005b) "Problematizing Wales". In J. Aaron, and C. Williams (eds), *Postcolonial Wales*. Cardiff: University of Wales Press.

9

Local Voices: The Regional Press and User-Generated Content

ANDY PRICE

Around the world many news producers are pursuing hyper-local (community level) online news strategies, increasing the depth and diversity of local news and information. This is based on the fact that social Web tools on news websites allow the simple creation of user-generated news, information and comment. This editorial strategy supports corporate objectives of generating greater revenue from digital platforms against a backdrop of falling newspaper sales and dramatically increasing online advertising revenue elsewhere.

Traditional media theory identifies the media as an essential part of modern democracy and considers that a healthy democracy requires informed and educated citizens, who need reliable sources of news and access to a range of opinions. This normative view is predicated on such news being free of political pressure, objective, impartial, accurate and full in its coverage (McQuail 2005). In a Habermasian sense this creates the environment for a functional public sphere, which in turn allows for the development of informed and deliberated public opinion, leading to effective democratic government.

The citizen requiring information and education on local matters does so on an equal basis with national or international provision (Aldridge 2007; Franklin 2006). As Aldridge says of local news: "The community of residences is, as Friedland so vividly expresses it in Habermasian terms, the seam between the system and the lifeworld." She also suggests that "ordinary citizens may not muse abstractly about the lifeworld but they demonstrate that news of the locality is valued both in their attitudes and by their behaviour" (2007: 161).

The growth of corporate digital news media, in the form of local newspaper websites, appears to be opening up new spaces for both increased information and opinion, often user-generated, from non-corporate sources (Allan 2006; Bruns 2005). This would suggest that a further development of the role of the media could be taking place, that citizens may be being better served in their civic needs and that the subsequent functioning of the public sphere and generation of public opinion could be being enhanced. This study will examine the developing emphasis on localness and hyper-local news in the regional press online in Britain and the corporate commercial strategies driving it. It will do so by examining in detail what could be considered the flagship Trinity Mirror Group website, GazetteLive!, based in Teesside in the north-east of England, in the development of greater of local content and hyper-local news. It will also consider implications for citizens from such changes. This is an exploratory study of one the new "hybrid spaces" identified by Deuze et al. (2007) that are seen to be developing between the top-down corporate world and bottom-up world of the reader/contributor. In particular, it will examine the pro-active policy of the publisher of GazetteLive!, the Gazette Media Company, in the creation of a blogging community.

The description of non-professional news production is still in flux, with labels such as "citizen journalism", "public journalism", "civic journalism" and "user-generated content" all being applied in one circumstance or another. This study considers the news contribution to the GazetteLive! website by users and its subsequent editorial strategy to be a form of participatory journalism (Deuze 2005; Bruns 2005; Nip 2006). Deuze et al. (2007) claim that "Participatory journalism is any kind of newswork in the hands of professionals and amateurs, of journalists and citizens, and of users and producers." And Bruns (2005) considers his collaborative model of gatewatching is also a form of participatory journalism. Nip also identifies that "participatory journalism represents an attempt by the news media to incorporate the change in the relationship between professional journalism and the people made inevitable by technological change" (Nip 2006: 230).

The analysis of participatory news sites offered by Deuze et al. (2007) uses the following evaluation criteria; "the degree of user participation, the role of the professional journalists, the motivation of suppliers and participants, conflicts between editors and users and the perceived success or failure of the project" (Deuze et al. 2007: 326). It is hoped that a close study of GazetteLive can further develop understanding of these issues. The writers also note that, while the concept of participatory journalism is still somewhat contested, there are also identifiable differences in approach to the subject in different news websites, particularly around the level of editorial control exercised and the contributory strategy being employed by the publisher. Bruns (2005) also identifies that there are examples of lesser or greater editorial involvement in this participatory approach, but that its collaborative nature is its essential characteristic.

Deuze et al. (2007) describe the two-tier development of participatory news as part of a convergence process "between top-down and bottom-up journalism" that is "driven by commercial pressures on existing news organizations". He describes a "third space" developing between the top-down, bottom-up interface and places this in the context of Jenkins's "convergence culture", where it is believed that media industries attempt to blur the boundaries between users and producers of content. This disruptive effect of digital technology certainly appears to be leading to a new collaborative approach towards news production. Nip makes an interesting point about the disruptive effects of technology when she says: "When the Internet offers the capability that could destroy the journalists' monopoly of news making, the news media are forced to respond by giving the news users a role in news making" (Nip 2006: 230). Deuze et al. believe that

> What is most important about these sites is that they provide clear and workable alternatives to the traditional separation of journalists, their sources, and the public. These are not utopian ideals (or, to some, dystopian horror scenarios). Instead, we have found practicable and (monetary, communal or intellectual) revenue-generating models for the production of news outside of or across the boundaries of the established news industry.

But they note that "Coping with the emergence of hybrid producer-user forms of newswork is easier for some than for others, and tends to clash with entrenched notions of professionalism, objectivity, and carefully cultivated arrogance regarding the competences (or talent) of 'the audience' to know what is good for them" (Deuze 2005).

In the case of this study, user-generated content is considered to be both participatory and created by citizens. Its form is the blog. Thurman (2008) identified a number of different modes of user-generated content production in his study of ten predominantly national UK new websites. As he says: "The survey . . . revealed seven major formats for participation: 'Polls', 'Have your says', 'Chat rooms', 'Q & As', 'Blogs with comments enabled', 'Pre-moderated message boards' and 'Post-moderated message boards'." (See also in this volume.) This study only examines the "Blogs with comments enabled" that are part of the *Gazette Communities* section of GazetteLive!, although the wider website does contain other user-generated content features such as "Post-moderated message boards", "Polls" and other "Blogs with comments enabled" produced by staff journalists.

Blood describes blogs as "frequently updated websites, with posts arranged in reverse chronological order, so new entries are at the top" and writes that the weblog is "arguably the first form native to the Web" (Blood 2006: 61). Bruns (2005) considers the blog to be a unique publishing phenomenon, one that has a variety of forms and content. He notes that variations in blog content are most important to their understanding. In particular, he suggests that in news production there are two major forms: comments on news or "annotation at a distance" and the reporting on original news. In terms of GazetteLive! the community micro-sites explored can be seen as a form of "group blogs" (Bruns 2005), where original reporting and comments on the reporting are active features.

The *UK Press Gazette*, the trade paper for the UK newspaper industry, has regularly covered the growing movement into online hyper-local news across the regional newspaper sector, with headlines such as "Northcliffe Rolls Out New Generation of Geocoded Websites", "Archant Website Geo-Tagging Will Provide Personalised Local News" and "Associated 'Hyperlocal' Sites To Broaden Regional Empire". These highlight the fact that similar hyper-local strategies to that of Trinity Mirror are being pursued by other regional newspaper groups.

GazetteLive! is the companion website to the *Evening Gazette*, the daily evening newspaper for Middlesbrough and the Tees Valley published by the Gazette Media Company, which is a wholly owned subsidiary of Trinity Mirror PLC — Britain's largest regional newspaper publisher (Newspaper Society 2008). The *Evening Gazette* has an audited circulation of 52,900 and a readership of 158,000 (*Evening Gazette* 2007). There are seventy journalists attached to Gazette Media Company titles in Middlesbrough.

The Tees Valley is a conurbation along the banks of the River Tees that includes Middlesbrough, Stockton, Redcar, Hartlepool and Darlington, with a combined population of over 650,000. This area of the north-east of England suffered severe economic hardship over the later part of the twentieth century with the decline in its traditional manufacturing industry.

Structured interviews were carried out in the spring and summer of 2008 with staff of Trinity Mirror directly responsible for the delivery of the hyper-local news strategy. These included Neil Benson, editorial director, Trinity Mirror Regional Newspapers, Darren Thwaites, editor, *Evening Gazette,* and Julie Martin, assistant editor (multimedia), *Evening Gazette*/GazetteLive!. These examined the corporate strategy behind a hyper-local approach, together with the local implementation and professional perceptions of the changing relationships of readers and publishers.

The regional press in Britain is an often overlooked element of the UK media industry and is rarely an object of study (Aldridge 2007). This is surprising, considering its relative commercial success and significant social role in people's lives. A critical approach to ideas such as local public spheres, local identity, community and social cohesion would be well advised to consider the role of both analogue and digital platforms in local and regional news provision.

According to Newspaper Society research, "Eighty-four per cent of adults, 40.5 million people, read a local newspaper, making it the most widely read medium in the country", and "as a source of information about the local area in which people live, local newspapers are three times more popular than the next medium BBC TV news". In terms of online publishing, regional newspapers have a significant presence in the UK. Once again the Newspaper Society says that: "There are more than 1,300 local newspapers and 1,100 associated websites in the UK". And it emphasizes that: "Local newspapers and their associated websites are 49 per cent more trusted and relied upon than the nearest medium, commercial TV" (Newspaper Society).

The regional press, although very profitable, is in long-term decline, with readership dropping year-on-year (Franklin 2006). Developing digital publishing is seen as one way to address this and most regional press groups have ambitious targets for digital revenue. As the 2007 Trinity Mirror PLC Annual Report and Accounts state, the group's aim is "to increase substantially digital revenues as a proportion of total group revenues". The Newspaper Society reported in 2007 that regional press advertising stood at £2.70 billion, with 16.15 percent of total UK advertising spend, but this represented a decline of 1.8 percent over the previous year (UK Media Advertising

Expenditure 2007). The Internet Advertising Bureau reports that in 2007 online advertising spend was £2.8 billion, or 15.3 percent of the market (IAB Online Adspend Factsheet 2007). Both of these are respectable achievements, with the caveat that the online spend had grown 38 percent year-on-year, compared with an industry average of 4.3 percent. While it would be simplistic to extrapolate this trend into the future, it is clear that the dramatic growth of the online advertising market should be of particular interest to new media producers, such as regional newspapers.

Over the last two years GazetteLive! has received national industry recognition for its innovation in online news media. It was named Website of the Year in the *UK Press Gazette* Regional Press Awards 2007. And in the UK Association of Online Publishers Awards 2007, it was made Online Community Website of the Year and Consumer Website of the Year, with the judges describing the Gazette site as "A cut above the other community sites — a great example of how to make local news real, with relevant interactivity". Other plaudits were that it "sets a new benchmark for local news sites — worked seamlessly, personal — we felt that we were part of that community" (AOP Awards winners 2007). Peter Preston, writing in *The Observer* in March 2008, praised the local news strategy of GazetteLive!, describing it as a return to the traditional news virtues of a truly local paper with a "digital twist", being part of a "Trinity Mirror experiment that clearly works" (Preston 2008).

This is part of a corporate "online content strategy" developed by the Trinity Mirror Group as part of an effort to grow online audiences, online advertising and overall digital revenue. It is one that identifies locally managed and implemented user-generated content as a key element.

GazetteLive! is in many ways a typical example of the genre, in its diversity of content, design, navigation and information architecture. The main emphasis of the home page is on breaking news with the dominant upper-left central area given over to a rotating main news feature. The home page also has a horizontal navigation bar below the masthead with links to subsections of the main areas of reader interest, News, Boro FC (the local football team), Sport and "Gazette Communities". The centre of the home page consists of an interactive map of Teesside with links to 20 smaller postcode-defined areas. Clicking on one of these 20 links opens independent community news pages or micro-sites of hyper-local news. These neighbourhood community areas are presently serviced by 300 community bloggers, who produce a daily digest of post-moderated local news and information.

The assistant editor (multimedia), Julie Martin, explained that by June 2008 GazetteLive! was attracting 200,000 unique users and enjoying more than 2.2 million page impressions per month, compared with 166,000 unique users in June 2007 and 88,000 in June 2006. In addition, the community micro-sites achieved 145,000 unique users and 350,000 page impressions per month in June 2008, compared with 40,000 unique users and 140,000 page impressions in June 2007, a growth rate of around 250 percent per annum in page impressions and 360 percent in unique users (Martin 2008).

A template publishing system is used throughout the site to maintain aesthetic consistency and user experience with banner ads, text and links appearing in the same place on each page visited. All the content of the newspaper is published to the site and is archived for long-term access, via a content management system. The site contains a wide range of multimedia, with more than twenty journalists having received video production training.

At present the Community News Team, responsible for the Gazette Community micro-sites, consists of a community editor, deputy community editor, a senior video journalist, a content developer and a community co-ordinator.

Although the Gazette Communities are published via a different technology (Movable Type 4.0) from the main site, the integration is largely seamless and the user would be unaware of this. On entering a community micro-site the geographical or local name of the area becomes very bold, while the logo of the site (GazetteLive!) reduces in size, privileging the identity of the neighbourhood over that of the website. This is a subtle action, but one that illustrates, perhaps, the changing relationship between the publisher, the brand and the reader/contributor.

The Gazette Media Company describes GazetteLive! micro-sites as "interactive and accessible with the aim of turning readers into content providers through the use of blogging, video footage and photographs". This appears to be a genuine invitation to participate in news production. The micro-sites are also described as "a one stop shop for online information and news", an indication perhaps of the publisher's goal to be a significant provider of information as well as news (Gazettelive.co.uk 2007).

The editor, Darren Thwaites, outlined the economic case for online hyper-local news: "I just see this [hyper-local journalism] as an addition, an extra benefit and added value, added depth that it is difficult to reach cost-effectively in newspapers because of print costs." He adds that "doing it online allows us to do it more cost-effectively than investing in an awful lot of pagination" (Thwaites 2008). It is clear that the analogue-based business models of the past limited the scope for publishers in terms of what they were able to publish effectively to diverse audiences. The move to digital does to a degree challenge this situation editorially, but there is still the matter of profitably generating income from such online activities.

Thwaites (2008) explained the journalistic rationale behind the hyper-local sites:

People are very interested in what happens very close to where they live, that has a direct impact in their lives and its what we've always known with regional newspapers. Hyper-local takes it to the next level; small-scale news, news that would not be interesting outside the immediate environment — the news that is important to you because it affects your daily life.

He observed that this had traditionally been a challenge to editors and journalists alike with the ability "to really get in deep to every community being difficult". This again reflects the limitations of the analogue print industry, where the prevailing economies of scale precluded much journalism that would be considered "un-news worthy" (too parochial) and uneconomical to print.

Martin explained how the micro-sites began after a successful experiment that involved zoning house price information by postcode on the website in December 2006. To stimulate blogging and user-generated content, the Community News Team originally contacted likely contributors to solicit their support directly. She described it thus: "We used a mix of traditional methods and digital methods to attract them — we scoured directories, reporters' contacts books, and the Internet. We then sent out mail shots, email shots, contacted them by phone, and posted comments on their websites where applicable" (Martin 2008). By July 2008 the site had 300 bloggers, which they aim to turn into a 1,000.

The newspaper already had a successful print product, *Gazette People*, which was distributed with the Saturday edition with a significant amount of community-generated content. This perhaps indicates how the development of user-generated content could be seen as a natural development from the traditional print culture, rather than being the more revolutionary process that it is sometimes perceived as.

She explained that, editorially, "the sites allow GMC to drill down into our core communities like never before, providing lots of opportunity for reader interaction, encouraging community contributions, and sparking healthy debate . . . The sites are in line with the Trinity Mirror Group's editorial strategy — to create fully multi-media newsrooms able to grow audiences and drive revenue." She estimated that approximately seventy news items a day are presently posted to the micro-sites. These consist of "the contents of the *Evening Gazette* . . . then there are nibs, bloggers' entries, reader contributions which are sent by e-mail or post, contributions from [the] *Herald & Post*, and copy lifted from the *Times* series". The combination is of 40 percent pre-purposed and 60 percent original material, with a goal of 80 percent user-generated content. In terms of a distinction between material that was on the micro-sites and not in the newspaper, she explained that "The sites contain all kinds of stories, many of which would traditionally be off the news desk radar", but that "a great story will always be a great story, news values remain the same" (Martin 2008).

With regard to a traditional news list or agenda-setting, she identified an interesting distinction between the newspaper and the micro-sites in that "the sites don't have to produce a news list, there's no splash or page three lead. The sites are 'blogs' and, as such, the latest entry will be at the top of the page." But she added that "The only time we interfere with this running order is when there's a major news story on a particular postcode area, and then we manipulate the administration page to keep the entry at the top of the page until much later that day" (Martin 2008).

Software allows users to upload material themselves and for it to then be post-moderated by the Reader Content Team. Martin said that there had been few problems with this post-moderation and that interestingly "on the whole people use their common sense, they know that it's going to be read by the public and I think they are guided by the fact that it is on an *Evening Gazette* website, it is not something that they are doing personally". She added: "I think there is still a huge community feel on it [the website], but people tend to respect the fact that they are writing on a site that is owned by a newspaper" (Martin 2008).

This suggests that bloggers in this particular environment understand different forms of blogging and behave in different ways depending on whether they are "personal" or more institutional. Martin also pointed out that there were certain characteristics of the contributors: "people tend to be writing about subjects close to their

143

hearts, and groups that they are involved in . . . so there doesn't tend to be anything too contentious". She believes that, unlike the more widely recognized "stream of consciousness" blogs that populate the blogosphere, the contributors to the GazetteLive micro sites "publish when they have got something they want to say, rather than it be in a constant conversation". She did, however, describe an example of how one blog on a particular community micro-site about a proposal to open a takeaway restaurant, generated an intense online discussion between proponents and objectors to the proposal, to the point where the restaurant owner entered the debate to explain his struggle to develop a viable business in the area. It is hard to envisage how the traditional media could have covered an issue of such local interest in such depth and offered the opportunity for subsequent debate and discussion.

The editor agreed that there were "different types of user-generated content on the community sites" and that in terms of the style of a more institutional approach he perceived some bloggers were "behaving more like community correspondents", suggesting that "there is still a link to the traditional style of journalism" (Thwaites 2008).

Thwaites also observed that "by giving direct publishing access to community bloggers without any premoderation" the traditional institutional gatekeeping role had been effectively abolished in a world of post-moderated content. However, it would appear that self-moderation is at work on the site and that the present bloggers are consciously or unconsciously performing a "role" as proto-journalists in terms of the institutional style of their contributions. Peter Preston, in his *Observer* article, interestingly describes this as a form of "unmediated trust". The GazetteLive! model of post-moderation blogging appears very similar to Brun's model of gate-watching, where the editorial function is more of that of a facilitator than a traditional gatekeeper (Bruns 2005). Martin pointed out that "news values" equally seem to be consistent with the newspapers existing agenda, and it may be the case that the contributors see their role as matching or modelling what they see as existing editorial values, behaviours and norms. She believes that, owing to other online communities being based on communities of interested groupings — for example, those of school, work, pastimes and so on — the GazetteLive! micro-sites fulfil a unique function in terms of their geographical nature (Martin 2008).

Martin also emphasized the changing impact on professional journalistic practice:

I think that anybody who is involved in the industry will hold their hands up and say it's a change in mind-set right across the industry and I think the biggest thing is for people to grasp that it is about collaboration and conversation. You know, the Web 2.0: that's the whole ethos behind it. So to come from a print background, a newspaper print background, and grasp all the opportunities is going to take time. (Martin 2008)

She also added: "I think it's challenging, but I think it is hugely exciting, I think that it is the most exciting time in journalism in the last 100 years" (Martin 2008).

TRINITY MIRROR'S CHANGED ONLINE STRATEGY

It might be reasonable to conclude at this point that the strategy of progressively developing greater "localness" in news and delivering finer-grained more relevant content has been an organic process. However, this is not the case, and the present emphasis in regional digital media such as the *Evening Gazette* is in fact a return to a "localness" somewhat downplayed in Trinity Mirror's earlier online strategies.

Neil Benson explained that in 1997 "there was a realization that the Internet was going to be a mass medium, and that we [Trinity Mirror] needed to be a part of it". The strategy then was to develop small new media teams in individual newspapers and one of "saying 'localness is what we've got let's try and develop that'". However, this decentralized approach had a particular consequence in that "there was a big disconnection between the editorial department that produced the newspaper and this Internet thing" (Benson 2008).

The second major phase of the Trinity Mirror Group's strategy was developed from around 1999 onwards, with the creation of a network of IC (i-see) branded sites across each newspaper circulation area. Benson said: "We [Trinity Mirror Group] were following a national portal strategy, and I think that localness was seen as very much secondary." He added that the IC portal "became even more removed from the editorial departments". Local Trinity Mirror Group websites were redesigned to a standardized layout and structure and renamed such things as ICTeesside, ICNewcastle, ICLiverpool. This showed some relationship to a geographical community, but it did so by removing the relationship with the newspaper. As Benson pointed out, the debate over the use of analogue brands in digital environments raged within editorial and management teams.

In 2000, as result of an abandonment of a national portal strategy, regional management were given back responsibilities for their local IC website. Benson (2008) felt that in editorial terms "again the newsroom was probably further away at this point . . . than it ever had been". By 2006, however, things had changed again, when Trinity Mirror started to ask questions about developing their online brands. So what was asked was "what have we got that's unique in our market? And what we've got which is unique is more journalists than anyone else . . . We're certainly seen as trusted." This had implications for local editorial control, Benson says:

> So that really pushed my thinking . . . "let's get some companion sites up" because that way you give responsibility for them to the editors overtly. You know: "You're in charge of it, you and your team have got to populate it and engage them". It was a brand that they were responsible for in print . . . but that was the trigger that got the newsrooms engaged, involved and creating content. At that point, we started to focus much more on original Web content. (Benson 2008)

Reflecting on the previous portal policy, it is clear that the overt change in responsibility to local editors and managers is intimately linked to engaging the newsrooms in the digital platforms. In 2007 Benson and the senior Trinity Mirror Group editors agreed a set of guidelines for the strategic development of online content. The goal was to be able to

> move away from the previous heavy dependence on print-originated content, to focus much more strongly on unique Web content and interactivity. The key to success for our editors and senior journalists [was] to use their skills and judgement to select the most appropriate ways to develop particular stories, and then to employ the appropriate medium for delivery. (Benson 2008)

This was a clear indication of the enhanced and empowered role of local editors in the control and management of their digital platforms. Benson also stressed the significance of this approach, based, as it was, on greater knowledge and understanding of local digital audiences by the centre and titles alike. The new local companion sites produced were clearly related to their print partners and to their community and had a newfound emphasis on unique hyper-local content.

With regard to this, GazetteLive! is "one of our most innovative sites", Benson suggested. He identified its specific hyper-local strategy as one that was initiated and developed locally, but which fits within the corporate strategy of greater local content. He says of the hyper-local strategy:

> That came from the editor locally . . . we saw that it was a very good strategic fit with what we wanted to try and do, we wanted to be more and more local. The approach is that we'll layer the market, so the newspaper will get to a group of people, GazetteLive! will get to another group of people — hyper-local gets to this sort of grassroots level, which sort of burrows into a much more micro level of content than any kind of newspaper or newsletter can do. (Benson 2008)

He also made an interesting point about the thinking of major news organizations: "What's kind of interesting is that the more globalized we become, the more research shows that people want to have a sense of belonging, it may be geographic or it may be communities of interest" (Benson 2008).

In terms of the corporate strategy for an initiative such as hyper-local news and community blogging, issues such as transferability and scalability matter. For example, can the model developed on Teesside be easily replicated elsewhere? Benson identified the need for online newspaper websites to be successful by developing specific characteristics, tailoring them to the socio-economic character of their locality (Benson 2008). Julie Martin also speculated on the related problems of replicating the Teesside model in other, larger urban areas owing to the much greater number of neighbourhoods and the need to support each one individually (Martin 2008). This suggests that, while the basic currency of hyper-local news is a powerful device, its deployment (along with other digital features) will have to be undertaken carefully, working with the local cultural landscape. There are indications elsewhere — for example the "locavore" movement (Locavores 2007) — that other factors such as environmental concerns are driving a cultural recognition for the need to consume goods and services as locally as possible.

This not only further embeds the notion of localness but further generates demand for local information and news.

It appears that with GazetteLive!, Trinity Mirror Group's hyper-local news strategy has successfully increased citizen participation in both the creation of news and the consumption of that news, something that in itself would seem a positive democratizing development. However, culturally, the behaviour of these participatory journalists appears at present to being undertaken within existing news production conventions, which suggests that in terms of news values and diversity the full democratic potential is not perhaps yet being realized. Equally, the deliberative potential of the medium seems to be being exploited in only a limited way. However, with such a large and growing audience for the community sites, it can be assumed that citizens reading this material are reflecting on this user-generated content in some way and certainly feel a need for it, even if they are not yet driven to participate in writing.

In the interviews with editorial staff it was clear that their enthusiasm for this process was real and that they felt a genuine connection with the developing blogging community. Bruns (2005) contends that publishers that engage in a collaborative approach to newsgathering and publishing will ultimately provide more effective products than those that do not, provided that enough effort has gone into the process. The strategy employed by the Gazette Media Company and GazetteLive! appears to support this point, as it is evidently a significant part of newsroom practice and editorial policy. If meaningful revenue can be generated from this "third space", it would suggest that a sustainable participatory news model is possible that satisfies (to some extent) both commercial and democratic needs.

CONCLUSION

As mentioned earlier, Deuze et al. (2007) articulated an evaluation framework around such ideas as "the degree of participation of users, the role of the professional journalists, the motivation of the various parties, the conflicts between editors and users and the perceived success or failure of the project". This has proved very useful as an approach. For example, in the case of GazetteLive! there has been an observable change in the roles of journalistic staff both in their professional practice and editorial responsibilities.

The degree of user participation is similarly helpful but does have some limitations. The volume and variety of user-generated content being added to a site is reasonably easy to determine. Yet the inter-relationship between the users and journalists/editors is harder to discern, if the degree of participation is taken to mean the whole range of interactions possible through this process, not simply the posting of comments. For example, it was clear talking to the editorial team that there was, for example, an ongoing dialogue with users outside the blogs and posts that constituted another important dimension in their participation.

Equally, conflicts are unlikely to occur in public, for professional reasons and may be hard to observe — except when they do indeed reach a wider audience. It may be worthwhile considering editorial policy and the organizational approach to user-generated content, to see what is being encouraged and discouraged to understand possible areas of tension. Similarly, motivation is a vital component of context and analysis, but beyond the simple division of the commercial imperative/social benefit there is probably a wide range of important personal dimensions to this that are worth exploring further, both in terms of users and the editorial staff themselves.

The issue of success or failure is in some ways harder and easier to consider. For the publisher revenue targets are to be met and, if they are, that signals a commercial success – with the alternative being failure. However, from a broader social or narrower personal perspective, this is more difficult. The establishment of a healthy local public sphere of diverse voices and opinions would be seen by many as a success, but how do we really measure or evaluate that? And, from a personal point of view, the engagement, the empowerment, the emotional and psychological effects from this process are anticipated but, once again, difficult to determine.

References

Aldridge, M. (2007) *Understanding the Local Media*. New York: McGraw Hill.

Allan, S. (2006) *Online News*. Maidenhead: Open University Press.

AOP Awards Winners 2007 (2007) "Association of Online Publishers". Retrieved 8 June 2008 from: http://www.ukaop.org.uk/cgi-bin/go.pl/news/article.html?uid=1633.

Anon. (2006) "Associated 'Hyperlocal' Sites to Broaden Regional Empire", *Press Gazette*. Retrieved 1 February 2008 from: http://www.pressgazette.co.uk/story.asp?sectioncode=1&storycode=35180.

Anon. (2008) "Top 20 Regional Press Publishers (circulation)", *Newspaper Society*. Retrieved June 8 2008 from: http://www.newspapersoc.org.uk/Default.aspx?page=14.

Blood, R. (2006) "Weblogs and Journalism: Do they Connect?", *Nieman Reports*, Autumn 2006, pp. 61–3.

Bruns, A. (2005) *Gatewatching: Collaborative Online News Production*. New York: Peter Lang.

Deuze, M. (2005) "Towards Professional Participatory Storytelling in Journalism and Advertising", *First Monday*. Retrieved 8 January 2008 from: http://www.uic.edu/htbin/cgiwrap/bin/ojs/index.php/fm/view/186.

Deuze, M., Bruns, A., and Neuberger, C. (2007) "Preparing for an Age of Particpatory News", *Journalism Practice*, 1 (3), pp. 322–38.

Evening Gazette (2007) Retrieved 1 July 2008 from: http://www.gazettemedia.co.uk/downloads/MGCcore-July-Dec2007.pdf.

Franklin, B. (2006) *Local Journalism and Local Media*. London: Routledge.

Gazettelive.co.uk. (2007) Retrieved 1 July 2008 from: http://www.gazettemedia.co.uk/downloads/GMC%20Digital.ppt.

IAB Online Adspend Factsheet (2007) "Internet Advertising Bureau". Retrieved 3 July 2008 from: http://www.iabik.net/en/iabknolwedgebankadspend.html.

Jenkins, H. (2006) *Convergence Culture*. New York: New York University Press.

Locavores (2007) "The Locavores: Jessica Prentice, Sage Van Wing, Dede Sampson & Jennifer Maiser". Retrieved 6 July 2008 from: http://locavores.com/.

McQuail, D. (2005) *McQuail's Mass Communications Theory*. 5th edn. London: Sage.

Newspaper Society (2007) *UK Media Advertising Expenditure*. Retrieved 23 June 2008 from: http://www.newspapersoc.org. uk/Default.aspx?page=10.

Nip, Y. M. (2006) "Exploring the Second Phase of Public Journalism", *Journalism Studies*, 7 (2), pp. 212–36.

Preston, P. (2008) "According to Local Sources, This Could be a Real Winner", *The Observer*, 30 March. Retrieved 12 June 2008 from: http://www.guardian.co.uk/media/2008/mar/30/pressandpublishing.television.

Stabe, M. (2007) "Archant Website Geo-Tagging Will Provide Personalised Local News", *Press Gazette*, 11 May. Retrieved 1 February 2008 from: http://www.pressgazette.co.uk/story.asp?sectioncode=1&storycode=37547.

Stabe, M. (2008) "Northcliffe Rolls Out New Generation of Geocoded Websites", *Press Gazette*, 17 June. Retrieved 1 July 2008 from: http://www.pressgazette.co.uk/story.asp?sectioncode=1&storycode=41438.

Thurman, N. (2008) "Forums for Citizen Journalists? Adoption of User Generated Content Initiatives by Online News Media", *New Media and Society*, 10 (February), pp. 139–57.

⦃ CHAPTER ⦄
10

Changing Auntie: A Case Study in Managing and Regulating User-Generated News Content at the BBC

JANET JONES

There is an uneasy relationship between corporate news providers such as the BBC and the adoption of participatory journalism or "bottom-up" news sourcing routines. This chapter seeks to analyse the speeches of senior BBC news executives alongside official documents and examples of the BBC's user-generated news output (2007, 2008) in order to understand better how the corporation is learning to manage the increased flow of contributions from its publics. This is written in the light of the BBC's recent public pronouncements, which pay considerable attention to creating a second tranche of service dedicated to user-generated content (UGC).

By inviting viewers and listeners into the process by which they produce news, broadcasters can open a new dialogue with the potential to enhance relations between a broadcaster and its public as well as between citizens themselves. Yet, despite the Internet's potential to re-invent news production along more democratic lines, news outlets such as the BBC are more comfortable and accomplished engaging in "crowd-mining" and "crowdsourcing" newsgathering activities, while nervous of any move towards more open-source practices that might impinge on professional standards. The former phenomena include corporate, top-down, aggressive harvesting of ideas, product innovations and product feedback from users, as part of a gift economy. The latter open-source practice implies an attempt to produce news in an egalitarian and participatory manner where communication is often horizontal and there are few barriers to entry.

The BBC is beginning to make its own distinctions. It has dropped its wholesale references to citizen journalism and now prefers to use "public participation journalism". This is in acknowledgement that, in reality, it is engaging in a very different form of newsgathering exercise — that of crowdsourcing.

This chapter concludes that, in order for the BBC to fulfil its remit as a public service provider, able to host a diversity of voices, it needs to adopt more flexible news production hierarchies and adaptable work flows to counteract the well-established normative journalistic work routines common to twentieth-century practice. This will involve challenging dominant occupational norms and reconciling its top-down culture with the use of disruptive interactive technologies and finding a new balance between quality standards and open civic engagement.

Coleman talks of a newly revitalized BBC as central to hosting an "online civic commons" that would inspire and facilitate public participation in government (Coleman 2005). The corporation's survival may well depend on its success in engaging diverse publics, bringing them together through the latent power of new media and providing the legitimacy it needs to continue its present funding regime past its 2016 Charter review.[1]

A study in 2008 of how the British news media are struggling with user-generated content concluded that "UK newspaper websites are adopting a traditional gatekeeping role towards UGC" and that editors are undergoing an uncomfortable transition in integrating user media (Hermida and Thurman 2008: 1). It cites one major reason as the "aggressive–defensive culture" common to the news industry (Reader Institute Culture Report 2000). This works well when the pace of technological change is slow but becomes a barrier to change when faced with "surging competition and revolutionary advances in technology" (Hermida and Thurman 2008: 6).

The BBC is one of the most recognizable and revered broadcasting brands internationally, and the need to protect it from any damage that might result from user-generated content is an important public relations issue. Traditionally, journalists and editors are trained to gather and filter. This approach affords the maximum control. Yet there is an irreconcilable contradiction between the working model of broadcast news and true interactivity. The balance of power cannot strictly shift from the centre to the periphery because the producer cannot relinquish control. In a commercial environment interactivity is inevitably grafted on to commercial media products.

This chapter suggests that, in its attempt to embrace participatory journalism, the BBC has created more of a democratic façade around its national news programming that falls short of the ideals underpinning the Internet as civic commons, although new experiments at the very local level may hold the key to shifting the locus of control.

CULTURAL HISTORY

The Internet has been hailed as the ultimate democratic medium. Yet Carey (2005: 443) argues that amid the promise of the Internet, users and critics fail to see how changes in systems of production and dissemination can just as easily create new borders as break down old ones. Technology in and of itself, he affirms, is not necessarily liberating. Certainly the social structures that surround news production do not seem to be changing as fast as the new technologies used in the production process.

Technology may not always be liberating, but it often gives that illusion. At its best, technology is neutral, neither empowering nor disempowering. All technology fundamentally derives its use value from the collective actions of its gatekeepers. Yet, as each new medium takes hold, there remains a promise of technological transcendence — the dawn of a new, empowered communications environment.

At its onset, radio was heralded as an empowering medium, a community medium, but as it began to take hold early last century, it soon became clear that this new communications channel was in fact disempowering. The main reason was down to basic economics. Airwaves were a scarce resource, often controlled by governments or proxies to government such as the BBC, thereby creating an elite group of gatekeepers.

Arguably, radio was a technological change that militated against an open market for ideas and universal access, whereas its predecessor, publishing, was far more liberating. When Caxton invented the printing press, in theory, all citizens had a voice, where before they had none. You didn't need one central public service provider to control and filter the free exchange of views. As the American Oliver Holmes declared, "the best test of truth is the power of the thought to get itself accepted in the competition of the market" (cited in Curran 2001: 225).

By the turn of the twenty-first century it cost approximately £20 million to establish a new national broadsheet (Curran 2002: 226), disqualifying all but a wealthy minority from having a voice. Yet with the digital age came interactive platforms ideal for harnessing public participation and encouraging robust debate. Suddenly there were few barriers to entry, and once again it was cheap to publish and "groups of ordinary people could set up their trestle-table, so to speak, in the main market place of ideas" (Curran 2002: 226). At the outset broadcasting was a product supplied by the state and, once the state got its hands on it, it was very reluctant to let it go. In most democracies the state was less able to control what went on the printing press or how it was distributed. The fact you had one newspaper didn't prevent the publication of others. Even with government censorship and repression of printed material it was not difficult for rogue publishers to operate clandestine presses, or to smuggle clandestine tracts into a country. Airwaves are more difficult for individuals to control and, although the UK experienced a period where pirate radio came into its own in the 1960s, it made very little impact. Therefore open-publishing and broadcasting have never enjoyed a rich tradition in Britain or other countries.

This has allowed the BBC to become habituated to a role where it has a loud voice in the production and dissemination of broadcasting goods in British society. It has, some say, become a little arrogant, and it was no coincidence that it earned the nickname "Auntie Beeb" — describing a matronly, well-intentioned but paternalistic body.

Yet over the last two decades technology has done a lot to individualize the broadcasting market-place and empower the individual. It is not, as yet, evident how this new era of empowerment translates into any meaningful change in working practices. The BBC announced in November 2007 that it was reorganizing BBC News to put the Web and user-generated content "close to the middle of the operation" (Horrocks 2007,

2008). This was hailed as part of a cultural, structural and physical transformation that would put the audience at the centre of BBC activity.

Like other media brands internationally, the BBC wanted to position itself to take advantage of what new technology has to offer. Happily for the BBC, it had been allowed to invest heavily in interactive infrastructure against the grain in the early 1990s. These activities were rooted in the institutional and programme policy renewals in the late 1980s and early 1990s spearheaded by John Birt, Director-General from 1992 to 2000. On his departure in 2000, Birt had developed Europe's most popular Internet site and the BBC had an excellent reputation in the area of online journalism.

"Bottom-Up" Corporate News

Many researchers have begun to explore the attitudes of traditional news media practitioners toward technologies that enable a two-way dialogue with audiences. At the outset the attitudes of reporters and editors tended to mix enthusiasm for the new media's potential with fear of, and resistance to, the challenges to journalistic traditions (Singer 1998; Williams 1998). Williams (1998: 31) states that the typical responses to new media include uneasiness and lamentation about traditional demarcations, such as "the firewall between advertising and news, the distinction between news and entertainment, and the separation of objectivity and opinion" (Williams 1998: 31).

Recent studies have shown that, despite the Web's potential for promoting dialogue between user and producer, use of this technique has been limited and the preservation of normative journalistic functions has largely prevailed (Quinn and Trench 2002; Matheson 2004; Gillmor 2004: 112; Lasica 2002).

Yet, the BBC no longer sees bottom-up news sourcing as a marginal activity relegated to alternative online news sites but has placed it at the heart of its *Creative Future's Strategy* (BBC 2006). This celebrates "a new editorial blueprint designed to deliver more value to audiences over the next six years and turn the BBC's public purposes laid out in the recent Government White Paper into quality content for the on-demand world". It is what Peter Horrocks (then head of BBC Television News) described as an "anti-elitist revolution", leaving behind an age when broadcasters told the public what to think and embracing the chance to host citizens' debate (2006).

Although the BBC may be applauded for stimulating information exchange and debate within an increasingly sterile public sphere, questions remain about how significant these pioneering efforts to change newsroom culture through audience contributions may be. The counter-argument is that BBC journalists are simply squeezing established routines and values into the new spaces opened up by electronic media, rather than introducing any fundamental shift in practices.

Horrocks (2006) states that part of the rationale for introducing aggressive user-generated content routines within the corporation can be traced to declining audiences for traditional news output, especially in the 16–34 age group. BBC News lost 2.5

million young adults to mainstream news over the last five years. The BBC projects that, unless something radical is engineered, its local and national journalism on all platforms (TV, radio and online) may only reach two-thirds of the population in five years time.

Horrocks (2006) terms this emotively the "lost audience" and argues that failing to entice these citizens back to the fold of public service broadcasting (PSB) would lead to a "democratic deficit for a disengaged and disenfranchised part of society". His argument centres on the desirability of "mass" rather than "niche" news provision. There has been a phenomenal growth in the use of tailored news services over the last five years that serve various minority interest groups and cater for highly specialized views and tastes. There is overarching concern that reliance on "niche" news prevents citizens from regularly coming across ideas that disagree with their personal worldviews. The decline of mass PSB news would thus impoverish and narrow the "range of information that society would hold in common" and "more people would only come across views that reinforced rather than challenged their prejudices".

This provides a strong and convincing reason to continue to support mass-reach public service news, and the hope is that audience engagement through user-generated content will reclaim those lost to public service news and reinvigorate a valuable part of the public sphere. In theory, interactivity should strengthen the bonds between broadcaster and audience, so this form of news sourcing has the duel benefit of both enriching the news agenda and attracting loyal listeners.

In its *Creative Futures Strategy Report* (2006) the BBC acknowledges the need to forge innovative relationships between producers, texts and audiences that take advantage of new technology to realize its stated "public value" goals of building a new civic commons and an active and informed citizenship (Thompson 2004). The report identifies opportunities and challenges created by the disruptive wave of digital technologies and talks of "seismic shifts in public expectations, lifestyle and behaviours". It stresses that unidirectional, linear discourses are not interesting for younger licence payers (those whom the BBC must attract to survive). The under-35s, it suggests, prefer to interact, to change and add content or ideas.

THE BBC'S QUANDARY

In his book *The Third Wave* Toffler describes the notion of a "prosumer" (producer-consumer) where the consumer moves up the value chain and becomes a producer helping to fashion the product he will ultimately buy (Toffler 1980). Picone prefers to use the word "produser" (producer-user) to describe the activities that surround online citizen journalism activity. As the production of news becomes part of the consumption of news, the user's role is thus re-conceptualized. "He does not merely consume news, but also shares it, rates it, searches it and produces it" (Picone 2007: 104). This inevitably upsets the power base and editorial decision base of any traditionally run news organization. Each must decide to what extent it wants to leverage audience participation and how committed it is to embracing audiences as "prod-users", integrating audiences into the production process — into the very formation of news.

The BBC, Britain's largest and most significant public service broadcaster, is in a quandary, illustrated vividly in a recent speech by its head of Multimedia News, Peter Horrocks, entitled *The Value of Citizen Journalism* (Horrocks 2008).

Underpinning Horrocks's vision for the BBC is a profound ambivalence towards participatory journalism. His remonstrations suggested that the organization is uncomfortable with fully embracing audiences as producers of news.

> I want to argue that the somewhat messianic and starry-eyed way in which public participation journalism is argued for needs some very careful consideration . . . We cannot just take the views that we receive via emails and texts and let them dictate our agenda. Nor should they give us a slant around which we should orient our take on a story.

There were many excellent reasons given for this discomfort, including issues of quality, impartiality, cyber-bullying, lobbying and professionalism. Yet the hype that surrounded the introduction of user-generated content at BBC News has grown exponentially over a very short period of time, raising expectations within the BBC's stakeholder group that a serious paradigm shift is under way that may genuinely dissolve boundaries between those that make the news and those that consume it.

The organization is wrestling with two very different models of news production that compete irreconcilably: top-down control versus bottom-up influence. It needs to be seen to promote civic interaction to justify the continuation of its licence fee. But evidence from Horrocks's speech suggests that the BBC is finding it increasingly difficult to balance these two competing ideals.

Horrocks relayed a powerful dilemma his news team faced just after Pakistan's former prime minister, Benazir Bhutto, was assassinated in December 2007. The newsroom quickly launched a Have Your Say forum, which is a facility for users to post and recommend comments. They were deluged by reactionary posts condemning the Islamic religion:

> That's the way politics works with The Religion of Peace.

> Religion of Peace strikes again.

> Is this another example of the wonderful tolerance for which, or so we are constantly being told, Islam is famous? It's time the rest of the world stopped making excuses for this barbaric, dark ages way of life and completely condemned the casual brutality continually perpetrated by so many of the religion's supporters. (Horrocks 2008)

As a consequence, the nervous BBC considered turning off the comment recommendation facility on the BBC News website. Horrocks (2008) said:

> It was only a fleeting suggestion, but that we could consider, however briefly, freezing this

important part of BBC News' service tells you something about the power and the potential danger of the new intensity of the interaction between the contributing public, journalists and audiences. And it raises the question of how much attention and resource news organisations should devote to this rapidly burgeoning aspect of our journalism. The vehemence and the unanimity of these opinions against the Muslim religion were striking. So why did we briefly consider freezing this forum? A small part of our thinking was that in the context of the death of a significant international figure, who was herself Muslim, we thought that the weight of remarks could be offensive to some users of the BBC News website. Might some readers believe that such views as "most recommended" represented an editorial line by BBC News? I suspect not, but there was at least that danger. But our real question concerned the editorial value of the comments and how far they should influence our coverage more widely. And the answers to that were: very little and hardly at all.

This shows the tension between a genuine desire to harness audience views and contributions and the need to control them. The message was not one that was particularly palatable for a state broadcaster to relay and yet it could not cut off the flow of feedback without being accused of censorship. The BBC has charged itself with growing and nurturing the community it serves, but Horrocks implies that it is afraid to open its gates too widely and allow disparate voices to be heard. Instead, the normative functions of the BBC newsroom struggle to reassert themselves against this unwelcome tide of "bilious vitriol" from its public.

User-generated content promises to challenge and enrich the way that news is produced. Boundaries between people, producers and text in news production that have traditionally been closed are starting to open, and organizations such as the BBC have actively created and promoted new opportunities for changing and realigning these boundaries. The assumption is, of course, that audiences would welcome this change. These representative public posts, following the online publication of Horrocks's speech, tell a different story. They were almost unanimous in wanting the BBC to abandon attempts to democratize the newsroom.

I think that the inclusion of such a high proportion of user-generated content and especially comment is a mistaken path for the BBC to be following.

We pay a licence fee to the BBC partly so that it can gather and present the news to us, and sometimes to analyse it. I trust its journalists and editors to be experts. Why is user opinion necessary at all in this process?

As someone who relies on BBC news on the radio and web for your (usually very good) coverage of the world, I don't feel included or empowered by this aspect of the site, but rather patronized and irritated by it. Just because the web can be more interactive than older media doesn't mean it should be.

The few instances you mention when readers were on the spot quicker than journalists are, I think, a separate issue, and I agree that in those special circumstances reportage or pictures from Joe Public fill a gap. Otherwise I'd rather that writing on the site was left to your journalists.

After reading Peter Horrocks's article I think these BBC fora should be discontinued as a waste of limited BBC resources. The BBC web medium is not suitable for reasoned discussion. The myths and misquotes gain credibility by much repetition.

I'd like to see an end to all this interactive rubbish. I pay my license fee to learn stuff from trained journalists and genuine experts. I don't want to hear the knee-jerk bigotry of anonymous texters. (Horrocks 2008)

Where is the prod-user in all of this? These comments are crying out for authority and reliability; they are not asking for a voice or any part in this brave new interactive world. This phenomenon has been observed in other studies. The Project for Excellence in Journalism quoted an expert who recognized that participatory media "must offer the possibility of interactivity without getting pervasive or obtrusive for the passive user" (quoted in Picone 2007: 105). US user research from 2006 concluded that "in most online communities, 90% of users are lurkers who never contribute, 9% of users contribute a little, 1% of users account for almost all the action" (Nielsen 2006).

One way to understand the disquiet amplified in the above comments is to unpackage the jargon that has built up around the term "citizen journalism". There appears to be a fundamental misalignment between the way user-generated content is packaged on the BBC and the way it is received by its stakeholder groups.

A Definitional Problem

The BBC actively solicits views, ideas, images and video from its audience and packages these requests up as "citizen journalism". The name "citizen journalism" implies some form of active engagement with the news and an expectation of publication. It covers an array of activities but tends to denote new ways of harnessing the Internet and mobile phone technology to change fundamentally the relationship between journalists, their sources and their readers.

The term "citizen journalism" has spawned many variations over the past five years and is commonly used interchangeably with "crowdsourced journalism", "participatory journalism", "stand-alone journalism", "networked journalism", "open-source journalism" and "community journalism". Each one of these terms defines a distinctive engagement that is rarely distinguished in common parlance.

These neologisms have aspects in common. First, they assume realignment between producer and consumer of news texts and, secondly, they suggest that contributors are willing and enabled to participate in the news production process as part of the gift economy.

The BBC now makes its own distinctions. It has dropped its wholesale references to "citizen journalism" and now prefers to use "public participation journalism". This is in acknowledgement that, in reality, it is engaging in a very different form of news-gathering exercise — that of crowdsourcing. To help make this distinction clear, the two definitions below capture opposite ends of the "citizen journalism" spectrum.

Open-source news aims to be genuinely participatory. Sites such as OhmyNews (South Korea), Wiki News or the Independent Media Centre Network come the closest to this ideal whereby anyone can potentially contribute a news story and see it appear instantly in the pool of stories publicly available. Ideally, readers can see editorial decisions being made by others. They can see how to get involved and help create content. If they can think of a better way for the software to help shape that process, they can copy the software, because it is free, and they can change it and start their own site. If they want to redistribute the news, they can, preferably on an open publishing site.

Crowdsourcing is a neologism for a business model that depends on work being done outside the traditional company walls: crowdsourcing relies on a combination of volunteers and low-paid amateurs who use their spare time to create content, solve problems or even do corporate research and development. The term was coined by *Wired* magazine writer Jeff Howe and editor Mark Robinson in June 2006. Crowdsourcing presumes that a large number of enthusiasts can outperform a small group of experienced professionals. In this new model of collaboration the results of the global efforts return only in the organization that leads the project. A good example of crowdsourcing is what Horrocks terms "the accidental journalist". This covers those members of the public who send the thousands of images to the newsroom capturing fires, natural disasters and newsworthy events of all descriptions: for instance, pictures sent capturing the London Underground bombings of 7 July (2005), the Asian tsunami (2004), the Virginia Tech shootings (2007) and 9/11 (2001).

WHO IS ALLOWED A VOICE ON THE BBC?

The comments actively solicited by the BBC under the umbrella of "public participation journalism" have the potential to introduce fresh voices into the national discourse. Yet BBC journalism is hidebound by its cultural heritage, its operating practices and also, as the preceding quotes attest, by its audience. The organization values its traditional practices and its ability to adhere to a firmly established set of editorial standards. The values of egalitarianism and subjectivity compete with control, filtering and impartiality. Incorporating citizen voices within a regulated commitment to impartiality is proving a challenge.

In the world of conventional news there exists a core consensus on who has the right to speak and who can be trusted to speak. Traditional journalistic practice uses a narrative structure that privileges a singular, authoritative author and a fixed storyline (Bolter and Grusin 1999; Joyce 1995; Landow 1997; Murray 1997). But this reporter's privilege is coming under increasing attack through the rise of bloggers and citizen journalists, making it difficult to define who counts as a reporter entitled to invoke this privilege.

Horrocks acknowledged this in his speech, caught in a quandary where he remains afraid to gatekeep but just as nervous about what might happen if the gates were allowed to open. On the one hand, he pushes the notion of radical impartiality, where the BBC is allowed to host variant voices.

> I have argued previously that the traditional model — safe, middle of the road, balancing neutrality — is now outdated and that we need to embrace the idea of "radical impartiality", that is, of a much broader range of views than before. (Horrocks 2008)

This is the reason Horrocks gave for not turning off the "Have Your Say" feature after Benazir Bhutto's assassination. Yet this competes irreconcilably with the corporation's need to control the input flow as it receives an average of 10,000 emails or posts in a day to its "Have Your Say" site alone — a figure that rises substantially on a big news day.

> Rather than playing the numbers game to drive our agenda, I instead encourage our teams to look for thoughtful and surprising views and opinions . . . simply orienting ourselves to the wealth of audience input is never going to be as straightforward as the propagandists of citizen journalism suggest . . . We need to be able to extract real editorial value from such contributions more easily. We are exploring as many technological solutions as we can for filtering the content, looking for intelligent software that can help journalists find the nuggets. (Horrocks 2008)

The position that Horrocks had adopted positively aligns the BBC News ethos with the definition of crowdsourcing. Essentially he is using technology to harvest a new and "rich" source of news: the public. The voices are thus subsumed into the normative practices of the BBC Newsroom and staff groomed to package these voices in the most acceptable manner, through what Horrocks calls "an expert journalistic prism". The aim is to do this with the utmost efficiency. Sorting the "wheat from the chaff" is an expensive and time-consuming business.

BEAN COUNTING

Overall, the message the BBC is transmitting is that it likes email correspondence because it enjoys counting the numbers as a quantitative exercise, even though it finds it extremely difficult to manage the numbers qualitatively. BBC's Head of Interactive News, Vivian Taylor, remarked: "You know you've touched a nerve when after 15 minutes you have 50 emails in the inbox . . . After the Danish Cartoon story, we had as many as 1900" (Taylor 2007).

This is a politically opportune strategy as long as the BBC can get it right. It does raise the question of what happens to all those contributions that never get an airing. Many voices inevitably fall into a large black hole, and if this happens too frequently, it may not be long before contributors turn away, recognizing that the apparent two-way conversation is actually only one-way and the return path is too limited to make the conversation valid. The challenge the BBC faces in the short to medium term is how to manage this relationship effectively without alienating its millions of online and mobile text contributors.

INDYMEDIA

The alternative to the more opportunistic crowdsourcing model, and at the other end of the citizen journalism spectrum, is open-source journalism. This encompasses radical, fragmented, pluralistic forms where readers, listeners and viewers are seen more as collaborators than consumers. Indymedia is self-defined as the largest, open-source, global, public, democratic media news network in existence and has survived almost ten years, with 150 international sites.

While this radical news organization does represent one of the best models of open-source journalism, whereby anyone can potentially contribute a news story and see it appear instantly in the pool of stories publicly available, Indymedia also grapples with difficult editorial dilemmas not dissimilar to the BBC's.

Jones and Martin (2007) conclude that what ideally defines Indymedia's relationship with its users is its decentralized organizational structure, aimed at empowering individuals through the interactive nature of open publishing. However, practical restraints mean that even at Indymedia there are significant limits to its open-access editorial policy.

Whitney (2005) states that when everyone is empowered to have their say in an unrestrained and anonymous environment, the output is potentially chaotic. A lack of accountability produces opinion-based content and "fact-checking is often met with cries of censorship". In addition she observes that the content is often badly written and presented, lacking basic journalistic skills.

Indymedia struggles to come to terms with filtering the myriad of voices, especially since there are those who would take advantage of open-source publishing to spread hate and extreme views. The technological and philosophical base underpinning open-publishing systems such as Indymedia simultaneously promotes both inclusivity and exclusivity. While initially encouraging free, ubiquitous, horizontal interactions, it also triggers an equal and opposite limiting reaction imposed through the necessity of coherent, legal publishing.

So even in the most radically reengineered news environment it is impossible to ignore the need for back-room censors to hide posts that are illegal, badly written or somehow inappropriate. Very much like mainstream news providers, Indymedia is also forced to gatekeep. Yet the editorial processes involved in hiding posts are often far from transparent, leading to heated arguments about the validity of those acting as gatekeepers (Jones and Martin 2007).

Among several disputes posted between 2004 and 2005 on the Indymedia UK process pages, the following case is symptomatic of the problems it faces. An article appeared and was immediately "cleaned", contravening its rigid advertising policy, because it mentioned where readers might purchase a particular book that exposed a "right-wing conspiracy". The censored individual wrote:

> So who hid it? The BNP, The World Bank, NATO . . . or was it Mr Smith's mate that hid it — another anonymous player of "pass the password" . . . lying/ditching editorial guidelines to cover his tracks. (Jones and Martin 2007: 18)

Thus, it's naïve to idealize alternative media as "free spaces", mysteriously liberated from the everyday structural considerations of the practice of journalism. Old gatekeepers are replaced by new gatekeepers. Worse still, the new hierarchies of power that emerge may be invisible and, as such, unaccountable.

DELIVERING TO THE STAKEHOLDER

Indymedia and the BBC face similar problems. They have to match stakeholder expectations with what they can properly deliver. In Indymedia's case, it is selling an ideologically based, free space with equality of access and minimal gatekeeping. It cannot easily live up to this ideal and is struggling to rationalize the need to filter with the promise of ubiquitous and free-flowing communication. The BBC, on the other hand, celebrates participation and heavily promotes audience-based journalism, but in very restrictive corporate terms. Both organizations need their prod-users, and neither can risk alienating these crucial stakeholders.

Horrocks believes that only 1 percent of the BBC's audience participate as active bottom-up contributors and even fewer do so regularly. This is the rationale the BBC use for being highly selective in the handling of this material.

> We need to be aware that the bulk of the people who pay the licence fee are always likely to be non-participative so our activities in handling audience content and harvesting the best material from the web must generate editorial value for the non-participators as well as the participants. (Horrocks 2008)

Hence selectivity becomes the principal operational definition of crowdsourcing, as opposed to open-sourcing. Since the BBC's brand reputation is predicated on accuracy and impartiality, the challenge is to reconcile truth and accuracy while simultaneously courting the polyvocal, fragmented universe the Internet facilitates.

Indymedia recognizes that a significant proportion of its users are active and not simply lurkers (those who engage with the content in a view-only mode), and it relies on their unpaid labour to survive. In Platon and Deuze (2003: 345) an unnamed Indymedia journalist is cited:

> The main advantage of open publishing is you get direct accounts. They do not have to be true *per se*. This is a little bit beside the point. I believe it is the truthfulness of the person saying it that matters. It is the very image of that person, reporting what he/she really believes. And that strikes some chord inside most people.

The "truthfulness" of the account is paramount to the BBC, and subsequently its systems must remain tightly filtered and closed. As the moderation of professionals is lost, so the argument goes, so are technical quality, dramatic content, intellectual stimulus and cultural significance. The instinct is for newsmakers to take control of the UGC and redefine it in their own terms.

A New but Trivial Toybox

The BBC is still unsure of how to manage the sifting process while simultaneously harvesting the potential of the crowd and promoting a sense of community involvement. From time to time it tries new experiments. Like a new toy in the toybox, user-generated content is exciting to play with.

Jeff Jarvis, an associate professor and director of the interactive journalism programme at the City University of New York's Graduate School of Journalism, was recently speaking at a blogging conference, where he enthused about the idea that news organizations should be commissioned or assigned by their audience to report on stories.

As it happened, Peter Barron, from *Newsnight* (the BBC's flagship nightly current affairs programme), was in the audience and was quite taken with this idea. Jarvis reported on the outcome in his daily blog (Jarvis 2007). The *Newsnight* blog that afternoon ran:

> You can tell our editor's just returned from a blogging conference. Fresh-faced and with fists clenched, he's pushing another *Newsnight* experiment in audience participation. It's quite simple — opening up the *Newsnight* running order to the people who watch us.

And so for the next three mornings *Newsnight*'s daily output editor shared with users their morning email to the production team outlining the potential running order for that night's programme. A comment to the blog post on Wednesday highlighted how the running order changed that night to include a story about lifestyle/cancer risk:

> We won't always be able to oblige, tomorrow for example we have a long film from Mark Urban in Pakistan whether you like it or not, but there's no doubt that what you tell us will help us form our thoughts. If you'd rather leave it to us that's fine; if you're worried that what others say is unrepresentative, get on here and lobby for what you'd like to see us do.

After the first few nights the experiment petered out. Again, similar to the aftermath of the Bhutto assassination, the door was thrown open, but the results were unsatisfactory. News agendas according to the number of hits or posts, as the BBC's flagship *Newsnight* discovered, is an untenable practice.

Another experiment involved a broadcast on Radio 4, the BBC's premiere radio news service. The makers of its early evening news and current affairs programme *PM* decided in November 2007 to expand its Saturday offering with *iPM*, a new brand designed to actively encourage its listeners to contribute ideas for stories. What's iPM?

> iPM is a weekly programme as well as a podcast. The "i" stands for interactive and "i", as in something personal. You can discuss ideas with the production team on this blog, and during the course of the week you can view and comment on stories that are being lined up for Saturday's programme. iPM is an experiment. It'll take advantage of the huge number of conversations and sources that take place every minute of every day. Our intention is to distil the very best and produce the type of programme that you'll find interesting and engaging. (iPM 2008)

The first week featured two main items: "Motor Scooters" and "Painting Voices". These items had a slightly eccentric or absurd feel, as if they were the postscript to the real news. They were essentially entertainment-based. They had a personal and dramatic quality, intentionally heightening their appeal.

"Mr Blog" was then introduced. He only had a first name — Chris. Chris had a light and bubbly personality as he recounted the week's blogging highlights. By depriving him of a surname, his status was lowered. It was as if he was afforded a different rank from his more serious colleagues who deliver the "real" news. This is not an uncommon way of packaging user-generated content within news contexts. Output connected with the public is often reduced to sub-news, with a strong tendency to report in only trivial contexts.

Six months later the iPM format had matured somewhat, and it became increasingly frequent for the programme to foreground and celebrate the occasional big news "scoop" provided by its listeners through the website. This suggests that, within the thousands of contributions from its publics, there will always be a nugget of gold to be exploited and privileged. Other communications are commonly used as "vote" fodder, revealing quantitative figures on interests, opinions and attitudes. This BBC Radio 4 experiment in public participation journalism began as an inert public space, but has slowly developed into something more genuinely participatory. The programme-makers are testing limits daily, discovering what can be successfully harvested within the news crowdsourcing model.

A QUESTION OF LEGITIMACY

The trend to harvest user-generated content at the BBC effectively encourages thousands of voices to speak up at once; but a narrow filter is subsequently applied so only a very few voices get through. As time goes by, the filter becomes more powerful and more sophisticated and the stories are sifted from a wider and more diverse range of speakers — but filtered none the less.

It certainly doesn't change the basic gatekeeping structure at the heart of all BBC news operations. It simply makes it more challenging for the production team to apply the filter successfully in the full glare of publicity. It appears that, at least for now, the BBC is simply carrying its old forms and processes into the new world of interactivity.

Chris Anderson (the journalist who coined the term "journalism's long-tail" and who now edits *Wired* magazine) is slightly more honest about how crowdsourcing has really changed the news editorial process.

> The old form of being a tastemaker, and a filter and an editor and a gatekeeper is that you had to guess at what people wanted. Every month you would guess, and I'm hired for my taste and judgement and experience, because people think I can guess better than somebody else. The Internet is a fantastic information-gathering exercise, and it does make my job easier now the guesswork is gone. (Anderson 2005)

This acknowledges that the role of the news editor hasn't changed significantly. It's always been about negotiating the relationship between news and audiences, but now editors have more tools in their armoury to do just this.

Luoma-aho (2007) states that the BBC has to balance two potentially irreconcilable goals: legitimacy and credibility. Legitimacy it gains from involvement of the stakeholders (the licence paying public) and credibility from its investment in traditional working practices. Public relations scholars have studied this critical stakeholder relationship and suggest that to succeed it needs careful management with "a shared culture, shared norms and expectations as well as suitable and transparent practices". Weber (1994) writes that this dynamic is in constant flux and studies have shown that the appearance of legitimacy may be more important than legitimacy itself. The BBC must cautiously manage its user-generated content relations to try to balance these conflicting ideals and it could be argued that its courtship of "citizen journalism" has on the surface at least been very effective, although the proof of this will reside in its ability to lure back the "lost" audience it vitally needs to sustain its legitimacy.

CONCLUSION

The BBC is preparing itself for an age of participatory journalism, but how far is it really willing or able to go? It is dependent on public trust, which, until recently, has been built top-down through authority and credibility disseminated through a strong corporate ethos of impartiality. But trust and audiences are both diminishing (Horrocks 2006; BBC World Service 2007). What may be wrong is not the principle of democratized news but the fact that the explosion has happened too quickly and the implementation is too crude. Our news culture has not had time to adapt properly. Both traditional audiences and traditional news producers are still uncomfortable with the notion of bottom-up news. What we have now is a slight softening of the walls, a gradual disintegration of the barriers and gates, making the boundaries more porous.

In 2003 the American Press Institute asked its principal gurus of participatory journalism from academia and industry to report on the phenomenon of participatory news media. The report laid out a number of essential transformative steps that all corporate news providers should consider to adapt to what the authors see as the unstoppable force of bottom-up news.

The last and perhaps most important step for a media company to take, is to relinquish control. News media are geared to own a story. They shape it, package it and sell it. But that mindset might make organizations blind to the larger opportunity. (Bowman and Willis 2003: 60)

Bowman states that the opportunities the authors evangelize are predicated on an open news platform that supports social interaction around the stories created (2003: 53). They argue that, in a networked world, the primary value of the media lies in their ability to connect people. Bowman suggests that newsrooms need to be empowered to grow communities of interest online and "as the value of their communities grows, so will it enhance the value of the media organization" (2003: 59).

We are reminded that the "Internet-aware" younger generation may not be so tolerant of media that are one-way. They are uniquely habituated to communication routines that demand an interactive, two-way traffic flow. And, once the dissolution of boundaries is under way and once expectations are created that the public has a voice, it may be difficult to quiet.

It is significant that the BBC has recently chosen to invest a considerable amount of time and money in its local news services. In 2008 it maintained sixty local sites across the UK devoted to delivering on-demand news, and these are well placed to become community networks that reach beyond the opportunistic nature of crowd-sourcing.

ITV Local has also investing heavily in its local Web news services. Mark Waddington, Channel Manager for ITV Local in Yorkshire, reported at a conference in early 2008 that "we can no longer carry the old forms into the new world". He was particularly conscious of the problem around the definitions of "quality" and how these definitions must change for news producers to accept community involvement (Waddington 2008). The local level is where much of the genuine experimentation in participatory media will take place. It is here that content producers are closest to their audiences and that rules can be broken without attracting too much attention. These initiatives have been defined as "hyper-local or microsite and are typically, devoted to stories and minutiae of a particular neighbourhood, ZIP code or interest group within a certain geographic area" (Picone 2007:102).

As corporate news invests in these small public sphericules where conceptualizations of news quality and impartiality are being reworked, the culture of these large organizations may be allowed to change from the bottom up, challenging attitudes that are over-cautious and conformist.

Yet in a commercial environment interactivity is inevitably grafted on to commercial media products. It will be a brave BBC editor who can cope with truly altering the relationship between authors and readers. This kind of re-conceptualization of roles in the newsroom currently remains untenable, and, for now at least, the nickname "Auntie Beeb" is still fitting.

Note

1   The current Charter can be accessed at http://www.bbc.co.uk/bbctrust/framework/charter.html.

References

Anderson, C, (2005) "The Long Tail, Pre-filters vs. Post Filters". Retrieved 10 October 2007 from: http://longtail.typepad.com/the_long_tail/2005/07/prefiltering_vs.html.

BBC (2006) "BBC Creative Futures". Retrieved 6 June 2007 from: http://www.bbc.co.uk/pressoffice/pressreleases/stories/2006/04_april/25/creative.shtm

BBC World Service (2007) "Global Report into the Perceptions of Media Freedom". Retrieved 12 December 2007 from: http://news.bbc.co.uk/1/shared/bsp/hi/pdfs/10_12_07_worldservicepoll.pdf.

Bolter, J. D., and Grusin, R. (1999) *Remediation: Understanding New Media*. Cambridge, MA: MIT Press.

Bowman, S., and Willis, C. (2003) *We Media: How Audiences Are Shaping the Future of News and Information*. Reston, VA: The American Press Institute.

Carey, J. W. (2005) "Historical Pragmatism and the Internet", *New Media & Society*, 4 (4), pp. 443–55.

Coleman, S. (2005) "New Mediation and Direct Representation: Reconceptualising Representation in a Digital Age", *New Media and Society*, (7) 2, pp. 177–98.

Curran, J. (2002) *Media and Power*. Oxford: Routledge.

Gillmor, D. (2004) *We the Media: Grassroots Journalism by the People, for the People*. Sebastopol, CA: O'Reilly.

Hermida, A., and Thurman, N. (2008) "A Clash of Cultures: The Integration of User-Generated Content within Professional Journalistic Frameworks at British Newspaper Websites", *Journalism Practice*, 2 (3). Retrieved from: http://reportr.files.wordpress.com/2008/09/hermida_thurman_a_clash_of_cultures.pdf

Horrocks, P. (2006) "The Future of News". Retrieved 3 December 2007 from: http://www.bbc.co.uk/blogs/theeditors/2006/11/the_future_of_news.html.

Horrocks, P. (2007) "Multimedia News". Retrieved 14 November 2007 from: http://www.bbc.co.uk/blogs/theeditors/2007/11/multimedia_news.html.

Horrocks, P. (2008) "The Value of Citizen Journalism". Retrieved 29 January 2008 from: http://www.bbc.co.uk/blogs/theeditors/2008/01/value_of_citizen_journalism.html.

iPM website, BBC, Retrieved 23 January 2008 from: http://www.bbc.co.uk/blogs/ipm/2007/10/whats_ipm_1.shtml.

Jarvis J. (2007) Personal blog. Retrieved 23 January 2008 from: http://www.buzzmachine.com/2007/11/02/you-assign-the-journalists/.

Jones, J., and Martin R. (2007) "Crypto Hierarchy and its Discontents". In *Making Our Media*. Cresskill, NJ: Hampton Press (forthcoming). Also retrieved 12 November 2007 from: http://docs.indymedia.org/view/Global/ImcEssayCollection.

Joyce, M. (1995) *Of Two Minds: Hypertext Pedagogy and Poetics*. Ann Arbor, MI: University of Michigan Press.

Landlow, G. P. (1997) *Hypertext 2.0*. Baltimore, MD: Johns Hopkins University Press.

Lasica, J. D. (2002) "The Promise of the Daily Me", *Online Journalism Review*. Retrieved 12 November 2007 from: httm://www.ojr.org/ojr/lasica/1017779142.php.

Lilley, A. (2007) "Blueprint for the PSP", *Television*, February 2007.

Luoma-aho, V. (2007) "Making Stakeholders, Gaining Legitimacy". Paper presented at Reader and User Oriented Communication, Demands, Applications and Criticism, Vaasa University, Finland, December 2007.

Matheson, D. (2004) "Weblogs and the Epistemology of the News: Some Trends in Online Journalism", *New Media & Society*, 6 (4), pp. 443–68.

Murray, J. (1997) *Hamlet on the Holodeck: The Future of Narrative in Cyberspace*. New York: Free Press.

Newsnight (2008) *Newsnight* blog. Retrieved 23 January 2008 from: http://www.bbc.co.uk/blogs/newsnight/2007/10/what_do_you_want_in_wednesdays_programme.html.

Nielson, J. (2006) *Participation Inequality: Encouraging More Users to Contribute*. Retrieved 30 March 2008 from: http://www.useit.com/alertbox/participation_inequality.

Picone, I. (2007) "Conceptualising Online News Use", *Observatorio Journal*, 3 (2007), pp. 93–114.

Platon, S., and Deuze, M. (2003) "Indymedia Journalism: A Radical Way of Making, Selecting and Sharing News?", *Journalism*, 4 (3), pp. 336–55.

Project for Excellence in Journalism (2007) "The State of the News Media: An Annual Report on American Journalism". Retrieved 30 March 2008 from: http://www.stateofthenewsmedia.com/2007/aboutthestudy.

Quinn, G., and Trench, B. (2002) "Online News Media and Their Audiences: Multimedia Content in the Digital Age". Retrieved 30 March 2008 from: www.mudia.org.

Readership Institute (2000) "Culture Report: A Profile of the Impact Newspapers and their Departments". Retrieved 10 February 2007 from: http://www.readership.org/culture_management/culture/data/final_culture_report.pdf.

Singer, J. B. (1997) "Still Guarding the Gate? The Newspaper Journalist's Role in an On-line World", *Convergence: The Journal of Research into New Media Technologies*, 3 (1), pp. 72–89.

Singer, J. B., (1998) "Online Journalists: Foundations for Research into Their Changing Roles". Retrieved 30 March 2008 from: http://jcmc.indiana.edu/vol4/issue1/singer.html.

Stabe, M. (2006) "Journalists Should Understand 'Long Tails'". Retrieved 7 July 2007 from: http://www.pressgazette.co.uk/story.asp?sectioncode=1&storycode=35548.

Taylor, V. (2006) Notes from speech at Citizen Journalism Conference, Birmingham, hosted by Media Skills, 26 January 2007.

Toffler, A. (1980) *The Third Wave*. New York: Morrow.

Waddington, M., (2008) "Broadcast News and the Active Citizen", University of Leeds Conference, 7 January 2008.

Weber, M. (1994) *Political Writings*. Cambridge: Cambridge University Press. Cited in Luoma-aho (2007).

Whitney, J. (2005) "What's the Matter with Indymedia?" Retrieved 28 July 2005 from: http://www.alternet.org/module.

Williams L. (n.d.) *Frontiers of Innovation in Community Engagement: New Organisations Forge New Relationships with Communities*. Center for Citizen Media. Retrieved 30 March 2007 from: http://citmedia.org/reports/newscommunities.pdf.

Williams, W. S. (1998) "The Blurring of the Line between Advertising and Journalism in the On-line Environment". In D. Borden and K. Harvey (eds), *The Electronic Grapevine: Rumor, Reputation, and Reporting in the New On-line Environment*. Mahwah, NJ: Lawrence Erlbaum Associates, pp. 31–41.

CHAPTER 11

A Free Market of Ideas? The Utility of Citizen-Generated Content

LIAN ZHU

Our world is changing, facilitated by the rapid development of communication technology. Soldiers in Iraq send back mobile footage to reveal prisoner abuse; ordinary people take the first on-the-spot pictures, before professional journalists have a clue that a story is unfolding; and people from Burma set up their own blogs to tell the stories that the state media would never divulge. With all this happening, we might imagine that we are finally seeing the rise of a truly democratic forum at a global scale, where everybody can be a journalist, participate in politics and public affairs, and have his or her views expressed and heard by the world. This could be a challenge to the long-established norms. However, to accept this argument, in its extreme form, is to risk drifting towards a form of technological determinism.

When the excitement about citizen media gradually fades away, people may start to acknowledge that citizen journalism has not dealt a fatal blow to the established media. Rather, both forms of journalism "complement each other, intersect with each other and play off one another" (Lasica 2003: 73). This could be positive for the practice of citizenship, but some have questioned whether citizen-generated content is journalism (see Hudson and Temple in this volume). Others argue that a large amount of the content is no more than compelling eyewitness testimony and only valuable to the mass audience when something extraordinary happens, such as the Asian tsunami. An interview with news editor Liesl Smith-So (2007) from BBC South Today echoes this view: "It is dangerous to call people citizen journalists . . . I don't think that by taking a few shots and being in the right place at the right time constitutes being a journalist." Even worse, citizen journalism may not be fairly representative of the wider public (Horrocks 2008). Moreover, Allan's study (2006) exposes how little power that public, and its citizen journalism, has in exercising citizenship and asserting control.

While examining the commercial potential of citizen journalism, Allan argues that the mainstream media utilize digital technologies and citizen journalism as an effective marketing tool. This has also become prominent in a content analysis of BBC and ITV local news, as well as interviews with local editors.

In the light of my research I shall argue that there are two main forms of citizen journalism. On the one hand, there is journalistic content produced by non-professionals but delivered via professional media outlets, such as broadcasting and newspapers, the websites of the mainstream media and news agencies that distribute content to the mainstream media. On the other, both professionals and non-professionals produce independent journalistic content as members of the public and disseminate it through non-professional sites on the Internet. Both these forms of citizen-generated content, however, are increasingly used for audience-building and commercial gain, leaving the public nowhere near the centre of power.

FROM THE NINETEENTH CENTURY TO THE MODERN DAY

In the UK in the nineteenth century the government was seen as the biggest enemy of freedom of speech, and many people fought a bitter battle against a stamp duty on newspapers that was seen as a tax on knowledge. This campaign succeeded in 1855, as the stamp duty was abolished. However, many have argued that a free market of ideas did not really emerge, as had been expected (for example, Curran 2000). Nor did a public sphere follow, where, ideally, people would have universal access, equality of participation in a critical and rational debate about public affairs and possibly influence the decision-making process of the powerful. The subsequent media system was funded primarily by advertising, which extended the influence of capital. Despite being able to break free from the government, the commercial media system was subject to pressure from important advertisers wishing to promote their own agendas or censor unfavourable publicity, and privilege mass readership or wealthy niche markets (Herman and Chomsky 1988).

In the meantime, media companies increasingly concentrated in fewer and fewer hands. This challenged the ideal that journalism operated in the service of democracy. This system also discouraged innovation and diversity in media production, with further commercialization putting an emphasis on low cost and popular appeal (Murdock 2000). In addition, journalism employed simple narrative devices to reduce the complexity of events, in order to encourage mass audience involvement (Tulloch 2000). It is therefore suggested that economic power has joined government power in controlling press operations, to the extent that "the media *are* big business" (Curran 2000: 122). Thus, "a strategy is needed that defends the media from both public and private power, and enables the media to serve the wider public through critical surveillance of all those in authority" (2000: 127). This is to challenge a market dynamic and the financial motives that have come to dominate the media system and jeopardize the practice of citizenship.

People are autonomous citizens with the rights "to participate fully in existing patterns of social life and to help shape the forms they may take in future" (Murdock 2000: 121). In other words, citizenship is dependent on a citizen having: civil rights, which are necessary for individual freedom; political rights, in order to participate in the exercise of political power; social rights, which facilitate access to a modicum of economic welfare and security; and cultural rights, to access information, gain knowledge, be represented, communicate and contribute to the circulation of public information. Further, Isin and Wood extend the idea of citizenship to a global level by arguing that "there is a degree of cultural interpenetration, hybridity and fluidity across different localities around the globe" (1999: 91). The practice of citizenship is seen to be the basis of modern democracy, while the media are supposed to help to fulfil the rights of citizens in order to maintain a healthy democratic society, and, according to some, "address audiences not as consumers of politics but [as] producers" (Berger 2000: 86). To make it possible for citizens to become active providers and participate in politics, it is essential to have a free flow of information that is transparent and properly contextualized, which allows people to comprehend the issues at stake. But it is also required that there is extensive cultural diversity in media representation and the participation of citizens in journalistic production.

Commercialization is still a major global media trend, where the majority of the media organizations are governed by market dynamics and financial gain. However, some writers (Kahney 2003; Gillmor 2004) have seen the opportunity for people to fight back, practice citizenship, and even democratize journalism and influence policies. They have been excited about the rise of citizen-generated media and grassroots journalism, enabled by the rapid development of communication technologies, such as the Internet and camera phones. It is argued that everybody can be a journalist, challenging the monopoly of the established media, voicing their independent opinion in the virtual public sphere — in other words, the Internet — and debating important issues around the world. The lack of regulation and censorship on the Internet also enables personal campaigns and cyber-activism. Personal blogs and participatory news sites have proliferated around the world, ranging from sites that consider serious issues, such as the 2005 London terrorist bombings, to those containing more entertaining and amusing footage, such as YouTube.

This participatory journalism has been so influential that, on one occasion, one of the citizen sites, OhmyNews, famously overcame the hostility of the mainstream media to help elect a presidential candidate (Gluck 2003). In other words, individuals have been seen to be empowered with freedom of speech. The high cost of entering the media market and the conservative agenda of the mainstream media suddenly become irrelevant to people who want to be heard. The Internet is, instead, turned into a free market of ideas where public affairs can be openly discussed by anybody who has access. Greater equality of participation can be achieved regardless of the wealth of the participant and a wide range of perspectives can be reflected. This, at least in theory, leads to more enriched practices of citizenship and a healthier democracy. Moreover, the mainstream media are joining in, desperately wishing to interact with their consumers or audiences by setting up websites along with their major outlets and asking the public to report for them or comment on their stories. Among these are CNN's iReport in the US and

Channel 5's Your News in the UK, while major broadcasters and newspapers are expending much effort developing multimedia reporting on their websites.

Participatory journalism, however, is nothing new. In the late nineteenth century one of the strategies the media moguls adopted to create a closer relationship with readers was to make readers central to the process of generating editorial content. They invited the readers to write in, send jokes and generally collaborate in the creation of publications (Tulloch 2000). It was cheap for the owners and popular with the public, and therefore a successful marketing strategy. A century later, in 1987, CNN started its News Hound hotline to encourage the audience to call in with scoops and send in amateur camcorder footage (Calabrese 2000). These were early examples of user-generated content.

At first glance it might appear that the public have been able to participate in the production of media content. At closer inspection, however, it becomes clear that, first, the public have been effectively exploited as cheap labour for raw information and exclusive stories, rather than being respected contributors to the production and, second, that the primary reason to include user-generated content in everyday production has been to enhance connectivity with the audience and readers. This is one consequence of commercialization. The question we have to ask now is whether the rapid development of communication technology has brought new dimensions to participatory journalism, with citizens empowered and public communication breaking free from both political and commercial constraints.

INDEPENDENT CITIZEN MEDIA

Easy access to the Internet and essential software has enabled independent journalistic content to be produced and disseminated by both professionals and non-professional members of the public. Many have argued that compelling eyewitness testimony and subjective personal opinions dominate public contributions on the Internet. Moreover, the creators of this content "may be campaigning about something, or they could be funded by sponsors" (Britton 2008). These contributions can hardly be considered to be journalism, as it is often hard to tell whether the information is accurate and reliable or whether there is an agenda behind their inclusion. Yet the audience could view them as journalism. Indymedia, for example, arguably fills a void left by traditional journalism, by preaching an open-source philosophy, styling itself around an idea of advocacy and allowing users to pursue their own biases. The danger is that "questions of quality are unlikely to be answered in strict journalistic terms when for many of the reporters involved what matters most is the message being communicated" (Allan 2006: 128). Even worse is the display of violent and indecent material via the Internet and websites showing user-generated content. On 16 July 2007, for example, a self-recorded sexual video even made it on to YouTube's "top favourite" page in a thumbnail picture form, available to view by any user. Similarly, a one-minute pornographic video clip was removed from Yahoo Korea's video-sharing page in March 2007, after more than 25,000 people had viewed it (*The Korea Times* 2007). In the UK the BBC's

Panorama programme (2007) managed to shock its audience with an investigation into websites displaying user-generated content that showed clips containing "senseless and excessive violence" towards children.

It may be that the absence of traditional journalistic quality explains the relatively poor reach of citizen journalism in comparison to the mainstream media. Opinion polls consistently suggest that the attraction of citizen media may not be as wide as some may have expected, as a significant majority of the public is more likely to trust, and still get their news from, well-known and established news brands (Pecquerie and Kilman 2007: 11). Economic and survey data in the US also show that the biggest online audience numbers "are generated by the sites owned and operated by the richest media companies" and "most Americans, when they go online, are still consuming news that adheres to time-honoured principles of fairness and accuracy" (Vaina 2007: 27). Moreover, the "digital divide" between the information-rich and the information-poor, which has led to a new form of social inequality, certainly does not help enable citizen media to enter the mainstream.

Limited reach inevitably reduces the power of citizen media but has not, as yet, dimmed their financial potential. Many of the sites that host citizen-generated content undoubtedly have a potential commercial value, including the most visible ones, such as OhmyNews (Kim and Hamilton 2006). This, in the long term, could mean that such citizen sites could be commercially developed with the power of capital, which would jeopardize independent journalistic practice and the practice of citizenship in democracy. Furthermore, the emergence of some citizen media sites, such as OhmyNews, has already "attracted the attention of media giants around the world" (Newsweek 18 June, 2004). This is because they have demonstrated in their success the commercial potential of utilizing citizen-generated content to engage with audiences and readers, especially the younger ones.

Google, for example, acquired YouTube, for $1.65 billion in a stock-for-stock transaction. This acquisition has allowed YouTube to "operate independently to preserve its successful brand and passionate community" and to take advantage of Google's expertise in "organizing information" — "creating new models for advertising on the Internet" and distributing content to "reach a vast new audience" (Google 2006). However, it has also introduced YouTube to a commercial world driven by financial motives. For example, Google has introduced video advertising to YouTube, to be embedded in user-generated content. In fact, in the US and Canada, YouTube has opened up a "partnership programme", offering select content creators the ability to incorporate YouTube InVideo advertisements into their content. It has also offered them the opportunity to receive a share of the revenue from those advertisements that run along with their content (Karp 2007; YouTube 2007). Moreover, given Google's reputation in expanding its business around the world by negotiating with local governments, it is only reasonable to expect that some kind of agenda, be it financial or political, will be imported in to how YouTube filters the content it supplies. More importantly, with more and more big businesses being attracted to citizen media and citizen-generated content, it could be expected that both will have a huge impact on mainstream journalism practice.

COLLABORATION WITH THE MAINSTREAM

In fact, some mainstream media are hungry for user-generated content. They recognize the importance of ordinary people providing content that the newsrooms can, in turn, distribute more widely. They also acknowledge that the public can provide a useful new source of exclusive content (Thurman 2008: 149), especially with a breaking story. The BBC and ITV (the oldest commercial television network in the UK), for example, have both used this form of journalism in their national and regional evening news. Impressed by the advanced technologies that offer large memory and high editorial capacity in small devices such as mobile phones, Robin Britton, Head of News for ITV Thames Valley, even sees the potential for citizen journalism to cross over fully into television (Britton 2007). Although the BBC's regional editorial staff are reluctant to go that far (Smith-So 2007), the teaching material from its College of Journalism has confidently foreseen future BBC news programmes being dominated by user-generated content. News agencies are catching up too, with Reuters trying to incorporate the use of camera phones into journalistic practice, as well as launching the You Witness News site with Yahoo! in 2006, which expected to offer its clients a feed of user-generated images (Walker 2006). Associated Press also partnered NowPublic.com in 2007 to bring citizen content into AP newsgathering (cyberjournalist 2007).

It is clear that advanced technologies offer ordinary citizens increased opportunities to participate on an equal footing in daily news reporting. This helps fulfil the cultural rights of citizens. In the meantime citizen journalism, by supplying raw information to traditional journalism's news desks, also supplements the established media system and increases cultural diversity in media representation. As Golding and Elliot note: "even in highly equipped and financed news organizations there is an enormous reliance on the news gathering of agencies and on a few prominent institutional sources" (1999: 115). They also suggest that the emphasis on news production is "for most part passive . . . selecting from already limited supplies of information" (1999: 118). This means that "a great acreage of UK life simply remain untouched" (Davies 2008: 77). It is, therefore, only reasonable to expect that collaboration between mainstream media organizations and citizen-generated content would lead to more aspects of social life being reflected in newsroom production. More importantly, it could be that what was left out by the mainstream media owing to political or financial motives might now be picked up by this very system and the public could finally become active providers and producers of politics, as critics have hoped. The optimistic expectation from this is that minority groups might be pushed to the forefront and there would be more diversity in the mainstream.

THE RAW DATA

A total of eight weeks' worth of evening news programmes from BBC (*South Today*) and ITV (*Meridian Tonight*) from 2008 and an equal amount of the same programmes from one year earlier were studied to consider the involvement of user-generated content in mainstream regional TV. The results suggest that, apart from input from the public as eyewitnesses being interviewed by journalists, the most consistent use of user-generated content on the sample programmes was limited to individuals sending weather pictures and personal comments on particular issues discussed in programmes, posted on the organizations' websites or texted to the newsrooms. In the 2007 sample of BBC *South Today*, for example, it was true that there were news items filmed by members of the public who were equipped with essential skills and were receiving help from the professionals. This, however, decreased in 2008. In fact, in the 2008 sample studied there was no single news item produced directly by the public. ITV used citizen-generated footage in their news items in both 2007 and 2008. However, members of the public never directly produced the news items. Britton (2008), reflecting on the ITV Thames Valley footage, explained that there wasn't an editorial decision not to use amateur footage, but that broadcasters "don't get a lot [of user-generated content]" or actively search on the Internet for amateur contributions, "unless it's a major story". As Pecquerie and Kilman observe, citizen journalism is "increasingly disappearing, to be replaced by the more comprehensive notion of user-generated content" (2007: 10). This, according to Horrocks (2008), is because there is "no evidence that raw audience interaction or unvarnished news direct from the audience is more attractive than professional news".

So why weather pictures? Using user-generated content, according to Sambrook (2005), is about providing value to the audience, but Smith-So (2007) makes the point more clearly — "in weather stories, people want to feel involved". In other words, the inclusion of citizen journalism — or, more accurately in this case, user-generated content — has been rarely employed to enhance audience involvement and connectivity. Audience levels are crucial to news programmes. The BBC needs rating figures to prove its popularity and therefore be in a better position to maintain its licence fee, while commercial media needs the same to compete in the market-place and gain more advertising in return. As Smith-So (2007) says, "the audience is paramount in what we do and is centre to what we do. So we try not to ignore them."

While acknowledging that having new technology and less complicated editing software available to the public acts as an impetus, Britton (2008) considers the main reason for using citizen journalism is that if the "public is interacting with us, the rest of the public see that we encourage this. So we build connections with the audience, and then we get more stories. It's a self-fulfilling prophecy." Furthermore, almost all major media companies now have their own websites designed with space to accommodate user-generated content and interactivity with their audiences and readers. Apart from asking for comments and hosting blogs, ITV, for example, gets people to register online with their phone numbers and the areas they live. This is so that when a story breaks near them, they can be texted with a picture request (Britton 2007). The websites of other long-established media present a similar picture.

There are two concerns, though. On the one hand, only a small number of public contributions have found their way to actual news programmes. ITV local online Your News, for example, is a virtual space for members of the public to upload pictures and video clips. In the first two weeks of July 2008 the Your News section for Meridian, the ITV regional station for southern England, had 123 items from the public, and only one of them was shown on the evening news (Britton 2008). Journalists' reluctance to use items uploaded directly by the public is also evident in AP's newsgathering. Despite the collaboration with NowPublic.com since 2007, until July 2008 AP's archive only had two news items from public sources — both about a shooting in Finland that happened in November 2007 (AP 2008). This suggests that the calls for citizen journalism on websites that are owned and operated by mainstream news organizations, again, may well be just a business strategy to strengthen their relationship with the audience. They could well be there to help build up a popular image of being close to the public and willing to include them in news practice as producers as well as audience. In actual practice, public contributions are not presented as equally valuable as news items produced by the professional team, unless the content creators happen to be early on the scene and acquire valuable footage to which the professionals don't have access. On the other hand, this online space does not necessarily demonstrate wider participation from the public. In the case of ITV Local's Your News, only 17 people produced the 123 public contributions uploaded — and one person provided just over half of these (62 items) (ITV Local 2008).

Online posts and texts may provide a wider range of perspectives from the public. However, the discussions that were published on the websites run by major media organizations are mostly comments and opinions, with reasoned critique "sometimes lost in a flurry of heated rants and diatribes" (Allan 2006: 127). Moreover, sometimes those "heated rants and diatribes" can be offensive, and the most visible "public opinion" on the Web does not necessarily provide a fair representation of the wider public. As discussed in the last chapter, hours after the death of Benazir Bhutto, for example, the BBC News website launched an open discussion on their Have Your Say forum to gather reactions from the public. As a result, vehement and unanimous opinion hostile to the Muslim religion — some of which was factually incorrect — became the most popular and visible, whereas the valuable insights offered by people who had met Bhutto or knew her ended up buried in the huge volume of comments (Horrocks 2008).

This incident also raises the question of gatekeeping. While independent citizen media are likely to suffer from financial constraints or intervention from big business, the collaboration with the mainstream also leaves citizen-generated content in the hands of traditional gatekeepers. As argued earlier, the quality and reliability of citizen contributions are not always satisfactory. Although some news organizations claim not to edit users' comments on their websites, many use different techniques to monitor, or even editorially moderate public contributions to maintain the reputation of their organizations. These techniques range from persistent monitoring, to editorially moderating, to cleverly restricting the type of debates the online platforms host — in order to minimize the risk of "dodgy" comments (Thurman 2008). This, according to some, is often the result of an editor's mistrust of non-professional contributions and a desire to retain editorial control (Gillmor 2004; Thurman 2008). More importantly, this control enables the media organizations to secure their reputation in the marketplace by delivering "good" journalism with traditional core characteristics, so that they retain public trust and, in return, market share. However, any degree of intervention is likely to challenge the free expression offered by the Internet, allowing corporate interests and values to dominate public contributions and the flow of information, and, eventually, absorbing citizen journalism into the established information system.

CONCLUSION: COMMERCIAL DRIVE VS. CITIZENSHIP

On the positive side, the Internet does provide a huge amount of information — perhaps much more than we have ever experienced. Moreover, new communication technology allows for a great degree of public interactivity and intervention, potentially pressing the established media into providing greater accountability and openness (Sambrook 2005; Horrocks 2008). It could be argued that it is now more difficult to conceal a piece of information than ever before. Technological advancement has also enabled people to contextualize news stories by creating links to background information, relevant articles and commentary. As a result, the public can have a better understanding of the world. The Internet may not represent the wider public or have a wider reach in the public domain. However, it is undeniable that it provides the public with a cheap platform to voice their views, if they wish to and have the means. This inevitably enhances cultural diversity to some extent. More importantly, new technology allows ordinary people to become producers and content providers, and forces the mainstream media to collaborate with this new emerging power.

This optimistic view, however, depends on "[a] deterministic definition of new media that assumes that technological transformations in and of themselves make regulatory, corporate and consumer change necessary and inevitable" (Freedman 2006: 276). In fact, the reality has not changed as fundamentally as one might have expected.

First, audiences and readers still need the traditional media — perhaps more so than ever — as an increased quantity of easily accessible information does not necessarily mean a higher level of quality. Overwhelmed by the flood of information, many people have turned to traditional journalism that offers a selection of the most relevant and useful information, seeking help to sort out "the wheat from the chaff" (Hafez 2007). This takes power away from citizen media and user-generated content, while enhancing the significance of traditional journalistic practice.

Second, commercialization is still a major trend in the media world, be it traditional or online citizen media. Rejecting technological determinism, Hirst and Harrison argue that "like any business, the commercial reality of journalism is that new technology often means a change in the way work is managed; with new and different skill-sets being required and in some cases a reduction in staffing levels" (2007: 246). Neither the structure nor the nature of the media system changes, and it is still capital that rules. As suggested above, commercial outlets will increasingly recognize the attractiveness of citizen journalism to the public and its relatively cheap costs:

> the types of cost-cutting strategies associated with bottom line pressures sharply reduce the scope for innovation and improvement. In the meantime, it is likely that citizen journalism will be increasingly recognized by commercial sites for its attractiveness to users (its pulling power

being sold, in turn, to advertisers), as well as for the relatively modest operational costs involved. Both are crucial considerations in the eyes of managers, especially those inclined to consider serious, investigative newsgathering to be too expensive to justify further investment from shareholders. And yet . . . both similarly promise to curtail the very aims, values and commitments which citizen journalism, at its best, represents. (Allan 2006: 142)

The danger is that financial interests will eventually challenge the ideal of citizen journalism that allows citizens freely to express their opinions to a wider public by using advanced technologies such as the Internet. The Web may not be as heavily regulated as other media, but a large part of it is now guided by commercial motives.

It is therefore fair to conclude that, although public contributions and interaction are important to the mainstream media, the public is nowhere near the centre of power. It is still the long-established media, which are often driven by market dynamics, that decide what to show to most of the public, and how. In order to secure a sizeable market share, a media company has to attract an audience to sell to its sponsors. With the mainstream media experiencing a downturn in consumer-driven advertising (Garside 2008), the use of digital technology and user-generated content is no more than a breakthrough in marketing. Many journalists may use the public's contributions as a source, but this is often about having a better connection and strengthened relationship with the audience and, in return, staying competitive in the market-place, especially when facing the "YouTube generation" (Britton 2008). After all, giving the audience what they want is far more convenient and financially sensible than guessing what they want.

The rapid development of technology may have advanced public communication and led to a heated debate about how far it could go to extend freedom of speech for even the most powerless. At its best, as far as the mainstream media are concerned, this could be a win-win situation. On the one hand, it opens up the mainstream media to the public, so that the citizens can have more opportunity to participate equally in the practice of journalism and have a more effective input in public affairs. On the other hand, the media can utilize the technologies available to engage with more of the audience and, in return, attract more advertising. Nevertheless, with a rather narrow representation of the wider public offered by user-generated content, a continued commercialization strategy extended onto the Internet and the old low-cost-plus-high-appeal commercial strategy at the heart of media operations, we have not really advanced significantly from the nineteenth century. A free market of ideas is still yet to be seen.

References

Allan, S. (2006) *Online News*. Maidenhead: Open University Press.
Berger, G. (2000) "Grave New World? Democratic Journalism Enters the Global Twenty First Century", *Journalism Studies*, 1 (1), pp. 81–99.
Britton, R. (2007) Interview with Robin Britton, Head of News, ITV Thames Valley.
Britton, R. (2008) Interview with Robin Britton, Head of News, ITV Thames Valley.
Calabrese, A. (2000) "Political Space and the Trade in Television News". In C. Sparks, and J.

Tulloch (eds), *Tabloid Tales: Global Debates over Media Standards*. New York/Oxford: Rowman and Littlefield, pp. 43–61.

Curran, J. (2000) "Rethinking Media and Democracy". In J. Curran and M. Gurevitch (eds), *Mass Media and Society*. London: Arnold, pp. 120–54.

Cyberjournalist. (2007) AP Partners with Citizen Journalism site. Retrieved 13 July 2008 from: http://www.cyberjournaloist.net/news/004043.php.

Davies, N. (2008) *Flat Earth News: An Award-Winning Reporter Exposes Falsehood, Distortion and Propaganda in the Global Media*. London: Chatto and Windus.

Freedman, D. (2006) "Internet Transformations: 'Old' Media Resilience in the 'New' Media Revolution". In J. Curran, and D. Morley (eds), *Media and Cultural Theory*. London: Routledge, pp. 275–90.

Garside, J. (2008) "Pressing Matter of Advertising Spend", *Daily Telegraph*, 16 June.

Gillmor, D. (2008) *We the Media: Grassroots Journalism by the People, for the People*. Sebastopol, CA: O'Reilly.

Gluck, C. (2003) "South Korea's Web Guerrillas". Retrieved 19 September 2006 from: http://news.bbc.co.uk/1/hi/world/asia-pacific/2843651.stm.

Golding, P., and Elliot, P. (1999) "Making the News (Excerpt)". In H. Tumber (ed.), *News: A Reader*. New York/Oxford: Oxford University Press, pp. 112–20.

Google (2008) "Google to Acquire YouTube for $1.65 Billion In Stock". Press release, 9 October.

Hafez, K. (2007) *The Myth of Media Globalisation*. Cambridge: Polity.

Herman, E. S., and Chomsky, N. (1988) *Manufacturing Consent: The Political Economy of the Mass Media*. New York: Pantheon Books.

Hirst, M., and Harrison, J. (2007) *Communication and New Media: From Broadcast to Narrowcast*. Oxford: Oxford University Press.

Horrocks, P. (2008) "Value of Citizen Journalism", *The Editor*. Retrieved 10 July 2008 from: http://www.bbc.co.uk/blogs/theeditors/2008/01/value_of_citizen_journalism.html.

Isin, E., and Wood, P. (1999) *Citizenship and Identity*. London: Sage.

ITV Local (2008) Retrieved from: www.yournews.itvlocal.com.

Kahney, L. (2008) "Citizen Reporters Make the News". Retrieved 19 September 2006 from: http://www.wired.com/culture/lifestyle/news/2003/05/58856.

Karp, S. (2008) "How Google Will Monetise YouTube without User Generated Content". Retrieved 13 July 2008 from: http://publishing2.com/2007/12/11/how-google-will-monetise-youyube-without-user-generated-content.html.

Kim, E., and Hamilton, J. W. (2008) "Capitulation to Capital? OhmyNews as Alternative Media", *Media, Culture and Society*, 28 (4), pp. 541–60.

Korea Times (2008) "Korea: Porn on YouTube Alerts Local Portals", *Korea Times*, 27 July 2008. Retrieved 30 August 2008 from: http://www.asiamedia.ucla.edu/article.asp?parentid=74176.

Lasica, J. (2003) "Blogs and Journalism Need Each Other", *Nieman Reports*, Autumn 2003, pp. 70–75.

Murdock, G. (2000) "Money Talks: Broadcasting Finance and Public Culture". In E. Buscombe (ed.), *British Television: A Reader*. Oxford: Clarendon Press, pp. 118–41.

Pecquerie, B., and Kilman, L. (2007) "From Citizen Journalism to User-Generated Content", *Ejournal USA*, 12 (12), pp. 9–11.

Sambrook, R. (2005) "Citizen Journalism and the BBC", *Nieman Reports*, pp. 13–16.

Smith-So, L. (2007) Interview with Liesl Smith-So, then Assistant News Editor, *South Today*.

Thurman, N. (2008) "Forums for Citizen Journalist? Adaptation of User Generated Content Initiatives by Online News Media", *New Media & Society*, 10 (1), pp. 139–57.

Tulloch, J. (2000) "The Eternal Recurrence of New Journalism". In C. Sparks, and J. Tulloch (eds), *Tabloid Tales: Global Debates over Media Standards*. New York and Oxford: Rowman and Littlefield, pp. 131–46.

YouTube. (2008) "You Drive the YouTube Experience". Retrieved 26 June 2008 from: http://www.youtube.com/blog?entry=rqpnstzbgqm.

Vaina, D. (2008) "New Media versus Old Media", *Ejournal USA*, 12 (12), pp. 25–8.

Walker, D. (2006) "Reuters and Yahoo Calling All Citizen Photojournalists". Retrieved 13 July 2008 from: http://www.pdnonline.com/pdn/search/article_display.jsp?vnu_content_id=1003468115.

Watt, J. (2008) "World's First Internet President Logs On". Retrieved 28 September 2006 from: http://www.guardian.co.uk/technology/2003/feb/24/newmedia.koreanews.

⟨⟨ CHAPTER ⟩⟩
12

The Blog in Mainstream Slovenian Journalism: Gatekeeping, Audience and Citizenship

IGOR VOBIČ

Over the last decade it has become possible to map three phases in the shifting relationship between journalism and blogging. At first, the mainstream media was fearful of blogging. This was followed by a period in which the traditional media embraced blogs as a source of information. And, most recently, bloggers have become producers of content alongside staff journalists (Tremayne 2007; Thurman 2008). These shifts have taken place in parallel with an emerging crisis in the classic paradigm of the journalist as a gatekeeper of news (Hardt 1996: 21; Iggers 1999: 75–91; McNair 2000: 7–8). Thus the blog has been presented as a threat to journalism, an opportunity for journalism or a bit of everything (Lowery 2006; McNair 2006: 118–136).

This chapter sets out to ask three interrelated questions concerning the online journalism of Slovenian mainstream media organizations:

- How do blogging and similar interactive forms affect the gatekeeping roles of journalists and others in the newsroom?
- Do these interactive forms bring about a reshaping of the audience from being passive to becoming interactive?
- How does the implementation of these interactive forms affect the Slovenian media's construction of its audience in the context of a consumer–citizen divide?

The investigation is based on an analysis of six leading websites of traditional media organizations in print media, radio and television, and the findings are supported by interviews with the editors who manage these sites. The selected sites were the online newspapers of three most-read quality dailies — *Delo*, *Dnevnik* and *Večer* — the online newspaper of Žurnal24 (Zurnal24.si), which is the largest-circulation free daily, the public broadcaster Radiotelevizija Slovenije (Rtvslo.si) and the largest commercial television stations, POP TV and Kanal A (24ur.com). I explore whether journalism can be revitalized if audiences engage as citizens as well as consumers — bridging the gap between online citizens and those offline in such a way that a connection between the two "communities" can be built.

Recently the online activity of the mainstream media in Slovenia has started to include various forms of interactive communication (Oblak 2005). The major online Slovenian media — 24ur.com, Rtvslo.si, Delo.si, Dnevnik.si, Vecer.si and Zurnal24.si — have incorporated blogging on several levels. Blogs have been included: first, as a permanent part of online newspapers in the traditional media; second, as a form of interactive communication that invites and includes members of the audience of online newspapers in the standard production process; third, as a source of information in the news production process; and fourth, as offering members of the audience the opportunity to create their own blogs and posts within the newspapers' sites. Here I analyse some of this activity between 1 August 2008 and 1 September 2008, revealing that traditional Slovenian media organizations offer an array of interactive forms: online auctions, online games, the ability to send messages to the newsroom, opinion polls, comments on articles, rating of articles, chats, discussion forums and blogs. Furthermore, most of the online newspapers offer links where members of the audience can publish their own "news".

However, my analysis of the websites and interviews with the editors demonstrates that interactivity has not been required in the standard production process. Nevertheless, there have been rare cases where some dialogue has taken place between members of the audience and journalists or editors. Much of the literature dealing with blogging in journalism suggests a shift in the power relationships between journalists and their audience and, in turn, a shift in the role of the journalist as gatekeeper. Indeed the Project for Excellence in Journalism argues that:

> Power is moving away from journalists as gatekeepers over what the public knows. Citizens are assuming a more active role as assemblers, editors and even creators of their own news. Audiences are moving from old media, such as television or newsprint, to new media online. Journalists need to redefine their role and identify which of their core values they want to fight to preserve — something they have only begun to consider. (Project for Excellence in Journalism 2006)

Nip (2006) and Dahlgren (2008) also suggest that the evolution of online communication opens new spaces for the audience to participate in journalistic activity as citizens. However, the success or failure of journalists in dealing with the changing role of technology in their work must also be set against the history of their professional identity, the shifts in the institutional structure of the industry and the fragmentation, or even disappearance, of the audience (Deuze 2007: 157–8).

Deuze (2007: 157) argues that, overall, journalists tend to embrace technology as long as they perceive this will enhance their status or prestige, and that the new practices correspond to the way they did their work before. However, as Garrison (2001: 234) demonstrates, news organizations tend to be reluctant to adopt new technologies early. This, he argues, is because they fear time will be lost while training takes place and that the new resources will be costly. The question of reshaping journalism and, simultaneously, its audience toward interactivity is thus very complex — embracing the effects of more general communication aims, the preferences of journalists, their employers and the audience (Oblak 2005: 99).

As journalism faces a crisis, some suggest the pursuit of interactive journalism could be a driving force leading to its revitalization. For instance, Robinson (2007: 317) stresses that news, in the context of the interactive audience, is becoming "more authentic". The transformation of the audience from a passive into an interactive entity is therefore a question of journalistic culture determined by its institutional and organizational surroundings in politically, economically and culturally specific social contexts.

The transformation of the journalist's gatekeeping role and shifts in the role of the audience theoretically merge in a debate on the divide in audience engagement, between audience-as-consumers and audience-as-participative citizens. According to some in the traditional media, citizens are groomed to expect little that is of serious political use, while members of the audience are addressed as consumers rather than citizens, thereby undermining their identity — and discouraging them from taking action as citizens (Iggers 1999; Campbell 2004; Dahlgren 2007).

However, Couldry, Livingstone and Markham (2008: 119) stress the subtle role of "ordinary consumption" in sustaining citizen engagement, suggesting that members of the audience cannot exclusively be regarded as consumers or as citizens. Indeed, one argument suggests that incorporating blogs and other means of audience participation engages people more as citizens by promoting public deliberation (Nip 2006; Deuze 2007). Nevertheless, this can also be seen as a simultaneous attempt to increase readership, with its attendant economic benefits (Allan 2006: 122).

A Comparative Study of Different Types of Traditional News Media in Slovenia

A study of Internet use in Slovenia, *Raba interneta v Sloveniji 2007*, showed that almost two-thirds of Slovenians between the ages of ten and seventy-five regularly use the Internet. That is more than a million citizens and approximately half the population of Slovenia (Vehovar and Brečko 2008). According to another study *Merjenje Obiskanosti Spletnih Strani*, the websites of both main TV broadcasters have the largest number of different visitors per three weeks: 24ur.com has 700,000 and Rtvslo.si, which is a public service broadcaster providing radio and television, has approximately 460,000 (Slovenska Oglaševalska Zbornica 2008).

Online newspapers

The print press has been at the forefront of introducing opportunities for audience participation. Every three weeks the websites of two national dailies, Delo.si and Zurnal24.si, have a reach of approximately 250,000 each, Vecer.si has 147,000 and Dnevnik.si has approximately 120,000 different visitors. Editorially speaking, the online versions of the newspapers are autonomous, but, even though they have their own news production and content base, they still rely on the journalistic activities of their parent media organizations. And their news production is, likewise, primarily based on rewriting already published agency and other media news.

Delo.si

The daily newspaper *Delo* began in October 2005 and became the first among the traditional media to invite members of the audience to visit Delo.si and open a blog — with the advertising slogans "Have One Too!", "You, Too, Can Blog!" and "Famous Slovenes Also Know How to Blog!". Erika Repovž, editor of Delo.si, says their website is going through a "rationalization" of production. With this, journalists and editors are to concentrate on the production of content — mostly by recycling agency and other media stories — leaving blogs, forums and other interactive environments to the moderators. He says that the blog runs "without any editorial intervention and loyal readers publish within it". However, "Delo.si does not use any content from the blogs in journalistic reporting, because *Delo* is a serious newspaper concentrated on serious news" (E. Repovž 2008).

    Delo's professional journalists and editors can write their blogs, but these are not separated from other blogs.

> The original idea was that the blogs would be written by journalists and editors. The sense of a blog is that it is written by people who can explain the background and other things that cannot be published in the print edition. At present it is very difficult to get in-house writers [to do this]. If the work is not mentioned in the job assignments, and it is unpaid, there is no interest . . . Interactivity is not our focus — it does not popularize. Most of the visitors are attracted only by fresh news and journalists feel vulnerable responding to people's comments, because their identity is not hidden. (E. Repovž 2008)

However, Delo.si has recently created a page called "Delo's Opinions" ("Delova mnenja"), where members of the audience have the chance to comment, express opinions and analyse articles from the print edition. "With Delova mnenja we want to expose leading *Delo* commentators and to praise them. The goal is to attract visitors and preserve the quality level. Responses from the commentators are not intended", says Repovž.

    On these sites technologically implementing interactive forms does not by itself bring interpersonal interactivity, but rather creates a pseudo-interactivity. Despite being oriented towards audience interaction, this pseudo-interactivity remains monological, with the flow of communication predominantly in one direction — from journalists to the audience or *vice versa*.

Zurnal24.si

The online newspaper Zurnal24.si was set up in September 2007, when the free print daily *Žurnal24* started publishing. While *Delo* appears to value neither content generation by the public nor a dialogue between journalists and citizens, Zurnal24.si goes some way towards using the public as content providers. On this site blogs are separated into three parts: Blogs ("Blogi") for members of the audience, Blogs of Celebrities ("Blogi zvezdnikov") with blogs of celebrity columnists, directors, models and others, and the Editors' Blog ("Blogi urednikov"), with blogs from the editors of the online and print editions of *Žurnal24*. The online newspaper Zurnal24.si also has an interactive mechanism, ŽurnalUGC (as in user-generated content), through which it generates content from individual members of the audience via email, text and telephone. Online journalists use this channel as a permanent source of information for producing news stories.

According to Milena Kalacun Lapajne, editor of Zurnal24.si, they also plan to include audience blogs in every section of the online newspaper (News, Sport, Magazine, Scene, Life and Auto). In these cases:

> Some amateur bloggers would become commentators and even opinion-makers . . . Blogs are a trend, however. Nowadays [it] is not enough that they are a part of an online newspaper. The blogs of our readers should be an integrated part of the journalistic content and not completely separated from it . . . However, the editors and journalists would remain those who primarily assemble, select, and produce news. Bloggers will still be just an additional value. (Lapajne 2008)

Indeed, like Delo.si, Zurnal24.si does not cultivate interpersonal interactivity between the journalists and the readers. As Lapajne puts it: "We [will] respond to [a] collective push by the readers, [but] journalists usually do not respond to individual comments, unless they are explicitly asked for an explanation. Journalists primarily inform, visitors primarily read."

Nevertheless, he goes on to say:

> By including people in [the] journalistic experience they feel [a] stronger affiliation to [the] virtual community within Zurnal24.si. This is especially important because we strive to have many loyal visitors. News is business and profit is our goal. Our prime responsibility is to the owner. Of course, we have also a big responsibility to the public. (Lapajne 2008)

Vecer.si

The online newspaper Vecer.si provides "Večer's Blogosphere" ("Večerova blogosfera"), where members of the audience can open their own blogs and navigate over 2,800 blogs, using a search engine to take them to the most-visited and commented-on blogs and posts. Darko Šterbenk, editor of Vecer.si, takes a similar position to Lapajne of Zurnal24, saying:

> We have included blogs because we think that Vecer.si readers should have an option to express their opinions. However, further integration of bloggers with journalistic content is difficult, because their content is predominantly less important than serious news. (Šterbenk 2008)

However, according to Zvone Štor, who is the editor responsible for "Večerova blogosfera", Vecer.si uses its own blogosphere as a recruitment tool. "Three former bloggers have become members of the newsroom. We observed them for a while and then slowly introduced them to journalism by asking them to write stories on a specific topic" (Štor 2008). Vecer.si has also used information from bloggers as a basis for its news production process. Furthermore, Vecer.si provides guidelines on how to write, take photos and shoot videos. According to Štor: "In the context of citizen journalism it is a problem when [the] subjectivity of bloggers is taken to an extreme. Therefore, we draw attention to basic journalistic criteria and ethical norms. Some bloggers take this seriously and they are aware that the know-how of traditional journalism is useful."

Večer and Vecer.si journalists and editors do not have their own blogs. "Journalists and editors have the print edition to write in. It is important that we give space to people from the street; to those who have something to say and are unable to do so in the traditional media. The posts of certain bloggers are also published in the print edition," says Štor. He selects posts that are to be published in the print newspaper on the basis of frequency of visits, the number of comments and linkability. They are printed with all the typos, spelling, grammatical and other errors, and the bloggers receive a token payment.

Again, interpersonal interactivity is not an institutional requirement within Vecer.si:

> Journalists do not have time to respond, because they have to produce pieces one after another. Their task is to inform the audience professionally about the problems in the community. The organization of our small newsroom just does not allow anything more. However, in theory, every journalist should long for interaction with the readers. (Šterbenk 2008)

Thus Štor and Šterbenk both stress that visitors are important primarily for commercial reasons — and not so crucially to enhance interactivity.

Dnevnik.si

Dnevnik.si is the website of the national daily *Dnevnik*. During the period of research this site received the lowest number of regular hits. Dnevnik.si has a page entitled "Your Articles" ("Vaši prispevki"), divided in to "Tell What You Think" ("Povej, kaj misliš"), where readers are explicitly invited by the editor's questions to express their opinion on a given subject, and "Your News" ("Vaše novice"), where stories by readers are published and commented on.

Dnevnik.si journalists have access to a blog to publish stories that depart from traditional journalistic norms. Milan Slana, editor of Dnevnik.si, says:

> Those journalists who do not have opinion articles in the print edition have an opportunity to express their opinions. The blog also offers the opportunity for representatives of civil society, that is, marginal groups and those who are otherwise excluded from the mass media — but . . . [there has not been] . . . much response. (Slana 2008)

The online newspaper does not offer blogs to the general audience. "Blogs for visitors will not be a part of the vision, as we were somewhat delayed [in appearing]. There are already many blogs in Slovenia, and those who want to create a blog have already done so," stresses Slana. He adds, regarding "Your Articles": "This page is a compensation for the exclusion of the forum from Dnevnik.si — moderation is much easier. Now we have more control over content sent by the readers. We publish only legally and morally suitable content." The editor of Dnevnik.si stresses that interactive forms are important for community-building. "It is necessary to have a community and *pro et contra* discussions if Dnevnik.si wants to retain the number of visitors and to survive," claims Slana. He suggests there are three main reasons for the lack of interactivity: first, content is only sent by a small section of the audience; second, the relationship between the anonymous members of the audience and the visible journalists is undeveloped; and third, there is a lack of time owing to the standardization of the production process (Slana 2008).

Rtvslo.si

Blogs were first integrated into the website of the public broadcaster Radiotelevizija Slovenija (RTVS) in September 2006. Since then the website has gone through minor changes and blogs remain separated on a page called "My Web" ("Moj Splet"), which also offers links to chat-rooms, a forum and a link to Second Life, where Rtvslo.si has its own island. The blogs are separated in three categories: blogs written by members of the audience under the heading "Your Blogs" ("Vaši blogi"), blogs of well-known individuals (musicians, academics, writers, models and others) under "Guests" ("Gostje") and blogs of voluntary journalists, editors, anchors and others from RTVS under RTV.

Igor Pirkovič, editor of Rtvslo.si, says:

> User-generated content should be completely separated from the journalistic content, but users . . . should feel that they co-develop the content. Users are not professionals and their autonomy is limited — in terms of respect of others and good taste. [The] editor is the one who is responsible for everything published within Rtvslo.si. (Pirkovič 2008)

Nevertherless, hyper-local community news is published on the "Your News" ("Vaša novica") page. About this Pirkovič says: "We have to find as many stories from people's lives as possible. They are not important for the community, but people easily identify with them. The philosophy is simple: if people co-produce, they feel important and are part of this medium." Indeed, Zvezdan Martič, director of RTVS's Multimedia Centre, reveals that "as a public broadcaster we were almost required to offer blogs to our viewers, listeners and readers as a form of communication" (Martič 2007).

Within Rtvslo.si, then, interaction between journalists and members of the audience is rare. The only exception is that some journalists and other RTVS workers voluntarily write blogs for Rtvslo.si. They are, according to Pirkovič, not given an additional payment for blogging, and they operate independently of the broadcaster's editorial guidelines. Pirkovič says he is aware of the responsibility RTVS has in the Slovenian media system:

> We have to balance between quality and market needs. Human-interest stories generate most of the visits, but we have to remain on the level suitable for public service . . . Most of the journalists are too occupied with producing news and do not have time to interact. We should be cautious of furthering interactivity because of the uneven power being given to journalists and visitors — the latter have the right to be anonymous, the former do not have this right. We cherish interactivity only among visitors. (Pirkovič 2008)

24ur.com

The news programmes of POP TV and Kanal A and the news portal 24ur.com are produced by Pro Plus, which is jointly funded by the US-owned media organization CME. The website offers most of the interactive forms mentioned above. Pro Plus television journalists have been invited to write blogs but have not done so, owing to the fact that engaging in blogging and similar practices are not part of their contracts. 24ur.com has recently closed down its "Your News" ("Vaše novice") page, where members of the audience were asked to send their "news" with the invitation: "Have you been witness to an event that would interest the public? Has something that bothers you fallen on deaf ears among those responsible for it? Send us your news!"

Barbara Repovž explains that members of the audience predominantly sent photographs of children, pets and sunsets. "When a traffic accident or natural disaster happened people sent us information, photos, and videos — but not via Vaše novice, but via email or telephone." Instead, the opportunity to interact is offered to the audience under the heading "Friends and Flirts" ("Frendi in Flirt"). In this section blogs take the form of personal comment and diary entries narrowed to the specific interests of members of the audience and are separate from journalistic content. Barbara Repovž, editor of 24ur.com, comments:

> Frendi in Flirt attracts a substantial amount of visitors, and 24ur.com has it because the bosses want it. Moderators very rarely inform us about interesting content, photos or videos useful

in further journalistic work. A large majority of information on the blogs is useless. (B. Repovž 2008)

As Repovž explains, interactivity is not part of their newsroom culture:

Online journalists do not have time for interactivity. Online journalism is an industry. Furthermore, there are only a few visitors' responses worth responding to. We check their feedback, but that is all. However, interactive forms within 24ur.com are important for building a community and regularizing people's visits. The bosses' happiness increases with the number of visits. If the bosses are happy, I am happy. (B. Repovž 2008)

Conclusion

The research presented here suggests that the answers to my research questions are far from straightforward. Indeed, it seems that Splichal's assertion still stands: "New communication technologies may indeed have a revolutionary character in the technological sense, but all its social consequences cannot transform the cultural, political and economic continuity" (1999: 312). Looking at the problem of interactivity and the opportunity for audiences to become active participants in the construction of news, it would appear that blogging has to some extent become normalized as an everyday part of the online newspaper environment. However, the technological functioning of this and the other interactive forms considered does not by itself bring about a dialogical interconnection. Instead, what is offered is an illusion of interactivity. Whether it is from the journalist to the audience, or *vice versa*, the flow of communication is predominantly unidirectional and monological in nature.

It would appear then that the traditional Slovenian media are ambivalent towards incorporating blogging and other interactive practices into the production process. Furthermore, the pseudo-interactive communication offered by online newspapers limits any transformation in the traditional journalist's gatekeeping role. It denies communitarian ideas of changing the news audience into interactive citizens who can dynamically enter the news production process — either to deliberate with journalists or to suggest solutions to communal problems. In considering the question of gatekeeping, it would appear then that there has been little shift in the traditional role of the journalist.

We also asked how the incorporation of blogging and other interactive forms may have affected the news organizations' construction of the audience as consumers or citizens. The current position is to some extent summarized by Milan Slana's revealing distinction between professional journalistic content and the prospect of audiences as content providers: "So-called citizen journalism is a threat to journalism because it uses mainstream media as an information source to build a critique of traditional journalism." What, then, is the purpose of offering these monological interactive forms? On the basis of the evidence here, I would argue that the traditional media is primarily striving to attract numerous visitors who will return frequently.

The "rationalization" of the news production process by traditional Slovenian media organizations has tended to treat the production of news as a particular industrial process. Here journalists are positioned as industrial workers within the traditional gatekeeping hierarchy and members of the audience are located as passive consumers of news, rather than as a community of (actualizing) citizens. There is not much evidence of the democratic potential promised by incorporating blogging as a form of communication — offering the possibility of connecting to the community, engaging individuals as citizens and helping public deliberation. In this regard, Slovenian online journalism by itself has not brought fundamental changes to the journalist's gatekeeping role or provided any dramatic transformations in the notion of the audience or the grounding of citizens in a new public communication.

References

Allan, S. (2006) *Online News*. New York: Open University Press.

Campbell, V. (2004) *Information Age Journalism: Journalism in an International Context*. London and New York: Arnold.

Couldry, N., Livingstone, S., and Markham, T. (2008) "'Public Connection' and the Uncertain Norms of Media Consumption". In: Soper, K., and Trentmann, F. (eds), *Citizenship and Consumption*. Basingstoke: Palgrave MacMillan, pp. 104–20.

Dahlgren, P. (2007) "Introduction: Youth, Civic Engagement and Learning via New Media". In P. Dahlgren (ed.), *Young Citizens and New Media: Learning Democracy*. New York: Routledge, pp. 1–15.

Dahlgren, P. (2008) *Media and Political Engagement: Citizens, Communication and Democracy*. New York: Cambridge University Press.

Deuze, M. (2007) *Media Work*. Cambridge: Polity.

Garrison, B. (2001) "Diffusion of Online Information Technologies in Newspaper Newsrooms", *Journalism*, 2 (2), pp. 221–39.

Hardt, H. (1996) "The End of Journalism: Media and Newswork in the United States", *Javnost/The Public*, 3 (3), pp. 21–41.

Iggers, J. (1999) *Good News, Bad News: Journalism Ethics and Public Discourse*. Boulder, CO: Westview Press.

Lapajne, M. K. (2008) Interview with the author, 2 September.

Lowery, W. (2006) "Mapping the Journalism–Blogging Relationship", *Journalism*, 7 (4), pp. 477–500.

Martič, Z. (2007) Interview with the author, 8 January.

McNair, B. (2000) *Journalism and Democracy: An Evaluation of the Political Public Sphere*. London and New York: Routledge.

McNair, B. (2006) *Cultural Chaos: Journalism, News and Power in a Globalised World*. London and New York: Routledge.

Nip, J. (2006) "Exploring the Second Phase of Public Journalism", *Journalism Studies*, 7 (2), pp. 212–36.

Oblak, T. (2005) "The Lack of Interactivity and Hypertextuality in Online Media", *Gazette*, 67 (1), pp. 87–106.

Pirkovič, I. (2008) Interview with the author, 3 September.

Project for Excellence in Journalism (2006) "The State of the News Media 2006: An Annual Report on American Journalism". Retrieved 1 June 2008 from:

http://www.stateofthenewsmedia.org/2006/narrative_overview_intro.asp.

Repovž, B. (2008) Interview with the author, 5 September.

Repovž, E. (2008) Interview with the author, 5 September.

Robinson, S. (2007) "'Someone's Gotta be in Control Here': The Institutionalization of Online News and the Creation of a Shared Journalistic Authority", *Journalism Practice*, 1 (3), pp. 305–21.

Slana, M. (2008) Interview with the author, 4 September.

Slovenska Oglaševalska Zbornica (2008) *Merjenje Obiskanosti Spletnih Strani. MOSS – Pomlad 2008*. Retrieved from: http://www.soz.si/uploads/MOSS_Pomlad_2008_Dosegi.pdf.

Splichal, S. (1999) *Public Opinion: Developments and Controversies in the Twentieth Century*. Lanham, MD: Rowman and Littlefield.

Štor, Z. (2008) Interview with the author, 2 September.

Šterbenk, D. (2008) Interview with the author, 2 September.

Tremayne, M. (2007) "Introduction: Examining the Blog-Media Relationship". In M. Tremayne (ed.), *Blogging, Citizenship and the Future of Media*. London and New York: Routledge, pp. ix–xix.

Thurman, N. (2008) "Forums for Citizen Journalists? Adoption of User Generated Content Initiatives by Online News Media", *New Media & Society*, 10 (1), pp. 139–57.

Vehovar, V, and Bre ko, B. N. (2008) *Raba interneta v Sloveniji 2007*. Retrieved 1 September 2008 from: http://www.ris.org/uploadi/editor/1210328301Uporaba%20interneta 2007.pdf.

A Study of Journalistic and Source Transparency in US Online Newspaper and Online Citizen Journalism Articles

SERENA CARPENTER

Transparency has been heralded as a journalistic principle that can promote the relationship between journalists and news users. It has been touted as the value that is expected to flourish as news outlets begin to understand better how online is different from traditional offline news publications (Gillmor 2006). The principle of transparency essentially means openness. The Center for Citizen Media (2007) defined transparency in the form of a verb — the act of disclosure. The act of disclosing hypothetically encourages communication between journalists and news users. Openness can encourage interaction because people are more likely to engage in dialogue if they trust the source (Plaisance 2007). If journalists were transparent, Plaisance (2007) argued, news users might begin to identify with and trust them. The application of transparency in newsrooms has been said to be one approach in repairing the credibility of the field of journalism (Harris Interactive Poll 2007; Ziomek 2004).

To assess whether news organizations are encouraging full disclosure, a quantitative content analysis was conducted of online newspaper and online citizen journalism articles. The Aspen Institute (Ziomek 2004), an international non-profit organization that addresses the impact of communications, has argued that transparent behaviour for journalists consists of completely identifying sources and offering opportunities for news users to communicate with journalists. For this investigation, an examination of source and journalist transparency was conducted on 962 online articles. The research operationally defined source transparency by measuring whether sources were fully identified in articles, while journalistic transparency was recorded by identifying whether journalists provided an email address, a phone number, a comment opportunity or a profile of themselves near each article.

The online citizen journalism articles selected for this study derive solely from sites that focus their coverage on a geographic area of the US, rather than on an issue (for example, politics or education). For the purposes of this chapter I have defined an online citizen journalist as "an individual who intends to publish information online that is meant to benefit a community". In the US it is a First Amendment right to publish, and any infringement on that right goes against the ideals of the First Amendment. "Intent" protects the rights of journalists as they gather information. "Community" refers to "the interconnected relationships among people who share a common goal, neighborhood, and/or relationship" (Kurpius 2000: 340). "Benefits" indicates that journalists should publish information meant for the good of the public, rather than to misinform them.

This research had two goals. First, it assessed to what extent journalists in the US are being transparent. Second, comparisons were made to determine to what extent online citizen journalists and online newspaper journalists differed in their inclusion of transparent information.

ONLINE CITIZEN JOURNALISM AND TRADITIONAL JOURNALISM

Many of the constraints that traditional media providers face are dissimilar from the constraints of online citizen journalists. These are likely to contribute to differences in content. For the purpose of this investigation, traditional news media are defined as commercial news organizations that have historically focused on the daily delivery of information concerning a geographic (for example, local, state, national or international) area in either a textual, audio or visual format offline. Traditional journalists who work for an organization are more likely to conform to organizational norms and thus behave in a more predictable manner, because traditional journalists share the organization's goals and values, while online citizen journalists are likely to experience a greater degree of independence (Shoemaker and Reese 1996).

There are few studies conducted on online citizen journalism publications; however, differences in content may be attributed to the perceived variation in their consumers (Carpenter 2007; The Institute for Interactive Journalism 2007). Citizen-generated content is likely to be published for smaller, more homogeneous audiences on a less regular basis, which encourages citizen journalists to produce content dissimilar from that of daily newspaper journalists (Johnstone et al. 1976; Tichenor, et al. 1980). Daily newspapers journalists cater their content to a larger diversity of people.

Research conducted on alternative, neighbourhood, weekly, urban, dissident and community-oriented publications can shed light on citizen journalism publications (Duncan 1952; Janowitz 1952; Hindman 1998; Gladney 1990; Kessler 1984; Reader 2006; Ward and Gaziano 1976). These types of publications can be categorized as "smaller" publications. Smaller publications primarily cover issues, people or events that affect smaller communities, neighbourhoods or suburban areas. In many cases these types of publications are available to the public at no cost (Lacy 2002). Smaller publications, whether urban or rural, tend to emphasize community consensus over conflict, advocacy over objectivity and interpretation over straight reporting (Gladney 1990; Hindman 1998; Janowitz 1952; Johnstone et al. 1976; Reader 2006; Tichenor et al. 1980; The Institute for Interactive Journalism 2007). Smaller publications balance their community's needs with their desire to produce professional journalistic content; however, their allegiance typically teeters toward their community (Reader 2006; Weaver et al. 2007), and content reflects their own and their local community leaders' viewpoints (Hindman 1998; Janowitz 1952). Recent survey research supports this community-booster role: many online citizen journalists feel that their online publications create opportunities for dialogue (82 percent) and build a connection to their community (74 percent) (The Institute for Interactive Journalism 2007).

TRANSPARENCY

The principle of transparency is related to the notion that journalists strive to produce the truth. The principle of truth is correlated with the principle of veracity. Getting to the truth requires journalists vigorously to question the reality presented by biased sources. Kovach and Rosenstiel (2001) suggest that journalism should embody certain values, for example by verifying information offered by sources and being accountable for the information presented. The authors argue that verification is what separates journalists from other information providers.

The hope is that the application of transparency in newsrooms will encourage readers to question information offered by sources and journalists. By fully revealing all facets of a story, journalists can encourage readers to allow themselves to be vulnerable enough to participate in and critique the news process (Tompkins 2003). People process information differently, and the presence of transparent information can help people understand an issue on a deeper level if journalists provide access to the same information that was used to construct a story, rather than just providing their edited interpretation of an issue. However, O'Neill (2006) warns that being transparent should not mean that the information provider *disseminates* the information, but rather they must *communicate* it. Otherwise, the mere presence of additional information online may create confusion because it sometimes can only be found and interpreted by people with relevant expertise. Thus, transparency has the potential to worsen communication.

But, used appropriately, transparency can protect against biased sources manipulating the news media to their benefit (Kovach and Rosenstiel 2001). Most journalism codes of ethics stress the importance of identifying sources fully (APME 1994; AP 2006; BBC 2008; CBC 2004; RTNDA 2000; SPJ 1996). Providing the full identity of a source illustrates to users how journalists' stories are built and allows users to assess the validity of information presented (Plaisance 2007). In this study, source transparency was defined by measuring the presence of anonymous sources in articles and whether journalists fully identified their sources in articles.

ANONYMOUS SOURCES

The use of anonymous or unnamed sources undermines the credibility of information presented to the public, which fuels the loss of confidence in journalism, according to the Nieman Reports (2005). The Pew Research Center for the People and the Press (2005) revealed that a little more than half (52 percent) of the people that it surveyed believed that the reliance on unnamed sources could lead to faulty or unreliable information. Nevertheless, past survey and experimental research has shown that people do not perceive anonymous sources as less credible than fully identified sources (Rains 2007; Wilson et al. 1997). Rains (2007) speculated that people make inferences about why people conceal their identity, and they believe that their veiled inclusion is justified in order to protect themselves. However, Riffe (1980) found that, over time, readers have become less willing to accept journalists' use of anonymous governmental sources. He argued that using veiled sources made news stories far less believable. Categories of news such as war, national security and US government tend to feature more anonymous sources than entertainment or lifestyle categories (Martin-Kratzer and Thorson 2007; Zhang and Cameron 2003).

For the most part, US newspaper publications do not contain a proportionately high number of anonymous sources (Zoch and Turk 1998). This may be because traditional journalists are trained to identify a source fully. But research has shown that US national publications are more likely to cite anonymous sources than smaller publications (Project for Excellence in Journalism 2006). Culbertson (1975, 1978) found that *The New York Times* and *The Washington Post* were more likely to contain anonymous sources than six dailies in the state of Ohio. This may be because they tend to cover more government and national security topics than smaller publications (Shim 2006).

SOURCE TRANSPARENCY

Even if sources are named, the amount of information provided about a source can vary. Critics have urged news organizations to become more transparent in their reporting by identifying their sources fully, including their titles and their association to the story (Moeller et al. 2007). If a person's title or full name is not available, news users may not understand their connection to the story and they may not be able to confirm whether the information they provided is reliable.

JOURNALIST TRANSPARENCY

Transparency includes revealing the background information not only regarding a source, but also the background information concerning a journalist. Bias is inevitable. However, what is more important is that a journalist or an organization reveals the background that they bring to a story. Shoemaker and Reese (1996) contend that how journalists see themselves, including their biases, ultimately affects content. Providing full disclosure of a journalist's background reflects how accountable the journalist is willing to be towards their work. If a news organization does not reveal this information, it is difficult for the reader to assess the qualifications of the author (Hovland et al. 1953).

Computer-mediated communication and interpersonal theory can be used to understand to some extent the importance of disclosing one's identity. Online news is evolving into a two-way conversation, which means that both mass communication and interpersonal literature can be utilized to help understand the importance of relationship-building online (O'Sullivan 1999). Self-disclosure has been a widely studied variable in interpersonal communications because it is a key component in relationship building. Self-disclosure can be defined as communicating a message about oneself to another (Cozby 1973; Wheeless 1978). The online environment can be referred to as a "reduced-cues environment". In other words, some of the informational cues that would be available in face-to-face communication are not available. Thus people must compensate for the lack of non-verbal and contextual information. To further a relationship or trust online, one must disclose more information about oneself to make up for the absence of nonverbal information (Walther and Bunz 2005). Social information-processing theory suggests that the contribution of additional information in a computer-mediated environment is necessary to reduce uncertainty among communicators (Walther 1992; Walther and Burgoon 1992). However, Dan Gillmor, a leader in online journalism and director of the Knight Center for Digital Media Entrepreneurship, contends that the traditional news media have performed poorly in being transparent (Gillmor 2005) and that they will thus be likely to continue withholding information about their own background.

The posting of feedback opportunities online provides visual encouragement to news users to collaborate with journalists. Many news organizations produce quality journalism every day. However distrust can still occur (Harris Interactive Poll 2007). There is increased distrust when there is a lack of communication (Insko et al. 1993). The posting of a journalist's phone number, direct email address and profile may prompt citizens to access the journalist. The presence of phone number is desirable in situations where the user needs to access the journalist immediately, and a journalist's email address is attractive when expediency is not a concern (Ramirez, Walther, Burgoon and Sunnafrank 2002). General email addresses can be used to direct the user's comment or question to the newsroom (Domingo 2008). However, rarely do traditional journalists respond, even if a direct email address of a reporter is posted, because news people are not allotted enough time and resources to respond to consumers and also because much of their email content is spam and press releases (Domingo 2008; Fishman 1988; Randle et al. 2006; Ye and Li 2006).

This analysis not only assessed the transparency by examining the availability of an email address and a journalist profile, but it also recorded the commenting capabilities adjacent to each article as well. The Radio-Television News Directors Association (RTNDA) code of ethics states that it is the news organization's responsibility to respond to public concerns (RTNDA 2000). Communication opportunities are related to an increase in civic knowledge (Nichols et al. 2006). Comment links or boxes present readers with a more transparent approach to communication with journalists. Based on observations, a public conversation can evolve when a journalist responds to a person commenting by using the comment function adjacent to an article. The comment option offers users a choice to publicly communicate with journalists regarding the quality of their reporting, and it allows the journalist the opportunity to respond to any critique or comment (Gillmor 2006; Lowrey and Anderson 2005). This option to express one's views publicly has been regarded as a highly necessary element of journalism (AP 2006; ASNE 2006; Kovach and Rosenstiel 2001; SND 2006; SPJ 1996). However, the comment option can increase a news outlet's workload (Domingo 2008). Many news organizations have comment-screening policies in place for fear of publishing offensive comments (Walters 2007). Offensive comments may actually hinder discussion among news users for fear of negative attacks from other people who comment. In addition, the presence of user comments may also affect the willingness of sources to be cited within a news article.

RESEARCH QUESTIONS AND METHOD

In order to gain a greater understanding of the differences between online citizen and newspaper journalists, this research was guided by three questions:

- Will online citizen journalism or online newspaper articles differ in their use of anonymous sources?
- Will online citizen journalism or online newspaper articles differ in their use of identifying background information of sources?
- Are online citizen journalists or online newspaper journalists more likely to publish biographical information about the author and contact opportunities?

This study employed a quantitative content analysis of articles from English-language daily newspaper and citizen journalism websites in the US. This investigation was restricted to newspapers that had an online presence and did not include websites for radio and television outlets. Newspaper websites were preferred to radio and television news websites because online newspaper sites are greater in number and geographic diversity.

The unit of analysis for this investigation was the individual text article located on the home page of the news website for one day's time. Articles also included editorials, opinion pieces, blog posts and columns. Analysis was restricted to the home page because to examine deeper into the website would be difficult owing to the growing complexity of news sites. In addition, limiting the analysis to the home page was intended to encourage uniformity in coding (Greer and Mensing 2006; Ha and James 1998).

In this national sample, wire articles were excluded because many of the online publications featured the same articles across publications, diminishing the variability in content. Article categories also excluded from the analysis included sports articles and weather forecasts, because rarely does coverage of such topics change over time, according to The Project for Excellence in Journalism (1999). In addition, other articles excluded were calendars of events, obituaries, wedding announcements, advertisements, multimedia without text (for example, information graphics, maps, videos, audio, photos, graphics, slide-shows), horoscopes, birthdays, letters to the editor, photo of the day, Dow Jones, top emailed stories, most popular articles, magazine articles, open threads, reader feedback, article corrections and comments adjacent to articles.

ONLINE CITIZEN JOURNALISM SAMPLE

Online newspaper articles were compared with online citizen journalism articles. In this study, both publication types concentrated on creating content that is focused on community issues, events and people. The use of online newspapers for comparative purposes can highlight the value of both publication types, especially during a time when negative assumptions are being made regarding the reliability, accuracy and fairness of content produced by both citizen journalists and newspaper journalists (Brown 2005; Harris Interactive Poll 2005; Shaw 2005).

A purposive sample of online citizen journalism sites was selected because no master online citizen journalism site list exists. To begin the selection process, Cyberjournalist.net was consulted. Cyberjournalist.net is a site that is dedicated to examining how technology affects the news media. In the early spring of 2007 Cyberjournalist.net listed 77 US "citizen media initiatives" (Dube 2007). Each site was placed in two categories, based on the home city of the publication from the Cyberjournalist.net list of "citizen media initiatives". The goal was to find two citizen journalism websites to represent all fifty states (one "small" and one "large" community from each state in the US). To accomplish this task of selecting two sites to represent each state, one site was selected because it covered a city with a total resident population of more than 100,000, and the other because it covered a city with fewer than 100,000 people (Demers 1994). For example, the MyMileHighNews, based in Denver (population 557, 917), and the Glenwood Blog, based in Glenwood Springs (population 8,564), represented the state of Colorado.

However, the master Cyberjournalist.net list of seventy-seven sites did not provide a diverse or large enough number of sites to represent all fifty states. To supplement the master sample list from Cyberjournalist.net, Placeblogger.com was used. Placeblogs are sites devoted to covering a particular neighbourhood, city or region (Williams 2006). There were 1,011 placeblogs listed in the US in the early spring of 2007. The final list of online citizen journalism sites totalled seventy-two sites; 51 percent of the sites were extracted from the Placeblogger directory. Iowa was the only state that had no citizen journalism site representing it and twenty-one states had only one citizen journalism site representing their state.

ONLINE NEWSPAPER SAMPLE

After the online citizen journalism list was complete, a matching technique was used to populate the online newspaper list. For the online newspaper sample, an online newspaper was matched to each citizen journalism site city. For example, in Alabama, the Birmingham Blog online citizen site's counterpart was *The Birmingham News* online newspaper. An online daily newspaper was not included in the final sample if a newspaper was not found to represent the home community of the citizen journalism site. A total of fifty online daily newspapers were found to match the online citizen journalism publication's home city.

SAMPLING PROCEDURE

Once the online citizen journalism and online newspaper lists were complete, the sampling procedure was determined. Analysis of online daily newspaper websites is difficult because news can be updated hourly (Greer and Mensing 2006). This creates content analysis challenges because citizen journalism content is updated less often than online newspapers.

This study utilized two different sampling techniques because of the likelihood that online daily newspaper content would be over-represented. To compensate for the expected fewer numbers of articles available daily, online citizen journalism content was captured every day for one month (March 2007), while online newspaper articles were captured every day for a period of one week during that same month. More specifically, a constructed one-week sample was collected for online newspapers. A constructed week is a randomly selected week. According to Riffe, Aust and Lacy (1993), one constructed week for daily newspapers is an efficient sample for a six-month period, and the constructed week is used as a control for days that feature a greater number of articles. Articles were printed off at the same time each day.

NEWSPAPER AND ONLINE CITIZEN JOURNALISM STORY SAMPLE

This sampling procedure produced a total of 6,485 articles — 2,221 from citizen journalists and 4,264 online newspaper pieces. To make the study more manageable while maintaining the meaningfulness of the data, articles were randomly reduced to 500 for online citizen journalism sites and 500 for online newspaper sites. From the available 1,000 articles selected from the 50 online newspaper sites and 72 online citizen journalism sites, some articles were discarded because they featured sports, wire articles or other excluding factors. After extracting the unusable articles from the 1,000-story samples, 962 articles were available for analysis (480 online newspaper articles and 482 online citizen journalism articles).

CODER RELIABILITY

To establish inter-coder reliability, two graduate students coded 9 percent of the total sample — that is, 91 articles. Reliability is the extent to which coders agree on the operational definitions of variables when coding content. This process helps ensure that author bias does not affect the results of the study. Training of coders took approximately twenty-five hours, and training was not conducted on content included within the sample. Coders used a standardized codebook to determine how to proceed when coding variables. To determine inter-coder reliability for variables, Pearson's correlation was used. Riffe, Lacy and Fico (2005) suggest using Pearson's product-moment correlation coefficient to determine ratio level inter-coder reliability. Pearson's correlation above a .80 level is a sufficient level for reliability. Inter-coder reliability for ratio level variables ranged from .83 to .86.

To determine inter-coder reliability for nominal level variables, Scott's Pi computation was selected for nominal level variables because it corrects for chance agreement. In addition, Scott's Pi is a conservative index because it assumes that proportions are not true proportions, but rather the result of agreement among coders. Finally, Scott's Pi is useful for nominal-level categories when two coders are used (Lombard, Snyder-Duch and Bracken 2002). The reliability of nominal level variables ranged from .85 to 1.0.

CODING CATEGORIES

Source Anonymity

An article was considered to have anonymous sources if such anonymity was explicitly granted in the story to a source, or if sources were referred to with only unidentifiable attribution (for example, "sources said"). The identity of the source was impossible to establish. Coders also identified the number of anonymous sources used in an unofficial (for example, bystanders) capacity and an official (for example, White House aide) capacity.

Source Transparency

A source was considered transparent when the full identification of the source was cited, including the identification of how the sources were connected to the story. Source transparency enables a person to seek the information from same source as the journalist. Coders determined whether a full name and a title of the source were available, and if not, identified whether it could be determined how the source was directly connected to a article. For example, a source that has a name but no title was classified as a non-transparent source (Project for Excellence in Journalism 2006).

Serena Carpenter

Journalist Transparency

This variable involved holding the journalists accountable for their own reporting. Coders recorded whether a direct Web address for the journalist (for example, rob.davis@news.com), a general email address (editor@news.com), an author profile or a phone number was located adjacent to the article.

RESULTS

The final sample included 480 online newspaper and 482 online citizen journalism articles. More than half (55 percent) of the online citizen journalism articles were blog posts, while 5 percent of the analysed online newspaper articles were blog posts. Blog content in most newspapers is likely to be similar to their article content. Wall says journalism blogs should be constructed like a column in a newspaper with highly personal and opinionated comments from bloggers (Wall 2005). However, many news organizations do not allow the inclusion of reporter opinion in their stories. For example, two US newspapers, *The Washington Post* and *The Arizona Republic*, do not allow reporter opinion in their blogs (Leach 2007; Manning 2008). If a news organization does allow journalists to include opinion, this inclusion may put journalists in an uncomfortable role because many journalists have been trained to be objective observers of news (Schudson 2003). Thus, blog and news content are likely to be similar in nature on traditional newspaper home pages.

The use of sources by publication types varied. Almost one-third (32.6 percent) of online citizen journalism publications did not contain a source, while 11.9 percent of online newspaper articles did not contain a source. Online newspaper articles were more likely to have on average more sources (3.64) than online citizen journalism articles (1.37).

Table 13.1 Presence of Anonymous Sources in Articles

	Online Newspapers	Online Citizen Journalism
Source Type	n=480	n=482
Anonymous	21.0%	16.6%
Official Anonymous*	18.8%	4.6%
Unofficial Anonymous*	4.2%	12.9%

*p > .01, difference in proportions tests

The first research question asked how these publications differed regarding their use of anonymous sources. Based on a difference in proportions test, online newspaper articles (21 percent) were more likely to contain an anonymous source than online citizen journalism articles (16.6 percent). However there was not a significant difference between each publication type. There was a significant difference related to the presence of official and unofficial anonymous sources in articles (p < .01). Online newspaper journalists were more likely to cite official anonymous sources (18.8 percent) than online citizen journalists (4.6 percent), while online citizen journalists (12.9 percent) were more likely to cite unofficial anonymous sources than online newspapers (4.2 percent) (See Table 13.1 on previous page).

The second research question addressed whether publication types differed in how they identified sources in articles. A difference in proportions test revealed that online newspaper journalists (84.4 percent) were significantly more likely to cite transparent sources in articles than online citizen journalists (46.6 percent) (p < .01) (See Table 13.2). However, there was no significant difference related to the inclusion of non-transparent sources in online newspaper (34.8 percent) and online citizen journalism (33.8 percent) articles.

Table 13.2 Presence of Transparent and Non-transparent Sources in Articles

Source Type	Online Newspapers	Online Citizen Journalism
	n=480	n=482
Transparent*	84.4%	46.6%
Nontransparent	34.8%	33.8%

*p > .01, difference in proportions tests

The transparency of a journalist reflects the willingness of the journalist to stand behind his or her story by being available to answer questions regarding the veracity of its content. The third research question addressed this willingness on the part of the journalist or organization. The most open form of communication online is the comment opportunity. A difference in proportions test indicated that online citizen journalists (87.3 percent) were significantly more likely to provide an opportunity to publicly respond to their work than online newspaper journalists (19.4 percent) (p < .01). Online citizen journalists (20.5 percent) were significantly more likely to provide a journalist profile adjacent to the article than newspaper journalists (0.8 percent). While citizen journalists preferred the comment option, newspaper journalists (59.8 percent) were more apt to communicate with their readers via a direct email address than citizen journalists (29.9 percent). (See Table 13.3.)

Table 13.3 Presence of Journalist Transparency Article Attributes

Transparency Attributes	Online Newspapers	Online Citizen Journalism
	n=480	n=482
Direct Journalist Email*	60%	30%
Journalist Phone*	33%	0%
Public Comment*	19%	87%
General Journalist Email	3%	3%
Journalist Profile*	1%	21%

*p > .01, difference in proportions tests

Discussion

In summary, online newspaper journalists were more likely to include transparent sources but were less likely to be as transparent themselves as online citizen journalists. There were no differences in the use of anonymous sources between the two publication types. However, there was a difference in the use of official and unofficial anonymous sources. Newspaper journalists preferred to communicate via a direct email address, while online citizen journalists preferred to engage in dialogue using the "open comment" function.

There was no difference related to the presence of anonymous sources in articles between online citizen journalism publications and online newspapers, but there was a difference in the use of official and unofficial anonymous sources. Online citizen journalists were more likely to cite unofficial anonymous sources, while online newspaper journalists were more likely to include official anonymous sources.

Kovach and Rosenstiel (2001) have warned against citing anonymous sources as the first quote in a story or incorporating anonymous sources who express their opinion of another person. Further analysis was conducted to identify how information publications used anonymous sources. This sample revealed that online citizen journalists never used anonymous sources in this manner. And rarely did online newspaper journalists cite an anonymous source as a first quote (2.9 percent) or cite an anonymous source that was quoted as giving an opinion of another person (0.6 percent).

Transparency of a source requires identifying the background information of a source. Online newspaper journalists were more likely to include the background information of a source. This may be a reflection of either newspaper journalist training to include background information, or it could be that online citizen journalists may not feel that they need to include a source's background information because they perceive that their target audience is already familiar with the source's identity. A greater amount of information is necessary for larger audiences to understand the source's relationship to a story. In smaller communities the journalist may not feel that they need to be as transparent because local readers may already know the person featured in the article, making the title an unnecessary inclusion.

Traditional journalists push other people and organizations to be transparent. However, journalists themselves tend not to be transparent (Kovach and Rosenstiel 2001). Online newspapers were not as likely to provide a publicly available forum for news consumers to express their views on stories. On the other hand, online citizen journalists provided the opportunity to comment on almost all of their stories. This research indicated that the organizations' preferred way to communicate with the public was via the newspaper journalist's email address. However, the appearance of an email address does not necessarily mean that communication will occur between the sender and the receiver. An email address is more of a secretive approach to engaging in dialogue with the news audience — and many traditional journalists do not respond to the person who sent the email (Randle et al. 2006; Ye and Li 2006).

Traditional journalists face numerous pressures that affect the time they have to respond to comments from a much larger audience compared with citizen journalists

(Shoemaker and Reese 1996). Online citizen journalists may be more transparent because the credibility of their reports is associated with their willingness to answer questions from the public (Gillmor 2005; Lowrey and Anderson 2005).

Online citizen journalists provided access to a user profile on more than one-fifth of their articles. The availability of a user profile does not necessarily mean that online citizen journalists are behaving in a more transparent way. This research did not assess whether the user profile contained an accurate or a full name. In fact, blogging survey research reveals that more than half of bloggers use a pseudonym, but that figure encompasses all types of blogs, including personal ones (Lenhart and Fox 2006). Thus, future research should identify different levels of anonymity to determine the transparency level of online journalists.

However, the masking of the identity of a journalist may be arguably necessary to encourage the contribution of extreme viewpoints, especially when the public availability of the author's identity could cause him or her harm. An anonymous source who posts sensitive information can still have a good reputation online because users may put a high value on the sharing of information contributed. However, in most cases, it is likely that anonymous sources are not worried about being physically harmed, but instead, they want to protect their reputation.

CONCLUSION

This study sets the foundation for future studies in the area of citizen journalism. For example, it analysed online newspapers and online citizen journalism sites focused on a geographic area. So it would be of informational value to make comparisons using content produced by online citizen journalists who write about specific issues, rather than a geographic area, or to examine how broadcast organizations differ from online citizen journalists to understand more fully the value of citizen journalism's content to society. This analysis was also limited to sites in the US, and thus more research needs to be conducted to reflect differences beyond the US borders to determine whether the findings of this study hold true for online citizen journalism sites hosted in other countries.

The news media are an establishment built on the idea that the content that exists within each publication reflects who we are as a society. To accomplish this task effectively, the material found inside each publication should strive to reflect the truth accurately. Dissatisfaction with the news media occurs when news users feel that established media are not accurately reflecting their community (Harris Poll 2007). Online citizen journalism and online newspaper publications should encourage people to communicate virtually, which can encourage people to behave as a collective in the physical world (Nichols et al. 2006). To profit, news outlets should invest in producing content that reflects the notion of community, because trust and online loyalty can occur when people perceive that the content reflects them (Meyer 2004). Some traits of community include geography, involvement, sharing and awareness (Christensen and Levinson 2003; Chyi and Sylvie 2001; Kurpuis 2000; Lacy and Simon 1993). If these elements truly define community, it appears that the application of transparency in information organizations can promote involvement, sharing and awareness. And, by being more open, this practice may encourage conversation and knowledge-sharing beyond a circle of elites, journalists and sources so as better to reflect the reality of all people.

References

American Society of Newspaper Editors [ASNE] (2006) "ASNE Statement of Principles". Retrieved 15 June 2007 from: http://www.asne.org/kiosk/archive/principle.htm.

Associated Press [AP] (2006) "The Associated Press Statement of News Values". Retrieved 15 June 2007 from: http://www.ap.org/news values/index.html.

Associated Press Managing Editors [APME] (1994) "Statement of Ethics". Retrieved 15 June 2007 from: http://www.apme.com/ethics/.

BBC (2008) "Accuracy". In *Editorial Guidelines in Full*. Retrieved 8 March 2008 from: http://www.bbc.co.uk/guidelines/editorialguidelines/edguide/accuracy/anonymoussource.s html.

BBC News (2007) "Deaths Rise as U.S. Storm Spreads", *BBC News*, 15 January. Retrieved 28 February 2007 from: http://news.bbc.co.uk/1/hi/world/americas/6262533.stm.

Brown, F. (2005). "'Citizen' Journalism is Not Professional Journalism", *Quill*, 93 (6), pp. 42–3.

Canadian Broadcasting Corporation (2004) "Journalistic Standards and Practices". Retrieved 8 March 2008 from: http://cbc.radio-canada.ca/accountability/journalistic/index.shtml.

Carpenter, S. (2007) "United States Online Citizen Journalism and Online Newspaper Stories: A Content Analysis of their Quality and Value", *Dissertation Abstracts International*, 68 (09). (UMI No. 3282070).

Center for Citizen Media (2007) "Transparency", *Principles of Citizen Journalism*. Retrieved 28 February 2007 from: http://citmedia.org/principles/transparency.

Christensen, K., and Levinson, D. (2003) *Encyclopedia of Community from the Village to the Virtual World*, vols 1–4. Thousand Oaks, CA: Sage.

Chyi, I. H., and Sylvie, G. (2001) "The Medium is Global; The Content is Not: The Role of Geography in Online Newspaper Markets", *Journal of Media Economics*, 14 (4), pp. 231–48.

Cozby, P. C. (1973) "Effects of Density, Activity and Personality on Environmental Preferences", *Journal of Research in Personality*, 7 (1), pp. 45–60.

Culbertson, H. M. (1975) "Veiled News Sources — Who and What Are They?" *American Newspaper News Research Bulletin*, No. 3, pp. 3–23.

Culbertson, H. M. (1978) "Veiled Attribution: An Element of Style?", *Journalism Quarterly*, 55 (3), pp. 456–65.

Demers, D. P. (1994) "Effects of Organizational Size on Job Satisfaction of Top Editors at U.S. Dailies", *Journalism Quarterly*, 71 (4), pp. 914–25.

Domingo, D. (2008) "Interactivity in Daily Routines of Online Newsrooms: Dealing with an Uncomfortable Myth", *Journal of Computer-Mediated Communication*, 13 (3), pp. 680–704.

Dube, J. (2005) "Citizen Media Initiatives List", *Cyberjournalist.net*. Retrieved 11 January 2007 from: http://www.cyberjournalist.net/news/002226.php.

Duncan, C. T. (1952) "How the Weekly Press Covers News of Local Government", *Journalism Quarterly*, 29, pp. 283–93.

Fishman, M. (1980) *Manufacturing the News*. Austin, TX: University of Texas Press.

Gillmor, D. (2004) *We the Media: Grassroots Journalism by the People, for the People*. Sebastopol, CA: O'Reilly.

Gillmor, D. (2005) "Dan Gillmor on Grassroots Journalism, Etc.", Center for Citizen Media blog. Retrieved 15 January 2007 from: http://dangillmor.typepad.com/dan_gillmor_on_grassroots/2005/01/the_end_of_obje.html.

Gillmor, D. (2006) "We the Media: The Rise of Grassroots, Open-Source Journalism". Presented at the Ohio University Institute for Applied and Professional Ethics Seminar, Athens, OH.

Gladney, G.A. (1990) "Newspaper Excellence: How Editors of Small & Large Papers Judge Quality", *Newspaper Research Journal*, 11 (2), pp. 58–72.

Greer, J. D., and Mensing, D. (2006) "The Evolution of Online Newspapers: A Longitudinal Content Analysis 1997–2003". In X. Li (ed.), *Internet Newspapers: The Making of a Mainstream Medium*. Mahwah, NJ: Lawrence Erlbaum Associates, pp. 13–32.

Ha, L., and James, E. L. (1998) "Interactivity Re-Examined: A Baseline Analysis of Early Business Web Sites", *Journal of Broadcasting & Electronic Media*, 42 (4), pp. 457–74.

Harris Interactive Poll (2007) "TV Network News Top Source of News and Information Today", Retrieved 5 August 2007 from: http://www.harrisinteractive.com/harris_poll/index.asp?PID=768.

Hindman, E. B. (1998) "'Spectacles of the Poor': Conventions of Alternative News", *Journalism & Mass Communication Quarterly*, 75 (1), pp. 177–93.

Hovland, C. I., Janis, I. L., and Kelley, H. H. (1953) *Communication and Persuasion: Psychological Studies in Opinion Change*. New Haven, CT: Yale University Press.

Insko, C. A., Schopler, J., Drigotas, S. M., and Graetz, J. (1993) "The Role of Communication in Interindividual-Intergroup Discontinuity", *Journal of Conflict Resolution*, 37 (1), pp. 108–38.

Janowitz, M. (1952) *The Community Press in an Urban Setting*. New York: Macmillan.

Johnstone, J. W. C., Slawski, E. J., and Bowman W. W. (1976) *The News People. A Sociological Portrait of American Journalists and Their Work*. Urbana, IL: University of Illinois Press.

Kessler, L. (1984) *The Dissident Press. Alternative Journalism in American History*, vol. 13. Newbury Park, NJ: Sage.

Kovach, B., and Rosenstiel, T. (2001) *The Elements of Journalism*. New York: Three Rivers Press.

Kurpius, D. D. (2000) "Public Journalism and Commercial Local Television News: In Search of a Model", *Journalism & Mass Communication Quarterly*, 77 (2), pp. 340–54.

Lacy, S. (2002) "Competition for Readers among U.S. Metropolitan Daily, Nonmetropolitan Daily, and Weekly Newspapers", *Journal of Media Economics*, 15 (1), pp. 21–40.

Lacy, S., and Simon, T. F. (1993) *The Economics & Regulation of United States Newspapers*. Norwood, NJ: Ablex.

Leach, J. (2007) Personal communication, 22 November.

Lenhart, A., and Fox, S. (2006) "Bloggers: A Portrait of the Internet's New Storytellers". Retrieved 20 June 2007 from: http://www.pewinternet.org/pdfs/PIP%20Bloggers%20Report%20July%2019%202006.pdf.

Lombard, M., Snyder-Duch, J., and Bracken, C. C. (2002) "Content Analysis in Mass Communication. Assessment and Reporting of Intercoder Reliability", *Human Communication Research*, 28 (4), pp. 587–604.

Lowrey, W., and Anderson, W. (2005) "The Journalist behind the Curtain: Participatory Functions on the Internet and their Impact on Perceptions of the Work of Journalism", *Journal of Computer-Mediated Communication*, 10 (2), pp. 1–20.

Manning, J. (2008) Personal communication, 25 February.

Martin-Kratzer, R., and Thorson, E. (2007) "Use of Anonymous Sources Declines in U.S. Newspapers", *Newspaper Research Journal*, 28 (2), pp. 56–70.

Meyer, P. (2004) "The Influence Model and Newspaper Business", *Newspaper Research Journal*, 25 (4), pp. 66–83.

Moeller, S. D., Melki, J., Lorente, R., Bond, M., Cutler, J., and Johnson, M. (2007) "Openness & Accountability: A Study of Transparency in Global Media Outlets". Retrieved 24 June 2007 from: http://www.icmpa.umd.edu/pages/studies/transparency/main.html.

Nichols, S. L., Friedland, L. A., Rojas, H., Cho, J., and Shah, D. V. (2006) "Examining the Effects of Public journalism on Civil Society from 1994 to 2002: Organizational Factors, Project Features, Story Frames, and Citizen Engagement", *Journalism & Mass Communication Quarterly*, 83 (1), pp. 77–100.

Nieman Reports (22 June 2005) "Offering Anonymity Too Easily to Sources", *Nieman Reports*.

O'Neill, O. (2006) "Transparency and the Ethics of Communication". In C. Hood, and D. Heald (eds), *Transparency: The Key to Better Governance*. New York: Oxford University Press, pp. 75–90.

O'Sullivan, P. B. (1999) "Bridging the Mass—Interpersonal Divide", *Human Communication Research*, 25 (4), pp. 569–88.

Pew Research Center for the People and the Press (2005) "Public More Critical of Press, but Goodwill Persists", *Pew Research Center for the People and the Press*. Retrieved 28 February 2007 from: http://people-press.org/reports/display.php 3?ReportID=248.

Plaisance, P. L. (2007) "Transparency: An Assessment of the Kantian Roots of a Key Element in Media Ethics Practice", *Journal of Mass Media Ethics*, 22 (2 and 3), pp. 187–207.

Project for Excellence in Journalism (2006) "The State of the News Media 2006". Retrieved 13 March 2007 from: http://www.stateofthenewsmedia.com/2006/.

Radio Television News Directors Association [RTNDA] (2000) "Code of Ethics and Professional Conduct". Retrieved 20 January 2007 from: http://www.rtnda.org/pages/media_items/code-of-ethics-and-professional-conducts48.php?g=36?id=48.

Rains, S.A. (2007) "The Anonymity Effect: The Influence of Anonymity on Perceptions of Sources and Information on Health Websites", *Journal of Applied Communication Research*, 35 (2), pp. 197–214.

Ramirez, A., Walther, J. B., Burgoon, J. K., and Sunnafrank, M. (2002) "Information-Seeking Strategies, Uncertainty, and Computer-Mediated Communication", *Human Communication Research*, 28 (2), pp. 213–28.

Randle, Q., Davenport, L., and Lunt, S. (2006) *Walkin' the Walk; Talking the Talk: Reporters' Online Interaction with Readers*. Proceedings of the Annual Convention of the Association for Education in Journalism and Mass Communication Conference. San Francisco, CA.

Reader, B. (2006) "Distinctions that Matter: Ethical Differences at Large and Small Newspapers", *Journalism & Mass Communication Quarterly*, 83 (4), pp. 851–64.

Riffe, D. (1980) "Relative Credibility Revisited: How 18 Unnamed Sources Are Rated", *Journalism Quarterly*, 57 (4), pp. 618–23.

Riffe, D., Aust, C. F., and Lacy, S. (1993) "The Effectiveness of Random Consecutive Day and Constructed Week Samples in Newspaper Content Analysis", *Journalism Quarterly*, 70 (1), pp. 133–9.

Riffe, D., Lacy, S., and Fico, F. (2005) *Analyzing Media Messages: Using Quantitative Content Analysis in Research*. Mahwah, NJ: Lawrence Erlbaum Associates.

Rosenstiel, T., Gottlieb, C., and Brady, L. A. (1999) "Local TV News Project 1998: What Works, What Flops, and Why. What is a 'Good' Newscast?" *Project for Excellence in Journalism*. Retrieved 15 March 2007 from: http://www.journalism.org/node/377.

Schudson, M. (2003) *The Sociology of News*. San Diego, CA: University of California Press.

Shaw, D. L. (27 March 2005) "Media Matters: Do Bloggers Deserve Basic Journalistic Protections?" *L.A. Times*, E14.

Shim, H. (2006) "The Professional Role of Journalism in U.S. Press Reportage from 1950 to 2000". Ph.D.diss., University of Texas at Austin. Retrieved 8 May 2007 from: http:hdl.handle.net/2152/532.

Shoemaker, P., and Reese, S. (1996) *Mediating the Message: Theories of Influences on Mass Media Content*, 2nd edn. White Plains, NY: Longman.

Society for News Design [SND] (2006) "The Society for News Design's Code of Ethical Standards". Retrieved 5 July 2007 from: http://www.snd.org/about/organization_ethics.html.

Society of Professional Journalists [SPJ] (1996) "Code of Ethics". Retrieved 5 July 2007 from: http://www.spj.org/ethicscode.asp?.

The Institute for Interactive Journalism (2007) "Citizen Media: Fad or the Future of News?" Retrieved 28 February 2007 from: http://www.kcnn.org/research/citizen_media_report/.

Tichenor, P., Donohue, G., and Olien, C. (1980) *Community Conflict and the Press*. Beverley Hills, CA: Sage.

Tompkins, P. S. (2003) "Truth, Trust, and Telepresence", *Journal of Mass Media Ethics*, 18 (3 and 4), pp. 194–212.

Wall, M. (2005) "'Blogs of War': Weblogs as News", *Journalism: Theory, Practice & Criticism*, 6 (2), pp. 632–57.

Walters, P. (2007) "Dealing with Comments: A Few Interesting Approaches". Retrieved 1 June 2007 from: http://poynter.org/column.asp?id=103&aid=123155.

Walther, J. B. (1992) "Interpersonal Effects in Computer-Mediated Communication: A Relational Perspective", *Communication Research*, 19 (1), pp. 52–89.

Walther, J. B., and Bunz, U. (2005) "The Rules of Virtual Groups: Trust, liking, and Performance in Computer-Mediated Communication", *Journal of Communication*, 55, pp. 828–846.

Walther, J. B., and Burgoon, J. K. (1992) "Relational Communication in Computer-Mediated Interaction", *Human Communication Research*, 19 (1), pp. 50–88.

Ward, J., and Gaziano, C. (1976) "A New Variety of Urban Press: Neighborhood Public-Affairs Publications", *Journalism Quarterly*, 53, pp. 61–7.

Weaver, D. H., Beam, R. A., Brownlee, B. J., Voakes, P. S., and Wilhoit, G. C. (2007) *The American Journalist in the 21st Century: U.S. News People at the Dawn of a New Millennium*. Mahwah, NJ: Lawrence Erlbaum Associates.

Wheeless, L. R. (1978) "A Follow-Up Study of the Relationships among Trust, Disclosure, and Interpersonal Solidarity", *Human Communication Research*, 4 (2), pp. 143–57.

Williams, L. (2006) "What's Going on Around Here?" *Placeblogger*, 25 October 2006. Retrieved 30 January 2007 from: http://www.placeblogger.com/location/directory.

Wilson, S. L., Babcock, W. A., and Pribek, J. (1997) "Newspaper Ombudsmen's Reactions to Use of Anonymous Sources", *Newspaper Research Journal*, 18 (3 and 4), pp. 141–53.

Ye, X., and Li, X. (2006) "Internet Newspapers' Public Forum and User Involvement". In X. Li (ed.), *Internet Newspaper: A Making of a Medium*. Mahwah, NJ: Lawrence Erlbaum Associates, pp. 243–59.

Zhang, J., and Cameron, G. T. (2003) "Study Finds Sourcing Patterns in Wen Ho Lee Coverage", *Newspaper Research Journal*, 24 (4), pp. 88–101.

Zoch, L. M., and Turk, J. V. (1998) "Women Making News: Gender as a Variable in Source Selection and Use", *Journalism & Mass Communication Quarterly*, 75 (4), pp. 762–75.

Zoimek, J. (2004) "Journalism, Transparency and the Public Trust", *The Aspen Institute*. Retrieved 14 February 2008 from: http://www.aspeninstitute.org/site/c.huLWJeMRKpH/b.612049/k.612F/Communications_and_Society_Program.htm.

The Role of Citizen Journalism

⑊ CHAPTER ⑊
14

Seeing the Unseen: Is New-Media Journalism Reshaping Questions of Race?

AARON BARLOW AND ANNIE SEATON

"Race", in the American optic, is always a question of seeing the unseen, or, perhaps, of being the unseen. Lamenting this, Ralph Ellison sings what Michelle Wallace calls the "invisibility blues":

> I am an invisible man. No, I am not a spook like those who haunted Edgar Allan Poe; nor am I one of your Hollywood-movie ectoplasms. I am a man of substance, of flesh and bone . . . I am invisible, understand, simply because people refuse to see me. Like the bodiless heads you see sometimes in circus sideshows, it is as though I have been surrounded by mirrors of hard, distorting glass. (Wallace 1988: 3)

Does Ellison already take us to a science fiction world? Are blacks, *a priori*, "virtual"? It sure can seem like it.

This brings up a number of important questions: what is the relationship between a distorted, invisible subject and the question of citizenship, with its implications of visibility and "men" not just "man"? If black "virtuality" precedes Web journalism and new media, how does it affect both *de jure* and/or figurative notions of "the citizen"? After Obama's election, these questions are, paradoxically, more unsettled than ever, for a variety of reasons.

The heavy symbolism of the ultimate American fact of "citizenship"— to be president — is undermined, potentially, in a host of ways in which even this accomplishment was achieved. This was not realized with the full significance of blackness, but rather with its cancellation or erasure via a notion of what is often called the "post-racial", but could also be another name for a kind of postmodern racial "passing". This is where all of the negative aspects of race are said not to belong to the post-racial person in question and which still leaves certain notions of race intact. For if there are those who are "post" racial, this term is understood not to refer to everyone — and, still more absurdly, it only refers, in the first place, to those who are already "racialized". Whites are not, for instance, ever post-racial, because they were never racialized to begin with. Thus, the notion of post-racial marks out a certain terrain of inclusion — or citizenship — just as it also implies that there is a terrain of exclusion, and, further-more, that to be "racial(ized)" is to be backward. This is, of course, particularly interesting given the link between the "post" racial and the "new" media — which are both spaces in which aspects of the racialized body or, for that matter, bodies in general — will undergo shifts in meaning. If we are, for instance, "post-human", then wouldn't it follow, almost necessarily, that we would be "post-racial"? And yet, it seems that we are simultaneously, somehow, still back in the 1940s, as the strong link between Ralph Ellison and Barack Obama's ways of thinking about racialized selves suggests.

N. Katherine Hayles characterizes post-human as privileging "informational pattern over material instantiation, so that embodiment in a biological substrate is seen as an accident of history" (Hayles 1999: 2). She goes on to write that a post-human point-of-view considers "the body as the original prosthesis . . . [that] can be seamlessly articulated with intelligent machines. In the posthuman, there are no essential differ-ences or absolute demarcations between bodily existence and computer simulation" (1999: 3). The assumption would be that race, too, is a prosthesis — an artificial exten-sion that replaces a missing body part — although the situation is, of course, far from so simple.

The visual distortion experienced by Ellison's nameless narrator is also existential and social — a series of masks, riddles and identities that all add up to one thing: a lack of a stable, "real" self. Paradoxically, Barack Obama — responding to the same discourses of distortion and invisibility — has described himself, similarly, as a "blank screen" (2006: 11) on which other people's hopes are projected. So, despite everything, Obama's sense of his own subjectivity is quite Ellisonian, and, one could say, "virtual".

What's left is a masked self that shifts in meaning, depending on the viewer or reader. This self is both unstable and controversial. This isn't just fiction: It really seems to describe, powerfully, what it means to be African-American, or to be what Patricia Williams, in *Seeing A Color-Blind Future: The Paradox of Race*, refers to as being racially "impugned". It also makes the subject of "race" something more than just a body: Blacks are invisible, surrounded by mirrors, part human, part machine, with surreal effects of distortion. The social effect of race, then, results in a parody of the Cartesian self: "I am not, because I am not seen ⤙ or am I?"

Are African-Americans, then, the first cyborgs, located somewhere between human and machine — an early version of Ridley Scott's Philip K. Dick-inspired *Blade Runner* androids? Harriet Jacobs' nineteenth-century novel *Incidents in the Life of a Slave Girl* seems to suggest this: "These God-fearing machines are no more, in the sight of their masters, than the cotton they plant, or the horses they tend," argues Jacobs' narrator (Jacobs 1861: 5). Half-human, half-machine — slaves were, in fact, the first industrial workers and the precursors to the post-human. In the "sight" of their masters these hybrid human-machines are, like Ellison's subject, masked. Sight, then, is a powerfully important metaphor for the way race functions, and it is the viewing of race that the Internet appears, at first glance, to eliminate. But here, once again, this apparent elimination of the (racialized) body is actually something both familiar and new.

We are seeing an undefined universe open to ownership by whoever defines it: an "informational pattern", to use Hayles's term, replacing a "material instantiation" with no carry-over sense of possession. In many ways the Web is the blank slate the Europeans imagined they saw as they entered the Americas. With, as William Bradford wrote, "no freinds [sic] to wellcome them, nor inns to entertaine or refresh their weatherbeaten bodys, no houses or much less townes to repaire too, to seeke for succoure" (Bradford 1899: 94–5), the assumption is that all waits for the taking, that the landscape can be imprinted as one wishes.

In this reading, the Web becomes, paradoxically, a kind of "nature" in the Emersonian sense of a wild, untamed landscape: "In the woods, we return to reason and faith. There I feel that nothing can befall me in life — no disgrace, no calamity, (leaving me my eyes,) which nature cannot repair" (Emerson 2000: 6). Almost unnoticed, at the end of this passage, lurks a series of remarks that link the disembodied experience of Emerson's famous transparent eyeball firmly to an experience of power, which hints at the forms this turn will take later on: "master or servant, is then a trifle and a disturbance", says Emerson (2000: 6), moving from this "disturbance" to the statement that "I am the lover of uncontained and immortal beauty". In the same way that "theories of races" initially function as a disturbing presence in the beginning of Emerson's *Nature*, the racial order embedded in the phrase "master and servant" also presents a detour, which transcendental vision must overcome. The transparent eyeball sees *through* and beyond the relationship of master to servant, but only because of a certain structural ability to do so. Emerson's blank slate is only "blank" because he wills it to be so — free of Native Americans and unconstrained by the presence of slavery, this "America" is, like the notion of a free and open "Internet", a cultural construction whose truth-value is a matter of point of view.

Rather than any perfect freedom of information or public sphere for free discussions among citizens, the Internet and its "domains" appear to be a series of reflections, distortions and "masked" versions of the "real" world. This is, of course, a deceptive dichotomy and rarely recognized. When online newsmagazines and blogs such as Salon.com and Huffingtonpost.com, with their apparent freedom from the multinational corporate media, maintain somehow the same kinds of racial hierarchies found elsewhere — virtually entirely white writers, editors and so on — then the way to think about "race and new media" is clearly not by imagining that it leaves the body — or race — behind, or that it fundamentally changes racial equations. Yet, simply repeating that the "new" media is still "white" isn't very interesting. What this chapter will seek to do, instead, is to elaborate how race, in its "virtual" mode, works — specifically in relation to the Internet and Web journalism — and *vice versa*. It will consider the following questions: Are there new forms of citizenship here? Or are there just the same old forms, re-cast in the virtual?

Patricia Williams describes an eleven-year-old Puerto Rican computer whizz who loves computers because, he says, "nobody judged him for what he looked like, and he could speak without an accent" (Williams 1997: 38). Williams, evidently sceptical, wonders "what to make of this freedom as disembodiment, this technologically purified mental communion as escape from the society of others, as neutralized social space" (1997: 38). Is there freedom in disembodiment? Does technology offer an escape from "the society of others?" Probably not.

In *How to Build a Universe that Doesn't Fall Apart Two Days Later* the science-fiction writer Philip K. Dick quotes Heraclitus: "The nature of things is in the habit of concealing itself" (Dick 1985: 18). No other line from Classical philosophy better cautions contemporary examination of the Internet or of what the Web has done to questions of race, citizenship and information. Just so, no other writer of the twentieth century anticipated the questions raised by the World Wide Web as well as Dick did: "unceasingly we are bombarded with pseudo-realities manufactured by very sophisticated people using very sophisticated electronic mechanisms. I do not distrust their motives; I distrust their power" (1985: 4). Today that power, along with the ability to hide behind Web masks, makes even exploration dangerous. Masks never mean to show things as they are; even with the best of intentions, they deceive. Opposite to, as well as the complement of, Ellison's "invisibility", they can be understood, for the purposes here, through the concept of "blackface", the disguising of race for performance (and disparagement) worn, at times, over both black and white visages.

Later in his essay, Dick reflects on a headline:

SCIENTISTS SAY THAT MICE CANNOT BE MADE TO LOOK LIKE HUMAN BEINGS. It was a federally funded research program, I suppose. Just think: Someone in this world is an authority on the topic of whether mice can or cannot put on two-tone shoes, derby hats, pinstriped shirts, and Dacron pants, and pass as humans. (1985: 2)

The question today becomes: What does it mean to *be,* not simply look, human on the Web? What is the human reality — what one *is* elsewhere, or what one *seems* online? Are mice in derbies any different on the Web from whites (or blacks, for that matter) in online "blackface"? If they are all accepted as human, as peers and citizens, shouldn't that be all that matters?

After all, an "avatar" — that word for some of the masks that the Web allows — does make metaphoric mice roar, in some instances scaring many, including the lions, for example, of the older community of professional journalism.

Fake realities will create fake humans. Or, fake humans will generate fake realities and then sell them to other humans, turning them, eventually, into forgeries of themselves. So we wind up with fake humans inventing fake realities and then peddling them to other fake humans. It is just a very larger version of Disneyland. (Dick 1985: 6)

On the Web the mice and the lions might both be fake. Yet they are easy to create — and this is where the problem comes in. In 2002 Paulie Abeles, a white woman, concocted Cassandra Mays-Lewis, a 67-year-old black woman, "in a bid to keep descendants of a reputed [Thomas] Jefferson mistress out of . . . [a Jefferson] family reunion" (Kahn 2003). All she had to do was establish a Yahoo! account in the new name and Ms Mays-Lewis was born.

Just as the Web was forming, John Perry Barlow warned that: "Digital technology is detaching information from the physical plane, where property law of all sorts has always found definition" (Barlow 1994). He was writing specifically of ownership of intellectual property, but the sense of detachment he mentioned has become so associated with the Web that even theft stops seeming as serious and value becomes meaningless. As the fake becomes real, it stops responding to established frameworks for negotiating reality, further complicating ownership and position, not to mention revenue. Today, for example, no one wants to pay newspapers to get to readers who are more reachable cheaply in online manifestations, where the readers can find the content they want there, for free.

There's real danger in this change, for it removes all gatekeeping. In this new online environment access can mask the user and the creator, allowing for creation of an online persona without even the evident fictionality of an avatar, making even race subject to fiction. Andrew Keen, author of *The Cult of the Amateur: How the Internet Is Killing Our Culture*, sees a usurpation — the amateur to replace the professional — but the real danger concerns accountability, not the level of skill or experience.

Writing in the mid-1990s, Esther Dyson presented a naïve vision of what one's image on the Web *should* be:

> You can't hide. And the image you project — on your Web home page or elsewhere — will and should be true. It's not just outsiders peering in, it's your own employees out in the electronic world: they are the company. As both physical and intellectual products lose their value . . . the interactions with your company will be what you sell. And the quality of the interactions you foster will be what draws employees to your firm or community. People want to buy information-based services and products from visible companies that operate as partners. They do not want commodity products from black boxes. (Dyson 1995)

What we are seeing instead is a funhouse of deception — or a gigantic minstrel show where we often can't tell if it is a white, black (or human) face behind the make-up.

Oddly, the masking of identity on Web news venues can be justified in the US through the logic behind "shield laws": laws that protect journalists from forced revelation of sources. They typically cover

> a person [who] regularly engages in collecting, photographing, recording, writing, editing, reporting, or publishing news, for gain or livelihood, who obtained the information sought while working as a salaried employee of, or independent contractor for, a newspaper, news journal, news agency, press association, wire service, radio or television station, network, or newsmagazine. (Florida 2008)

Like most descriptions of journalism, the Florida law fails. It assumes an economic model for journalism that is now being superseded and, as a result, provides no place for the truly independent journalist, one working for oneself and publishing oneself — such as a blogger. The situation could change, state by state or if a proposed federal protection law is enacted. For now, however, protection for online journalists remains problematic.

Those essaying journalism on the Web, feeling unprotected by law, often resort to creation of their own shields, the avatars, masks and simple pseudonyms that grew from early discussion boards. This, of course, makes it difficult to determine who should really be considered a journalist and who is merely one of Keen's amateurs or, more insidiously, a propagandist. Neither is it clear who is a legitimate voice for a particular segment of society and not simply someone donning "blackface".

The tools of the Internet itself, then, also fundamentally change the way race is considered. The avatar, that which stands in for the person speaking and symbolizes them, has become a metaphor for this transformation. An avatar is, by definition, a way of crossing between various symbolic worlds. "Avatar" originates in the Sanskrit *avatarah* ("descent"), itself derived from *avatarati* ("he descends"). The Sanskrit prefix *ava-* means "away", while *tarati* signifies "he crosses over". The *Oxford English Dictionary* (*OED*), characteristically, stresses the power inherent in the notion of the avatar, as "presentation to the world as a ruling power of object of worship". "Loosely", continues the *OED*, an avatar can also refer to a "manifestation, display; or phase". Merriam-Webster's last entry for avatar is, however, the most relevant to this enquiry: an electronic image that represents and is manipulated by a computer user (as in a computer game). The *OED*, in its most recent edition, has failed as yet to note this leap in usage. An avatar is a paradoxical notion — a reflection that can also be an apotheosis — and, therefore, suited to the unstable nature of the representation of race that we began with, as well as to the ever-evolving nature of the Internet.

The avatars of interest here, though, are those that appear on social networking sites such as Facebook and MySpace, blogs and discussion boards. These spaces both overlap with and help to construct the space of what can now loosely be called "journalism", as the difference between the "new" media and the old media is increasingly irrelevant. Thus CNN and *The New York Times* both link directly to blogs, as well as making their own attempts at creating a simulation of the "new" media in their own online spaces, while "new" media bloggers, such as Markos Moulitsas of *Daily Kos*, appear on network news programmes as commentators. Facebook groups, in turn, spawn newspaper articles or function as political organizations. These spaces are a mix of citizen journalism, activism, performance and undefined public/private space — a veritable public sphere.

In this chaotic, undefined space avatars say: "You have no idea who this is. You have no idea where you are. Am I real? Are you real?" Avatars set up a notion of the self as performative, substitutive and always masked, or in question. But they do much more than that, particularly in relation to questions of race.

Avatars are visual icons attached to either proper names, like Jack Krohn, or to user names, like Anniewilde (a virtual persona of Annie Seaton). The split between the visual and the verbal is often violent, as in the black woman porno star icon created by that user Jack Krohn on Brooklynian.com. A careful reading of the Brooklynian.com website reveals, beyond a reasonable doubt, that Jack Krohn is a white man.

The irony of this is compounded by the fact that the image of a black woman in a sexually open and inviting pose, lifting her hair and open-mouthed, pouting, with what appears to be dried-up semen on her arm, appears next to comments by Jack Krohn that often have offensive content. For "she" *is* "Jack Krohn". Given the history of the black woman's body in US visual history, law and sexual politics, the use of such an image invokes a complicated and potentially ugly sense of violation and appropriation — even though, in the minds of many, the "separateness" of the online "world" makes such invocation irrelevant.

The presence of the avatar appears, in the most literal sense, to "authorize" the black woman's icon as a co-creator of Jack Krohn's posts — while the same presence also makes "her" an unwilling witness to this writing. Like the apparently willing image of her sexually submissive body, her presence as avatar appears to function somewhere between consent and violation.

On a post "rating" the sexual attractiveness of various Brooklyn neighbourhoods, in response to a topic titled "rate neighborhoods for girl/boy-watching", the Jack Krohn avatar/persona declared the following: "For Bushwick, Jack Krohn gives the women a "7" rating, especially along the stretch of Wyckoff Avenue between Dekalb Ave. and Halsey Street." For Crown Heights, he is even more generous, giving an "8" to the inhabitants: "Utica Avenue, between Eastern Parkway and Empire Boulevard, is always a sure bet." Krohn also likes Flatbush, which he gives a "10", declaring that it is "always chock full of gorgeous women. Flatbush Avenue itself is great, as is the long walk on Church Avenue between Flatbush and Utica Avenue," according to Krohn.

Without being over-literal and humourless, the notion of a white man "dressed" in the virtual body of the exploited, violated body of a black woman, while sexually rating the attractiveness of, specifically, Brooklyn neighbourhoods that are well known to be almost entirely populated by people of African descent, is phenomenally striking. A little later on, a user called Young Snitch, with an "Ayatollah" icon that is also blatantly ethnically coded, has the following to offer: "my boy swears that women from flatbush have asses that can be picked out of an ass-lineup and identified as being from flatbush. young krohn, is that true?"

What is perhaps most astonishing about this is the perceived licence to step beyond historical context that, in some minds, the Internet provides. Of course, only a few hundred years ago African-American women *were* lined up, and their bodies *were* rated on a variety of attributes — size, colour, age, firmness, shape and so on — so that they could be bought and sold, to be used in whatever ways their masters desired. Such women were thing-like humans or embodied objects, both property and person — not legal subjects but subjected to the law; more often the targets of representation than its origin. Replicating slavery's relationship to black bodies and subjects is considered to be problematic in polite (non-racist) conversation. Because of this, overt racial imagery and/or conversation is, generally, somewhat more veiled than in the following conversation, which ends with Jack Krohn's comment: "Young Snitch: Yes, it's true about the women in Flatbush. Everytime I'm there I cannot believe that the women are real."

The use of the category "real" in this conversation is particularly arresting. In this virtual space two men, self-identified as white in other Brooklynian.com posts, both use, as avatars, representations of *differently raced* selves, not to mention the racial implication of a "young snitch", a term of derision in many urban neighbourhoods, alluding, among the black underclass, to those who "tell" on the drug dealers, who are more aligned with the "oppressive" authorities than with the people of their blocks.

Do these avatars, the Ayatollah and the Porn Star, somehow facilitate or embolden the notion of black women's bodies as pure objects to be discussed in whatever way the "characters" in question wish? Certainly in many public spaces such a conversation would be difficult — for a variety of reasons. In the workplace it would violate sexual harassment guidelines or even, at certain universities, hate speech policies. But, more blatantly, such conversation both implies the total absence of people of colour from this space, as well as ensuring that this space is coded as a racially offensive and, therefore, a whites-only virtual landscape.

In fact, the prevalence of whites using avatars of colour operates like a kind of virtual "blackface" with all of the implications of separation its use in whites-only Vaudeville contained — in the form of avatars that represent people of colour as somehow innately funny or absurd. This is what, of course, blackface is about in the first place — the notion that the body of a person of colour is *prima facie* ridiculous.

Why do Jack Krohn and Young Snitch both have avatars that represent non-white "personae"? Would a white woman porn star not have worked for Jack Krohn's avatar? Or would that have carried, simply, an implication of sexism — would it have offended the white women who also populate Brooklynian? And, similarly, why an Ayatollah image for Young Snitch? Why not a white Catholic or Episcopalian priest, or a white evangelical minister?

Avatars are a way of speaking of race without talking about it, and in such a tense, charged environment they speak volumes — and become emblematic of the place of race on the Web and in Internet journalism. Whenever, over the last few years, anniewilde tried to critique what she saw as overt racism, she was called "racist" and basically driven off discussion boards, although she is an actual, not virtual, African-American. In the Brooklynian.com world, for example, anybody who is anti-racist, particularly if they have self-identified as a person of colour, becomes a "racist" as soon as they raise issues of race, while the atmosphere of racial dominance and hostility of the board in general maintains the silence of the status quo, accepted and enforced by the moderators as well as the inhabitants. Attacks, hidden behind avatars and online identities, can get quite nasty, especially since the "reality" behind any professed identity can be questioned. Is it not, then, a reasonable thing to say that a preponderance of avatars of colour assumed by white users signals a form of virtual racism, a means of using the image of the black race to belittle that race — just as was done with blackface? Is this virtual racism all the more significant, or interesting, because it represents a throwback that is now being reinvigorated via cyberspace?

Avatars aren't the only way that the virtual world gets racially configured. Brownstoner.com, like Brooklynian.com, is a Brooklyn site driven by unabashed fixation on real estate property and everything that goes along with it (money, skin colour, class and cultural pretensions). "Writing about an unhealthy obsession with historic Brooklyn brownstones and the neighborhoods and lifestyles they define" is the tag line for this website, offering frenzied commentary on Victorian-style architecture and the money it takes to inhabit it. There's a thin veneer, on the site, of architectural history and artsy-fartsiness, along with some pretensions of "eco"-friendliness, but mostly this is a blog about being rich enough to buy, renovate, "flip" (that is, buy a property intending to sell it quickly for a profit) and speculate. Authored by "Brownstoner" (Jonathan Butler), the blog's comments have also become semi-famous, particularly those by a person who refers to himself as "The What". The What usually rails against the housing market, yuppies and the American economy.

On 17 March 2008 a major New York investment bank fired thousands of employees. The What launched a series of apocalyptic tirades, invoking Schopenhauer to claim the status of an unacknowledged prophet. Another commentator responded: "Now we know The What is a white guy, he's quoting Schopenhauer." This speculation about The What's racial identity, which is supposed to be "invisible" (although it is often easy to determine a person's "actual" race online, through verbal clues), was meant, one supposes, to be funny — but in the context of a blog written about gentrification in the extensively racially segregated New York City it didn't seem that amusing. Property values have been directly driven by the skin colour in that city for centuries and do so today for those who inhabit particular brownstone neighbourhoods. Whiteness equals money in terms of real estate, and the only thing brown in the most desirable Brooklyn areas is the stones.

Another Brownstoner.com conversation, on 7 October 2007, featured the topic of "Brownstoner Pride". An openly gay commenter wanted to bring up the idea of sexual orientation — which certainly seems to go along with the Brownstoner tag line about "lifestyles they (Brownstones) define". Not so, evidently. "I'm all for gay rights, but why do you have to segregate yourselves[?]" asked one poster. Another said: "I as a straight guy wish to start an all straight meet and greet" and continued with "I mean really, whats [sic] next? All black brownstoner forum, all working class brownstoner." The joke is, of course, that neither the majority of African-Americans nor working-class people of any race can afford the $2–5 million prices of the brownstones on Brownstoner.com. In fact, many of the neighbourhoods (or "nabes", as the Brownstoners like to say), are undergoing what some might call a property-driven version of ethnic cleansing. This is why, perhaps, the comments continued in this vein: "But I just am tired of the double standard. I am white, stright [sic] and lived in park slope and south slope [sic] for the last 7 years. I would love to compare how many times white Park Slopers are bashed on this site compared to gays. I bet the statistics would be staggering." When a poster finally suggested that "if someone feels excluded the thing to do is include them and make them feel like they do belong; talking about irrelevant issues that straight white men go through isn't exactly helpful", another flurry of comments followed. These were epitomized by this one: "This site is about brownstone Brooklyn (Or supposed to be) why does it need to become a forum where race, sexual preference, socio-economics, etc., becomes the overriding factor?"

There's a drive to purify the Internet, precisely because, frankly, no one knows actually if The What is white. Self-identification as "other" leads demonstrably to back-lashes on many sites in the "liberal" (yet dramatically racially and economically segregated) webspaces of New York City. Identification comes at a risk: "outing" your-self (as gay, black, Muslim etc.) will be at a cost, it seems. This very drive, however, leads to a blacklash. There are many ways that identification works in the absence of either bodies or overt self-identification as "other", and these are beginning to appear more frequently online, and in ways that are often missed by the white majority, leading to misunderstandings as comical as the mistaking of a Barack and Michelle Obama "fist bump" as a terrorist gesture.

The ALL CAPS phenomenon operates as another form of representation and, in fact, as another form of symbolic embodiment along with the avatar. Taken together, they help structure a way of thinking about race, virtual citizenship and how the meaning and function of representation itself may be changing as a result of the new media and its slippery, complex and ever-changing domains.

In the new rhetoric of the online world, speaking, for instance, in ALL CAPS is a way of marking your online body as — classed, raced and definitely not part of the "straight, white" mainstream that the posters of Brownstoner and Brooklynian bravely claim as a kind of embattled and besieged identity. A quick glance at Craigslist.org's New York City "women seeking women" personals shows that the ALL CAPS world has expanded as a code for race even there. A post, "SEXY DIME SEEKS SAME (JERZ)", uses not only all capital letters but also a certain kind of associated language: "ATTENTION ALL SEXY LADIES . . . LOOKING FOR A FRIEND WITH BENE-FITS...SOMEONE I CAN SHOP WITH, GO TO DINNER WITH, GO CLUBBING WITH, AND SHARE MY CURVY BODY WITH." While writing in all capital letters, on certain parts of the "Net" world, once may have simply meant "shouting", it is used here for a completely different purpose. It invokes a certain kind of urban speech, one associated with blackness, although spoken by people of various races, a slangy, hip-hop aesthetic with its own developing grammatical rules. A "BLACK AND DOMINICAN FEMAG" insists that she "DONT LIK BEING CALLED MA MAMI SWEETIE OR ANY OTHER GIRLY SHIT LIK DAT". Over on the "men seeking women" side, a man looking for "SMALL UP TOP AND ROUND ON THE BOTTOM" says he's a "GREAT KISSER, VERY SMART, AN INTENSE TAKE CHARGE BROTHA".

Clearly, not all people of colour write in the heavily coded ALL CAPS discourse. Even most white people know that somebody calling themselves a "BROTHA" is prob-ably African-American. But does mentioning Schopenhauer, as The What did, really make you white? Is it possible that a white person could write in ALL CAPS, just as there are blacks who could "pass", unmarked, as virtually "white"? Certainly ALL CAPS allows for a way of marking something like "race" and "class" without pictures, and in the way that Schopenhauer — and any number of other signals — does the same thing.

So when African-American rap star Kanye West was offended by criticism and wrote in ALL CAPS on his blog, CNN's website rewrote West's words, while noting their shape — "Writing Tuesday on his blog at www.kanyeuniversity.com in almost all caps", reported CNN of the rapper's missive. While CNN rewrote Kanye's blog post, minus capital letters and profanity, media website *Gawker.com* did the opposite, quoting Kanye's original and even tweaking his words parodically. "YOU UNGRATEFUL HIPPIE BASTARDS", Kanye says in Gawker's "rewritten" version.

There were 332,000 Google hits for "kanye west all caps" — most of them expressing petulant cyber-shock and a kind of virtual linguistic puritanism. A black man yelling, even in his blog, is evidently unacceptable. A Craigslist poster from the Bronx, though, sees it differently: in her post of 9 July 2008, in the "women seeking women" section, she wrote: "Hopefully since this is my last post I could finally find what I'm looking for. I'll write what I'm looking for in caps so that it wouldn't be avoided" — which she then followed up with an ALL CAPS sequence.

"Wouldn't be avoided": perhaps it is the fear of being avoided that energizes much of what passes for journalism on the Web today — both by the old-time professionals and by the "new" Internet journalists. Before the introduction of the World Wide Web, professional journalism could not be avoided in the "developed" world of Europe and North America. It was a constant presence in all media except the movies. Once the number of available choices for media consumption exploded towards infinity, the professional journalism community found it had a smaller piece of the pie and discovered it was also being eclipsed by those able to shout louder — in ALL CAPS and otherwise.

By the same token, the expansion of possibilities has created a situation where questions of race are also transformed. Online, American blacks (among others) can no longer demand a presence: "We're here, so get used to us." In fact, blacks can be avoided almost completely, if that is so desired — leading to paradoxical situations such as those where even the mention of race leads to accusations of racism. "I don't see colour; I only see the individual" was one of the nonsense statements uttered by well-meaning American whites in the fifties and sixties, as though ignoring the fact of race could eliminate the experiences of generations that make up the individual. By trying to use the fact of the mask over each Internet user as a means of reaching beyond questions of race, many on the Web have, instead, retreated to the dead end of that older, smug statement. Furthermore, they have enabled those who wish to turn images of race to their own ends, making it acceptable for a white person, for example, to hide behind a black avatar.

Scared of what can appear to be an anarchic free-for-all, some in journalism, the older profession most immediately affected by the Web, set up a disparaging stereotype of the new online journalists, especially bloggers, calling them "pajama-wearing partisan ranters living in Mommy's basement. There they wile away their underemployed time obsessing" (Garofoli 2006). Yet among these are legitimate journalists as well as those of hidden and duplicitous purpose.

Want to be a journalist on the Web? Just a few years ago there were none, so all one had to do was set up shop and claim to be one. Want to be an African-American but you are Irish-Italian? Create a persona and learn how to "speak" the online lingo associated (such as the use of ALL CAPS), and that's what you are. Journalists also have used the Internet in order to misrepresent. This authority, abused, can have real political effects. This follows, in a certain sense, the logic of the "avatar". The story of

221

NewsMax.com and Andy Martin is an example of this. Posing as a neutral source of articles obtained from other sources, the website is actually a heavily partisan tool. Martin's Emersonian freedom in the Internet's "Wild West" is, for his targets, an all too familiar game, as an appearance of his on Sean Hannity's Fox News show *Hannity's America* on 5 October 2008, just a month before the presidential election, illustrated. Martin argued then that Barack Obama wanted to overthrow the American government, raising eyebrows and prompting claims about Martin's past (Greenwald 2008, Rutenberg 2008).

Martin, a self-described "Internet journalist", was identified in *The Washington Post* as a source of an email first claiming Obama was a Muslim. Institute for Advanced Study researcher Danielle Allen, on seeing polls showing that "the number of voters who mistakenly believe Obama is a Muslim rose — from 8 percent to 13 percent between November 2007 and March 2008" tracked the rumours to him, the newspaper said (Mosk 2008). Martin's influence on American perceptions of Obama has been substantial, although it was not ultimately overwhelming.

Obama's presidential campaign took hits from those who leverage other distinctive Internet features. Outsiders now have greater access to what were once seen as private conversations, as the Internet redefines the space of the local vs. the global. What could be more local than one's neighbourhood church? For Obama's former pastor, Jeremiah Wright, however, YouTube served as the medium by which his religious and discursive privacy was deconstructed by an offended American public. Once digitally recorded, his sermons were, obviously, no longer statements made among friends; "God damn America", a decontextualized sound-bite from a sermon Wright delivered in 2001, was endlessly replayed. Obama repudiated Wright, and Wright's theology was called "racist and anti-American". Obama, finally, ended up referring to YouTube in a famous speech on race given after this event — probably a first for an American political candidate.

Michelle Obama's undergraduate thesis at Princeton, written for a small, insular community (the Princeton faculty and, by extension, Princeton students and alumni) and entitled "Princeton-Educated Blacks and the Black Community", has been used similarly. Political columnist Christopher Hitchens derides the thesis:

> To describe it as hard to read would be a mistake; the thesis cannot be "read" at all, in the strict sense of the verb. This is because it wasn't written in any known language. Anyway, at quite an early stage in the text, Michelle Obama announces that she's much influenced by the definition of black "separationism" offered by Stokely Carmichael and Charles Hamilton in their 1967 screed *Black Power: The Politics of Liberation in America*. What Michelle Obama actually wrote was that "Stokely Carmichael and Charles Hamilton's [sic] (1967) developed definitions of separationism in their discussion of Black Power which guided me in the formulation and use of this concept in the study. (Hitchens 2008: 26)

Online, Michelle Obama's thesis and Jeremiah Wright's sermons were combined during the election campaign to make an assemblage consisting of as much fiction as fact: "While researching into the life of Stokley *(sic)* Carmichael, the mentor of Michelle

Obama, the first thing that popped out at me was an amazing similarity between the rantings of Carmichael and the ravings of spiritual mentor to Barack Obama, Jeremiah Wright. It is no coincidence that both Obamas have an affinity for this black separatist mentality," wrote blogger Larry Johnson.

I learned over the weekend why the Republicans who have seen the tape of Michelle Obama ranting about "whitey" describe it as "STUNNING". I have not seen it but I have heard from five separate sources who have spoken directly with people who have seen the tape. It features Michelle Obama and Louis Farrakhan. They are sitting on a panel at Jeremiah Wright's Church when Michelle makes her intemperate remarks. (Johnson 2008)

In fact, no such tape existed, but the false reports were not hampered by this "detail".

Much of race, on the Internet, like much of journalism, is similarly created; fiction out of whole cloth, an appearance of order out of chaos. It is information, yes, but information cut off from any connection back to the "reality" it purports to reflect. Whether both race and journalism on the Web will continue to be dominated by masks is yet to be seen. Whatever happens, perceptions of both are being substantially altered by the seen and unseen behind the Web, as is the very concept of citizenship, once limited by race and later defined through journalism — and now reshaped by new relations to information.

References

Barlow, J. P. (1994) "The Economy of Ideas", *Wired*, 2 March. Retrieved from: http://www.wired.com/wired/archive/2.03/economy.ideas.html.

Bradford, W. (1899) *Bradford's History "Of Plimouth Plantation": From the Original Manuscript. With a Report of the Proceedings Incident to the Return of the Manuscript to Massachusetts.* Boston: Wright & Potter, state printers.

Brownstoner.com Archives: http://www.brownstoner.com/brownstoner/archives/2008/03/monday_links_95.php.

Brooklynian.com Forums: http://www.brooklynian.com/forums/viewtopic.php?t=5923%3Cbr%3E%3C/a%3E. Craigslist.org.

Dick, P. K. (1985) "How to Build a Universe That Doesn't Fall Apart Two Days Later" in *I Hope I Shall Arrive Soon.* Garden City, NY: Doubleday, pp. 1–23.

Dyson, E. (1995) "Intellectual Value", *Wired*, 3 July. Retrieved from: http://www.wired.com/wired/archive/3.07/dyson.html.

Ellison, R. (1952) *Invisible Man.* New York: Random House.

Emerson, R. (2000) "Nature". In *The Essential Writings of Ralph Waldo Emerson.* New York: Modern Library.

Florida State Statutes (2008) Retrieved from: http://www.leg.state.fl.us/statutes/index.cfm?App_mode=Display_Statute&Search_String=&URL=CH0090/sec5015.htm.

Garofoli, J. (2006) "The Truth about Blogging". *SFGate*, 20 July. Retrieved from: http://www.sfgate.com/cgi-bin/article.cgi?f=/c/a/2006/07/20/MNGU1K2AVF1.DTL.

Gibson, W. (1984) *Neuromancer.* New York: Ace Books.

Greenwald, G. (2008) "Sean Hannity, Robert Gibbs and anti-Semitism: How to go on Fox

News", *Salon*, 5 October. Retrieved from: http://www.salon.com/opinion/greenwald/2008/10/08/fox_news/.

Hayles, N. K. (1999) *How We Became Posthuman: Virtual Bodies in Cybernetics, Literature, and Informatics*. Chicago: The University of Chicago Press.

Hitchens, C. (2008) "Are We Getting Two for One? Is Michelle Obama Responsible for the Jeremiah Wright Fiasco?" *Slate*, 5 May. Retrieved from: http://www.slate.com/id/2190589/.

Jacobs, H. (1861) *Incidents in the Life of a Slave Girl*. Boston, MA: published by the author. Retrieved from: http://xroads.virginia.edu/~hyper/jacobs/hj-cover.htm.

Johnson, L. (2008) "Michelle Obama and Louis Farrakhan Take On Whitey", *No Quarter*, 2 June. Retrieved from: http://noquarterusa.net/blog/2008/06/02/michelle-obama-and-louis-farrakhan-take-on-whitey/.

Jones, K. C. (2008) "Missouri Mom to Be Arraigned on Cyberbullying Charges Related to Teen's Suicide", *Information Week*, 16 June. Retrieved from: http://www.informationweek.com/news/internet/social_network/showArticle.jhtml?articleID=208404145.

Kahn, C. (2003) "Web Spying Puts Twist on Jefferson Saga", *redOrbit*, 3 May. Retrieved from: http://www.redorbit.com/news/technology/5888/web_spying_puts_twist_on_jefferson_saga/index.html.

Keen, A. (2007) *The Cult of the Amateur: How the Internet Is Killing Our Culture*. New York: Doubleday.

Mosk, M. (2008) "An Attack That Came out of the Ether", *The Washington Post*, 28 June, p. C01. Retrieved from: http://www.washingtonpost.com/wp-dyn/content/article/2008/06/27/AR2008062703781.html?hpid=topnews&sid=ST2008062703939&pos=.

Newman, J. (1993) "In re Anthony R. MARTIN-TRIGONA, Movant. In re George SASSOWER, Movant". United States Court of Appeals, second circuit, docket nos. 93-5008, 93-3041. Retrieved from: http://bulk.resource.org/courts.gov/c/F3/9/9.F3d.226.93-3041.93-5008.html.

Norman, B. (2003) "Operation Baghdad", *New Times: Broward-Palm Beach*, 31 July. Retrieved from: http://www.browardpalmbeach.com/2003-07-31/news/operation-baghdad/.

Obama for America (2008) "The Truth about Michelle", *Fight the Smears*. Retrieved from: http://my.barackobama.com/page/invite/notape.

Obama, B. (2006) *The Audacity of Hope*. New York: Crown.

Obama, B. (2008) "Barack Obama's Speech on Race", *The New York Times*, 28 March. Retrieved from: http://www.nytimes.com/2008/03/18/us/politics/18text-obama.html.

Obama, M. (Michelle Lavaughn Robinson) (1985) *Princeton-Educated Blacks and the Black Community*. Princeton, NJ: Princeton University. Retrieved from: http://www.scribd.com/word/full/2305083?access_key=key-16chi42k62njmues30ly.

PaganPower (2008) "Michelle Obama: More than They Want You to Know", *No Quarter*, 14 June. Retrieved from: http://noquarterusa.net/blog/2008/06/14/the-whole-enchilada/.

Rutenberg, J. (2008) "The Man Behind the Whispers about Obama", *The New York Times*, 12 October. Retrieved from: http://www.nytimes.com/2008/10/13/us/politics/13martin.html.

Second Life home page. Retrieved from: http://secondlife.com/.

Simpson, J. A., and Weiner, E. S. C. (eds) (1989) *The Oxford English Dictionary*. Oxford: Clarendon Press.

Smith, A., and Raine, L. (2008) "Reports: Public Policy/The Internet and the 2008 Election", *Pew/Internet: Pew Internet & American Life Project*, 16 June. Retrieved from: http://www.pewinternet.org/report_display.asp?r=252.

Wallace, M. (1988) "Invisibility Blues". In R. Simonson and W. Scott (eds), *Multi-Cultural Literacy*. St Paul, MN: Graywolf http://www.graywolfpress.org/.

West, K. (2008) "I'm 'Most Offended I've Ever Been", Associated Press article, Cnn.com, 25 June. Retrieved from: http://www.cnn.com/2008/SHOWBIZ/Music/06/25/music. kanyewest.bonna.ap/index.html?iref=mpstoryview.

White, B., and Medusa (2008) "Michelle Obama off Tape", *No Quarter*, 13 June. Retrieved from: http://noquarterusa.net/blog/2008/06/13/michelle-obama-off-tape/.

Williams, P. J. (1997) *Seeing a Color-Blind Future: The Paradox of Race*. New York: Farrar, Straus and Giroux.

⟨⟨ CHAPTER ⟩⟩
15

Citizen Journalism Online: Promise of an Alternative Conflict Discourse?

DMITRY EPSTEIN AND DOR REICH

"The major cause of violence is inattention to the subjective reality of the famous other."
(Galtung 2000)

The blog-dedicated search engine Technorati is tracking more than 35 million sites at the time of writing. The popularity of personal blogging is just one aspect of a wide spectrum of developments taking place in the online environment. These developments are viewed by the social scientific community as challenging traditional journalistic practices and institutions (for example, Regan 2003; Wall 2005; Lowrey 2006). In 2005, more than 7 percent of Americans who used the Internet reported that they had created a blog, and the readership of the blogosphere at that time was estimated at 27 percent, with a high proportion of them younger people (Lee Kaid and Postelnicu 2007). In 2007, 8 percent of US adult Internet users reported that they had created or worked on their own online journal or weblog (Horrigan 2007).

In journalism and media scholarship focusing on the "new" media, some consider blogging to be a form of "citizen journalism", also known as "participatory journalism". This type of journalism views citizens as "playing an active role in the process of collecting, reporting, analysing and disseminating news and information" (Bowman and Willis 2003). One of the emerging paradigms regarding citizen journalism is that it offers an alternative to the mainstream media in terms of structure and, consequently, in terms of discourse. Some scholars suggest that, unlike traditional journalism, caught in a web of institutional constraints, the blogosphere offers an environment where "high" journalistic values may flourish, such as those concerning the depth and representation of multiple perspectives (Tremayne 2007a).

The coverage of conflict situations provides a particularly interesting area of analysis in this respect. On the one hand, structural elements of conventional journalistic practice, such as market pressure, lead the media to focus on violence and to take sides in a conflict, while suppressing deeper and more inclusive discussion (Galtung 2000). On the other hand, the Internet, as a platform, possesses the features required to host open and inclusive coverage and analysis (Bowman and Willis 2003). Thus an interesting question arises: has a different kind of discourse evolved online, or is the Internet, like any other medium, subject to social, cultural, political and economic constraints, which impose similar, war-oriented coverage of conflicts?

In this chapter we analyse a subset of discourse surrounding the Israeli–Palestinian conflict in the blogosphere, using "peace journalism" as our conceptual frame of analysis. It is important to emphasize that we are not concerned with scholarly debate about the substance of "peace journalism" as a construct, its legitimacy as a journalistic practice or its ethical aspects. Instead, we are employing this concept as a normative analytical framework to assess the discursive nature of conflict coverage in the blogosphere and question the structural explanation of that discourse.

We start by describing the blogging phenomenon and its relationship with traditional journalism, especially in the context of social, political and military conflicts. In this review we are particularly interested in revealing the socio-technical structural differences between the mainstream media and the blogosphere, which can lead to production of different types of discourse. Then we describe the concept of peace journalism as a prism for assessing discourse prevailing in conflict coverage. This approach emerges from a substantial literature on how structural constraints operate on journalistic practice and on the resulting discursive patterns. Next, based on our discussion of structural differences, we investigate whether different structural settings will generate different kinds of discourse. More specifically, we ask if the blogosphere hosts a discourse that is more oriented towards peace, given that it is freed from many institutional constraints thought to shape the war-oriented discourse of the mainstream media. We focus on the Israeli–Palestinian conflict as our case study.

We conduct a discourse analysis of a sample of blogs, using a heuristic offered by Lynch and McGoldrick (2005a; 2005b) and further developed by Shinar (2004), which suggests a number of criteria to distinguish between communication oriented towards peace and war. Finally, we offer directions and questions for future research of the "new" media environment, online discourse and civic engagement.

ONLINE JOURNALISM, PARTICIPATORY JOURNALISM AND THE BLOGOSPHERE

The Internet's rapid growth over the last two decades has offered an additional platform for news information collection, analysis, verification and distribution. Since the beginning of the massive commercialization of the Internet during the 1990s, leading mainstream media figures have been interested in adapting it for their use (Boczkowski 2004; Schiller 2000). Media companies initially applied traditional mass communication archetypes and business models to the online environment (Schiller 2000). They ensured their presence in the virtual environment, for example, by creating online replicas of printed newspapers and online radio. In addition, journalistic practices started to change owing to technological advancement, allowing more visual and instant coverage of events worldwide (Boczkowski 2004).

However, the unique characteristics of the Internet's infrastructure as a distributed system, as well as its underpinning philosophy of decentralization, contributed to users' independence and their ability to creatively express themselves online. Since the explosion of the "dot.com bubble" at the start of the new millennium, we have witnessed a gradual rise of the "Web 2.0" paradigm, which, despite being primarily a marketing concept, grants internet users, or "netizens", a greater opportunity for agency compared with traditional media users (O'Reilly 2005). For example, talkbacks (or readers' comments) have been introduced on to traditional news websites. Moreover, there are websites such as YouTube, Wikipedia, Digg and others that provide a platform for their users to supposedly take control of content production.

Recent developments provide an excellent example of the interdependence between the architecture of the platform and the agency granted to the users. In April 2007 the Advanced Access Content System (AACS) licensing administrator started issuing warnings against websites hosting information that contained an encryption key for a new format of high-definition DVDs. The encryption was broken in December 2006 and, since then, the key has been circulating the Internet in various forms. One of the warnings was sent to a technical news ranking website Digg — a platform that allows its users to rank what they consider newsworthy items from any source on the Web, including blogs and other user-generated content. In an attempt to comply with the warning based on the Digital Millennium Copyright Act (US Public Law 105-304 1998), the website started deleting items containing the encryption key and also published an announcement with an explanation to its users. As a result, users reacted in unexpectedly creative ways, ranking as many news items and Web pages containing the key as possible. The "revolt" escalated to the extent that Digg's founders gave up[1] and agreed to comply with their users' will, against the demands of AACS.[2] In other words, the infrastructure of Digg and its social norms allowed its users to take control of the website's content, despite the owners' attempts to censor it. This is an example of the potential of the new media environment, which was impossible in traditional mass-media settings.

The changing nature of the Web has repercussions in the coverage of social, political and military conflicts. A particularly interesting phenomenon is that of citizen, civic or participatory journalism. Bowman and Willis define participatory journalism as:

> the act of a citizen, or group of citizens, playing an active role in the process of collecting, reporting, analyzing, and disseminating news and information. The intent of this participation is to provide independent, reliable, accurate, wide-ranging and relevant information that a democracy requires. (Bowman and Willis 2003: 9)

In other words, in the case of participatory journalism, the reader is also the author and the editor. Readers are encouraged to participate in creating news content and to react to each other's materials (Tremayne 2007a). Some claim that participatory journalism creates a symbiotic relationship between the "journalist" and the "news-consumers", thus challenging the authority of the classical archetype of a trained "journalist". Participatory journalism is essentially a grassroots phenomenon that has recently started attracting professional journalists and established media institutions (Bowman and Willis 2003).

Weblogs, or blogs, are considered the flagship of participatory journalism, owing to their increasing popularity in recent years (Gillmor 2006). The phenomenon dates back to the start of the new millennium. By 2004 more than 8 million people were publishing their own blogs. In 2006 Mishne and Glance (2006) estimated that blog posts were added at a rate of 700,000 a day (including spam and inactive blogs), and, in addition, the readers of the blogs left around 150,000 comments on a daily basis. Technorati reported in the autumn of 2008 that it was monitoring more than 1.2 million registered blogs.[3] Earlier, in March 2008, media buying agency Universal McCann released a report estimating that more than 184 million people worldwide have started a blog and 346 million read blogs. Moreover, the report stated that 72.8 percent of active Internet users have read blogs at least once (Smith 2008). In addition to "traditional" blogs, today blogs can be found as part of established online news outlets, social networking websites, corporate websites and other sites. In other words, blogging is a growing phenomenon, which generates significant scholarly, political and commercial interest.

Interestingly, conflicts and scandals signified milestones in the development of blogging as a journalistic phenomenon. In the late 1990s the Clinton–Lewinsky scandal marked the birth of online journalism. In a similar fashion, the September 11 attack can be viewed as the point where blogging emerged as a widespread phenomenon (Herring, Scheidt, Kouper and Wright 2007; Tremayne 2007a). In times of national crisis, mainstream media discourse is reduced to a single dominant voice, which is often one-sided and unbalanced. During the post 9/11 period, one could rarely find a voice critical of the US government in the American mainstream media. In this context, blogs provided an accessible and timely alternative for those who were searching for additional points of view (see also Williams, Trammell, Postelnicu, Landreville and Martin 2005).

Although there is an ongoing debate about the news value of blogs and the status of bloggers as self-proclaimed journalists (Bentley et al. 2007; Papacharissi 2007; see also Hudson and Temple in this volume), it is difficult to overestimate the growing significance of blogosphere in the media environment. Tremayne (2007a) suggests three different patterns of influence that the blogosphere has over traditional media. First, he suggests that the blogosphere can influence the traditional media through the media themselves. In this case, bloggers influence priming by creating further visibility to issues originally published in the established media, thus making these issues more accessible and lucid to the public (for an account of priming see Iyengar, Peters and Kinder 1982; and Roskos-Ewoldson, Roskos-Ewoldson and Dillman Carpentier 2002). The second pattern, in fact, operates by circumventing the media. Here bloggers engage in independent investigations that generate a "buzz" in the bloggers' community, thus influencing actual events directly or entering mainstream media debate. Finally, Tremayne notices that after initially rejecting the new platform, established mass media are now adopting it, with blogs linked to, and facilitated by, companies such as *The Washington Post*, CNN and others (see elsewhere in this volume for further discussion).

In spite of the growing interrelationship between the blogosphere and the mainstream media, the image of citizen journalism that is emerging is substantially different from its mainstream media counterpart. Particularly, focusing on confrontational situations, we can anticipate finding a richer and deeper discussion and analysis of conflict in the blogosphere, compared with the mainstream media. This difference can be attributed to the distinct socio-technical structure of the blogosphere. Whether or not this expectation is borne out remains an open question, which we are trying to grapple with in this chapter. In the next section we consider peace journalism as a normative analytical framework for assessing news coverage of conflicts, in terms of discourse oriented towards war and peace. Using this framework, we will then test a hypothesis regarding the nature of the discourse of blogs covering conflict situations.

REPORTING CONFLICT AND "PEACE JOURNALISM"

There is a *de facto* consensus among researchers that coverage of international conflicts is dominated by confrontational discourse, whether the conflict is of a political, social or military nature (for example, Cohen and Wolfsfeld 1993; Hackett 2006; Lee and Maslog 2005; Shinar 2007; Wolfsfeld 2004). In recent years, however, there has been an intense debate over the possibility of there being alternative paths of conflict coverage. The core premise of this approach, labelled "peace journalism", "constructive conflict coverage" or "ethically responsible journalism", is that the mass media, as a powerful social institution, significantly shapes the conflicts it covers (Galtung 2000; Peleg 2006; Shinar 2004; Tehranian 2002). According to Lynch and McGoldrick:

> Peace Journalism is when editors and reporters make choices — of what stories to report and about how to report them — that create opportunities for society at large to consider and value non-violent responses to conflict. (2005a: 5)

Galtung (2000) describes peace journalism as news coverage that focuses on people and voices the opinions of all the parties involved. The reports are oriented towards providing solutions and peace is defined in terms of non-violence and creative conflict resolution, which does not necessarily include "victory" of one of the sides. Peace journalism coverage aims to make the conflict transparent, by providing background information and a wider context to any particular issue covered in a single report. According to this notion, each side has an opportunity to present its aims, positions and ideas in a manner as free from editorial intervention as possible. The intention is to allow the usually silenced, authentic voices from both sides of the conflict to be heard.

At the same time, peace journalism aims at highlighting peace initiatives and action that would prevent conflicts from escalating.

One can see peace journalism as offering a view of social responsibility that encourages journalists to play an active role in helping resolve conflicts, thus explicitly affecting journalistic practice (Galtung 2000; Lynch and McGoldrick 2000). Identifying conceptual blocks for assessing the media discourses surrounding the coverage of peace and conflict processes, Shinar (2004) points to media frames as being one of the more influential aspects that constitute normative journalism. In mainstream journalism reporters and editors are under pressure to get their reports in front of audiences. In the process a set of approaches, often called media frames, have established themselves as appealing ways for how a certain story gets told. In Shinar's analysis, war-oriented metaphors are one of those frames. So, as Shinar sees it, framing issues in terms of war is not just one viable way to address viewers, it's a particularly compelling one and, as such, is becoming fundamental to news discourse (see also Shinar 2007). In other words, Shinar implicitly suggests journalistic practices and routines as one of the most meaningful forces shaping the nature of conflict coverage.

To an extent, this perspective resonates with the amalgamation of two classic arguments by Tuchman (1973) and Galtung and Ruge (1965). On the one hand, Tuchman suggests news people use different news categories and typifications to systemize dealing with seemingly unexpected streams of events. As such, journalists aim to routinize news reporting, she argues. On the other hand, Galtung and Ruge suggest a set of criteria that are applied to events to assess their newsworthiness. Interestingly, the extent to which an event has a negative impact constitutes one of the pivotal factors, which helps simultaneously to satisfy a set of other criteria, such as unambiguity, consensuality and unexpectedness (see also Harcup and O'Neill 2001). Relying on these two foundations — that journalists tend to places stories into pre-existing schema and to prioritize the negative — we can comprehend the vicious cycle of war discourse that dominates the coverage of social, political and military conflicts in the mainstream media. The remaining question is: can an alternative pattern of coverage emerge in a different institutional setting?

BUILDING A STRUCTURAL ARGUMENT

The cultural, social, political and economic settings of journalistic activity have been recognized as structural factors influencing journalistic practice, while simultaneously being shaped by it. Tehranian (2002) suggests viewing the peace/war discourse of conflict coverage in these structural terms. He argues that interaction between mutually dependent technological, social and cultural transformations in the last few decades has created a world where media and information exchange play a pivotal role, particularly in understanding the "other". He argues: "In our largely mediated world, reality is often constructed out of the interplay of three different realities, including media, existential, and social construction of reality" (2002: 75).

However, that same interplay has shaped the environment in a way that "communication, power, and conflict are thus inextricably tied together" (2002: 75). Hence the structural factors, and profound ties between them, favour a war discourse, through routinized practices of domination and control. In other words, Tehranian argues that "the structure is the message" and media structure is the most "efficacious method of ensuring individual, corporate, and government ethical behavior" (2002: 34).

Blasi (2004) allows us to link the structural argument back to the news production perspective. According to Blasi, there are six factors involved in maintaining sustainable journalism practice. These include the structural aspects of media, the features of the situation that is being reported, personal features of the journalists, the political climate and the effect of lobbying, and the nature of the audience. Interaction between these factors determines news production processes, resulting in what can be defined as either war or peace journalism (see Figure 15.1).

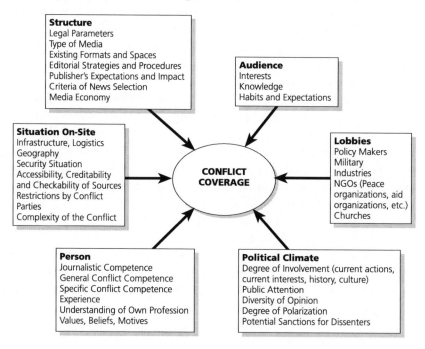

Figure 15.1 Six factors influencing conflict coverage production. (Blasi 2004: 5)

Building on Blasi's model, one can argue that online grassroots journalism offers a supposedly unique institutional setting, thus suggesting a "liberation" from traditional constraints. Particularly relevant for this study are the structural elements such as existing formats, editorial strategies, economic constraints and so on, which are mentioned across peace journalism literature as impacting on the discourse. As a result, one would expect that features of peace journalism, suppressed by the above constraints, would be enhanced in online, citizen-driven environments.

The case of the war in Iraq provides a particular example where citizen journalism fits such a projection (Wall 2005). During the early phases of the war the world was exposed to the insider view of an Iraqi named Salam Pax, whose blog, "Where is Raed?"

attracted the attention of the mainstream media. Compared to the embedded media that followed the US forces, his blog presented to the Western public what seemed to be an authentic and unfiltered point of view of an ordinary Iraqi (Johnson and Kaye 2007; Piper and Ramos 2005).

In their 2005 article, Piper and Ramos identify a rich segment of the blogosphere that addresses the ongoing war in Iraq. They distinguish between general war blogs, war news blogs, milbloggers and Iraqi blogs. General war blogs deal with analysis of the military aspects of the conflict, including its politics and casualties. War news blogs feature primarily journalists and former journalists who provide insights on the war and react to the mainstream media coverage. Milbloggers, or soldiers' blogs, are reflections of coalition soldiers, both male and female, on their personal experience in Iraq. The complex relationship between communicating their personal views and belonging to the military requires many of the bloggers to remain anonymous, and some of them were forced to stop blogging. The fourth category is the blogs of Iraqis themselves, ranging from pro-American to highly critical ones, which present a supposedly unfiltered and raw on-the-spot view (Piper and Ramos 2005). The actual blogging scene addressing the war in Iraq is probably even richer if one accounts for blogs that are not in English and thus not covered by Piper and Ramos. Nevertheless, among the English-speaking audiences, these blogs have generally enjoyed a high degree of authority and trust (Johnson and Kaye 2007).

The examples above suggest that the nature of discourse in the blogosphere differs from that of the mainstream media. Yet we are left to hypothesize about the potential reasons for this. A limited analysis of the structural elements of the blogosphere suggests that it has different features from the mainstream media. For example, explaining the mutual influence and tension between the grassroots online media and the mainstream media, Tremayne mentions a number of factors:

> First, they [bloggers] have outsider status. Like television news in the 1950s, they are seen by users as conduits to raw information, somehow less corrupted by power than their predecessors. Second, some have attained a large audience. Regardless of whether they "should" have an audience, they do, and with it comes power. Third, they have "the power of collective" . . . Even if many individual blogs have just a few hundred regular readers, collectively the blogosphere can generate a louder "buzz" . . . Through individual links choices, this collective bestows upon a select few the "power of authority". (2007a: xvi)

From this, we can consider the structural differences between the blogosphere and the mainstream media. As a grassroots phenomenon, the blogosphere is perceived to lack the traditional hierarchical structures and profit-oriented models geared to maximize audiences. Lowrey suggests a number of additional distinctions, arguing that "the organization of production is [the] most fundamental distinction between journalism and blogging" (2006: 480). Comparing mainstream journalism to blogging, Lowery shows that the organizational structure of the former enables a more standardized and routinized production process, while the later lacks the expertise, legitimacy and access to resources. At the same time, because they do not face mainstream journalism's organizational constraints, bloggers have less need to compromise on their values or to conform in order to reach larger audiences. They can focus on smaller but more detailed stories and are not constrained by production cycles. According to Lowery, these structural factors, combined with the subjective qualities of each occupation, result in differences "in content, work processes, tone, values and format" (2006: 480).

Clearly, blogging is different from news media not just in tone or format, but at a structural level. Following Tehranian's (2002) and Blasi's (2004) argument that the prevalence of war discourse in news is a function of the structures within which journalists are socialized, our question is: what kind of discourse would evolve in a different structural setting? We have demonstrated that the blogosphere is an emerging institution that interacts with both real world events and mainstream media institutions. We have also shown that the blogosphere is different to a degree that allows us to argue that it can produce a different kind of content. Now we can move to a concrete case in order to examine our hypothesis that different institutional settings would host different types of discourse. Specifically, we are interested in exploring the nature of the discourse in the blogosphere concerning the Israeli–Palestinian conflict, as a particular case to shed more light on that conceptual causal link.

Knowing that previous studies identified a war bias in mainstream media (Keshev 2004; Lee and Maslog 2005; Lynch and McGoldrick 2005a; Lynch and McGoldrick 2005b; Peleg 2006; Shinar 2007), will we find patterns of peace discourse in online participatory journalism as expressed in blogs? According to Lynch and McGoldrick (2005a; 2005b), the peace discourse should be open to creativity and to a variety of solutions. It should present a complex picture of the wider context and allow different voices to be heard. Lynch and McGoldrick contend that peace discourse must encourage a re-thinking of established conventions about the "other" or the "enemy". It should not make assumptions about the intentions of other people, but instead ensure an open and understanding mindset with regard to their motives (Lynch and McGoldrick 2005a; 2005b). In the next section we will discuss the procedures used to apply the peace journalism heuristics, as it was presented by Lynch and McGoldrick (2005a; 2005b) and then further developed by Shinar (2004).

THE STUDY

Our examination of the peace/war discourse in the blogosphere employs a critical text or linguistic analysis, as described by Phillips and Hardy:

> As with social linguistic analysis, critical linguistic analysis also focuses on individual texts, but with stronger interest in the dynamics of power that surround the text . . . It thus shares the concerns of critical discourse analysis but focuses more closely on the microdynamics of texts. Individual pieces of text are examined to understand how structures of domination in the local or proximate context are implicated in the text. (Phillips and Hardy 2002: 27)

More specifically, we employ procedures informed by Fairclough (1995; 2001), as they appear in Van Dijk (1993) and in Phillips and Hardy (2002). Our study is aimed at identifying discursive structures in a subset of blogs focusing on the Israeli–Palestinian conflict. It asked whether the content created online bears features closer to the peace journalism model proposed by Lynch and McGoldrick (2005a, 2005b) and Shinar (2004), as opposed to that of traditional journalism oriented towards war and violence. More specifically, it looked for textual constructs characteristic of journalism oriented towards: peace vs. war/violence; truth vs. propaganda; popular vs. elite; solution vs. victory-oriented; and war framing, trivialization and ritualization vs embryonic and sporadic peace discourse (see Table 15.1).

Table 15.1 Based on Lynch and McGoldrick (2005a; 2005b) and Shinar (2004)

Peace/Conflict Journalism	War/Violence Journalism
I. *Peace/Conflict-oriented*	I. *War/Violence-oriented*
Explore conflict formation; x parties, y goals, z issues general 'win win' orientation	Focus on conflict arena; 2 parties, 1 goal (win), war general zero-sum game orientation
open space, open time; causes and outcomes anywhere, also on history/culture	closed space, closed time; causes and exits in arena, who threw the first stone
making conflict transparent	making wars opaque/secret
giving voice to all parties; empathy, understanding, conflict/war as problem, focus on conflict creativity	'us-them' journalism, propaganda, voice, for 'us' see 'them' as the problem, focus on who prevails in war
humanization of all sides; more so the worse the weapon	dehumanization of 'them'; more so the worse the weapon
proactive; prevention before any violence/war occurs	reactive; waiting for violence before reporting
focus on invisible effects of violence (trauma and glory, damage to structure/culture)	focus only on visible effect of violence (killed, wounded and material damage)
II. *Truth-orientated*	II. *Propaganda-orientated*
Expose untruths on all sides / uncover all cover-ups	Expose 'their' untruths / help 'our' cover-ups/lies
III. *People-orientated*	III. *Elite-orientated*
Focus on suffering all over; on women, aged, children, giving voice to voiceless	Focus on 'our' suffering; on able-bodied elite males, being their mouth-piece
give name to all evil-doers	give name to their evil-doer
focus on people peace-makers	focus on elite peace-makers
IV. *Solution-orientated*	IV. *Victory-orientated*
Peace = non-violence + creativity	Peace = victory + ceasefire
highlight peace initiatives, also to prevent more	conceal peace initiatives; before victory is at

235

war focus on structure, culture, the peaceful society aftermath; resolution, reconstruction, reconciliation	hand focus on treaty, institution, the controlled society
	leaving for another war, return if the old flares up again

V. *Peace-Oriented Media Framing*	V. *War-Oriented Media Framing*
Embryonic, sporadic peace discourse	Framing Peace Stories in War Discourse
experimental demonstrations of peace discourse	trivialization
Style: Media Event Techniques Redefining Rules of Journalism	ritualization
adapting narrative style; conquests, contests coronations	
adapting performance styles; equal access humanization, dramatic coherence, interpretation of context and symbols	
Content: textual analysis genres "Master-frames", "super-texts", made of peace-related 'products'	
Constitutive rhetoric Assignment of meaning to new symbolic entities/processes (i.e. peace), through reality construction and combination of social and historical narratives with ideological objectives	

In order to pursue this, 150 blogs were sampled during a period of fifteen days, between 19 May and 2 June 2006. The main limitation of this sample is its short time-span. However, this sampling period has its strengths, as there were no significant political developments in the region at that time; as such, it served as a suitable time frame that minimized "noise" resulting from external influences on the discursive patterns. The blogs were selected through technorati.com, using a search string "(Palestine OR Palestinian) AND (Israel OR Israeli)" and the authority-ranking mechanism offered by the website.

The search criteria demonstrate one of the major challenges facing those researching the "new" media. By considering blogs containing both terms related to the conflict, we excluded the extreme blogs referring solely to one of the sides or using different, less politically correct, terms to define the parties. Moreover, our search did not include posts in languages other than English, which could have further skewed the data. In this way, our sample might have been biased towards the peace journalism discourse or not related to conflict at all. At the same time, one could also view it as focusing on mainstream blogosphere discourse, particularly given the dominance of the English language in the Internet.

In addition, we used Technorati's ranking system to select each day ten posts from the blogs that had the highest authority. Since the authority-ranking mechanism constitutes one of the unique features of Technorati, the company does not reveal its exact formula. However, from publicly available information on the company's blog, we can ascertain that it is primarily based on the number of incoming links to a particular blog in a given period of time. This approach to assessing the authority of blogs is widespread in the blogosphere (Tremayne 2007a; Java, Kolari, Finin and Oates 2006). It is, in fact, similar to the logic behind calculating the impact factor of academic journals, based on how often articles published in them are cited (for example, see Chen, Xie, Maslov and Redner 2007; Mingers and Harzing 2007). We have no information as to whether or not the fact that the sampling was conducted from an Israeli IP address influenced the results.

FINDINGS

Analysing the texts, our first striking observation was the degree to which bloggers regurgitate mainstream media reports — a tendency also observed by others such as Lowrey (2006), Rutigliano (2007) and Tremayne (2007b). Most of the blogs on our sample contained quotes, links or commentary from mainstream media news items. For example, a blog titled "A Daily Briefing on Iran" started its post on 25 May with the title "Israelis Aim to Sue Ahmadinejad", followed by a direct quote from a BBC News report: "A group of Israeli diplomats wants to sue Iran's President". Another example is a blog titled "Jihad Watch", which starts its 29 May post titled "Israeli Retaliates to Attacks, Bombs Bases in Lebanon" with a direct quote from Reuters. In these cases, the mainstream media item is used either as is, or is followed by a commentary that then generated an intense discussion with and among readers of the blog.

The discussion surrounding the mainstream media items is similar to the discussion one can find on the talkback pages of established news websites. For example a 30 May post at "Dhimmi Watch" was titled "Israel 'to Allow Arms to Abbas'" and cited a BBC article about military support for Mahmoud Abbas's forces. This post caused responses such as the following:

Where did this guy Olmert come from? This is a world leader that only Muslims and liberals could love. (posted by Ironman Hondo)

Give them all [Palestinians] a gun, with one bullet each, the gun can only be fired once, retreat to safe distance. (posted by IceDragon)

I thought every Palestinian already owned an AK47 and/or an rpg. (posted by MP)

As we can see, these reactions do not offer a discussion, but are more a collection of "dead-end statements" expressing readers' opinions, sometimes in a sarcastic way.

237

Moreover, they do not address the post itself or the cited item but use them as an excuse for expressing personal prejudices.

However, in other blogs we found criticisms of the mainstream media's coverage. For example, on 31 May a blog "Liberty and Justice" quoted Ha'aretz's report about an Israeli defence forces' preventive attack in the Gaza Strip. In the commentary following the citation, the blogger wrote:

> The Dutch MSM⁴ seldom reports about Palestinian organizations trying to kill Israeli civilians. We hear about what Israel does, but everything the Palestinians do, seems to mostly be ignored or it's, in some way or another, Israel's fault anyway.

Another interesting example can be found in a 27 May post at Yourish.com, which was dedicated to a critique of *The New York Times* editorial from 25 May. The post itself is interesting because it uses comparison to the blogosphere as a tool of critique:

> And it happened reading this editorial in NYT. Wow, man! You get, like, a blog of your own, but a) you get paid a good buck and b) lotsa folks are going to read it. And all the other conveniences of the blog: anonymity (it is NYT that has written it, after all, not a specific bloke — go and clean the clock of all the flunkies there — quite a sweaty undertaking), ability to write any bullshit that comes to mind and stuff.

In this case, the comment space was also utilized to criticize *The New York Times* further:

> I stopped reading the *Times* some years ago. This editorial is a reminder that I made the right decision. (posted by Jack Rich)

> Thankfully the last time I purchased the *New York Times* was back in February 2004. Never Again! (posted by Joel)

Extended reference to and open criticism of the mainstream media suggest a complex relationship between them and the bloggers. On the one hand, the mainstream media can be viewed as agenda-setters for the blogosphere, but, on the other hand, the bloggers often identify themselves as in an opposition to institutionalized journalism. We refer again to this complexity in the discussion of our results, as it will help us to understand other findings as well as develop a future research agenda.

Analysing the posts and their comments through the lens of a peace journalism model (Lynch and McGoldrick 2005a; 2005b) reveals a complex view of the conflict, with some trends emerging. We can see that the blogosphere is capable of hosting views consistent with a very extreme version of war journalism, particularly in the war/violence-oriented domain. For example, on 27 May a blogger named "PC Free Zone" published a post titled "'Hezbollah, Hezbollah,' Chanted the Iranian Crowd of Suicide Bombers". The post consisted of pictures from a demonstration supporting suicide bombing in Teheran, featuring men and women wearing headbands identifying their willingness to sacrifice their lives. One of the images featured uniform lines of men in white clothes, their arms crossed on their chests, their faces completely covered with distinctive scarves bound with red headbands stating "There is no God but Allah, and Muhammad is his prophet" in Arabic. The caption under that image read: "Iranian men wear white shrouds to indicate their willingness to give their lives to defend their country and Islam, during a gathering in Tehran on Thursday, May 25, 2006." The other image pictured a woman holding a little girl on her lap, both wearing traditional clothes and green headbands with the same quote from the Qur'an. The caption under that image read: "An Iranian woman and her daughter wearing headbands reading: 'There is no God but Allah, and Muhammad is his prophet' as they attend a suicide bombers gathering in southern Tehran."

The images in the example above suggest a homogenized view of the "other" as a faceless mob. They also dehumanize the people shown by presenting a mother socializing her daughter into the culture of martyrdom. This perspective is further emphasized in the text, which included direct quotes from a *Forbes* article:

A huge banner used as a backdrop showed flag-covered coffins. And a message — in English — promised to "damage the U.S. worldwide" in retaliation for any attack on Iran . . .

Volunteers mingled around monuments to attackers, including a Palestinian suicide bomber, an Iranian militiaman killed by the U.S. forces in Iraq and two commandos who helped carry out the 1983 blast at Marine barracks in Beirut that killed 241 U.S. servicemen. An almost simultaneous bombing killed 56 French peacekeepers . . .

"I only have one son and he's volunteered as a martyr", said Marium Nematzadeh, 56. "I have deep belief in my religion and my leaders. I would even become a bomber if asked."

Although the post does not address the Israeli–Palestinian conflict directly, it is mentioned there in the context of the debate on suicide bombing, where the conflict plays a prominent role. The choice of the event and the way it is presented portray the conflict in the broader context of the Middle East. However, it is still described in terms of war journalism. The post focuses on propaganda, emphasizing the propaganda of the "other" side. Thus it implies a sharp division between "us" and "them", portraying "them" as a problem, as warmongers promoting violence and focusing on "their" victory.

Taking into account our previous observation about the relationship between bloggers and the mainstream media, one could suggest that the violent discourse stems from the fact that the post described above is actually a replica of an article from the mainstream media. In this case, the *choice* of re-publishing the specific article becomes particularly interesting. While most research on online discourse focuses on what people write, less attention has been paid to what people re-post. However, that re-posting of a mainstream media article, even if it is done without any explanation or commentary, can still be read as a communicative act, although not an easy one to interpret. Considering the ease with which articles can be re-posted or linked to, this gesture of redistribution would be worth examining, but it is out of the scope of the current study. At the same time, viewing some of the personal commentary by bloggers also suggests similarly powerfully war-oriented discourse. For example, a blogger "Right on the Right" posted the following commentary on 21 May, under a title "Another Terrorist Bastard Dead":

I'm tired of the Leftist Liberals who consider Palestinians "Freedom Fighters" and call Israel "Occupiers". Look at their tactics, and look at their ideology, and you tell me which side is full of terrorists and which side is full of innocent people. The Israelis are fighting to secure their sovereignty while the Palestinians aren't fighting for a homeland, but rather because of a radical Islamofascist agenda. I hate the Palestinian Terrorists, and I hope they all die.

Following the commentary, the blogger posted an unidentified news item about a successful assassination of a member of Islamic Jihad in Gaza. Then he continues:

For those of who that don't know [sic], Islamic Jihad is a radical terrorist para-military group with ties to groups such as Al-Qaeda and Hamas. All of these groups also receive moderate support (sometimes in the form of weapons) from the terrorists in Iran. If you don't think Israel is assisting in the War on Terror by doing this, you need to learn about the Global Jihadist Movement going on in the Middle East. Another terrorist bastard is dead, which is good for the world, and good for the United States.

Carefully examining this post, one can see a language oriented more towards extreme violence and victory than the previous example. The blogger is praising the death of an "enemy", treating one group of people again as a homogeneous mass whose sole purpose is violently fighting "us". The mixture of the news item that actually describes elimination of the "enemy" and the commentary amplifies the war aspects of the discourse. There are many examples of war discourse among the posts:

Israel will crush them with an iron fist [. . .] There's a sense that Bush and Olmert are enjoying their vicious game of punishing the Palestinians for their choice at the ballot box.[. . .] The US and Israel are determined to achieve their narrow objectives even if it means sacrificing the lives countless women and children. This isn't policy; its barbarism. (posted by Global War)

The Jews don't want peace, they want to kick us to Jordan [. . .] Israelis are the main enemy and the main source of suffering. (posted by Michael J Totten)

[Palestinian] leaders have bombed women and children, using children as the suicide bombers, for years. Their "culture" seems to be built on corruption and brutality. (posted by The Strata-Sphere)

Nonsense [—] it is an ancient Arab propaganda lie. Israel never had any imperial ambitions, the Israelis only wanted to be left to live in peace, something the Arabs have never allowed them. In this lie we see the Arabs' projection onto the Israelis of their own vicious ambitions. (posted by Yourish.com)

Ahmadi may talk about genocide, but genocide has been already committed by Jews, and if it were not for their protector and colony (called USA), all their leaders would be tried for genocide and hung by their balls. (posted by A Daily Briefing on Iran)

In general, more than 60 percent of the posts analysed presented a war-oriented discourse. In some instances the war discourse is created mainly through the readers' commentary. For example, on 1 June, a blog named "Hot Air" published a post titled "Pali PM Haniyeh: Bush Administration is the Enemy of All Muslims". The post addressed Hamas leaders' comments regarding George W. Bush, and the language was oriented towards war. However, the comments of the readers provided an even more inflammatory discourse, which at times some could even be classified as racist:

No matter what you do to help Muslims and/or Arabs, no matter what you do to be friends with them, to explain yourself to them, to get closer to them, no matter what you do, they will hate you and they will seize any chance to destroy you. (posted by CatholicConservative)

This is the first time we have ever faced an enemy that truly believes that if we ALL die, including they themselves . . . THEY WIN. Remember the old saying that there is no one more dangerous than someone who no longer gives a s**t? Welcome to post 9-11, folks. (posted by horsepower_1st)

Damn straight. The enemy is ISLAM!!! (posted by ecamorg)

The Muslim Faith is the Enemy of the Entire World. (posted by MaiDee)

The so-called "founder" of their evil cult — Islam — was a mass-murder [sic], that tells it all. Hitler, compared to Muhammad, is an angel. (posted by CatholicConservative)

However, the blogosphere also presents more complex examples, as in the following instance. On 22 May a blog named "Captain's Quarters" posted a claim that accused the Palestinians of creating the situation in the West Bank: "This is what happens when people elect terrorists to office, and when they produce no choice other than terrorists or crooks."

Again, we can see in this statement how the text focuses on closed time and context-less causes. It portrays "them" as a problem, while viewing Palestinians as a dehumanized, homogenous mass. However, looking at the readers' comments, we can find the following statement: "You're referring to Hamas with this statement, but it just as well refers to Fatah. Westerners need to shed our belief that Fatah is a viable partner for peace" (posted by Jeremiah).

This comment reveals an interesting phenomenon. On the surface it continues the war discourse in an attempt to homogenize the enemy. However, by doing so, it raises

241

the awareness of potential differences among Palestinians, which resonates with another comment: "My guess is that Hamas will chase Fatah out of Gaza and that if Abbas shows some spine, Fatah will chase Hamas out of the West Bank" (posted by TimK).

Thus we can see that even though the overall language used in both the post and the readers' comments remains war/violence-oriented, the interaction between different actors creates a more complex picture of the Palestinians as enemies. The internal politics within Palestine has particular importance in this instance.

Furthermore, in a limited numbers of blogs we came across a few expressions characteristic of the peace journalism discourse. Those usually featured peace initiatives and political discussion and are still focused on covering elite figures or elite news sources. For example, on 26 May "Israpundit" published a post containing the following: "realignment comes not to bury the road map, but to push it forward".

Part of another blog, "Tikun Olam", had the following text on 26 May: "Israel and the U.S. . . . called on Hamas to accept the Hadarim peace proposal . . . this could be a turning point that gets us closer to final status negotiations happening in months rather than years or even decades." A more explicit peace journalism discourse can be found in posts focusing on ordinary people as opposed to those focused on the elite. A blog by Michael J. Totten, "The Other Side of the Green Line", consists of 4,519 words and 22 colour pictures. It is a personal journal of Mr Totten's visit to Ramallah. The post quotes civilians and a number of Palestinian politicians, thus presenting a complex picture of the current conflict, which focuses on the people involved and their feelings:

> "It will be good for everyone when Israel is accepted as part of this region", he said. "The other countries will get some of Israel's technology. Everyone will benefit from more money and tourism."

> "I have Israeli friends", he said. "I tell them things that I don't tell some of my Arab friends. It depends on the person, not the nationality."

However, instances such as that presented above are rare. The bloggers' reliance on the mainstream media and the relative anonymity provided by the Internet appear to reinforce each other as attributes generating a discourse oriented towards war. The lack of structural constraints does indeed seem to generate a different type of discourse. However, contrary to our hypothesis, this discourse, in most observed cases, has the hallmarks of war journalism, which are, at times, more extreme than those one can see in the mainstream media.

DISCUSSION AND CONCLUSION

Building on a body of knowledge showing that the blogosphere is constituted by, and operates in, a structural environment different from that of the mainstream media, we expected to find in it patterns and elements of different, peace-oriented, discourse. Yet our preliminary results show that the online environment hosts a surprisingly hostile discourse.

In general, the bloggers' presentation and discussion of the Israeli–Palestinian conflict tends to diverge towards the extremes. Even when the blogs present a complex picture and employ a relatively moderate discourse, comments on their posts use arguments oriented towards war and violence. The dominant discourse thus matches what Hanitzsch (2004a) and others label as "journalism of attachment" or, simply put, journalism that is taking a side in a conflict.

Another example is a phenomenon where many posts refer to or duplicate items from the mainstream media. As such, they replicate the war discourse presented in mainstream news coverage. Moreover, in many instances the violent discourse is amplified by comments left by users who do not hesitate in taking sides. At the same time, some posts are critical of the mainstream media, with comments tending to reinforce that perspective. Interestingly, Israeli bloggers adopted a similar pattern in criticizing the mainstream media during the second Lebanon war in the summer of 2006 (Tautig 2006).

Even though the blogosphere seems to promise a platform conducive to constructive and peace-oriented discussions, the emerging picture is that of a complex environment bearing many of the characteristics of war and populist journalism. One possible explanation for this apparent contradiction lies in the cultural realm. Hanitzsch (2004b) suggests that peace depends on media users and their culture, beliefs and perceptions. As such, he claims, we cannot expect from journalists greater engagement with peace than we expect from their audiences. Extending this argument to our analysis of the blogosphere, one may view journalists and their audiences as participants in the same culture. Accepting that proposition, we can better understand the lack of peace discourse in the grassroots media. Since grassroots journalists are not part of a peace culture, the discourse created in the blogosphere will be more oriented towards violence and war.

We do find peace discourse when the topic of posts is related to peace initiatives. However, similar to Shinar's observation (2004), these efforts are still framed in war journalism terms. The more explicit elements of peace journalism are found in posts addressing personal experiences, such as the example of Michael J. Totten described above. These posts tend to focus on individuals affected by the conflict, but at the same time they present the context of the conflict and focus on the importance of its resolution. Such posts are usually framed in non-violent language, and they acknowledge suffering and motivations for action on both sides. As such, those examples can be viewed as instances of peace-oriented discourse or peace journalism. In other words, the blogosphere as a platform is open to peace-oriented discourse, but human agency is the determining factor regarding the type of emerging discourse. Bloggers bring into the blogosphere different socio-cultural practices, and those practices shape different kinds of coverage and discussion surrounding the conflict. This observation, again, resonates with Hanitzsch's argument (2004b) about the importance of cultural context for journalistic practices. At the same time, this observation can suggest that traditional media and their institutional settings act as filtering mechanisms that do not allow extreme views penetrating the mainstream discourse. The lack of such mechanisms in the blogosphere unleashes both extremely violent and extremely peaceful discourses.

Although limited, the current study raises important questions and suggests a number of potential directions for further research on peace journalism and especially the new media domain. Working on this study and focusing on the blogosphere, we saw a need for both more breadth and depth of inquiry. First, we see a need to map the terrain of the blogosphere dealing with a particular conflict. Understanding the inter-connectivity between different bloggers, and between bloggers and the mainstream media covering a specific conflict, will provide additional context for the discourse analysis proposed here. In addition, a quantitative study is needed, similar to those carried out on the mainstream media. Developing this direction could allow for comparative studies to address the idea of civil journalism further in the context of peace journalism studies and beyond. At the same time, research needs to extend the scope of inquiry to include blogs that are not written in English, but especially in Hebrew and Arabic, as native languages of the conflict parties. One could argue that together with the mainstream media monitoring initiatives, such as "Keshev" and "Miftah" (Keshev 2004), there is a need for longitudinal follow-up on grassroots online discourse.

In addition, pointing to the need for to further study of the blogosphere, our analysis raises questions regarding other factors shaping the grassroots online discourse. Hanitzsch (2004b) suggests cultural elements as possible features. Building on Tehranian (2002), one can suggest the need for further inquiry into social structures governing cyberspace, particularly the blogosphere and participatory domains. Another interesting question arises about the role of the technological infrastructure itself. For example, one of the researchers is currently involved in a project looking into the effectiveness of collaborative platforms, such as wiki-based engines, in promoting dialogue and reaching consensus. In this context blogs can be viewed as an isolated creative process, compared with the socially interactive nature of collaborative work in a wiki.

To conclude, our study is one of the first steps in exploring the peace journalism paradigm as applied to the new media. It raises many questions, particularly regarding the role of technology and its associated social structures as mediators of discourse surrounding social, political and military conflicts. It shows the potential strength of communication technologies, but it also emphasizes the importance of human agency in this process. More research is necessary in this domain, bearing in mind the importance of communication in public life and peace processes.

Notes

1   For an official announcement in the company's blog see: http://blog.digg.com/?p=74.
2   The incident received wide media exposure. For some examples see Wired: http://www.wired.com/entertainment/hollywood/news/2007/05/digglegal, Forbes: http://www.forbes.com/technology/2007/05/02/digital-rights-management-tech-cx_ag_0502digg.html, BBC: http://news.bbc.co.uk/1/hi/technology/6615047.stm and others.

3   Since 2004 Technorati has been publishing periodical "State of the Blogosphere" reports. Earlier reports (up to 2007) are available online at: http://www.sifry.com/ stateoftheliveweb/. The last report (2008) is available online at: http://www.technorati.com/ blogging/state-of-the-blogosphere/ and provides interesting insights into the phenomenon of blogging.
4   MSM is a widely used by bloggers abbreviation for mainstream media.

References

Bentley, C., Hamman, B., Littau, J., Meyer, H., Watson, B., and Welsh, B. (2007) "Citizen Journalism: A Case Study". In M. Tremayne (ed.), *Blogging, Citizenship, and the Future of Media*. New York: Routledge, pp. 239–60.

Blasi, B. (2004) "Peace Journalism and the News Production Process", *Conflict & Communication Online*, 3 (1 and 2). Retrieved from: www.cco.regener-online.de.

Boczkowski, P. (2004) *Digitizing the News: Innovation in Online Newspapers*. Cambridge, MA: MIT Press.

Bowman, S., and Willis, C. (2003) *We Media: How Audiences are Shaping the Future of News and Information*. Reston, VA: The American Press Institute. Retrieved 17 March 2006 from: http://www.hypergene.net/wemedia/.

Chen, P., Xie, H., Maslov, S., and Redner, S. (2007) "Finding Scientific Gems with Google's PageRank Algorithm", *Journal of Informetrics*, 1 (1), pp. 8–15.

Cohen, A. A., and Wolfsfeld, G. (1993) *Framing the Intifada: People and Media*. Norwood, NJ: Ablex.

Fairclough, N. (1995) *Critical Discourse Analysis: The Critical Study of Language*. London: Longman.

Fairclough, N. (2001) *Language and Power*. Harlow: Pearson Education.

Galtung, J. (2000) "The Task of Peace Journalism", *Ethical Perspectives*, 7, pp. 162–7.

Galtung, J., and Ruge, M. (1965) "The Structure of Foreign News", *Journal of Peace Research*, 2 (1), pp. 64–91.

Gillmor, D. (2006) *We the Media: Grassroots Journalism by the People, for the People*. Sebastopol, CA: O'Reilly.

Hackett, R. A. (2006) "Is Peace Journalism Possible? Three Frameworks for Assessing Structure and Agency in News Media", *Conflict & Communication*, 5 (2).

Hanitzsch, T. (2004a) "The Peace Journalism Problem: Failure of News People — or Failure of Analysis?" In T. Hanitzsch, M. Loeffelholz, and R. Mustamu (eds), *Agents of Peace? Public Communication and Conflict Resolution in an Asian Setting*. Jakarta: FES, pp. 185–209.

Hanitzsch, T. (2004b) "Journalists as Peacekeeping Force? Peace Journalism and Mass Communication Theory", *Journalism Studies*, 5 (4), pp. 483–95.

Harcup, T., and O'Neill, D. (2001) "What is News? Galtung and Ruge Revisited", *Journalism Studies*, 2 (2), pp. 261–80.

Herring, S., Scheidt, L., Kouper, I., and Wright, E. (2007) "Longitudinal Content Analysis of Blogs: 2003–2004". In M. Tremayne (ed.), *Blogging, Citizenship, and the Future of Media*. New York: Routledge, pp. 3–20.

Horrigan, J. (2007) *A Typology of Information and Communication Technology Users*. Washington, DC. Retrieved 10 August 2007 from: http://www.pewinternet.org/pdfs/PIP_ICT _Typology.pdf.

Iyengar, S., Peters, M. D., and Kinder, D. R. (1982) "Experimental Demonstrations of the "Not-So-Minimal" Consequences of Television News Programs", *American Political Science Review*, 76 (4), 848–58.

Java, A., Kolari, P., Finin, T., and Oates, T. (2006) "Modeling the Spread of Influence on the Blogosphere". In *Proceedings of the 15th International World Wide Web Conference*. Edinburgh, ACM Press.

Johnson, T., and Kaye, B. (2007) "Blog Readers: Predictors of Reliance on War Blogs". In M. Tremayne (ed.), *Blogging, Citizenship, and the Future of Media*. New York: Routledge, pp. 165–84.

Keshev (2004) "Media Monitoring Project". Retrieved 11 October 2007 from: http://keshev.org.il/siteEn/FullNews.asp?NewsID=74&CategoryID=3.

Lee Kaid, L., and Postelnicu, M. (2007) "Credibility of Political Messages on the Internet: A Comparison of Blog Resources". In M. Tremayne (ed.), *Blogging, Citizenship, and the Future of Media*. New York: Routledge, pp. 149–64.

Lee, S. T., and Maslog, C. C. (2005) "War or Peace Journalism? Asian Newspaper Coverage of Conflicts", *The Journal of Communication*, 55 (2), pp. 311–29.

Lowrey, W. (2006) "Mapping the Journalism–Blogging Relationship", *Journalism*, 7 (4), pp. 477–500.

Lynch, J., and McGoldrick, A. (2000) "Peace Journalism: How to Do It?" Retrieved 19 September 2007 from: http://www.transcend.org.

Lynch, J., and McGoldrick, A. (2005a) *Peace Journalism*. Gloucestershire: Hawthorn Press.

Lynch, J., and McGoldrick, A. (2005b) "Peace Journalism: A Global Dialog for Peace and Democracy". In R. A. Hackett, and Y. Zhao (eds), *Democratizing Global Media: One World, Many Struggles*. Boulder, CO: Rowman and Littlefield.

Mingers, J., and Harzing, A. (2007) "Ranking Journals in Business and Management: A Statistical Analysis of the Harzing Data Set", *European Journal of Information Systems*, 16 (4), pp. 303–16.

Mishne, G., and Glance, N. (2006) "Leave a Reply: An Analysis of Weblog Comments". In *Proceedings of the 3rd Annual Workshop on the Weblogging Ecosystem: Aggregation, Analysis and Dynamics*, 15th World Wide Web Conference. Retrieved from: http://staff.science.uva.nl/~gilad/pubs/www2006-blogcomments.pdf.

O'Reilly, T. (2005) "What is Web 2.0? Design Patterns and Business Models for the Next Generation of Software". Retrieved 19 September 2007 from: http://www.oreillynet.com/pub/a/oreilly/tim/news/2005/09/30/what-is-web-20.html.

Papacharissi, Z. (2007) "Audiences as Media Producers: Content Analysis of 260 Blogs". In M. Tremayne (ed.), *Blogging, Citizenship, and the Future of Media*. New York: Routledge, pp. 21–38.

Peleg, S. (2006) "Peace Journalism through the Lens of Conflict Theory: Analysis and Practice", *Conflict & Communication Online*, 5 (2). Retrieved from: www.cco.regener-online.de.

Phillips, N., and Hardy, C. (2002) *Discourse Analysis: Investigating Processes of Social Construction*. Thousand Oaks, CA: Sage.

Piper, P., and Ramos, M. (2005) "Blogs of War: A Review of Alternative Sources for Iraq War Information", *Searcher*, 13 (2), pp. 15–22.

Regan, T. (2003) "Weblogs Threaten and Inform Traditional Journalism", *Nieman Reports*, 57 (3), pp. 68–70.

Roskos-Ewoldson, D. R., Roskos-Ewoldson, B., and Dillman Carpentier, F. (2002) "Media Priming: A Synthesis". In J. Bryant, and D. Zillmann (eds), *Media Effects: Advances in Theory and Research*. Hillside, NJ: Lawrence Erlbaum Associates, pp. 97–120.

Rutigliano, L. (2007) "Emerging Communication Networks as Civic Journalism". In M. Tremayne (ed.), *Blogging, Citizenship, and the Future of Media*. New York: Routledge, pp. 225–38.

Schiller, D. (2000) *Digital Capitalism: Networking the Global Market System*. Cambridge, MA: MIT Press.

Shinar, D. (2004) "Media Peace Discourse: Constraints, Concepts and Building Blocks", *Conflict*

& *Communication Online*, 3 (1 and 2). Retrieved from: www.cco.regener-online.de.

Shinar, D. (2007) "Media Diplomacy and Peace Talk: The Middle East and Northern Ireland", *Gazette*, 62 (2).

Smith, T. (2008) *Power to the People: Social Media Tracker (Wave 3)*. Industry report, Universal McCann. Retrieved 8 September 2008 from: http://www.universalmccann.com/Assets/wave _3_20080403093750.pdf.

Tautig, S. (2006) "The Online Media (Hebrew)", *The Seventh Eye (Ha'ain ha'shviit)*, 64, pp. 26–8.

Tehranian, M. (2002) "Peace Journalism: Negotiating Global Media Ethics", *Harvard Journal of Press/Politics*, 7 (2).

Tremayne, M. (2007a) "Introduction: Examining the Blog–Media Relationship". In M. Tremayne (ed.), *Blogging, Citizenship, and the Future of Media*. New York: Routledge, pp. ix–xix.

Tremayne, M. (2007b) "Harnessing the Active Audience: Synthesizing Blog Research and Lessons for the Future Media". In M. Tremayne (ed.), *Blogging, Citizenship, and the Future of Media*. New York: Routledge, pp. 261–72.

Tuchman, G. (1973) "Making News by Doing Work: Routinizing the Unexpected", *American Journal of Sociology*, 79 (1), pp. 110–31.

US Public Law 105-304 (1998) "Digital Millennium Copyright Act". Retrieved 6 September 2008 from: http://frwebgate.access.gpo.gov/cgi-bin/getdoc.cgi?dbname=105_cong_ public_laws&docid=f:publ304.105.pdf.

Van Dijk, T. (1993) "Principles of Critical Discourse Analysis", *Discourse Society*, 4 (2), pp. 249–83.

Wall, M. (2005) "Blogs of War", *Journalism*, 6 (2), pp. 153–72.

Williams, N., Trammell, K., Postelnicu, M., Landreville, K., and Martin, J. (2005) "Blogging and Hyperlinking: Use of the Web to Enhance Viability during the 2004 US Campaign", *Journalism Studies*, 6 (2), pp. 177–86.

Wolfsfeld, G. (2004) *Media and the Path to Peace*. Cambridge: Cambridge University Press.

⦃ CHAPTER ⦄
16

Rehearsing Democracy: New Media, Political Freedoms and Censorship in Uganda

RYAN BOWMAN

In a warehouse on the north side of Kampala's industrial area sits a 1960s' Goss Urbanite printing press. This monstrous, royal blue contraption, dotted with a bewildering and seemingly endless array of dials and official-looking buttons is serviced by a group of frantic but efficient technicians dressed in bright green overalls, each one emblazoned with "MONITOR" in bright red letters. This particular machine was shipped second-hand to the *Daily Monitor* newspaper from India in 1995. Its arrival was an important moment in Ugandan media history. As one of the seven original founders of the *Monitor*, Charles Onyango-Obbo[1] told me, the first thing the group did when the *Monitor* turned a profit was to buy land and a printing press (2007). As he pointed out, possessing an independent means of printing, and a privately owned space in which to do it, made it significantly more difficult for the Ugandan government to shut the paper down.

Monitor Publications Ltd (the umbrella group for the *Daily Monitor*, its website and popular radio station KFM) still sits on the same piece of land Onyango-Obbo helped purchase nearly fifteen years ago. The compound, set defensively atop one of Kampala's seven hills, surrounded by a deep ravine on one side and a 15-foot, barbed-wire-topped wall on the other, pays tribute to the *Monitor*'s unique and embattled position in Ugandan culture. In 1986, when former Defence Minister Yoweri Museveni emerged from a five-year bush war against the oppressive regime of Milton Obote into the open arms of a tired and tortured public, one of his first moves as president was to ban the formation of political parties.[2] In this political vacuum the *Daily Monitor*, founded in July 1992 by seven Ugandan journalists, became, as the only viable and financially and politically independent voice in the country, the *de facto* home of the country's small and beleaguered opposition.[3] As such, it has suffered mightily. In 1993 the government banned its departments (which represented the bulk of the country's purchasing power) from placing advertisements in the *Monitor*, resulting in a 70 percent loss of revenue for the paper. In 1997 the ban was finally lifted, only to be replaced by a steady stream of government interference including various raids, arrests, trials and, at one point, a week-long shut down (Tabaire 2007).

While the situation has more recently stabilized, following the Supreme Court of Uganda's decision in 2004 to annul a long-standing and pernicious law making the publication of false news a crime, the *Monitor* still suffers under the weight of consistent government intrusion (Onyango-Obbo 2004). While I was there in early 2008, working on a relaunch of the newspaper, five prominent members of staff were arrested and interrogated following an investigative report on the pay packet of a government official. The story was extremely detailed, carefully balanced and merely reported what one government department was saying about another (Gyezaho 2007a). One of the "Monitor 5" (as they were dubbed), Emmanuel Gyuzaho, called it "a poorly disguised form of intimidation and harassment by the State" (2007b). The case was eventually dropped, but not before key members of the *Monitor* staff, including the managing editor, were forced to spend days away from their jobs to deal with the charges (Buwembo 2008).

Many Ugandan journalists believe that the ultimate goal of this programme of "soft-censorship" is to create an atmosphere that makes self-censorship the preferred alternative to government intrusion. Bernard Tabaire, managing editor of the weekend editions of the *Monitor* and one of those arrested, characterizes the government strategy as two-fold: "One, use the courts of law to pile pressure on nosy journalists and force them to self-censor. Two, target [the] *Daily Monitor* and use it to send a message to opponents of any kind, but primarily political [foes]" (Tabaire 2007: 36).

One reading of the government's treatment of the *Monitor* is that this so-called soft-censorship is a sophisticated attempt to transform the paper into an independent version of the other prominent newspaper in the country, the government-owned *New Vision*. That is, the *Monitor* would be nominally free to express limited political criticism but be generally compliant and operate under a silent regime of self-censorship.[4]

Given this tenuous position of the independent press in Uganda, the question I want to ask is: how viable are alternative media as a replacement for the political discourse and "democracy in action" that papers like the *Monitor* try, but ultimately struggle to provide? In particular, given the restraints on the Ugandan people — relative poverty, significant censorship, a low literacy rate[5] and insignificant Internet penetration — I want to examine the ability of new media, specifically the Internet, FM radio and mobile telephony, to act as a significant democratizing force, especially in relation to the current system of commercial mass media.

Radio Katwe and the Internet

Internet access in Uganda, especially outside the capital city, Kampala, is the province of the elite. The Uganda Communications Commission records only 15,000 subscribers in the whole country, almost all of them in Kampala.[6] Internet penetration lags well behind mobile telephony and radio access. However, two high-speed fibre-optic cables, the East Africa Submarine Cable System (EASSy) and a Kenyan-funded effort originating in Oman, are currently snaking their way towards East Africa and are projected to be commercially viable by the middle of 2010 (EASSy 2008). The cables, while much delayed, promise to leapfrog broadband speeds and will fundamentally change the way the Internet is used in Uganda and all of East Africa. Indeed, the cables have taken on mythical proportions to many Ugandan Web professionals, and rightly so. Office buildings of 200 workers routinely share the equivalent of a 2mb line and generators are necessary two to four times a day just to keep key technological components online. The cables, and the next generation connections they allow for, could spark a mini Web revolution. In the next ten years Uganda will see a jump in Internet access rates comparable to the recent mobile phone revolution, which saw a 200 percent increase in mobile penetration over just four years (Uganda Communications Commission 2008). It is easy to envision a Uganda where villagers share Internet terminals and cheap, pay-as-you-go broadband access in much the same way they do phone boxes and radios now. When the cables are finally operational, Uganda has the cultural and societal tools to enter the digital era quickly.

As in the West, newspapers in Uganda were the first to have a Web presence and are well placed to take advantage of the upcoming boom. The *Daily Monitor* and the *New Vision* boast two of the most popular and profitable sites in the country. According to internal documents and interviews with key personnel, both sites have detailed, long-term plans to vault the Uganda new media establishment into the twenty-first century.

Currently, the *Monitor* dedicates exactly zero members of its editorial staff to the website, leaving only one overworked man, named Ronald, who laboriously uploads the contents of the newspaper after it has gone to press. It is easy to see why: monitor.co.ug, as it now stands, is a strictly international website, a replication of the paper for an outside audience. Internal figures show that only 11 percent of the *Monitor*'s substantial traffic (more than a 200,000 unique users a day) is Ugandan-based (Monitor Publications 2008). The site is a hugely commodified space that still works on a newspaper model of advertising — where companies buy space on the page for a specific period of time — giving it a cluttered, busy feel.

Despite the site's sparsely populated chatrooms and forums, upper management understand that reader interaction and the Web are important aspects of their operation, and the print version of the *Monitor*, at least, reflects this insight.[7] It has a sophisticated and successful programme of interaction[8] encouraging readers to post, email and send SMS submissions to the paper (customers can also hand a note or message to their local street vendor, who will pass on the contribution at the end of his shift). The majority owner of the *Monitor*, the Nation Media Group, based in Nairobi, has made digital progress a priority and has recently completed a major overhaul of its Kenyan-based newspaper Web portfolio. The *Monitor* sites will enjoy the same facelift sometime in the near future. Indeed, internal documents show plans to overhaul the site in 2008 to include more user content, premium services, blogs and podcasts (Monitor Publications 2008). The plans, which have not yet been made public, share the ethos of the paper itself. A major new initiative, tentatively called Parliament Online, will take advantage of the immediacy and unlimited storage space of the Web to perform a minute-to-minute parliamentary and presidential watchdog service (Monitor Publications 2008).

The *Monitor*'s counterpart, the government-owned *New Vision* is better funded and marginally more dedicated to its Web presence.[9] The Web presence is essentially the same as the *Monitor*'s, if slightly better organized. One key difference is the forum, which attracts a significant number of comments every week. It is a lively discussion centre that prefigures the future of the Internet in Uganda. Crucially, the paper has a Web team of two and a significantly more sophisticated content management system.

Neighbour and big sister Kenya dominates the whole of the eastern border of Uganda and plays a hugely influential role in the region, both politically and culturally. Its digital industry is by far the most advanced in the region and is possibly the most advanced in sub-Saharan Africa (excluding South Africa). It boasts a wide variety of journalistic websites, run by both newspaper and independent sources. *The Daily Nation*, one of Kenya's main newspapers, features numerous blogs that routinely warrant comments numbering in the high hundreds for a single post.[10] In comparison, meanwhile, neither Ugandan newspaper runs even one blog or any other sort of Web-specific content for that matter (although several members of the *Monitor* staff run active and entertaining blogs alongside their print work).[11] Indeed, the content of the sites is essentially a replica of their respective print editions. The only genuine innovation comes from outside the major media outlets. Small, unapologetically controversial blog-like sites, which are nimble and elusive enough to avoid government interference, have captured the imagination of the country.

One such site, RadioKatwe.com, is a prominent blog run by a secretive group of ex-journalists who work from locations outside Uganda. Usually referred to as a political gossip site, Radio Katwe is something like the UK celebrity newsletter popbitch, only for the political class. It runs three or four stories a day, with staff posting items from readers and occasionally writing their own material. It has a hard-earned reputation for reporting the "true rumours" that almost never emerge in the mainstream media but have a strong presence on the street. In some ways Radio Katwe exists to print what you might hear in a café or bar in Kampala. It encourages reader participation, has an easy-to-use file submission system on its front page and makes a point of publishing a compilation of its readers' thoughts and letters at least once a day.

Radio Katwe is named after Katwe, a region of Kampala where artisans construct elaborate handmade steel knock-offs of industrial goods. "Katwe" means "head" or "small head" in Luganda, and the region is known as the centre of innovation and craftsmanship for the country — literally the brains of the nation. An intrepid group once replicated a helicopter so perfectly that it flew almost too well and had to be tied to trees until the group could figure out how to fix the switch that slowed the rotors. It is this DIY aesthetic and the long tradition of dissent attached to the name — dating back to colonial times, when Katwe itself was a "hotbed of nationalist resistance" (Tamale 2001) — that the website taps into. Thus, people around Kampala speak of the idea of Radio Katwe as a spectre that rises in correlation to the oppression of the current regime. During the civil wars of the early 1980s Radio Katwe was a powerful force of information dissemination (Tamale 2001).[12]

Under the Museveni government it has become the centre of a rapidly burgeoning politically minded blogger community that takes advantage of a difficult-to-suppress medium to express itself. In fact, Radio Katwe, which is run primarily from outside the country and operates under complete anonymity, is built to resist government influence. Still, in 2006, prior to the election campaign, the government blocked access to Radio Katwe (and the 700 other sites that shared the same server). It was the first time that the government, so adept at closing newspapers and shutting off TV and radio transmitters, had used its powers to censor the Internet. It was a relatively fruitless endeavour, however, as the site quickly distributed a detailed message about using proxy servers to circumvent the ban. In fact, the site bragged later about experiencing a 100 percent growth in traffic in the month after the ban was enacted (RadioKatwe 2006).[13]

Radio Katwe is unique in three ways. First, it is a historically significant beacon of opposition to governmental oppression and censorship. Second, unlike the newspaper websites that are its closest compatriots, it is an open and interactive forum built for the Web that features content that only the Web could host. (This is true in both content and form — a recent article made fun of President Museveni for his sexual prowess and ran for more than 2,000 words — three or four times the average opinion piece in the *Monitor*.) Third, it is hosted via a decentralized, international medium that, unlike radio, print or television, is virtually impervious to governmental officials bent on dampening free speech. In all three ways it is a valuable tool for political discourse that exists in direct contrast to the current traditional media strategies.

EKIMEEZA AND THE EMBRACE OF RADIO

In a country where only the relatively well-off can afford the Ush1000[14] price of a news-paper, the *Daily Monitor* and the *New Vision* both have a daily circulation of about 30,000.[15] But both papers are far more influential than these numbers suggest and they tend to set the news agenda for the country. It is not unusual for radio stations to read entire stories aloud to their audiences to provoke discussion. Both newspapers have sophisticated and popular radio arms that they use liberally for cross-promotion. Indeed, the near-universal coverage of FM radio — more than 90 percent of Ugandans listen regularly[16] — makes these stations incredibly efficient evangelists for the reporting featured in each of the papers. Radio is not something that the Western media, caught up in promise of the Internet, generally recognize as "new media" *per se*. But I would argue that radio, with its cheap, reliable infrastructure, open-access platform and networking potential, has many of the same revolutionary qualities as the Internet. In addition, radio as a medium is literally a new media for the country. Although the government-owned Radio Uganda has been broadcasting since 1954, Uganda's first private radio station, Sanyu FM, did not go on air until December 1993. And it was not until 1996 and 1997 that the appropriate laws were passed to properly allocate frequencies and licences to operators. In places where online access is limited, these newly formed radio stations — there were seven by 1995, and there are more than 200 today, broadcasting in all major languages and boasting vibrant and interactive virtual communities (Kibazo 2007) — represent a crucial cog in political communication. As Peter Mwesige, a columnist for the *Monitor* and media critic, notes, "talk shows have opened up new political spaces that were unimaginable only a decade ago . . . [it] may not be democracy in action but it is an important rehearsal for democracy" (Mwesige 2005, cited in Tabaire 2007).

Since 1996, one form of talk show, called *ekimeeza* (or "round table"), described to me as a huge, outdoor, town hall discussion,[17] has dominated radio formatting and has revolutionized the way political discussions work in Uganda. Because the equipment needed for such a gathering is minimal, the shows can easily reach outlying communities and, for the first time, give rural people a public voice. According to reports, the initial shows were filled with pro-government voices but, as the practice spread and began to be held in local languages, things changed quickly. Later *ebimeeza* (plural) were marked by the frankness of the discussions, with its participants free for the first time to criticize the government in a way that would be impossible for a lone voice (International Press Institute 2002). As these *ebimeeza* became more and more popular, the government itself would enter into the dialogue, sending representatives or calling into the switchboard to defend its policies. Rumour has it that even President Museveni himself called into a CBS show and took questions for hours from all-comers.[18]

The gatherings generally focused on political issues and were widely seen as a hotbed of opposition to the Museveni government. Museveni himself is said to closely monitor the radio programmes, and there are dozens of documented cases of arrests stemming from *ekimeeza* broadcasts (US Department of State 2008). In 2002 the government banned the *ebimeeza* by claiming that radio stations were not licensed for outdoor broadcasts, limiting subsequent gatherings to crowded radio studios (Tabaire 2007). By hampering the key aspects of the talk shows — their mobility, ubiquity, openness and relative anonymity — the government hoped to sap some of their political power. But, as Mwesige notes, the *de facto* ban "provoked a louder public outcry than the occasional government muzzling of newspapers because they [the shows] have a much bigger audience, and also because they gave members of the public opportunities to participate". A petition gathered more than 6,000 signatures, the Uganda Law Society wrote to the government in protest (Mwesgie 2004) and the ban became law in name only. *Ekimeeza* continue to be popular today.

Although this ban was not completely successful, the government continues its attempts to rein in radio debate. In 2004 it announced stations that "abuse the President or use offensive language and fail to correct the behaviour" were to have their licence revoked. Earlier in the year KFM, the *Monitor*'s station, was shut down for allegedly seditious comment. More recently, the government has resorted to violent takeovers of radio stations and pouring acid on radio transmitters (US Department of State 2008). The government has also ordered an official ban of new FM stations in Kampala, citing dwindling frequency resources. However this rule, as with the *de facto* *ekimeeza* ban, is regularly flaunted without punishment (US Department of State 2008).

Ebimeeza have done much to open political dialogue to the 88 percent of rural Ugandans who live off the land and in relatively isolated locations (International Institute for Communication and Development 2008). It is an example of new media encouraging participation and democratic expression. Whereas old media, such as newspapers, are hampered by high barriers of entry, expensive final products and what Yochai Benkler characterizes as a "one-way, hub-and-spoke structure, with unidirectional links to its ends, running from the center to the periphery" (2006: 179), FM radio, with its universal uptake and relatively open platform, populated with innovative formats that work on a local level, provides a practical alternative to mainstream commercial media.

Importantly, radio, like the Internet, provides some limited buffer from governmental interference in the form of undeniable popularity. As we have seen in the cases of the failed bans of *ebimeeza* and the new stations in Kampala, the sheer ubiquity of radio has forced the government to accept its own inability to interfere with a country in conversation with itself.

Mabira and the Rise of Mobile Telephony

In today's Uganda, as in much of Africa, mobile phones have more than twice the penetration rate of the Internet and are ingrained in the culture in ways that the Internet and newspapers, with their relatively tiny circulation, simply cannot match (Uganda Communications Commission 2008). The prevalence of mobile telephony has rapidly changed the way society communicates with itself and with the world as a whole. Examples of mobile phones acting in the place of banks,[19] accountants,[20] doctors[21] and social organizers (as we will see) are remarkable but commonplace. One particular episode uniquely demonstrates the democratizing power of new media. An examination of a political issue that spans almost three years demonstrates that new media can be a defining contributor to the methods and efficacy of local protest and political participation. Importantly, the reaction to this particular event runs in parallel with the most remarkable growth in mobile phone penetration the country has ever seen, with the number of subscribers growing by more than 200 percent (Uganda Communications Commission 2007).

In late October 2005 the government received a letter from the Mehta Group, an Indian-based multinational that runs Lugazi Sugarworks, the country's largest sugar factory, located between Kampala and Jinja, in southern Uganda. The letter asked for more than a third of the neighbouring Mabira Forest Reserve to be turned over to the company for farming (Tenywa 2005). The reserve, which is surrounded by sugar fields on one side and tea fields on the other, is an animal sanctuary and a valuable tourist attraction for the south of the country (Alweny 2007). Almost immediately letters from Ugandans, sensitive to environmental concerns after a similar situation involving oil company BIDCO the year before, started to appear in newspapers (Nsangi 2006):

> I appeal to the President to listen to reason and leave the Kalangala and Mabira forests alone. (Tibaijuka 2005)

> I pray that they remember the significance of our precious environment. It does not only belong to us alone but to posterity as well — even to those not yet born! (Orach 2005)

The cabinet eventually quashed the proposed move in late November, saying that "a change of land use was out of the question" (Tenywa 2005b). Eight months later, however, President Museveni began the process again, ordering a study of how the land would be used in August 2006. Again there was a low level of dissent, as letters of protest appeared in papers and at least two separate groups organized small demonstrations (Tenywa and Okeowo 2006; Nalunkuuma and Mubiru 2006). The issue percolated for eight more months, with constant newspaper reports of cabinet meetings, announcements, reversals and plans. The general consensus from the letters pages was that the Mehta Group would get its land.

Meanwhile, for the first time in Ugandan history, a loose coalition of well-organized NGOs, taking advantage of the huge recent growth in mobile phone penetration, began to utilize new media to keep the issue on top of the news agenda and to mobilize the public (National Association of Professional Environmentalists (NAPE) 2007). They used a wide variety of strategies, including a smart mob tactic that left Kampala awash with the sounds of sympathetic car horns at exactly 5 p.m. on a Wednesday. The most prominent of the schemes, however, was an SMS campaign so thorough that one Ugandan I talked to said he received the same text message twenty-seven times in one day — "Save Mabira, Boycott Lugazi" (Appel 2008).

The fight culminated on 5 April, when the shadow minister for the environment Beatrice Anywar called for a demonstration to take place in Kampala in one week's time. This time, instead of urging a boycott, the coalition used a wide network of blogs and text messages to organize a group of determined protesters. The demonstrators, joined by prominent MPs and NGO supporters, marched from the centre of the city to the Clock Tower, a symbolic landmark of political protest in the west of Kampala. In response to the massive protest, the government formed a cabinet subcommittee to study the issues further and, a month later, decided to suspend the issue until further notice (Luggya 2007).

The organizational ability of mobile phones was key to the protesters' influence and, indeed, the very presence of the protesters. What began as a political issue that was eliciting ineffective, low-level dissent for a significant period of time was transformed, with the addition of new media tools, into a viable protest movement that ultimately forced the government to change course. It seems certain that the key mechanism to this reversal was the more than 200 percent growth in mobile phone penetration, which allowed people to be connected in a bi-directional way to each other (Uganda

Communications Commission 2007). Mobile phones are cheap, easy to maintain and increasingly essential to everyday life in Uganda. In no small part because it is free to receive text messages and calls, mobile telephony has become a valuable and viable real-time mass communications strategy in a way that newspapers, hampered by timeliness and production, and TV, hampered by its broadcast model, can never hope to match.

Conclusion

From the fifth floor boardroom of the *Daily Monitor* building, high atop the city, you can see the hazy outline of downtown Kampala from one window and, from the other, a faraway slaughterhouse with vultures circling. It is hard not to take these vultures as symbols for the difficult times ahead for the *Monitor* and other traditional media groups. The government has become extremely adept at enforcing a form of soft-censorship on newspapers and TV stations that has the effect of limiting media freedom and dampening political discourse. However, as we have seen, even under difficult circumstances Ugandans have managed to sculpt new paths of political expression from the relatively limited forms of new media available to them. In Radio Katwe we see the rise of increasingly self-sufficient and sophisticated media participants who can guarantee their anonymity and, through superior technical know-how, protect themselves from government censorship. In the *ebimeeza* we see how a majority can resist government intrusion via sheer numbers. At Mabira we saw that with universal access to communication networks comes remarkable participation. New media are a powerful tool in the fight for political and media freedoms in Uganda. Even as they are currently constituted, they are a viable alternative to the traditional media, and what we see now are just the faltering first steps of a media movement in its infancy. In fifteen years' time a mature new media environment will transform Uganda in ways that are unimaginable today.

Notes

1 Onyango-Obbo now lives in Kenya as the head of Digital Strategy for the Nation Media Group, which owns a majority stake in the *Monitor*.
2 In the interest of national unity, all candidates were to run on their own merit under one, overarching Movement "party". The ban was lifted just before the elections in 2006 (Muhanga 2005).
3 Its motto, then as now, is "Truth Every Day".
4 I should be careful not to mislead. Uganda is not alone in its struggle for media freedom against a powerful government. Indeed, no less an authority than Tabaire (2007: 30) endorses the notion that Museveni has been "infinitely more tolerant" than any of his predecessors. In fact, the situation in Uganda, ranked 96 out of 169 countries in the 2007 Press Freedom Index by Reporters Without Borders (2007), is relatively liberal when compared with similar nations. But this is not a forum for relativism. Every Ugandan journalist I have interviewed has bemoaned the state of media freedom in the country.
5 67 percent according to UNICEF (2008), though youth literacy is at 81 percent.
6 As hundreds of offices workers, or thousands at a café, can share one line (Uganda

Communications Commission 2008), this figure could, perhaps, be more realistically put at two million users.

7   It was a major part of our brief for the relaunch of the *Monitor* to increase interaction and opportunities for citizen journalism and to design the mechanism for the eventual in-paper promotion of a new and improved website.

8   This includes a lively letters page, a regular corrections column, regional weekly questions answerable by SMS, a mature citizen journalism selection that invites and receives stories (my first school, my childhood, the neighbourhood, etc.) and a noble and successful campaign to chronicle the story of each of the estimated 100,000 victims of gun crime during the Idi Amin regime.

9   The government has been proactive in technological policy in other ways, establishing Africa's first rural fund for universal access and generally embracing what seems to be liberal and effective policies toward technology (Uganda Communications Commission 2005b).

10 The *Daily Nation* sites, Kenya's largest and the region's most sophisticated, were designed by my company and are cutting-edge creations with a robust and sophisticated back end by one of the largest technological groups in Germany. They include, among other things, comments, voting, rating, numerous blogs and high-quality video, plus an easy and automated print-to-web operation.

11 As a whole, the Ugandan blogging community is relatively large and active. There are more than 2,500 listed on Blogger, although I suspect that this particular blogroll is a lot like the local coffee shop: packed with American "study abroad" students.

12 "The 'real' stories would circulate via informal media, the most influential being "Radio Katwe" (Tamale 2001). This historic Radio Katwe refers to an elaborate communication system transmitted by word of mouth among the local populace. Its "transmitters" dot the countryside in almost all trading centres, with local bus and commuter taxi parks being the main media of dissemination.

13 This was partially due to renewed international interest in the site as news of its closure spread. (It was even linked via the popular blog *boingboing*.) I was able to access the site from my hotel in Kampala.

14 At the *Monitor* staff canteen, it's enough to buy you lunch of stewed plantain and fish curry two times over.

15 *The New Vision* has an ABC circulation of 32,500 (New Vision 2008). The *Monitor* is slightly coy about its circulation, but it is approximately the same.

16 It was estimated in 2005 that "100% of the population had listened to the radio in the past year, 92.8% in the past seven days, and 73.7% as recently as the day before" (Khamalwa 2006: 15).

17 You can listen online to portions of an *ekimeeza* in English at: http://www.panos.org.uk/?lid=19869.

18 Several interviewees mentioned this rumour, but I cannot find any corroborating evidence, except on various blogs.

19 See Jan Chipchase's (2006) fascinating work on Sente, a method of using credit as a currency in rural Uganda.

20 Banks now allow citizens to pay bills via their phones (Ndiwalana 2008).

21 Charities have set up SMS HIV information centres (see http://texttochange.com) and even use the technology to increase drug compliance (see http://computrainer.com).

Ryan Bowman

References

Afemann, U. (2004) "Internet in Senegal". In R. M. Beck, and F. Wittman, (eds), *African Media Cultures*. Cologne: Rudiger Koppe Verlag, pp. 287–310.

Alweny, S. (2007) "Mabira Forest Lodge Wins Award", *Daily Monitor*, 31 October.

Appel, S. (2008) Personal communication, 5 April.

Benkler, Y. (2006) *The Wealth of Networks: How Social Production Transforms Markets and Freedom*. New Haven, CT, and London: Yale University Press.

Butagira, T. (2008) "Radio Journalists Paid By Newsmakers – Report", *Daily Monitor*, 12 May.

Buwembo, J. (2008) Personal communication, 4 April.

Castells, M. (2000) *The Rise of the Network Society*. 2nd edn. Oxford: Blackwell.

Chipchase, J. (2006) "Share Phone Practices". Retrieved from: http://www.janchipchase.com/blog/mt-search.cgi?tag=Sente&blog_id=1.

Committee to Protect Journalists (2006) "Critical Web Site Still Blocked on Eve of Presidential Election: CPJ News Alert". Retrieved 22 February 2006 from: http://www.cpj.org/news/2006/africa/uganda22feb06na.html.

EASSy (2008) "Project Milestones". Retrieved from: http://www.eassy.org/project%20milestones.html.

Gyezaho, E. (2007a) "IGG in Salary Scandal", *Daily Monitor,* 25 August. Retrieved 25 August 2007 from: http://www.monitor.co.ug/artman/publish/sun_news/IGG_in_salary_scandal.shtml.

Gyezaho, E. (2007b) "We are under Attack!" *Daily Monitor*, 30 January. Retrieved 30 January 2007 from: http://www.monitor.co.ug/artman/publish/Emmanuel_g/ We_are_under_attack.shtml.

Hyden, G., Michael, L., and Folu F. O. (eds) (2003) *Media and Democracy in Africa*. New York: Transaction Publishers.

International Institute for Communication and Development. (2008) "Uganda — Country Report". Retrieved from: http://www.iicd.org/countries/ghana/projects/countries/uganda.

International Press Institute (2002) "World Press Freedom Review 2002". Retrieved from: http://www.freemedia.at/cms/ipi/freedom_detail.html?country=/KW0001/KW0006/KW0181/&year=2002.

Khamalwa, J. W. (2006) *Uganda: African Media Development Initiative: Uganda – Research Findings and Conclusions*. London: BBC World Trust.

Kibazo, P., and Kanaabi, H. (2007) *FM Stations in Uganda "Quantity without Quality"*. Eastern Africa Media Institute.

Landow, G. (2006) *Hypertext 3.0: Critical Theory and New Media in an Era of Globalization*. Baltimore, MD: The Johns Hopkins University Press.

Luggya, J. (2007) "Cabinet Suspends Mabira Giveaway", *Daily Monitor*. Retrieved 22 May 2007 from: http://www.monitor.co.ug/artman/publish/news/Cabinet_suspends_ Mabira_ give-away_45570.shtml.

Muhanga, K. (2005) "Museveni Thanks Referendum Voters", *The New Vision*. Retrieved 2 August 2005 from: http://newvision.co.ug/D/8/13/448186/referendum.

Monitor Publications Ltd (2008) "Digital Strategy 2008" (unpublished)

Monitor Reporter (2008) "Daily Monitor Gets New Editor", *Daily Monitor*. Retrieved from: http://www.monitor.co.ug/artman/publish/news/Daily_Monitor_gets_new_editor.shtml 26 June 2008.

Mwesige, P. G. (2004) "Can You Hear Me Now? Radio Talk Shows and Political Participation in Uganda". Ph.D. thesis, Indiana University.

Nalunkuuma, M., and Mubiru, A. (2006) "Ssekandi Denies Knowledge of Mabira Case", *New Vision*. Retrieved 25 September 2006 from: http://www.newvision.co.ug/D/8/13/523194/ mabira%20demonstration.

National Association of Professional Environmentalists (NAPE) (2007) "The Ugly and Beauty of Mabira Forest Campaign in Uganda". Retrieved from: http://www.nape.or.ug/lib/The_ Ugly_Beauty_ofMabira_Campaign.pdf.

Ndiwalana, F. (2008) "Uganda: Mobile Phone as your Banking Hall". Retrieved 28 June 2008 from: http://allafrica.com/stories/200806301160.html.

Netanel, N. (2002) "The Commercial Mass Media's Continuing Fourth Estate Role". In Elkin-Koren, N., and Weinstock, N. (eds), *The Commodification of Information*. The Hague: Kluwer Law International, pp. 317–41.

New Vision (2008) "New Vision: About Us". Retrieved from: http://www.unicef.org/ infoby-country/uganda_statistics.html.

Nsangi, K. (2006) "Three More Forests in Kalangala Given to Bidco", *Daily Monitor*. Retrieved 1 September 2006 from: http://www.monitor.co.ug/artman/ publish/news/3_more_forests_ in_Kalangala_given_to_Bidco_54120.shtml.

Onyango-Obbo, C. (2004) "Onyango-Oboo and Mwenda vs. Attorney-General", Constitutional Appeal No. 2 of 2002, Supreme Court of Uganda 11 February.

Onyango-Obbo, C. (2007) Personal communication, 15 February.

Orach, B. (2005) "Uganda Does Not Belong to Us Alone!" *New Vision*. Retrieved 14 November 2005 from: http://www.newvision.co.ug/D/8/21/465757/mabira.

Radio Katwe (2006) "How Radio Katwe Has Changed Uganda". Radio Katwe. Retrieved 5 March 2006 from: http://radiokatwenews.blogspot.com/2006/03/how-radio-katwe-has-changed-uganda.html.

Reporters Without Borders (2007) "North Korea, Turkmenistan and Eritrea the Worst Violators of Press Freedom". Retrieved 16 March 2007 from: http://www.rsf.org/article. php3?id_article=19386.

Rheingold, H. (2002) *Smart Mobs: The Next Social Revolution*. Cambridge, MA: Basic Books.

Tabaire, B. (2007) "The Press and Political Repression in Uganda: Back to the Future?" *Journal of Eastern African Studies*, 1 (2), pp. 193–211.

Tamale, S. (2001) "'Duka-Duka!'1: Memories of the Ugandan Civil War", *AGI Newsletter*, 8. Retrieved from: http://web.uct.ac.za/org/agi/pubs/newsletters/vol9/duka.htm.

Temmerman, Els de (2006) "Letter from the Editor in Chief", *The New Vision*. Retrieved 30 November 2006 from: http://newvision.co.ug/D/8/20/535270.

Tenywa, G. (2005a) "Mehta Asks for Mabira Forest", *The New Vision*. Retrieved 4 November 2005 from: http://www.newvision.co.ug/D/8/12/464173/mabira.

Tenywa, G. (2005b) "Cabinet Rejects Mabira Takeover", *The New Vision*. Retrieved 30 November 2005 from: http://www.newvision.co.ug/D/8/13/468611/mabira.

Tenywa, G., and Okeowo, A. (2006) "'Save Mabira' Demo Halted", *The New Vision*. Retrieved 24 August 2006 from: http://www.newvision.co.ug/D/8/13/517164/mabira.

Tibaijuka, J. (2005) "Please Keep off the Forests!" *The New Vision*. Retrieved 8 November 2005 from: http://www.newvision.co.ug/D/8/21/464673/mabira.

Uganda Communications Commission (2008) "Market Review March 2008". Retrieved from: www.ucc.co.ug/MarketReviewMarch2008.pdf.

Uganda Communications Commission (2007) "Communication Sector Statistics". Retrieved from: http://www.ucc.co.ug/marketInfo/marketstatistics.php.

Uganda Communications Commission, (2005a) "Recommendations on Proposed Review of the

Telecommunications Sector Policy". Retrieved from: www.ucc.co.ug/UgTelecomsSectorPolicyReview_31_Jan_2005.pdf.

Uganda Communications Commission (2005b) *Funding and Implementing Universal Access: Innovation and Experience from Uganda.* Kampala: Fountain.

Uganda Securities Exchange (2008) "Stock Detail: New Vision Printing and Publishing Company Ltd". Retrieved from: http://www.use.or.ug/copindex.php?cat=lstofallco&subcat=lstcodir&cop=89.

UNICEF (2008) "Uganda – Statistics". Retrieved from: http://www.unicef.org/infobycountry/uganda_statistics.html.

US Department of State. (2008) "Country Reports on Human Rights Practices 2007". Retrieved from: http://www.state.gov/g/drl/rls/hrrpt/2007/100510.htm.

⟨⟨ CHAPTER ⟩⟩
17

Facilitating Participatory Communication in China: An Analysis of Citizen Journalists and Media Regulators in the Qiangguo Forum and its Discussions on Income Inequality

QIAN GONG

PARTICIPATORY COMMUNICATION AND CITIZENSHIP

Participatory communication, as an element of participatory democracy, is closely related to the notion of citizenship. In democratic societies it is fundamental for people to be able to "discuss social and political issues" based on their roles as citizens (Dahlgren 1996: x). Among the legal, civil, political, social and cultural dimensions of citizenship, participation primarily relates to the political dimension and considers the relationship between citizenship and the free flow of information and free expression. Participatory communication also connects to citizenship through the sense of inclusion; this is regularly argued when discussing democratic inclusiveness as an important corrective to contemporary politics. Indeed, it is a necessary condition for sustaining a healthy citizenship (Golding 1990; Dahlgren 1996; Fraser 1996; Coleman and Gøtze 2001). Situated in the broader context of the inquiry into participatory communication and democracy, this chapter assesses not only the freedom of expression of citizen journalists, but also the wider question of the inclusion of social classes in participatory communication.

Citizen journalism provides "bottom-up coverage" in which ordinary citizens effectively contribute by "offering their first-hand reports, digital photographs, camcorder video footage, mobile telephone snapshot or audio clips" (Allan 2006: 7). The notion of citizens, who are distinct from consumers and clients, places more emphasis on the political dimension, including participation in public affairs and contribution to public life. In this chapter I have combined these two aspects but placed more emphasis on political participation — how the bottom-up and alternative nature of citizen journalism pose a challenge to the mainstream media and facilitates a wider social inclusion. This is largely due to the fact that I am considering China, where the public are given few rights as citizens, in terms of freedom of expression, assembly and association. It is essential to understand how information and communication technology (ICT), such as online forums, can integrate a greater number of perspectives from citizens and can foster participatory political communication among the Chinese public.

BACKGROUND

The development of citizenship is influenced by many economic, political and cultural factors. In China the changing social conditions and the increasing use of ICT have been major factors in its emergence.

On the one hand, increasing social inequality and class stratification have challenged the legitimacy of the Chinese Communist Party (CCP). Responding to the strong demand for political participation since the 1980s, the Chinese government has initiated measures to construct an interest-based[1] social order with the aim of producing political benefits (Zheng 2004a; 2004b). This is reflected in two concepts developed by officials. The so-called "Three Represents"[2] is a idea whereby the party seeks support from entrepreneurs and the rising middle classes. The "Harmonious Society"[3] shifts the emphasis of social policies towards under-privileged social classes (*People's Daily* English 2005; 2007). The changing focus of government policies has represented a tension between high economic growth and increasing social inequality, as well as the CCP's response to the challenges to its legitimacy.

On the other hand, the Chinese public is increasingly being allowed to participate politically, with the aid of ICT. Technological developments such as the Internet and mobile phones have made government censorship extremely difficult. Public opinion, as expressed in online single-issue petitions such as those regarding SARS,[4] the Sun Zhigang case[5] and that of the black kiln[6] have been successfully integrated into political decision-making or policy-making (Jiang 2007; Teng 2007; Yang and Calhoun 2008; Zhao 2008). Indeed, the government has more recently started to consider the Internet as a reasonable barometer of public opinion. So on 20 June 2008, the president of China, Hu Jintao, visited the Qiangguo Forum (discussed in more detail below) and said he hoped to glean "some suggestions and advice proposed by our netizens to the government and the Party" (*People's Daily* English 2008).

One area where these two considerations have come together has been the increasing public discussion on the Internet of social class stratification and polarization. Tensions among the public, based on diverging social interests, have increased, as there has been no way of expressing these under authoritarian one-party rule. Instead, the Internet has provided a means of expression, nurturing a sense of autonomy, solidarity and citizenship. One effective expression of this notion of citizenship was the nationalism expressed online in response to the international relations crisis caused by NATO's bombing of the Chinese embassy in Belgrade in 1999. This online nationalism saw a form of "contracted citizenship" operating, as described by Prasenjit Duara (quoted by Shen 2007: 198). The government had allowed the Chinese public to have some rights as citizens as long as they affirmed their loyalty to the nation-state.

However, as I have argued elsewhere, it is also important to note that the Internet is also a place where different social interests compete (Gong 2008a; 2008b). The rising middle classes have been starting to claim their political rights and to become a potentially dominant social force. Whether this clash of interests is fostering participatory communication, which helps to reduce conflicts of interests, or is preventing certain interests being expressed, because of economic and political inequality, will remain a critical issue. Precautions need to be taken, Castells warns (1998), since ICT can widen inequalities in society. Therefore, as suggested by Dahlgren (1996: 23), it is important to assess participatory communication at two levels. First, we need to consider how citizen journalists see themselves as collectively representing the common interest of the public against an authoritarian government. Second, we need to assess how citizen journalists balance the collective interest of the general public and the specific interests of individuals and social groups.

This chapter investigates one of the most critical and popular online forums in China — the Qiangguo Forum (the "Strong China" Forum,[7] which discusses current affairs, and political and social issues), in particular by considering forum debates on income inequality. The Qiangguo Forum is one of the largest and most politically critical forums in China, yet is hosted by People's Net — the online community of the *People's Daily*, the official newspaper of the Chinese Communist Party.[8] Although the forum has strong connections with the government's party paper, it has a greater range of discussions on controversial social issues than forums on commercial portals or websites.[9] The Qiangguo Forum is in general very critical and has therefore attracted a substantial number of users. The average daily number of forum users is 300,000, although sometimes the number reaches 800,000.[10] Moreover, it provides a channel for direct dialogue between the public and the government. An increasing number of government officials, including the President of China, Hu Jintao, and Prime Minister, Wen Jiabao, have participated in live discussions on the forum.

METHODOLOGY

The data for this investigation came from interviews with seven forum participants who have posted extensively on the issue of income inequality, one interview with a forum administrator, one interview with the founder of the forum and interviews with two officials from the media regulatory bodies. These are the State Administration of Radio, Film and Television and the Central Propaganda Department of the Chinese Communist Party.

This chapter aims to provide a preliminary analysis of whether the Qiangguo Forum can facilitate participatory communication and therefore help include citizens more widely in socio-political discussions. China's media censorship system puts the forum participants and the regulators on opposite sides. Reflecting this, I have split the research question into two complementary sets of questions, covering the citizen journalists' perspective and that of the forum regulators. By considering the issue of income inequality debated on the forum, I analyse how participants take part in discussions and perform the role of citizen journalists, how the forum is regulated and administered and whether this regulation and administration facilitate any form of political participation.

So, from the citizen journalists' perspective, the questions to consider are:

- How do they contribute to the forum discussion in seeking to fulfil their roles as citizens?
- What are the criteria of forum participants when posting articles and comments on the forum?
- Can they contribute to public-government communication?
- Do they represent under-privileged social classes?

And from the regulators' perspective, the questions to be discussed are:

- What is the official attitude towards the forum and the Internet in general?
- Does the Qiangguo Forum have any mechanism to channel public opinion?
- How was the forum founded, and how is it administered?
- Does this allow an input of public opinion into the policy-making process?

Sources of Information and Trustworthiness

To answer these questions, first I asked forum participants why they had taken part in discussions on income inequality. They said:

My knowledge of this issue [income inequality] firstly comes from my own living environment. I live in a basement, but to my surprise there are long-term basement residents who have reasonable and stable incomes. I know one person who has been living here for five years. This is a first-hand experience. (A, interviewed on 28 September 2007)[11]

My information [about income inequality] is mainly from the Internet. But besides the Internet there is a more direct way [of getting the information] — I talk to people from other social strata such as cleaners. . . . The reason I've been adding posts on income inequality is that I hope the majority of the Chinese people can have equality; they are paid fair and square; and the under-privileged social groups can be helped. (E, interviewed on 6 October 2007)

Personal experience is clearly a major source of information. Interviewees valued other sources such as international publications (for example, UN data) highly, but they considered their own everyday life a more important source. Its importance is reflected in the fact that it is also used as the criterion to assess the authenticity of the posts on the forum. When asked whether they trusted citizen journalists on the forum, many participants had positive answers:

> I don't think there is much difference between the posts which are created by the forum participants and the posts which are reprinted [from other traditional media] in terms of authenticity. The posts are created by forum participants based on their knowledge and motivation. I think they are generally trustworthy, if there is no conflict of interests. (A, interviewed on 28 September 2007)

> I trust 100 percent the posts created by the forum participants, especially the ones relaying personal experiences. (B, interviewed on 24 October 2007)

> I believe the posts created by participants from their own life experiences or what they have seen. But sometimes, logically, you can tell some posts are made up and I really wonder whether the authors of such posts are people who work for the government. (C interviewed on 29 September 2007)

The rise of both Internet use and online citizen journalism in China is, as in many other countries, increasingly challenging traditional mainstream media institutions. Especially by using mobile telephones with built-in cameras, citizen journalists are more likely to provide their first-hand experiences and images for local new stories. As citizen journalists who "report" their own stories, forum participants seem most concerned about the authenticity of "reports". As we have seen, it is posts containing first-hand experience that are highly valued. The fact that first-hand experience, rather than the mainstream media, is cited as the ultimate reference point demonstrates the gap between public trust and the mainstream media controlled by the authorities. The issue of authenticity is at stake, but more in a sense of whether the news is manipulated in favour of the government by someone who secretly works for it than whether the news is faked by individuals for other reasons (for example, to make it more sensational or amusing).

This can be easily explained, as people tend to distrust the mainstream media, which are considered, in differing degrees, as propaganda tools. The high degree of distrust is reflected in the earlier quote in which the interviewee cast doubt on posts that seem to be made up by someone who works for the government, while in my interviews with the forum users, journalistic objectivity and impartiality are largely dismissed as the criteria for the trustworthiness of news stories. The high value that forum participants place on first-hand personal experience helps to enhance the credibility of citizen journalists. Moreover, the first two quotes have also shown a close connection between the forum users and the under-privileged social groups, despite the former's middle-class social status. As I will discuss in more detail in the second half of the chapter, the awareness of the living conditions of the under-privileged social groups has helped the forum users to develop a more rigorous agenda to represent the interests of the under-privileged social groups, which to some extent facilitates inter-class equality.

PUBLIC–GOVERNMENT COMMUNICATION

By prioritizing informative posts containing first-hand experiences, participants generally believe the forum can facilitate communication between the public and the government, despite its official status. In order to find out how they understand the interactive role of the forum, I asked them what they thought about government officials being invited onto live discussions on the forum:

> The interaction between the forum participants and government officials is necessary. Inviting government officials and scholars onto live discussions on the forum is an economical way [for the government] to get to know what the public think and receive feedback from the public. (A, interviewed on 28 September 2007)

> The reason that the forum can attract attention from the government is exactly because of its nature — it belongs to the online community of the official newspaper of the Chinese Communist Party — the People's Daily. (C, interviewed on 29 September 2007)

> Participation by government officials in the live discussion on the forum should be viewed in a positive light. It is a channel between the government and the public. But the guests [government officials, academics etc.] should be answering substantive questions, rather than being diplomatic. (D, interviewed on 22 August 2007)

While some participants see this official aspect of the forum as a "short-cut" to involvement in the political decision-making process, and the invitation of officials as an effective way of getting public feedback, some believe that much has yet to be done to make the forum a real conduit between the public and the government:

> I do not think this is a channel for communication, mainly because the guests do not answer substantive and challenging questions. And the moderators also pre-select the questions, which they should not. I was personally invited onto a live discussion (by a guest) and I had a low opinion of it. Nevertheless, issues discussed on the forum do get some attention from the government. Once I asked the Qiangguo Forum to forward my thoughts on a social problem — let's not mention what exactly this problem is — to the relevant department, because I believed the wording [of the problem] was incorrect. A week later, newspapers changed the wording. Later on, the Qiangguo Forum sent me a message saying they appreciated my trust. (E, interviewed on 6 October 2007)

From the responses above we can see that "communication" between the government and public is limited, largely reflected in the pre-selection of the questions and the diplomacy of the government officials. It is, however, important to acknowledge the interactive role of the forum, which opens up a direct channel for public–government communication. Although much criticism is levelled at the pseudo-communicative role of the forum, the government does at least partly acknowledge and consider public feedback internally, as illustrated in the previous quote. As a result, the interaction has enhanced participatory communication between the forum participants and the government. Another point worth mentioning is the interviewee C and his candid agenda of confronting the central official media. The tension between the public and media censorship can be manifested in a less confrontational way, such as boundary-pushing, a point I will return to shortly. In interviews with an official from the Central Propaganda Department and a forum administrator both parties acknowledged the existence of the government's "internal mechanism" and the role it plays:

> The Central Propaganda Department of the Party has not blocked public opinion on the Internet and, as a matter of fact, it is not possible. But we do have an internal mechanism that passes public opinion to the relevant . . . department. We have staff watching all kinds of information on the website. Once the information is significant enough, the problem is directed to the related government department(s). (F, interviewed on 18 October 2007)

> In March 2001, a participant named "Urban Villager" added a post headed "Railway, what's wrong with you?" on the forum. It was soon responded to by the Ministry of Railways. . . . We have many examples where the posts of forum participants have received responses from government departments. But the most common way to report issues raised by forum participants is through Internal Reference. (G, interviewed on 25 October 2007)

Internal mechanisms, such as the Internal Reference,[12] have contributed to channelling public opinion through to the government. However, the forum participants do not regard this "one-way" flow of information as transparent. This is because they are not sure whether their feedback or comments have been taken up or to what extent they have influenced political decision-making. The one-way flow process is explained by one official thus:

> The Internet is helpful in terms of understanding the problems. But it is not a panacea. Many things (for example, government misconduct) are very complicated and are related to institutional problems. For example, millions were spent on the decoration of a building which turned out to be a waste and the culprits are nowhere to be found. What are you going to do about that? Tell them [the public] this [bringing the culprits to justice] cannot be done? (H, interviewed on 22 August 2007)

Both government officials and forum participants (whom I will discuss later) have indicated that it is beyond the scope of the Internet to resolve many of China's social problems. What the Internet has exposed is only the tip of the iceberg of institutional problems. Without reforming the institutions, many problems are irresolvable and hidden behind closed doors, even if citizen journalists on the forum expose them. The complexity of the institutional problems has limited the potential of the forum, as the feedback and advice of participants are not necessarily followed up. The liberalizing potential of the forum itself and of the Internet in general is limited by the institution. It can only be developed with the correct timing and opportunities. As one of the media regulators pointed out:

> The mentality of Internet regulation is changing. The Internet is increasingly being considered as a mainstream medium which is under a stricter media control. The liberalizing potential of the Internet in regard to facilitating the expression of public interest under the media control is not totally incompatible with the way it is regulated. But it [the liberalizing potential] needs opportunities and conditions, because not too many people within the regulatory bodies have a liberal mindset. (H, interviewed on 23 August 2007)

> We allow critical posts, which are not posted by those with evil intentions, even ones which are "playing the edge-ball".[13] So long as there is no serious political problem, we would like the keep the forum as it is. And that is also why the forum is thriving. (G, interviewed on 25 October 2007)

The opportunities offered are made possible not only by forum participants who critically engage in public discussions but also by media regulators and practitioners such as forum moderators and administrators. Liberal-minded media regulators and practitioners, although small in number, constitute a liberalizing force from within, slowly pushing back boundaries and testing how far the party will go. They challenge party censorship in an incremental fashion and push for more critical media practices to be directed against the authorities. This is reflected in how the Qiangguo Forum was set up, as revealed by its creator below. As we shall see, the NATO bombing of the Chinese embassy in Belgrade provided the opportunity for the establishment of the forum:

> I wanted to create a space where people could talk in from the bottom of their heart. . . . Online forums were not considered acceptable by the leaders back then. They were like Big Letter Posters from the Cultural Revolution. These posters were used by both party leaders to attack their political opponents and by the public to attack their leaders. How could they possibly tolerate things like this? But with the chance offered by the NATO bombing [of] the Chinese Embassy in Yugoslavia, I created a forum called "Protest at the Violence of NATO Headed by the US Forum".[14] I knew this could not be [regarded as] wrong because it enabled the Chinese to express their nationalism. And this was in tune with our government's stand — we were not on good terms with the US anyway. And, of course, the leaders did not say anything against the forum, so I thought I could keep this forum going even after the anti-American wave [ended]. A month later, the forum was re-named the Qiangguo Forum from the "Protest at the Violence of NATO Headed by the US Forum". I knew this couldn't be [seen as] wrong either, as patriotism was also on the government/party agenda. (I, interviewed on 26 October 2007)

Similar to the interviewee C quoted previously, the creator of the forum is also astonishingly open about his intention to challenge the CCP. The tension between the CCP and its citizens, forum users or forum administrators is clearly demonstrated above. The approach of the forum creator may be more incremental in fashion and subtle in nature than the confrontational approach of the forum user (interviewee C), but it may be more effective as the former plays the game, knowing all the rules, such as timing and testing. As shown in the above transcript, the creator has been quite successful in setting up the first online forum in China.

As indicated by this, the official attitude towards the forum and the Internet in general tends to be fairly tolerant. The government's change in attitude has to be understood within the broader context of a national strategy aiming at constructing an information society. The Chinese government has invested a huge amount of money in building a telecommunication infrastructure, such as a fibre-optic network developed during the 1990s (Dai 2003: 13). It obviously plans that this will have a broader application than the development of discussion forums, but the falling cost of Internet access and the fact that "more than ten percent of the Chinese population use the Internet" provides the basis for participatory communication (CNNIC 2007). Whether this can be translated into some institutional changes in media control needs more empirical research to prove. Yet the public is more involved in social issues such as the petition over SARS, in which they pressurized the authorities to co-operate with the World Health Organization. Meanwhile the government, reflecting its policy goal of a "Harmonious Society", has become both more open to public input and more tolerant of social interests being expressed. Such expression is a prerequisite of participatory communication.

INCLUSIVENESS — REPRESENTING THE UNDER-PRIVILEGED SOCIAL CLASSES

In addition to understanding how forum participants engage in government–public communication as a whole, it is also important to understand how they balance the collective interests of the general public and the specific interests of individuals. In the discussion on income inequality, participants have generally considered under-privileged social classes as the victims of an unjust social system. Forum participants, who are mostly middle-class, hardly fall into this category. Therefore, forum participants' perception of the interests of under-privileged social classes is essential in gauging their sense of inclusiveness of other social classes. As a result, I asked them whether they felt able to represent the under-privileged social classes:

> Forum participants constitute only a small part of all citizens. Under-privileged people do not use the Internet. Those who are always online and talking about politics are the ones who have time and money. They cannot represent the under-privileged population. They are just onlookers. (A, interviewed on 28 September 2007)

> Forum participants cannot represent the under-privileged social groups. They [under-privi-

leged people] need to have their own channel to express their interests. (J, interviewed on 2 September 2007)

Both journalists and forum participants are very complex social groups. Although some of them have managed to speak up for the under-privileged classes in the newspaper or on the forum, it does not mean they can truly represent the under-privileged classes because of their own economic status. In the end it is merely [showing] "sympathy". And this cannot change the lives of these people. Under-privileged people can only be represented by themselves. (K, interviewed on 25 October 2007)

A good number of forum participants would [want to represent the social lower classes]. But they [the participants] cannot. They are not in the "powerful" social strata. (E, interviewed on 6 October 2007)

I add posts like this [on income disparity] not because I want to speak for the under-privi-leged people, but because I am interested in this question and it is a quite a serious social problem. (B, interviewed on 24 October 2007)

Most of the forum participants acknowledge that they cannot represent the interests of the under-privileged social classes, either because of their own socio-economic conditions or their low position in the power hierarchy. On the one hand, this demonstrates their awareness that there are distinctive social groups, based on socio-economic conditions. On the other hand, the fact that forum participants consider the issue of income inequality as a "serious social problem", and that they have had intense discussions on it, shows that they are actively engaging. And from another perspective, it shows inclusiveness as they consider the interests of the lower social classes as one of the social concerns that need addressing. Moreover, the fact that several posters have considered a need for a mechanism whereby the under-privileged social classes can express their political interests indicates that they have thought about a solution.

In addition, a hidden theme can be sensed from the quotes above: the need for political rights for under-privileged social classes. Although the Chinese government is increasingly tolerant of politically challenging content, political reform still remains a taboo. As result, no one has explicitly suggested a political reform that might challenge the legitimacy of the CCP. However, as I have argued elsewhere, the forum participants have powerfully, if only implicitly, criticized the unjust social system, resulting from the under-supervised political power (Gong 2008b). Instead of directly challenging the system, online citizen journalists in China have adopted a gradualist approach — consistently trying to legitimize the idea of political reform in the forum. This veiled but implicitly critical attitude of forum users has helped contribute to the forum's critical stance overall, despite its links to the party newspaper, the *People's Daily*. The forum users have covertly shifted the forum's agenda. Their sense of defiance, distrust and cynicism has been expressed through the forum. Moreover, participants have used the forum to systematically and consistently level criticism at political power, an unequal social system and corruption, which raises their criticism to a higher level.

In addition, we have seen that many forum participants tend to express considerable sympathy for low-income families. Yet within this middle-class-dominated forum, some do not identify with the under-privileged, showing distinct class interests. For instance, another participant explains why he posts against what he regards as an over-sympathetic attitude:

> I can't remember clearly what I posted. What I meant was we need to reconsider these problems from two directions. We shouldn't only criticize people with high incomes. The social structure is much more reasonable than it was a decade ago. It is reasonable that people with high education and skills get paid more in a society based on knowledge. On the contrary, people have low incomes largely because they don't have enough qualifications or they don't work hard enough. Right now the unjust social system is generally considered as the main cause of income disparity by the netizens. And society is over-sympathetic to people with low incomes, without regard to the reasons why they have low incomes, which I think is completely misleading. (B, interviewed on 24 October 2007)

This is obviously contrary to the dominant sympathetic discourse on the forum, as he is defending high incomes based on knowledge and skills. Competing interests are not a problem for participatory communication in the forum, as citizens do have different economic, political and social statuses, and citizens are not absolutely equal "as if they were social and economic peers" (Fraser 1996: 118). Another problem many participants identify is that there is not enough in-depth thinking and rational debate. Some believe that the fast pace of the forum discussions truncates serious thinking and debate: "The problem is that the forum is similar to chatrooms — high-speed, but without in-depth thinking. People tend to browse instead of participating" (E, interviewed on 6 October 2007).

CONCLUSION

The Qiangguo Forum, one of the most influential political forums in China, has demonstrated a number of dimensions in regard to citizen participation and social inclusion in its discussion on income inequality. Though linked to the Communist Party paper, the forum participants have an implicitly critical attitude towards the existing political system. Given the authoritarian nature of the Chinese political system, the fact that there is a degree of political expression, albeit articulated implicitly rather than explicitly, should be regarded an achievement of the forum. The findings here reveal that forum participants largely use first-hand experiences as the ultimate reference point in assessing the authenticity of posts. The posts created by citizen journalists on the forum are considered a reliable source of information by participants, facilitating the further development of citizen journalism on the forum or in other online media. This demonstrates that there is a gap between the public's trust of the mainstream media, controlled by the Chinese authorities, on the one hand, and the general acceptance of the citizens' perspectives on the other. This trust has, in return, underpinned the citizen journalists' practice and enhanced their sense of autonomy, solidarity and citizenship. Meanwhile, forum participants have an implicitly critical attitude towards the existing political system. Given the authoritarian nature of the Chinese political system, the fact that there is a degree of political expression, albeit articulated implicitly rather than explicitly, should be considered an achievement of the forum.

In developing the forum, both the media practitioners, such as the forum's creator and the users, have employed gradualist and indirect methods. Their incremental but open agenda of engaging, challenging and changing the official medium has high-lighted, on the one hand, the rigid media censorship and, on the other, the tension between the authoritarian political order and citizens' desire to participate. The role of the forum as a conduit between the government and the public has significantly enhanced political participation. The forum has also demonstrated, however, the competing interests of different social classes. Even though forum participants have acknowledged the limitations of representing under-privileged social classes, they have given considerable attention to the problem and to solutions. During the process of discussion, debates have been considered insufficiently in-depth. Nonetheless, the discussion has sufficiently unearthed citizens' experiences and perspectives in commu-nication both between the public and the government and among the public. As a result, in fulfilling the roles of citizen journalism, both with regard to disseminating information and political participation, the forum has facilitated participatory commu-nication through citizen journalists' active contribution. Information dissemination and political participation are further facilitated by the internal democratic mechanism set up by the media regulators, which collects critical views on the party and the government within the Qiangguo Forum.

Notes

1   Interest is understood as the fundamental force that motivates the action of the actor, and interest can include honour, glory, self-respect, an afterlife, economic advantage etc. (Hirschman, cited in Zheng 2004a: 62). From the perspective of the CCP, interest mainly referring to economic interest makes the society more predictable and governable (Zheng 2004a: 62).

2   The "Three Represents" is the term used in the official Chinese English newspapers. The "Three Represents" was first announced by Jiang Zemin, the former president of the CCP, in February 2000, when he inspected Guangdong Province. It was included in the party constitution in 2004. In the "Three Represents", Jiang suggested that the Chinese Communist Party should represent advanced social productive forces, advanced culture and the interests of the majority. The "advanced social productive forces" are largely consid-ered to be entrepreneurs and the middle classes.

3   The main objectives of the "Harmonious Society" are identified as economic growth, democracy, justice, the rule of law, equality, ideological construction and environmental protection.

4   In 2003 a news report in the *Southern Metropolis Daily* warning of the epidemic nature of SARS (Severe Acute Respiratory Syndrome) was widely disseminated on the Internet.

Internet BBS forums and text messages became major news sources for the public after the Chinese government blocked reports of SARS in the traditional media. Information disseminated online was picked up by the overseas media, which drew the attention of the World Health Organization. The international community pressed the Chinese government to cooperate with other countries to curb the disease.

5 In 2003 Sun Zhigang, a university graduate, was tortured to death during his detention in a police station in Guangzhou. Under great pressure from media reports and public concern expressed online, the local government fired twenty staff from the police station, health care authorities and the civil affairs administration. More importantly, Sun's death resulted in the National People's Congress reviewing the detention and repatriation rules. A year later the Chinese State Council repealed the rules.

6 In 2007 an online post that wanted to stop children working in sweatshop kilns in Shan'xi province was viewed hundreds of thousands of times on the Internet. This triggered large-scale rescues and a crackdown on child labour in Shan'xi, headed by the governor of the province.

7 "Strong China" is the English translation of "Qiangguo" in the Chinese English media. However, it does not fully reflect the original meaning of "strong", so in this chapter, "Qiangguo" is used instead of its English translation.

8 The *People's Daily* is the official newspaper of the Chinese Communist Party.

9 Commercial portals such as the Internet Content Providers (ICPs) and Internet Service Providers (ISPs) are held responsible by the regulatory bodies for any political subversive content appearing on their websites or servers. As a result, many ICPs and ISPs exercise very strong censorship on their own websites or servers. In fact, many of them avoid the problem by not having a forum for discussing political issues.

10 Personal interview with a forum administrator (G, interviewed on 25 October 2007).

11 Owing to the self-censorship in China, all interviewees are guaranteed full anonymity, and only letters of the alphabet are used to distinguish individual interviewees at the end of each transcript.

12 Internal Reference is a publication circulated internally among party members. Critical reports that would be seen to have a negative influence are prohibited in the public media but are allowed in the Internal Reference.

13 This refers to the idea that someone can avoid punishment if they break the rules only marginally. Here it refers to harsh criticism of the party or the government.

14 The original name in Chinese is also long and awkward. The description is to highlight the crime convicted by the US. (Interview with I, 26 October 2007). The precision of the wording also reflects the extremely caution of media practice under censorship.

References

Allan, S. (2006) *Online News*. Maidenhead: Open University Press.

Castells, M. (1998) *End of Millennium*. Malden, MA, and Oxford: Blackwell.

CNNIC (2007) "The 20th Statistical Report on the Internet Development in China". Retrieved 24 October 2007 from: http://www.cnnic.cn/en/index/0O/02/index.htm.

Coleman, S., and Gøtze, J. (2001) "Bowling Together: Online Public Engagement in Policy Deliberation". Retrieved 21 June 2008 from: http://bowlingtogether.net/.

Dahlgren, P. (1996) *Television and the Public Sphere: Citizenship, Democracy and the Media*. London, Thousand Oaks and New Delhi: Sage.

Dai, X. (2003) "ICTs in China's Development Strategy". In C. R. Hughes, and G. Wacker (eds),

China and the Internet: Politics of the Digital Leap Forward. London and New York: Routledge Curzon, pp. 8–29.

Fraser, N. (1996) "Rethinking the Public Sphere: A Contribution to the Critique of Actually Existing Democracy". In C. Calhoun (ed.), *Habermas and the Public Sphere.* Cambridge, MA, and London: MIT Press, pp. 109–42.

Golding, P. (1990) "Political Communication and Citizenship: The Media and Democracy in an Inegalitarian Social Order". In M. Ferguson (ed.), *Public Communication: The New Imperatives.* London, Newbury Park and New Delhi: Sage, pp. 84–100.

Gong, Q. (2008a) "Internet BBS Forum and News Reporting: Towards an Enhanced Public–Government Communication in China". In K. Prasad (ed.), *e-Journalism: New Directions in Electronic News Media.* New Delhi: B.R. Publishing.

Gong, Q. (2008b) "Extended Media Public Sphere in China? An Analysis of Media Coverage of 'Income Disparity' Issue in Four Media Discourses", *The 6th International Conference on Media Proceedings.* Athens: ATINER.

Jiang, H. (2007) "The Platform Shift of the Communication Discourse: From the Perspective of Significant Events", *Nanfang Media Research,* 9, pp. 81–7.

Nip, J. Y. M. (2007) "Exploring the Second Phase of Public Journalism", *Journalism Studies,* 7 (2), pp. 212–36.

People's Daily English (2005) "Building Harmonious Society Is Crucial for China's Progress". Retrieved 10 May 2008 from: http://english.people.com.cn/200506/ 27/eng20050627_ 192495.html.

People's Daily English (2007) "Three Represents". Retrieved 10 May 2008 from: http://english. people.com.cn/90002/92169/92211/6274616.html.

People's Daily English (2008) "President Hu Jintao Inspects People's Daily: First Live Online Chat with Netizens". Retrieved 20 June 2008 from: http://english.people. com.cn/90001/90782/6435851.html.

Shen, S. (2007) *Redefining Nationalism in Modern China: Sino-American Relations and the Emergence of Chinese Public Opinion in the 21st Century.* Basingstoke: Palgrave Macmillan.

Teng, P. (2007) "Hei Zhuan Yao Shi Jian Zhong De Yi Di Jian Du" (Non-Local Supervision in the Event of Black Kilns). In *Nanfang Media Research,* 9, pp. 88–96.

Yang, G. B., and Calhoun, C. (2008) "Media, Civil Society, and the Rise of a Green Public Sphere in China". In P. Ho, and R. L. Edmonds (eds), *China's Embedded Activism: Opportunities and Constrains of A Social Movement.* London and New York: Routledge, pp. 69–88.

Zhao, Y. Z. (2008) *Communication in China: Political Economy, Power, and Conflict.* New York and Plymouth: Rowman & Littlefield.

Zheng, Y. N. (2004a) *Globalisation and State Transformation in China.* Cambridge: Cambridge University Press.

Zheng, Y. N. (2004b) *Will China Become Democratic? Elite, Class and Regime Transition.* Singapore: Marshall Cavendish International.

}{ CHAPTER }{
18

Web-Oriented Public Participation in Contemporary China

RENA BIVENS AND CHEN LI

China is certainly not known for its tolerance of citizen protests or collective action. Yet the Chinese public is becoming increasingly involved in actions that have influenced government decision-making. Wider social and economic changes within China and the spread of new media technology, such as the Internet and mobile phones, have played a role in gradual social and political change.

This chapter assesses Web-related public participation, as a grassroots form of social activism, within the unique setting of China's authoritarian context. We examine some case studies from 2007 and 2008. The significance of these cases is their pertinence to the more general debate concerning citizenship, governance and new technology. In particular, they demonstrate how public participation in China has developed and how local government officials have responded by showing a growing willingness to appease some demands from the public. In this way we adopt Shi's argument that "high-level government agencies have become much more tolerant toward local collective resistance" in China, which represents at least a partial explanation for "the success of grassroots movements" (2008: 252), although it should be noted that the Chinese political perspective does not promote the construction of the type of democratic citizenship that has its origins in the West.

In this chapter we highlight three significant issues:

- the new technologies that are facilitating a rich eco-system, in which a form of civil society can be developed;
- the forms of public participation that Chinese citizens employ in order to influence government decision-making;
- the issues that are most likely to spark these actions.

The wider debate surrounding the potential progression towards a democratic dialogue can be examined through a broad range of perspectives. The literature is divided between optimistic and pessimistic frameworks, but many academics believe that political change in China will be necessarily gradual and incremental (see, for instance, Zheng and Wu 2005; and Ho 2007). The development of any form of democratic dialogue is, of course, limited by the governing system that is in place. In the context of China we argue that, while democratic dialogue is rare, despite the potential inherent within the new technology, citizenship has developed as public participation has increased — at least when people have reacted to very specific, local issues that have provoked a widespread emotional response.

New forms of civic engagement in contemporary China are helping to establish what is implicitly a "politics of expanding general public discourse". Public groups have formed around a wide range of single issues including, feminism, HIV/AIDS, cyber-activism and other rights more generally (Yang and Calhoun 2007; Shi 2008). The most prominent of these areas has been green politics (Yang and Calhoun 2007: 230). As Zheng and Wu (2005: 531, 532) argue, it was the introduction of the Internet in China that "enabled social forces to react to events more quickly and efficiently". With this, their influence over politics and policy practices increased, resulting in "incremental political changes".[1] Yang and Calhoun (2007: 211) also note several cases where "a high level of social concern" regarding the environment in the public sphere has, in turn, influenced government policies, especially through the use of the mass media and the Internet.[2]

Despite the fact that there are some environmental concerns involved in the case studies to be examined, overall they are not rooted in the broader environmental discourse. Instead, these cases demonstrate the Web-oriented nature of Chinese public participation. However, it is first necessary to consider some theoretical issues relating to democratic dialogue, new technology and a general framework for guiding the analysis of Chinese social action.

DEMOCRACY, THE PROMISE OF NEW TECHNOLOGY AND SINGLE-ISSUE CAMPAIGNS

Overall, Internet penetration has been rising steadily in most places in the world, and China is certainly no exception, with the largest number of Internet users in the world (298 million).[3] The largest growth has been within the under-eighteen and over-thirty age categories. It is also important to note that the percentage of rural netizens has been rapidly growing — of the 73 million new netizens appearing in CINIC's report, 40 percent were from rural areas.[4]

For some, the traditional computer is no longer essential for Internet access. According to a July 2008 report by Nielsen Mobile, 6.8 percent of China's population was said to access the Internet through mobile phones. This percentage is close to Germany's 7.4 percent but lags behind the US's 15.6 percent and the UK's 12.9 percent. China is also known for its high percentage of bloggers, with 49.35 million citizens currently updating their blog or personal space online (CINIC 2008). In addition to bloggers, the popularity of Bulletin Board Services (BBS) — otherwise known as online forums — is also quite high in China. Prominent examples, such as Tianya.cn, club.cat898.com or dzh.mop.com, provide Chinese netizens with virtual public spaces to share and discuss issues of concern.[5] Most of the debates over social, economic and political issues that we consider in this chapter have begun on such forums.

In general, new technological developments have been hailed as helping facilitate the most effective means of communication (see, for example, Dahlgren (1995); and Dahlgren and Sparks (1991)). However, it is a well-known fact that Chinese citizens find their use of new technologies constrained by the Great Firewall (netizens often refer to such censorship as being "GFW'd").[6] As such, particular topics and events become censored as well as entire sections of the Internet — although, for the more technologically savvy, there are relatively easy ways to get around the GFW. Still, the stipulation (or, indeed, threat) of mandatory identity registration for blogs and other online spaces also acts as a constraint.

Despite these controls imposed by the Chinese government, some spaces still exist for people to organize collective activities (see, for example, Zheng and Wu 2005). The more popular online forums, such as Tianya.cn, are not under significant threat of being shut down by the government, but posts are continuously deleted. For example, posts were removed from the *Tianya Miscellaneous Chat* forum in relation to the "Weng'an Mass Incident", where citizens accused local government officials of covering up the death of a young girl.[7]

The promise of citizen participation and democratic dialogue has perhaps unfairly dominated discussions since the emergence of the Internet in China. While many have greeted the Internet with (at times) fervent optimism (see, for instance, Loader 1997), others have considered it as harmful to any form of civic participation. Sunstein (2001) developed perhaps the most convincing argument supporting the latter perspective, after Negroponte (1995) imagined the concept of the *Daily Me*.

According to this line of thought, the Internet scarcely encourages important tenets of democracy. It neither helps expose users to information and opinions not chosen in advance, nor does it provide users with a common set of experiences (Sunstein 2001). Instead, the increasing use of the Internet has arguably led to audiences fragmenting, partly as a result of its inherent potential for content to be personalized and for citizens to access only a narrow range of information and opinions. As a result, "those who want to find support for what they already think, and to insulate themselves from disturbing topics and contrary points of view, can do that far more easily than they can if they skim through a decent newspaper or weekly newsmagazine" (Sunstein 2007: 9). However, Sunstein's argument relates to a broader notion of democracy within societies. His notions are focused on "deliberative democracy", where government representatives remain accountable, while the citizens (and the government) engage in "a large degree of reflection and debate" (2001: 38).

Yet Zheng and Wu (2005) see new technology as having influenced China's transition towards a "liberalized authoritarianism", as opposed to any semblance of democratization. That is, there may be an opportunity for collective action, but government officials are still scarcely accountable, and their power is not subject to fair and competitive elections. To Zheng and Wu, the Internet represents a communicative tool, a public space and a facilitator of collective action. As a result, the transformation occurring within China — and indeed illustrated in the case studies below — involves participation in very specific, typically locally based, issues.

What is common to the incidents of Web-oriented public participation in China are their "fragmentary, highly localised, and non-confrontational" nature, which was how Ho and Edmonds (2007: 332) described Chinese environmentalism in the years since it emerged in the early 1990s.[8] This analysis can also summarize the main characteristics of the interaction strategies identified by Zheng and Wu in connection with collective actions that are based on so-called "voice activities" — direct expressions of dissatisfaction to the relevant authority — as well as social activism in contemporary China more generally. In the context of information technology and the public space, Zheng and Wu (2005: 531) define "voice activities" as those "Internet-facilitated collective actions that do not pose a direct challenge to the state", adopting a strategy that is acceptable to both the state and society without any attempt to "undermine or overthrow the state".

Shi (2008: 235) sums this up by arguing that the recent examples of collective action do not aim to tackle large-scale issues: "The new neighbourhood-based resistance movements target local authorities and commercial organizations, focusing on particular economic and social problems (e.g., protecting neighbourhood environments) as opposed to macro socio-political issues." Such grassroots movements are said to "exert [a] considerable force on local politics" despite their micro-focus (Shi 2008: 235).

To explain why they are "non-confrontational", Zheng and Wu (2005) argue that the failure of previous attempts to challenge the state directly has led social activists to adopt a strategy that deliberately does not aim to undermine the state's legitimacy. This is because they know that "if a given collective action is perceived as undermining the legitimacy of the state, it is likely to invite a crackdown by the state" (2005: 531). Consciously avoiding confrontation, such "voice activities" respond to issues by means of a "depoliticized politics" and "self-imposed censorship" (Ho and Edmonds 2007: 336). To lobby over small-scale issues based at the community-level, Shi (2008) has noted that some citizens prefer employing social networks, such as contacts with friends or relatives of high-ranking authorities, when challenging local government.[9]

As discussed above, the instances where Chinese citizens have taken action are largely restricted to specific issues, as opposed to attempts to tackle larger social, economic or political subjects. The examples that follow therefore largely revolve around property issues — although this has brought environmental issues to the forefront — which have raised concerns for those who live in the specific areas. They have resulted in fragmented, highly localized and relatively non-confrontational collective action, all of which was facilitated by new media technology. The first case we will consider relates to the rise of citizen journalism, while the latter assesses processes of citizen action.

CITIZEN JOURNALISM, LIVE POSTING AND LOCAL PROPERTY ISSUES

What is critical about technological developments is that they have coincided with a transformation in public behaviour that has had a significant social and cultural effect. While this shift had come about largely prior to the introduction of the new technology (Kline and Burstein 2005), it is only now having a more significant impact because opinions and information can now spread much more visibly and become more influential. The rise of citizen journalists is one such example that also points to a potential awakening of civic society. While this activity has become increasingly popular across the globe, with most news organizations now actively soliciting user-generated content, the phenomenon has also appeared within China. Citizen journalists behave like other citizens when they now, almost instinctively, pull out their mobile phone (or another piece of technology) in order to document something. But what sets them apart is that they are also more likely to engage in discussion or at least provide some type of analysis of relevant issues.

China's first citizen journalist, allegedly (or at least the first to make it into the mainstream), was Zhou Shuguang, who goes by the name of Zola. His is one of the most significant cases among Chinese citizen journalists. Claiming to originally have been a vegetable farmer, Zola took on the role of "investigative reporter" in March 2007. This was to publicize a couple's fight to hold on their home in Chongqing, in south-west China, despite property developers and the local government insisting that they leave.[10] Their home was the only one left standing, as all their neighbours had vacated their houses, which had been bulldozed to the ground.[11] International news organizations and the more outspoken Chinese national (as opposed to local) news outlets had reported on this.[12] This case was particularly interesting because it arose immediately in the wake of the Chinese authorities passing a new property law.[13] The media was first attracted by the enormous number of photos that were circulated by Chinese bloggers of the "nail house" (so called because, like a nail which sticks up through a plank of wood, it was difficult to remove). Many of these also posted information about the homeowners.[14] This highlights the immediacy and interactivity possible with new media (Bivens 2008).

What made the blogger Zola stand out was his continued use of "investigative" tactics. These involved continuously updating his site using photos, videos, text and interviews with the homeowners to document the progress of the case up to the point when his blog was blocked on the day the "nail house" was finally demolished. The campaign was successful, inasmuch as a local court awarded the couple compensation. Several foreign mainstream media outlets, including Associated Press, also cited Zola's work.

Zola's efforts were significant since the Chinese government had requested that the traditional media cease reporting on the event on 25 March 2007 (the day before Zola began) and took the further step of shutting down related online discussions and deleting posts on online forums. Zola sought to report the stories that the traditional media were banned from covering. However, he was also concerned about the infringement of property rights.

With financial donations, as well as his own determination, keeping Zola afloat, the blog posts continued along with images and video that covered a wide range of issues, including the Xiamen PX project (discussed below), the Olympic torch relay, the Sichuan earthquake, which left nearly 70,000 confirmed dead, and even the Weng'an mass incident (see above).[15]

Clearly Zola was aware that his actions were pushing at the limits of what would be acceptable. Indeed, he was forced to tackle censorship of his blog and alleged physical assault. After six months of working to encourage others to become citizen journalists and passing on vital technological skills, these challenges (at least momentarily) led Zola to stop, writing that: "The task of saving yourselves is in your own hands now."[16] Nevertheless, potential danger looms for any citizen who chooses to follow the lead of a blogger like Zola, or who decides to merely record what has happened through using new media technologies. A tragic example of this was what happened to Wei Wenhua,[17] who was beaten to death by a local city administrator after using his mobile phone to record government wrong-doing.

MOBILIZATION: TEXTING AND LOCAL ENVIRONMENTAL ISSUES

Apart from discussion, debate and the sharing of information and images, public participation can also include mobilization and collective action to influence government decisions. In China many have used mobile phones and particularly texting or SMS to do this. Despite the fact that members of the public might have different reasons for doing this, there have been massive mobilizations organized by texting both locally and nationally. Similarly, instant messaging programmes such as MSN and QQ (the Chinese version of the instant messaging system ICQ) have also frequently been used to inform others and organize activities. This has included patriotic mobilizations. People added a "red heart" symbol and the word "CHINA" in front of instant messaging screen names to demonstrate solidarity during the Olympic torch relay.[18]

Sending and receiving texts, which Chinese mobile users routinely do, can easily be combined with other forms of media as a means of informing and campaigning. And it has also helped circulate information and opinions regarding Web-related issues. However, it has on occasion played a unique role as an alternative to the traditional media and the Internet, when neither has been deemed effective. This has happened when the authorities have silenced the traditional media[19] or when campaigners have considered both the media and the Web to be ineffective in influencing local government decisions.[20]

In common with the highly localized characteristic of Chinese public participation mentioned earlier, most collective action in contemporary China has been aimed, ultimately, at altering decisions made by local authorities.[21] In this sense, campaigners have used the national to influence the local. They have employed online forums and other forms of public participation as a means of publicizing their concerns beyond the local setting, so as to gain nationwide public support, in order to apply pressure on the relevant local authorities. Meanwhile, they have employed mobile phones as an effective way to inform and rally other phone owners to influence local officials, when more conventional democratic dialogue has not worked, as shown in the following case of the Xiamen P-Xylene protest.

In an episode that was hailed internationally as a victory for people power,[22] the citizens of Xiamen were eventually successful in halting the construction of an industrial plant producing the toxic chemical P-Xylene in their city in south-eastern China. They were concerned about the threat to the environment and the health risks in a city traditionally known for its clean air. The massive protest conducted was reckoned to be responsible for halting the local government's plans.[23]

A group of academics and members of the Chinese People's Political Consultative Conference (CPPCC) initiated the protest by proposing a halt to the project (*Southern Weekend* 2007). This launched the P-Xylene project into the public eye and created a kind of "greenspeak", considered to be one of the "three basic elements" of the Chinese green public sphere by Yang and Calhoun (2007: 212).[24] On this occasion a limited "public" of different social groups (social activists, journalists and bloggers) first conducted this so-called "greenspeak" in different media, which was only then taken up by citizens who shared similar concerns. As is always the case in contemporary China, this process was uneven, as is the extent to which citizens' involvement can influence the authorities' decisions. What happened in this case was that the campaign elicited little attention nationwide on what was seen as just a local issue. Only a few news reports and commentaries about the potential damage of the PX project appeared outside the Xiamen local press.[25] This minimal coverage failed to persuade the local government to halt the hugely profitable $1.35 billion project.[26]

However, the campaign eventually went beyond the normal level of public participation, leading to what was labelled "the cell phone campaign" (*Los Angeles Times* 2007). Concerned for their future health, citizens became frustrated as their local media were silenced and posts on the local online forums were deleted by the authorities.[27] So they started to send warning texts to relatives and friends, with the powerful plea that "we may fail but should show our concerns".[28] This was "mass self-communication" via the mobile phone (as termed by Castells, in an interview with Qiu 2008).[29] The following is an example of a text sent to Chinese citizens at the time:

> Once this extremely poisonous chemical is produced, it means an atomic bomb will have been placed in Xiamen. The people of Xiamen will have to live with leukaemia and deformed babies. We want our lives and health! (English translation of a SMS repeated more than 1 million times among citizens)

An outdoor protest, scheduled for 1 June 2007, was also organized, and relevant information was circulated through similar innovative strategies that helped to publicize the campaign and inform more people (*Global Voices Online* 2007; *Los Angeles Times* 2007; Lu and Sun 2008). Campaigners used the term "walking" instead of "protest" to lower the sensitivity of the authorities and to help the message circulate more effectively, both through the Internet and, especially, mobile phones. This large-scale public action far exceeded the traditional strategy of having influential journalists and activists sign a petition letter, as shown, for instance, in the Nu River case, which involved a dam-building project (Yang and Calhoun 2007).

Driven by deep concerns for their own well-being, the citizens in Xiamen were more willing to stand up to protect their interests — in a form of active citizenship — using new media technology. They also uploaded a plethora of "live" pictures and videos about the "walking" event and conducted "SMS-blogging" to online forums, *YouTube* and a Chinese version *Tudou* (*Global Voices Online* 2007). Following this, the plant's construction was halted, and all of the Xiamen citizens were named the *Southern Weekend* Person of the Year 2007,[30] which helped legitimize their action as a model that citizens in other cities could follow.

In January 2008 citizens used similar innovative tactics in their protests about a planned extension of Shanghai's Magnetically Levitated (Maglev) train into downtown Shanghai, over concerns regarding possible health effects and lowered property values. Protests included "harmonious collective walking" and co-ordinated "shopping". These were also used to protest at plans to extend the line to nearby city Hangzhou. They eventually forced the local authorities into postponing a decision on the project.[31] This time it was the new rising middle class and intellectuals who took part. Once again, new media strategies were adopted to inform and organize, after citizens became frustrated as the authorities silenced the local media and deleted online posts. As such, Shanghai citizens live-posted pictures and videos online, in order to publicize their cause.

CONCLUSION

Overall, this chapter has demonstrated the effectiveness of new media technology in the context of China. Citizens have launched successful collective action over single issues where government decisions have affected their daily lives. The cases chosen illustrate the general point that citizen participation within the public realm is necessarily limited. And the context of China is exceedingly complex. Yet it is still clear that, at least with some local single-issue campaigns, Chinese citizens are becoming increasingly empowered, while local authorities are acting in a conciliatory way as a result. Public spaces on the Internet — particularly within online forums — along with mobile phones to mobilize people, have been vital to this shift.

The Chinese political context does not facilitate or encourage citizenship in the sense of democratic ideals that largely originated within Western thought. However, it is important to consider the actions of those Chinese citizens who are aiming to influence government decision-making. In this way we can reflect on the changes within Chinese society. We can also track the ways in which the Chinese government is responding to these social upheavals, as well as the way people are employing new media technology.

This chapter has illustrated the Web-related forms of public participation that are emerging. Yet more ongoing analysis is required in order to consider the full range of public forms of participation and government responses. The few instances of social action that have been rooted in a more national setting may indeed require an alternative analytical framework (as suggested, for instance, in relation to the Carrefour boycott mentioned in an earlier footnote). Historical comparisons are also necessary in order to achieve a comprehensive investigation of the intersection between new technology, citizenship and governance within China.

With more rural Internet users and continued growth within the under-eighteen and over-thirty age groups (CINIC 2008), new technology may facilitate even greater public participation in China. And the specific issues that are currently garnering attention may expand into other areas of social, economic and political life. As such, the typical motivation to participate may extend beyond these local settings or alter the development of China's civil society in other ways than we have outlined here.

Notes

1 Zheng and Wu (2005) studied three cases. The first led to reforms to increase political transparency and accountability, while in the other two the government was pressed into abolishing old regulations and discriminatory practices against certain social groups.
2 For instance, months of heated public debates in 2004 resulted in a decision from China's state council to halt the dam-building project on the Nu River, owing to environmental concerns.
3 *Nielsen Net Review*, February 2009.
4 In the CINIC's 2008 report, 52.62 million Chinese rural netizens were recorded, which set the annual growth rate at 127.7 percent.
5 These sources have also become the main resources for the popular ESWN blog (EastSouthWestNorth; http://www.zonaeuropa.com). ESWN aims to report issues that are not covered by the mainstream media. Most posts are translated into English and as such have also become an important resource for foreign correspondents working in China (MacKinnon 2007).
6 For example, Human Rights Watch (2006) "'Race to the Bottom' Corporate Complicity in Chinese Internet Censorship", 18 (8). Retrieved from: http://www.hrw.org/reports/2006/china0806/china0806web.pdf.
7 In response, some bloggers transformed their text to the classical right-to-left vertical in order to avoid keyword censorship. Others satirically wrote and posted images of individuals doing push-ups, since one of the accused boys was allegedly doing push-ups on a bridge at the time of the young girl's death. For more information see: http://rconversation.blogs.com/rconversation/2008/07/wengan-riots-pu.html.
8 Ho and Edmonds (2007) criticize such concepts as "a state-led civil society" or "state corporatism" owing to the failure of such theories to explain the features of social activism in contemporary China and such concepts' fixation with the state.
9 Use of such social capital is typically referred to in China as *guanxi*.
10 Zola arrived at Chongqing on 26 March 2007; see more at his blog: http://www.zuola.com/weblog/?p=750.
11 The ruling appeared to be a satisfactory result for the homeowners, who agreed to accept the compensation offer by the developers and allow their nail house to be demolished on 2 April 2007.
12 Among the international media were CNN, *The New York Times*, *The Times*, Hong Kong Cable TV and Hong Kong Phoenix TV. The Chinese media included *Southern Metropolis*

Daily, TVS (Southern Television) — both from Guangdong — and *Modern Herald* (Xian dai kuai bao) from Hangzhou.

13 While the male homeowner stayed at his home to make sure developers did not demolish his property before the court's deadline, he put up banners that read "People's property cannot be breached", in order to emphasize the newly passed law. He also displayed a five-star red flag to show his determination, while his relatives used baskets to send him food. For more information see: http://news.163.com/07/0322/08/3A65DR6700011229.html.

14 According to the *Y Weekend* (29 March 2007), live SMS-posting was first introduced by a Chongqing netizen with the ID Naked Dog. He continued to update photos and videos, accompanied with text, along with six other netizens, via mobile WAP, in the forum *Mop.com* (see more analysis in Li 2007).

15 Zola's "investigative reportage" of site photos and interviews about the Weng'an mass incident had been circulated on the Internet, and was also reported by *The Wall Street Journal* on 7 July 2008. See more at: https://www.zuola.com/.

16 See his blog post: http://www.zuola.com/weblog/mobile.php?more=1&p=857.

17 The Blogger Shanghaiist writes about a man in Hubei Province who was killed for using his mobile phone to record a protest against a municipal waste dump: "Wei Wenhua, a manager at a local government-owned construction company, with no apparent connection to the protest, was driving through the area when he stopped to get a better look. At this point he took out his camera phone and began recording the incident. Once the chengguan ['official'] noticed his presence, he was yanked out of his vehicle and then brutally beaten unconscious over a period of ten minutes. He was carted off, along with other injured protesters, and died *en route* to the hospital." For information see: http://shanghaiist.com/2008/01/11/hubei_city_offi.php.

18 See *Southern Metropolis Daily*, 17 April 2008 for more information.

19 If a particular news event has been officially banned, the traditional mainstream media will replace it with an article from China's Xinhua news agency. Meanwhile, sensitive words become filtered on the Internet, appearing instead as "**".

20 In some cases, such as the Xiamen PX protest discussed in this section, reporting news may not be banned totally nationwide. Instead, a few media outlets may cover the issue and criticize relevant officials. Campaigners may still not consider this to be that productive, since local officials may still ignore such limited coverage and refuse to enter into a dialogue.

21 However, other instances of collective action, such as the anti-Japanese demonstrations in 2005 and the Carrefour Boycott in 2008, following the protests that occurred during the French leg of the Olympic torch relay, are not included in our discussions here. In essence, these cases have reflected the Chinese public's response to a series of international events, with nationalism largely being the catalyst. Nonetheless, new media technology (especially the mobile phone) has played a significant role in organizing and mobilizing the protests.

22 http://time-blog.com/china_blog/2007/12/xiamen_people_power_victory_to.html; http://www.opendemocracy.net/article/china_inside/china_protests_or_politics.

23 See Walter, P. (2007), "Text Protest Halts p-xylene plant :-o", *Chemistry and Industry*, 11, 11 June 2007, p. 5.

24 Yang and Calhoun (2007: 212) argue that "the emerging green sphere consists of three basic elements: an environmental discourse or greenspeak; publics that produce or consume greenspeak; and media used for producing and circulating greenspeak". A similar campaign to halt the dam-building project at Nu River was originated by a series of forums that were held to trigger debate among scientists and scholars.

25 Five prominent articles had been published before the local government's decision to halt temporarily the project on 30 May 2007, of which three were directly related to the proposal with particular emphasis on the potential environmental damage (Zheng Yanfeng, *China Youth Daily*, 15 March 2007; Qu Lili, *China Business Journal*, 19 March 2007; Shao Fangqing, *First Financial Daily*, 20 April 2007) and the other two were critical commentaries by professional journalist Lian Yue of the outspoken Guangdong-based *Southern Metropolis Daily*. The latter pieces involved severe criticism of government behaviour, especially that of the National Environmental Protection Bureau. All of these five articles had been put together and circulated around the Internet. For more information, see: http://www.bullog.cn/blogs/kanchai/archives/65737.aspx.

26 It was then also approved by the State Development and Reforming Commission.

27 Despite this, Xiamen netizens did not give up regularly posting similar messages on online forums, personal blogs and QQ groups.

28 For more information see: http://www.bullog.cn/blogs/kanchai/archives/65737.aspx.

29 Also described as Internet/wireless network-oriented public communication.

30 *Southern Weekend* and *Southern Metropolis Daily* enjoy a good reputation and credibility among readers for being outspoken as they publish both comments by critical intellectuals and investigative reports about local conflicts. For more information about the Xiamen citizens becoming 'Person of the Year' see: http://www.infzm.com/content/9749.

31 For more information see related reports at the *Beijing News*: http://www.chinanews.com.cn/gn/news/2008/01-19/1139208.shtml.

References

Bivens, R. (2008) "The Internet, Mobile Phones and Blogging", *Journalism Practice*, 2 (1), pp. 113–29.

Chen, W. (2007) "The Most Awesome Nailhouse Gives Birth to Citizen Journalism", *YWeekend*, 29 March, p. A04. Retrieved 12 April 2007 from: http://www.yweekend.com/webnews/070329/A04/070329A0401.shtml.

CHINA hong bian wang luo [Red China over Internet] (2008) *Southern Metropolis Daily*, 17 April, p. AA32. Retrieved 12 May 2008 from: http://epaper.nddaily.com/A/html/2008-04/17/content_442759.htm. (English translation can be found at: http://zonaeuropa.com/200804b.brief.htm.)

China Internet Network Information Centre (CINIC) (2008) "Statistical Survey Report on the Internet Development in China", January 2008. Retrieved June 10 2008 from: www.cnnic.cn/uploadfiles/pdf/2008/2/29/104126.pdf.

Dahlgren, P. (1995) *Television and the Public Sphere: Citizenship, Democracy and the Media*. London: Sage.

Dahlgren, P., and Sparks, C. (1991) *Communication and Citizenship: Journalism and the Public Sphere in the New Media Age*. New York: Routledge.

Ho, P. (2007) "Embedded Activism and Political Change in a Semi-authoritarian Context", *China Information*, 21 (2), pp. 187–209.

Ho, P., and Edmonds, R. (2007) "Perspectives of Time and Change: Rethinking Embedded Environmental Activism in China", *China Information*, 21 (2), pp. 331–44.

Kennedy, J. (2007) "Liveblogging from Ground Zero". Retrieved 1 June 2007 from: http://www.globalvoicesonline.org/2007/06/01/china-liveblogging-from-ground-zero/.

Kline, D., and Burstein, D. (2005) *Blog! How the Newest Media Revolution is Changing Politics, Business, and Culture*. New York: CDS Books.

Landsberg, M. (2007) "Chinese Activists Turn to Cellphones", *Los Angeles Times*, 1 June. Retrieved 10 December 2007 from: http://globaltechforum.eiu.com/index.asp?layout=rich_story&doc_id=10856&title=Chinese+activists+turn+to+cellphones&categoryid=30&channelid=4.

Li, C. (2007) *New Trends in Chinese Blogosphere: Producing Citizen Journalism and Interacting With Traditional Media*. Paper presented at the Institute of Communications Studies, University of Leeds.

Loader, B. (ed.) (1997) *The Governance of Cyberspace: Politics, Technology and Global Restructuring*. London: Routledge.

Lu, J., and Sun, X. (2008) "Xin mei ti zai di fang zhi li zhong de zuo yong: yi Xiamen PX shi jian wei li" [The Role of New Media in Local Governance: A Case Study of Xiamen PX Event], Retrieved 10 June 2008 from: http://academic.mediachina.net/article.php?id=5685.

MacKinnon, R. (2007) "Blogs and China Correspondence: How Foreign Correspondents Covering China Use Blogs". Paper presented at The World Journalism Education Congress, Singapore.

Negroponte, N. (1995) *Being Digital*. New York: Knopf.

Nielsen Mobile (2008) "Critical Mass: The Worldwide State of the Mobile Web", July 2008. Retrieved 10 June 2008 from: http://www.nielsenmobile.com/documents/CriticalMass.pdf.

Qiu, J. L. (2008) "Interview with Manuel Castells", *Chinese Journal of Communication*, 1 (1), pp. 3–6. Retrieved from: http://dx.doi.org/10.1080/17544750701861863.

Shi, F. (2008) "Social Capital at Work: The Dynamics and Consequences of Grassroots Movements in Urban China", *Critical Asian Studies*, 40 (2), pp. 233–62.

Sunstein, C. (2001) *Republic.com*. Princeton: Princeton University Press.

Sunstein, C. (2007) "The Polarization of Extremes", *The Chronicle Review*, 54 (16), p. 9.

Yang, G., and Calhoun C. (2007) "Media, Civil Society, and the Rise of a Green Public Sphere in China", *China Information*, 21 (2), pp. 211–36.

Zheng, Y., and Wu, G. (2005) "Information Technology, Public Space, and Collective Action in China", *Comparative Political Studies*, 38 (5), pp. 507–36.

Zhu H. (2007, May 28) "Xiamen guo duan jiao ting PX ying dui gong gong wei ji" [Xiamen calls an abrupt halt to the PX project to deal with the public crises], *Southern Weekend*. Retrieved 15 June 2007 from: http://www.nanfangdaily.com.cn/southnews/zmzg/200705280624.asp. (English translation can be found at: http://zonaeuropa.com/20070601_1.htm.)

⸨ PART ⸩
IV

Mainstream Journalism

}{ CHAPTER }{
19

Online Journalism: The Changing Media Ecology from an Indian Perspective

SAAYAN CHATTOPADHYAY

This chapter discusses the implications of India's emerging media ecology from two different viewpoints. First, it asks whether the arguably exclusionary forms of communication and limited technological infrastructure available in a developing country are capable of transforming the processes of newsgathering and news dissemination and — assuming they are — considers the impact of such a transformation on specific journalism practices and ideologies. Second, it looks at whether the democratic structure of developing countries such as India can truly accommodate "voices from below" and at how credible these voices are in an openly participatory atmosphere. With special reference to India, as the world's largest democracy, with a colonial past and a thriving media industry, this chapter critically analyses the various issues related to the implications of the emergence of the information society, participatory journalism and the political economy of new media.

Since independence India has undergone an impressive democratic development. The country's constitution, through the granting of assorted rights and freedoms, has helped empower its citizens to engage in this. Developments have ranged from the granting of freedom of the press, albeit via a circuitous route rather than a direct process,[1] to rapid liberalization and its corollary: the information technology boom.[2] Parallel to this, a number of the tensions that exist within Indian journalism are related to the acceptance of the news media as an entirely commercial venture and, more problematically, as a business with a public service aspect. It is a peculiar incongruity, especially in a developing nation, that the "fourth estate" is the only estate of democracy that is increasingly becoming privatized.[3]

In keeping with the corporatization of journalism, Web journalism in India has essentially become an extension of the already established news media business, producing, among other things, market-friendly soft stories and popular syndicated content. With news being treated as a commodity, both online and offline, this has led to the trivialization of serious political and economic matters and the sensationalization of non-newsworthy issues.

This was perhaps inevitable if one considers the trajectory of the media liberalization process and the way it was initiated in India. The move towards a liberal, or neo-liberal, economic policy from the 1980s onwards had its roots in a number of factors, ranging from India's fiscal crisis to the effect of increasing loans from the International Monetary Fund and the World Bank. Gradually, by implementing liberal economic reforms such as the loosening of import–export constraints, the introduction of new currency regulations and the encouragement of private capital and foreign direct investment in the public sector, India emerged as an attractive site for both media conglomerates and existing media entrepreneurs to exploit their already established position. Yet this policy of liberalization did little to protect the interests of the smaller press or local newspaper concerns. As Dipankar Sinha notes:

> The decision to adopt liberal economic reforms was passed in the world's largest democracy by a "minority" government, without any worthwhile debate in the *Lok Sabha*, the lower house of the parliament, composed of elected representatives of the people . . . When the then Prime Minister, Narasimha Rao, referred to the "broad consensus" prevailing in India, he identified the industry and business circles and the media as the repository of such consensus, having made no reference to citizens and civil society organizations. (2005: 143)

This consensus with regard to the liberalization process existed only among the affluent, influential, urban population — the section of the population corresponding to the contemporary socio-economic classes A and B — the major contributors to India's Internet market.[4] Thus while the Internet in general, and Web journalism in particular, has an intrinsically liberating and democratizing capacity, it remains an essentially exclusionary, state-controlled and commercially motivated form of journalism.

THE PERILS OF POST-COLONIAL MEDIA: INFORMATION SOCIETY AND THE DIGITAL DIVIDE

Although the importance of dialogue and discussion has been underlined in the history of many countries in the world, the fact that the Indian subcontinent has a particularly strong commitment to these is worth noting. However, it is important to point out that the denial of such dialogic communication is also a substantial part of Indian history. There are three reasons for this. First, India's nationalistic discourse, preoccupied with creating a homogeneous national identity, was not keen to allow increasingly divergent voices to threaten the integrity of the nation-state during the immediate, post-independence era of nation-building. Second, the state has acted like the patriarch of the collective Indian family, mediating, negotiating and excluding voices through the "tactics of illusion" (Sinha 2005: 147), while increasingly becoming less transparent and more contradictory. The rhetorical link between the family and the nation was a common one during the rise of Indian nationalism during the colonial period and has continued in the post-colonial discourse of the nation-state. The head of the household, commonly the senior male member of the family, commands, intercedes and negotiates with other members of the family. His communication may seem arbitrary, oppressive and exclusionary, but the other family members do not actively resist this, since it is presupposed that he is acting with the greater interests of the family at heart and perhaps for the long-term benefit of family members. This paradigm of communication is analogous to the state's communication with its citizens, which is similarly authoritarian, contradictory and aims to exclude. Third, with liberalization and technological advances, the post-colonial and post-liberalization nation-state's model of communication has often been challenged by alternative/parallel "new media" communications. This is because new media technology offers the possibility of a certain autonomy of production, processing and distribution, which at least has the potential to elude state intervention. Hence the post-liberalization nation-state may attempt to restrict the counter-hegemonic application of the online news media, but it has but little choice other than to act as a facilitator of communications for the emerging consumer-citizens.

The post-colonial Indian state sought to regulate its communications network, primarily because of the paternalistic nature of its post-colonial development. Instead of being citizens' representatives, successive leaders saw themselves as their guardians. They acted in a manner that reflected their view that the power of the state and the power of the people were polar opposites (Sinha 1999: 2233). This binary model led the Indian state to espouse a policy that strove to subsume any divergent antagonism, aggression or protest by the people. And when the democratic consensus of the government was particularly threatened, as happened in mid-1970s, when the Emergency was declared,[5] the state deployed the crudest and most unpredictable methods of suppression and exclusion, which violently suffocated dialogic communication.

On the other hand, while the state has implemented various policies in the "interests of the common people", it has done so unilaterally, without paying much attention to the needs of those whom the policies are meant to benefit (Sinha 1999: 2230). State-controlled communication has barely accommodated voices from below. The state made only a token effort through its traditional forms of communication to reach out to the people "down below", which, if it had been done in a planned and effective manner, might in turn have encouraged greater citizen involvement in the activities of the state. Instead, the majority of citizens have remained silent and inactive in influencing the functioning of the state.

Communications were similarly one-way and centralized until the liberalization phase in India. A number of policies and reforms introduced by the post-independence state and publicized by the traditional print and broadcast media, reflected this inadequate communication, which in turn excluded the disenfranchised. Nevertheless, since liberalization in the 1990s, the Indian nation-state has increasingly operated with a changing market economy and moved somewhat away from a paternalistic role towards that of facilitator. The subsequent development of "Information Communications Technology" (ICT) and the advent of Internet-mediated communication initially suggested the possibility of more democratic communications, but their inherently exclusionary nature soon became clear. The Internet may allow politically disenfranchised groups an alternative medium for communication, dissemination and organization, but those who might have benefited most from a counter-hegemonic use of the new media may well be precisely those who have least access to it (Abbott 2001).

There were various factors behind the development of the IT sector in India, and most of these factors were also influential in the development of India as a potential market. Hence the emergence of a strong service sector and the "informatization of the Indian economy" happened simultaneously. In contemporary India the most glaring evidence of this is in the markedly thriving "outsourcing" or "call centre" sector. There is also little doubt that the skill base necessary for development has existed since the 1980s, primarily owing to public investment in higher education and the creation of elite engineering schools. T. N. Srinivasan points out that "As in the United States, India's IT sector is also concentrated, located in clusters in Bangalore, Chennai, Hyderabad, Mumbai, New Delhi, and Pune. These cities also had the highest concentration of public sector R&D establishments (especially defence) as well as publicly funded engineering colleges" (Srinivasan 2005: 210). This development, intensely regulated by the state, provided for both the simultaneous expansion of the Indian economy, through informatization, and the emergence of a powerful service sector. But from the outset "information" was considered as a "commodity", since informatization was conceived entirely in economic terms. This progressively shaped the course of online journalism in India.

Moreover, both the introduction and development of the Internet in India were essentially different from that in developed countries, especially the US.[6] This has affected the perception of — and, to a certain extent, participation in — online news media. The techno-democratic development of the Internet, diametrically different from the commercialized Internet, has often encouraged a discourse endorsing the democratic sharing of information without barriers in some Western countries (Jayaram 2006: 303). In India, on the other hand, there was no such history, as the Internet, like most other technological innovations, had been "imported" from the West. The Internet, as one would expect, became another component in the market-based economic system that emerged as a result of liberalization. This initial positioning of the new media, confined as they were to the upper-class, upper-caste, urban, English-speaking elite, continues to influence the reception of and access to news content over a decade later.

THE POLITICAL ECONOMY OF THE NEW MEDIA AND WEB JOURNALISM IN INDIA

Communication, as a process, is intrinsically connected to the system of class domination. Economic and technological practices not only establish the cultural superstructure but also incorporate them into pre-existing social relations of power (Murdock 1980: 457). Such a multi-layered relationship between technology-mediated communications and citizen and production relations can be traced in the mediating processes of Web journalism in India.

Indian news media sites can be categorized into four different groups. The first group consists of the sites that are primarily Web extensions of the existing print media publication or news agencies: timesofindia.com, manoramaonline.com, hindustan-times.com, hinduonnet.com, indianexpress.com, tehelka.com and ptinews.com. The second comprises sites that are similar extensions of the recognized news broadcast media: ibnlive.com, ndtv.com, timesnow.tv, zeenews.com and aajtak.com. The third is the purely online news sites, which, besides the Google and Yahoo! India news services, include merinews.com, india-newsbehindnews.com, indiatogether.com and indianews.net. The fourth is the news portals, which are relatively popular in terms of traffic ranking: rediff.com, indiatimes.com, sify.com, oneindia.in, 123india.com and so on.

In the recent past the online news sites of India have managed to emerge from their initial dependence on non-resident Indian (NRI) traffic. Now more than half of the traffic is from India. Nonetheless, online news sites still have to struggle to generate revenue, since they can neither introduce profitable subscription plans, because of the economics of Indian online traffic, nor depend on advertisers. Advertisers' reluctance to include new media in their campaign plans has constricted media sites' revenues and led them to be more dependent on parent companies (Saxena 2007: 275).

Moreover, this dependence of Indian news websites on traditional media, such as print, television or even news agencies, can be attributed to three distinct factors that jointly influence, and are also influenced by, the cultural politics of Indian Web jour-nalism practices.

EXCLUSIVE CONTENT: THE APOLITICAL INDIAN YOUTH AND THE CONSUMER-CITIZEN

It is not surprising that, on average, three-quarters of an Indian news site's content is originally produced for its print version and that the rest is news stories, features, columns and syndicated content delivered from news agencies or sister concerns. Even a couple of years ago there were hardly any news stories reported independently by any Indian news sites. The reason for the dearth of exclusive news stories online in India is that there are few reporters working on online news stories. The Indian online news sites have yet to appoint many reporters to cover stories exclusively for the Web, which would create a significant impact. Moreover, most of the Web's exclusive content eschews hard news and political content and focuses predominantly on entertainment, sports and lifestyle reporting, primarily targeted at young people, who form the major chunk of the growing Internet user-base in India.[7]

Fifty-four percent of all active users of the Internet in India are between the ages of fifteen and twenty-nine (Shrivastava 2007). Almost half of India's population is within this age group, and the country is predicted to lead the world in youth Internet participation by 2010. "It is a demographic gold mine for marketers and a case study in [the] progress of democratic capitalism" (Kohli 2006: 29). However, a recent survey of Indian youth provided a clear indication that email (76 percent) and chat (56 percent) dominate their Internet usage, while a mere 13 percent of them access the Web for news (Kohli 2006: 60). Almost every major consumer goods company is attempting to tap into the world of these emerging young consumer-citizens with their growing purchasing power. News, like any other commodity in this vast Third World developing country, is being "packaged" and "selected" in such a way that it caters to the major market segment of "Youngistaan"[8] — the youth. In the US 52 percent of Internet users said they went online to get news or information about politics. Nationwide surveys also suggest that online consumers of political news grew dramatically from 18 percent of the population in 2000 to 29 percent in 2004 (Rainie, Cornfield and Horrigan 2005). In India, on the other hand, the majority of young people are considered to be absolutely uninterested in the details of politics and social change (Kamat 2005: 339), whether in the online or traditional news media.

As a consequence, the exclusive content on Indian online news sites is mainly soft news and information that cannot always be described as news (Saxena 2007; Jayaram 2006; Businessworld Survey 2006). Items such as photo galleries, special features, film reviews and gossip columns are considerably more popular than the news sections. Thus the "popular" or "amusing" rather than the "newsworthy" is selected to lure more traffic to the site. This not only explains the relative popularity of the news portals over the participatory journalism sites or typical news sites, but it also highlights the basis on which "exclusive news" content is selected on news sites that disregard newsworthiness.

Moreover, there has been an interesting shift in the political activism of Indian youth with the advent of online news sites. A significant number of students do not actually take to the streets now; instead, they demonstrate through online news portals, by registering, forwarding or merely by clicking to vote. Ndtv.com was the first to popularize such "clicktivism", initially through text messaging and later through its website, to garner support for a retrial in the Jessica Lal case.[9] Previously in 2002, in the aftermath of the Gujarat riot,[10] such online petitions, blogs and special online reports, which could not be published in the mainstream media, were published online. "Clicktivism" or "blogtivism", in support of political or social issues, is primarily an urban-centric phenomenon and may prove to be successful within a clearly defined upper-class, urban population. Yet it is predominantly an elite pastime, in contrast to more inclusive, across-the-board, political or social activism (Abbott 2001: 111). The impulse of the young, urban, consumer-citizens of India to "do something", without actually doing anything, is thus exploited by interactive news sites. As one veteran Indian journalist and author notes: "The Indian elites now have one more avenue to engage without getting their hands dirty" (Jayaram 2006: 307).

The Problem of Access: Vernacular Language and the Spiral of Silence

India has the largest English-speaking population in the world, with more than 350 million people able to carry on a conversation in English (Crystal 2004). But they are predominantly based in the major metropolitan areas, while 72 percent of the population reside in rural areas. Also, the rural literacy rate in India is 58.7 percent, compared with 79.9 percent in urban areas (Census India 2001). As a majority of the content (including news) accessible over the Internet is in English, familiarity with English acts as a major factor driving Internet usage — confining it to urban centres. Therefore, other than technological factors, the major limitation in accessing the Internet for news hinges on language. India, being home to about twenty-two regional languages, is, as yet, unable to provide the necessary infrastructure and accessibility to hardware and software for people to use the Internet and computers effortlessly in regional vernacular languages. Consequently, online journalism in India cannot accommodate regional-language journalists, who ideally might have provided exclusive local news stories from different parts of such a multilingual, multi-ethnic subcontinent. If one looks at the contemporary print media, the National Readership Survey (NRS 2006) reveals that there is not a single English-language newspaper in the list of the top ten daily newspapers circulated in India. Recent developments in page design software have made regional-language integration easier than in the past, but, as Jayaram notes:

> the delivery mechanisms still prove a huge barrier because of the inability to transfer and download language fonts with the same ease as English . . . and given the fact that most users typically use a public outlet such as a cyber café or office computer, where time spent online is expensive, the upshot of such delays is to prevent further attempts. (2006: 309)

Over the years the number of Internet users from non-metropolitan areas and small towns has increased steadily — from 5 percent to 29 percent in the last five years (Shrivastava 2007). However, only 15 to 31 percent of users use the Internet to seek information. How much of that "information" constitutes "news" is a critical qualitative issue, since development communication perhaps maintains a very thin line between what is considered as pure "information" and "news". The social structure of developing countries such as India, with its significant economic and social inequity and ethno-linguistic diversity, makes technology-aided dialogic communication difficult (Sen 2006: 75). Dialogic communication, through interactive online news sites, is possible if people have access to the media. But in developing nations people have limited or no access to such media. With only 1.2 percent Internet penetration in rural India (JuxtConsult 2008), the rural and small-town population constitutes a minority — a situation that is reinforced by the role of language, literacy, society, economics and even, in some cases, caste and religion. It becomes a vicious circle of inadequate access, as this minority status isolates the people, who fall into a "spiral of silence" (Noelle-Neumann 1993). And their preferences, views and interests, in operating and getting involved in a participatory dialogic communication through online news and information sites, are ignored.

THE CREDIBILITY ISSUE: DEPROFESSIONALIZATION FOR THE SUBVERSION OF DOMINANT IDEOLOGY

Credibility research has suggested a strong correlation between the perceived credibility of a medium and the use of that medium. If people do not trust the medium, they are less likely to pay attention to its contents (Gaziano 1988: 267). News sources that are needed to fulfil the requirements of "objective reporting", ostensibly linked to credibility, are usually drawn from existing power structures and therefore tend to support the status quo. Belief in objectivity in journalism is not just a claim about what kind of knowledge is reliable but clearly points to a direction of thinking that journalists are expected to engage in (Narrain 2007: 49). Consequently, the Indian media as an ideological state apparatus form a critical aspect of such traditional gatekeeping, given that disparate ideologies and values are struggling for dominance. In this context the issue of the credibility of Web journalism relates to whether or not the online news site is affiliated to or associated with any traditional, mainstream news medium. There is thus a vicious circle, where the alternative, subversive new media, epitomized by Web journalism and blogging, require backing by the same mainstream, traditional media, which reinforce the dominant power relations that the new media are struggling to subvert both ideologically and contextually.

The paradox of credibility became apparent when, in 1975, Indira Gandhi, the then prime minister of India, said in her characteristic forthright manner that "she did not understand what the concept of 'credibility' implied, since there was no doubt that AIR [All India Radio] was a department of [the] government and would remain so" (Chatterjee 1991: 106). The nation-state, obsessed with possessing and controlling such traditional print and broadcasting communication sectors and, at the same time, refusing to expand the "new" and alternative communication network, provides an interesting paradox. With Indira Gandhi's "straightforward" manner being replaced in contemporary times by a false devotion to media autonomy, the state of affairs has changed very little (Sinha 1999: 2232).[11] The most popular websites of Indian online news and media[12] (rediff.com, ibnlive.com, ndtv.com, hindustantimes.com, hinduonnet.com, mid-day.com and indiatimes.com) all publish news stories sourced from the national and international news agencies, such as the Press Trust of India (PTI), Asian News International (ANI), Indo-Asian News Service (IANS) and the established print media. Moreover, all the above-mentioned leading news sites, with the exception of rediff.com, are associated with successful offline media enterprises with a stake in both print and broadcasting.[13] The much-hyped notion that the new media provide some sort of alternative or substitute to the traditional media, which reflect the dominant political and social ideologies, remains a distant dream. This is because, as we have seen, the major Indian news sites are either online avatars of the print version, or most of their news stories are sourced from mainstream news agencies.

It is not surprising that empirical data have established that age and education have a negative effect on the perceived credibility of Internet news (Robinson and Kohut 1988: 174–89). The ideological state apparatus reinforces cynicism towards news and information sourced from outside the ambit of the established mainstream media enterprises. The credibility stemming purely from the news reports covered by "professional" journalists involved in traditional offline reporting becomes problematic for the very notion of online journalism. Perhaps in this transitional phase in the evolution of a developing country like India, it is only by deprofessionalizing journalistic practices that the basis will be provided for news content to be produced without the hegemonic restrictions of a nation-state, global market economy or ideologically motivated editorial policy. This is because only with this does it becomes less problematic properly to integrate citizen journalists, local stringers and dedicated Web reporters. Yet, in contrast, India has seen an upsurge of private and self-financed graduate, vocational and certificate courses in various facets of journalism and media. These institutionalize journalistic practices and reinstate a professionalization of journalism that refuses to acknowledge the altering notions of journalism and journalists (Muppidi 2007).

ALTERING NOTIONS OF JOURNALISM: CITIZEN AS JOURNALIST AND JOURNALIST AS CITIZEN

Reporting on the multi-party system in India, as opposed to the bipolar political formation that exists in many other countries, generally results in fragmented, often oblique, news reports in the traditional print media. Interestingly, some of the local language dailies in Hindi, Bengali, Gujarati, Marathi and other languages that engage in explicitly partisan journalism often enjoy a steady and substantial regional circulation. But the reports published in them are often contested by opposition parties. Such debates are facilitated by online journalism. This is because it is much easier to provide pluralism and to negotiate contradictions online than in the traditional media, which do not have the space to incorporate analysis, backgrounders and research reports and where there are technological limits on embedding multimedia content. Instead of readers following only the reporter's account, Huesca and Dervin (2003) note that the use of hypertexts in online reporting embraces notions of contradiction, fragmentation, juxtaposition and pluralism rather than pursuing the single "truth" that is at the centre of the traditional journalistic enterprise. Conceivably, online journalism is an ideal platform for democratic and credible communication in a country such as India, since the citizens are vested with far more power than in a traditional media scenario, allowing them to challenge established gatekeepers (Beckette and Mansell 2008; Jarvis 2007; Jayaram 2006; Bardoel 1996). The online tools and the nature of the medium itself provide options for the reader to "look over the shoulder" of the reporter by researching the original documents and easily comparing one reporter's story with those of others, by scanning news publications and archives throughout the country (Harper 2000).

In undermining the hierarchy of socio-economic strata of caste, class, language and gender — notwithstanding the restrictions previously discussed — the Internet provides a form of communication where initiating or getting engaged in a public discourse regarding any issue, even in a country like India, is far less difficult and faces little or no control by the authorities. It becomes a podium where ordinary citizens can become journalists and where journalists can write as ordinary citizens. This fairly new trend of "citizen journalism" or "participatory journalism" became popular among the traditional print and broadcast media and, more importantly, online news sites in India after the devastating Asian tsunami in 2004.[14]

Initially, citizen journalists from the Indian subcontinent contributed reports, photographs and information about natural disasters only when it was extremely difficult for the reporters to be "on the spot". Gradually, as the popularity of the trend increased, citizen reports on local and specific issues, ranging from traffic problems and environmental issues to festival celebrations and communal riots, have been regularly published in the "citizen journalism" sections of the major online news sites. Citizens with no prior journalistic training have, to some extent, de-professionalized journalistic practice — but only "to some extent", because the association with established media conglomerates rather nullifies the decentralized, egalitarian and libratory thrust of participatory journalism.

In contrast to "citizen reports" in mainstream news portals, blogging seems to be capable of absorbing comfortably the tenets of democratic participatory journalism. Independent blog sites are increasingly emerging as a platform for citizen reporters, while mainstream news portals in India are also integrating blogs, albeit primarily as a mere extension of the conventional "Letters to the Editor" section.

Nevertheless, despite having the potential to do so, independent blog sites in India are reluctant to tackle political, governmental and economic issues. A recent survey of some most popular blogs (Kohli 2006: 61) showed that most follow the familiar penchant for trivializing and downplaying serious political, economical concerns and instead focus largely on entertainment and humorous news. But perhaps to expect a serious journalistic approach from blog sites is to confuse form and content, as may become clear if we look at the phenomenon of celebrity blogging in India.

In the last couple of years India, with the world's largest film industry,[15] has witnessed an unprecedented expansion of celebrity blogging. As well as connecting with the fans, almost all celebrities seem to use their blogs to repudiate and belittle their critics and, above all, as a marketing strategy for their films and to bolster their own image. Moreover, putting sensational and controversial comments on their blogs ensures that they remain in the headlines. Whatever the purpose of the celebrity blog is, what is interesting is that, increasingly, these blogs are becoming sources for mainstream media news — perhaps because of their inherent credibility, since they are supposedly written by the actors themselves. Even on the political front in India, politicians from almost every party are increasingly exploring the blog as an add-on marketing ploy to sell their image. Whether it is Bollywood or politics, it needs to be clear that celebrity blogs and blogging by prominent politicians do not constitute journalism *per se*; rather, they may serve as a more credible source for journalists. Consequently, blogging may never pose a direct threat to journalism, but it may considerably transform the ways in which news is gathered and commented on. As Rajeev Masand (cited by Ray 2008), a journalist and film critic with ibnlive.com, observes, the significance of celebrity blogging is that it will, over time, transform the practice of film journalism.

The notion of participatory media becomes more complicated when we recognize that mainstream journalists are also citizens, who normally surrender their individual right to freedom of expression as a condition of employment at most newspapers. In the Indian blogging sphere it is noteworthy that a number of journalists have started publishing their own independent blogs (Indibloggies 2006), which engage in analysing news stories from various perspectives, generally with a strongly humorous undercurrent. In addition to this, mainstream online news sites also include blogging sections featuring their prominent reporters, generally with a note in small letters at the end of the page declaring that the content posted should be considered as the views and opinions only of the employees and not of the media corporation.[16] In reality, it would be misleading to think that these integrated blog sections by prominent journalists represent democratic pluralism in online journalism. Rather, none of the blog sections operates without gatekeeping.

The author of Mediaah Weblog, Pradyuman Maheshwari, who became the editor of the leading daily the *Maharashtra Herald* in 2003, gained worldwide attention when *The Times of India* threatened to bring a libel action against him. This was supposedly for offending the newspaper in his blog (Maheshwari 2005). This reflects an attempt to restrict the individual freedom of journalists online; restrictive codes of journalistic ethics may essentially eliminate from public discourse the most informed and eloquent voices of the citizenry — the professional journalists (Hulteng 1981: 30). Loosening restrictions on journalistic activism would have broader implications for the institutional functioning of the press. This could encourage both political and sociological diversity among journalists (Isralowitz 1992: 223). Therefore journalists, irrespective of the medium, should be given more liberty to explore their individuality as citizens, both within their profession and beyond.

CONCLUSION

The naïve faith that new technology will prove to be a panacea for the developing nations by democratizing communications while enhancing social responsibility is based on an undesirable homogenization of citizens. It also undermines the critical positioning of new media practices within production relations, which has continually to negotiate with the market-oriented global economy.

Within the changing media ecology, the reality of people's fear and reluctance to use the innovative tools of new media communication encourages us to question any celebration of "pull" technology against the "push" technology of the traditional media.[17] Operating such sophisticated applications to extract the true potentiality of online news/information sites requires skills that go beyond mere literacy and needs to take into account language, age, gender and a whole range of cognitive and technical competencies. Therefore, simply making available the tools of communication is not enough. Without the ability to operate such tools, their potential becomes untapped. This pull-capability consideration questions the technotopian notion of the information society.

As a lot of research shows, even after acknowledging all of these limitations of a

299

developing nation, the changing media ecology must not just aim to "install" such new modes of journalistic practice mediated by new technology. Instead, the changing journalistic practices must be organically "integrated" into the existing newsgathering and news delivery processes. In the light of increasingly liberal economic policies promulgated by the Indian government, it is sensible to speculate that cross-media ownership will benefit from the integration of online journalism within the traditional news media organizations.[18] This integration may prove to be one of the various initial ways of normalizing the Internet for more traditional activities in a country such as India, which is more comfortable with the notion of developing an alternative indigenous modernity.[19]

The notion of a journalist must also become more inclusive, to accommodate "prosumer" citizens. A lucrative category for media corporations, such prosumer citizens, with the aid of the emerging new media, may "produce" and "consume" media content. The hybrid, shifting identity of the prosumer encapsulates the fundamental nature of online journalism: a hybrid medium, which may provide the largest growth among the new media in the coming decades (Tunstall 2007: 274).

This fundamental transformation of the media ecology of a developing nation such as India poses some crucial questions regarding modernity and tradition. The legacy of modernity, based on standardization, essentially produces an assortment of trends aiming to become hegemonic, ranging from reductionist professionalism and commodification of news to ideological bigotry and socio-linguistic exclusion. This is the dilemma of this transitional phase, where the traditional binaries of journalism and journalists have collapsed. India has a somewhat curious political economy of news media, with its colonial past and rapid post-independent liberalization policy, highly hierarchical socio-economic strata and a powerful film and television industry — a major player in the regional media economy and also a large exporter of media content. These features essentially exacerbate the quandary in which this paternalistic nation-state finds itself in seeking a middle ground between "public service broadcasting" policies and commercial objectives. However, technology can never be neutral, and the notion of plurality may never entirely accommodate totality. Therefore, if such new media are substituting traditional journalism with modernity, that modernity will remain genuinely ambivalent, as Partha Chatterjee (1997) remarks:

> this ambiguity does not stem from any uncertainty about whether to be for or against modernity. Rather, the uncertainty is because we know that to fashion the forms of our modernity, we need to have the courage at times to reject the modernities established by others.

Notes

1   Freedom of the press was one of the constitutional guarantees persistently demanded by India's freedom fighters during British colonial rule. Surprisingly, freedom of the press is not explicitly mentioned in the chapter on 'Fundamental Rights' in the Indian Constitution. In a series of decisions from 1950s onwards, the Supreme Court of India has ruled that freedom of the press is implicit in the guarantee of freedom of speech and expres-

sion in Article 19(1)(a) of the Constitution. Thus there is constitutional status for freedom of the press.

2   India's record of sustained growth since 1980 is second only to China among large economies. In global trade in commercial services, which includes trade in information-technology-enabled services (ITES) and business process outsourcing (BPO), India has emerged as a major player. The total exports of the Indian IT sector in 2007 were worth $31.4 billion. By 2010 the Indian IT sector is expected to reach an export target of $60 billion.

3   According to the Registrar of Newspapers for India, out of 8,512 newspapers registered in 2005–6, as many as 6,686 were owned by individuals, 1,122 by joint stock companies, 260 by societies and associations, 222 by trusts and 150 by firms and partnerships. In comparison, central and state governments produced 41 newspapers. Co-operative societies, educational institutions and the like owned the remaining 31 (Registrar of Newspapers 2008). Similarly, the broadcasting sector, with an impressive 53 percent growth in cable and satellite connection, is predominantly in the private domain.

4   Socio-economic classification indicates the affluence level of a household to which an individual belongs. Socio-economic classification of an urban household is defined by the education and occupation of the chief wage-earner of a household. The classification is divided into eight categories: A1, A2, B1, B2, C, D, E1 and E2 (in decreasing order of affluence).

5   India's most terrible encounter with censorship occurred during the Emergency, declared by the Prime Minister, Indira Gandhi, on 25 June 1975. Censorship of the press was imposed for the first time in independent India by the circulation of a Central Censorship Order, dated 26 June 1975. Taking advantage of the Emergency, numerous repressive measures were adopted in the form of executive non-statutory guidelines and instructions issued by the censor to the press. One of the instructions of the censor was that "nothing is to be published that is likely to convey the impression of a protest or disapproval of a government measure". See Sorabjee 1977).

6   In the 1960s the initial users in the US were primarily researchers, academicians, librarians and students. Not only did they technically develop the communication network, but they also laid the groundwork for a decentralized communication network, which provided the possibility of escaping state control while connecting individuals, enabling them to share information without negotiating with the state. In other words, there was an ideal democratic information-sharing system, though directly funded by the government. From the early 1990s, when independent commercial networks began to grow, this marked a significant shift since commercial uses were initially prohibited unless they served the objectives of research and education directly (Howe 2007).

7   The arguments are based on my personal communication with the sub-editor and correspondents of kolkatamirror.com, the leading news and information portal from the Times Group (BCCL).

8   The recent nationwide advertising campaign from Pepsi features the long-time brand ambassador the film star Shah Rukh Khan, along with two debutant actors. Pepsi, primarily to reinvent itself to cater to young India, have come up with a new term, "Youngistaan". This is a portmanteau word (combining "young" + "Hindustan"), which encapsulates, along with globalization and consumerism, a common trend among urban Indian youth to adopt a "Hinglish" dialect — a colloquial mix of Hindi and English..

9   Initially, the Delhi court acquitted all nine accused, including Manu Sharma, the son of

former Union minister Vinod Sharma, in the case of the murder of model Jessica Lal in a restaurant in April 1999. The courts did ultimately order a retrial, but whether the online petitions made any material difference remains unclear.

10 In 2002 a violent riot took place in Gujarat in the aftermath of the Godhara carnage, where more than 50 people, mostly Hindu, were burnt to death in the coach of a train that had been attacked by a Muslim mob. The resulting collective communal violence left 2,000 people dead. A large number of women were raped, children were orphaned or became lost and others were brutally wounded or are still missing. The media coverage of the Gujarat riot was highly controversial. The media were banned within the state of Gujarat as they spoke up against the state government and the chief minister, Narendra Modi. The Indian media were accused of provoking the violence with their coverage. The online news media played a crucial role in publishing reports and news stories that were severely critical of the government. For further discussion of this see *Gujarat Carnage: The Aftermath* (http://www.onlinevolunteers.org/gujarat/).

11 This "false devotion" is reflected in the functioning of Prasar Bharati, the supposed autonomous broadcasting corporation of India, which has an extensive record of controlling and censoring media content. Likewise, the more recent and highly debated Broadcast Bill has imposed a number of regulating and restrictive legislative sanctions.

12 The ranking is based on the alexa.com ranking, retrieved on 7 June 2008.

13 ibnlive.com is a venture of Network 18, which owns TV news channels such as CNN IBN, IBN7, CNBC TV18, CNBC Awaz and IBN Lokmat. ndtv.com is a venture of NDTV Convergence Ltd, which owns news channels such as NDTV 24X7, NDTV Profit and NDTV India. hindustantimes.com is owned and managed by HT Media Ltd, which also owns the daily newspapers the *Hindustan Times*, *Mint* and *Hindustan*.

14 Backgrounders provide more detailed background information or history, either to substantiate the report or to offer an even more comprehensive insight into the issue.

15 According to merinews.com, which has claimed to be India's first citizen journalism news portal: "India as the world's largest democracy . . . sets forth newer challenges for us as a nation, towards building a responsible society. The evolution of technology and emergence of new modes of communication add bigger dimensions to this daunting task . . . Thus People to People (P2P) interaction is of paramount importance and rather inevitable . . . www.merinews.com is an effort to provide one such platform to interact and express. It is a news platform for collective wisdom 'of the people, by the people, for the people'" (merinews.com 2004).

16 The Indian film industry is the world's largest film producer, with 1,041 films produced in 2005 (CBFC 2006). Popularly but incorrectly identified simply as Bollywood ("Bombay" + "Hollywood"), in reality it includes several regional film industries in south and east India, along with low-budget film industries in other provinces, along with a leading Hindi film segment.

17 For instance, the popular blog section of CNN-IBN site notes: "All the content posted in the 'IBN Blogs' section, unless specified otherwise, are made by CNN-IBN employees. The content posted in 'IBN Blogs' does not follow routine internal CNN-IBN reviews and editorial processes and should be considered only as the views and opinions of the employees and not of CNN-IBN" (IBN Blogs, 2008). A similar disclaimer is published in almost all the other blog section of mainstream news sites.

18 "Pull" here refers to a reader's or viewer's efforts to pull in news or information according to his or her requirements with the help of new media technology, as opposed to the "push"

technology of the traditional media, which pushes the news or information irrespective of the reader's or viewer's needs or receptivity.

19 Examples of such cross-media ownership in India are those of Bennett, Coleman & Co. Ltd, popularly known as The Times Group, Living Media India and Network18. These are a few of India's foremost media conglomerates with interests in television, radio, print, the Internet, filmed entertainment, mobile content and allied businesses.

20 Partha Chatterjee notes: "The formulation of the nationalist project, as an ideological justi-fication for the selective appropriation of Western modernity, continues to hold sway to this day." The notion of Indian modernity hinges on the dichotomy of material/spiritual, inner/outer or alien/indigenous. As Chatterjee explains: "[F]orms of western modernity were put through a nationalist sieve and only selectively adopted, and then combined with the reconstituted elements of what was claimed to be indigenous tradition" (1997). This argument can be extended to the post-independence and post-liberalization discourse on Indian development and national modernity to question some of the significant cultural and social transformations, including the changing notions of journalistic practice.

References

Abbott, Jason. (2001) "Democracy@Internet.Asia? The Challenges to the Emancipatory Potential of the Net: Lessons from China and Malaysia", *Third World Quarterly*, 22 (1), p. 111.

Bardoel, J. L. H. (1996) "Beyond Journalism: A Profession between Information Society and Civil Society", *European Journal of Communication*, 11 (3).

Beckett, C., and Mansell, R. (2008) "Crossing Boundaries: New Media and Networked Journalism", *Communication, Culture & Critique*, 92 (104).

Census India (2001) Retrieved 15 June 2008 from: http://www.censusindia.gov.in/Census_Data_2001/India_at_glance/rural.aspx.

Chatterjee, P. C. (1991) *Broadcasting in India*. New Delhi: Sage.

Chatterjee, P. (1997) "Our Modernity". In *South-South Exchange Programme for Research on the History of Development (SEPHIS) and the Council for the Development of Social Science Research in Africa (CODESRIA)* (Rotterdam/Dakar, 1997). Retrieved 2 November 2007 from: http://www.sephis.org/pdf/partha1.pdf.

Crystal, D. (2004) "Subcontinent Raises Its Voice", *The Guardian*, 19 November 2004. Retrieved 22 May 2008 from: http://education.guardian.co.uk/tefl/story/0,,1355064,00.html.

Gaziano, C. (1988) "How Credible is the Credibility Crisis?", *Journalism Quarterly*, 65 (summer), pp. 267–8.

Harper, C. (2000) "Journalism in a Digital Age". Retrieved 9 February 2008 from: http://web.mit.edu/comm-forum/papers/harper.html.

Horrigan, J., and Rainie, L. (2003) "Counting on the Internet". Retrieved 2 March 2008 from: http://www.pewinternet.org/pdfs/PIP_Expectations.pdf.

Howe, Walter (2007) "A Brief History of the Internet". Retrieved 5 March 2008 from: http://www.walthowe.com/navnet/history.html.

Huesca, R., and Dervin, B. (2003) "Hypertext and Journalism: Audiences Respond to Competing News Narratives". In H. Jenkins, and D. Thorburn (eds), *Democracy and New Media*. Cambridge, MA: MIT Press.

Hulteng, J. L. (1981) *Playing It Straight: A Practical Discussion of the Ethical Principles of the American Society of Newspaper Editors*. Guilford, CT: Globe Pequot Press.

Indibloggies (2006) "Best Blog Sites". Retrieved 21 February 2008 from: http://myjavaserver.com/~indibloggies/ib06/Tally2006.html.

IBN Blogs (2008) "Disclaimer". Retrieved 9 August 2008 from: http://ibnlive.in.com/blogs/.

Isralowitz, Jason P. (1992) "The Reporter as Citizen: Newspaper Ethics and Constitutional Values", *University of Pennsylvania Law Review*, 141 (1), pp. 221–81.

Jarvis, J. (2007) "Networked Journalism". Retrieved 19 July 2007 from: http://www.buzzmachine.com/2006/07/05/networked-journalism/.

Jayaram, M. (2006) "News and the Digital Divide". In A. Mathur, *The Indian Media: Illusion, Delusion and Reality.* New Delhi: Rupa & Co.

Juxt Consult (2008) "India Online: Annual Syndicated Research on Internet Usage in India". Retrieved 8 August 2008 from: http://www.ibef.org/download/JuxtConsultIndiaOnline.pdf.

Kamat, A. (2005) "Youth and The Indian Media". In N. Rajan, *Practicing Journalism.* New Delhi: Sage.

Kohli, V. (2006) "The Mind of India's Youth", *Business World*, 26 (24), p. 29.

Maheshwari, P. (2005) "Operation Intimidation: Media Biggie Sends Mediaah! Legal Notice. Asks Us to Delete 19 Posts and Stop Defaming It". Retrieved 8 June 2008 from: http://mediaah.blogspot.com.

Muppidi, Sundeep R. (2007) "Relevance of Journalism Education in India", *Global Media Journal* (winter).

Murdock, G. (1980) "Misrepresenting Media Sociology", *Sociology*, 14, pp. 457–68.

Narrain, S. (2007) "The Problem with Media Reportage of Queer Lives". In N. Rajan (ed.), *21st Century Journalism in India.* New Delhi: Sage.

National Readership Survey (2006) conducted by National Readership Studies Council, India, constituted by: the Advertising Agencies Association of India, the Audit Bureau of Circulations and the Indian Newspaper Society.

Noelle-Neumann, E. (1993) *The Spiral of Silence: Public Opinion – Our Social Skin.* Chicago: University of Chicago Press.

Rainie, L., Cornfield, M., and Horrigan, J. (2005) "The Internet and Campaign 2004". Retrieved 23 May 2007 from: http://www.pewinternet.org/pdfs/PIP_2004_Campaign.pdf.

Ray, I. (2008) "Elo Blogger Morlo Reporter" [The Birth of the Blogger and the Death of the Reporter], *Anandabazar Patrika*, 14 June, p. 27.

Registrar of Newspapers for India (2008) "General Review". Retrieved 16 November 2008 from: https://rni.nic.in/pii.asp.

Robinson, M., and Kohut, A. (1988) "Believability and the Press", *Public Opinion Quarterly*, 52(2), pp. 174–89.

Saxena, S. (2007) "Online Journalism in India: 2000 to 2005 and Beyond". In N. Rajan (ed.), *21st Century Journalism in India.* New Delhi: Sage.

Sen, A. (2006) *The Argumentative Indian: Writings on Indian History, Culture and Identity.* India: Penguin.

Shrivastava, B. (2007) "I Cube 2007 Summary Report". Internet and Mobile Association of India. Retrieved 11 February 2008 from: http://www.iamai.in/Upload/Research/I-Cube-2007-Summary-Report-final.pdf.

Sinha, D. (1999) "Indian Democracy: Exclusion and Communication", *Economic and Political Week*, 34 (32), pp. 2230–35.

Sinha, D. (2005) "Information Society as if Communication Mattered: The Indian State Revisited". In B. Bel, J. Brouwer, B. Das, V. Parthasarathi,, and G. Poitevin (eds),

Communication Process, vol. 1: *Media and Mediation*. India: Sage Publication.

Sorabjee, S. J. (1977) *The Emergency Censorship and the Press in India, 1975–77*. New Delhi: Central News Agency (Pvt.) Ltd.

Srinivasan, T. N. (2005) "Information Technology Enabled Services and India's Growth Prospects". In L. Brainard, and S. Collins (eds), *Offshoring White Collar Work: The Issues and Implications*. Washington, DC: The Brookings Trade Forum.

Tunstall, J. (2007) *The Media Were American: U.S. Media in Decline*. New York: Oxford University Press.

❴❴ CHAPTER ❵❵
20

Let's Talk: How Blogging is Shaping the BBC's Relationship with the Public

ALFRED HERMIDA

Auntie, as the BBC is affectionately known, has been Britain's national instrument of broadcasting since its creation in the 1920s (Blumler 1992). Over its eighty-year history it has earned "a place in hearts and minds of British viewers and listeners by being a great cultural institution, a patron and purveyor of information, education and popular entertainment" (Grade, quoted in Barnett and Curry 1994: 5). Yet it has grappled with the issue of accountability. This chapter examines how the world's largest journalism organization, BBC News, has sought to incorporate blogging as a platform for greater accountability and transparency. This research spans seven years, from 2001 to 2008, when the BBC came under intense scrutiny over its editorial and ethical standards. After a period of experimentation with elements of blogging and an internal debate over the role of blogging in its journalism, the BBC launched its first blog in December 2005. Within a year, the number of blogs across the corporation had risen to fifty (Hamman 2006).

THE ROLE OF BLOGS

Blogs are of particular interest to researchers in the field of online journalism, as they are unique to the Web and provide an example of how the established media adapts to a new context (Matheson 2004). While blogging developed largely outside the mainstream, traditional media has increasingly adopted the blog format. Research shows that 95 percent of the top 100 newspapers in the United States offered at least one reporter blog in 2007, up from 80 percent in 2006 (Duran 2007). There has been a similar expansion of blogging in the British news media, with the number of blogs at the leading newspaper websites jumping to 118 in 2006 from seven in 2005 (Hermida and Thurman 2008).

Scholars contend that new media technologies such as blogs have the potential to change the way news is covered and reported (Barnhurst and Nerone 2001; Singer 2001). Advocates argue that bloggers are changing journalism by adopting a more conversational and decentralized form of news (Delwiche 2005; Sullivan 2004) and offering multiple, subjective perspectives in contrast to the institutional nature of news (Bruns 2005; Gallo 2004; Haas 2005). Scholars have begun to contend that new forms of journalism could emerge online (Landow 1997; Murray 1997; Wall 2005). Some, such as Gillmor (2004), have suggested that blogging can alter the nature of the relationship between journalists and audiences by creating a conversation between them. Scholars contend that transparency between the news industry and the audience can lead to a more equal and communicative relationship between the two (Andrews 2003; Singer 2003).

Blogs have been described as "evidence of journalism's attempts to rethink its values and relations with its publics" (Matheson 2004: 462). Historically, journalists have been reticent about letting the public see the inner workings of the profession, while at the same time holding others to account. There is some evidence to suggest that the mainstream media are experimenting with the blog format as a way of providing an insight into internal editorial discussions (Glaser 2004). However there are also indications that established media are seeking to normalize this emergent format within existing practices. Singer (2005) suggests that journalists are normalizing blogs by maintaining a traditional gatekeeper function, while others consider that "news organisations may be more interested in containing and directing the blogging phenomenon than in fostering democratic participation" (Lowrey 2006: 493).

ACCOUNTABILITY AT THE BBC

Accountability is one of the three public principles on which the BBC, as a publicly funded organization, is based: "Collective ownership confers on the British public the right of collective accountability and the power to monitor the performance and guide the future of the BBC through their civic institutions" (BBC 2004: 7). Despite a mandate to be accountable, the broadcaster is often described as a "bloated monolith" (Birt 2002) bearing "traces of its monopolistic origins" (Kung-Shankleman 2003). It has been accused of being culturally elitist and centralist throughout its existence (Born 2002), and branded by critics as complacent, poorly managed and lacking in entrepreneurial spirit (Blumler 1992). Senior BBC executives have acknowledged the corporation's struggle with openness:

> It's hardly something the BBC's famous for. Even our nicest buildings tend to have a slightly fortress-like quality, and I don't need a pile of research to know that the BBC can seem fairly impenetrable sometimes to both public and producers alike. (Keating 2008)

307

The roots of its relationship with the public lie in the elitist philosophy of the BBC's first director general, John Reith, who saw broadcasting as a social, cultural, educational and moral force (Born 2004). Early examples of audience interaction were symptomatic of the paternalistic tone associated with the broadcaster (Kung-Shankleman 2000). Initiatives in the 1990s largely took the form of a series of official statements that Born (2002) contends were less about listening to the public and more about shoring up the BBC's legitimacy. Pressure over the issue of accountability has increased in the new millennium, as the notion of a public service broadcaster has come under strain due to commercial competition, audience fragmentation, political disengagement and alternative digital delivery platforms (Born 2002; Enli 2008; Lee-Wright 2008).

BBC journalism, one of the foundations of the corporation's public service remit, came under strain following the Hutton inquiry into BBC reports about the British government's dossier about Iraq's "weapons of mass destruction". BBC Director General Mark Thompson described the Hutton inquiry as "the biggest crisis in BBC journalism's 80-year history" (Thompson, quoted in Douglas 2005). Policy documents speak of a need to "recapture the full trust of audiences and participants in BBC journalism" (BBC 2004: 12) and report that this trust "must be earned, day in and day out" (BBC 2004: 32) and that the "days of deference towards, or paternalism from, the BBC are over — or should be" (Bridcut 2007). It was considered that "Audiences know almost as much about the decision-making process as the broadcasters" (Bridcut 2007: 74), leading the BBC to conclude that greater openness would be necessary for "the maintenance of the audience's trust" (Bridcut 2007: 75). This chapter contends that the changing nature of the BBC's relationship with the audience created an environment that encouraged the rapid growth of blogging at the BBC, specifically as a platform for greater openness and transparency in its journalism.

METHODOLOGY

This study is based on an analysis of documentary evidence surrounding the BBC's adoption of blogs covering the period from 2001 to 2008. These include publicly available official documents produced by the UK government and documentation produced by the BBC and its governing body, the BBC Trust. The author also had access to BBC journalists' own internal documents on blogging strategy from 2005 and 2006. BBC News online sources (including the BBC News website and the BBC blog network from 2001 to the present) provided much of the documentary material for this study. The research also draws on the personal blogs of BBC editors and senior journalists who played a role in the development of blogging at the corporation. These blogs exist outside the technical framework of the BBC's Internet infrastructure and, as such, allow for multiple personal perspectives on the topic.

The documentary evidence is complemented by six asynchronous qualitative interviews that took place in non-real time using email. This involved sending out a list of questions to journalists, editors and senior executives selected for their involvement in drawing up and implementing the BBC's blogging strategy. These were:

- Rory Cellan-Jones, BBC technology correspondent
- Pete Clifton, former editor, BBC News website
- Robin Hamman, former head, BBC Blogs Network
- Steve Herrmann, editor, BBC News website
- Nick Reynolds, editor, BBC Internet Blog
- Giles Wilson, editor, BBC News blogs.

Email interaction is not comparable to verbal interaction, but scholars have argued it may alleviate some of the interpersonal problems commonly associated with conventional interviewing techniques (see Roberts et al. 1997; Spender 1995; Thach 1995).

THE DEVELOPMENT OF BLOGS AT THE BBC

BBC political editor Nick Robinson launched the corporation's first official blog in December 2005 (Robinson 2005). This was the first "real" BBC blog, run on blogging software and offering the format's key capabilities, such as the ability to comment in real time on a post. But BBC News had been experimenting with ideas drawn from blogging for some years. As early as 2001, the BBC News website described a political column as a weblog (BBC 2001), even though it lacked many of the features commonly associated with blogging. Other early experiments included coverage of the US 2004 presidential election (Anderson 2004) and the UK 2005 general election (BBC 2005). However the technical constraints of the Web publishing system the BBC used limited the capabilities of these initiatives.

Senior editors at the BBC News website had editorial concerns about presenting BBC content alongside contributions from the audience (Nixon 2008). The adoption of blogs at the BBC, and within its news operations specifically, took place against a background of institutional tension (Hermida 2008), summed up in this observation from Robin Hamman, a BBC producer who led the blogging initiative between 2006 and 2007:

> The idea of blogging — and by blogging I mean fully engaging in the use of blogs as a technique, not just as a technology — can, on the face of things, sit awkwardly alongside some of the BBC's editorial values: truth and accuracy, impartiality and diversity of opinion, editorial integrity and independence, serving the public interest, fairness, and privacy. (Hamman 2006)

Despite these concerns, many across the BBC adopted blogging following the creation of the Robinson blog in 2005 and the launch of the BBC's blog trial in December 2005 (Hooberman 2005). As of July 2008, the homepage of the BBC Blog Network at http://www.bbc.co.uk/blogs/ listed 74 blogs, with a third of these related to news and current affairs.

Alfred Hermida

Blogs and Accountability

The UK government's approval for the launch of BBC Online included a condition that it should use the Internet "to forge a new relationship with licence fee payers and strengthen accountability" (BBC Trust 2008). BBC management contends that "the flexible, open and public-facing nature of the website enables people to engage direct with individuals within the BBC". Yet managers admit that in the BBC's broadcast services, the space given to accountability has "generally been limited" (BBC Management 2007). However, reviews of the corporation's online activities have concluded that the BBC has not fulfilled its commitment to be more accountable (BBC Trust 2008). The development of blogs, nevertheless, is seen as one way that the BBC may be able to live up to its promises. Audiences' use of the blogs has outstripped that of the BBC's corporate site and its "Have Your Say" message boards (BBC Trust 2008), with 1.2m weekly visitors to BBC blog sites (BBC Management 2007). In particular, The Editors blog from BBC News has "rapidly grown to become a key point of engagement between the BBC's journalists and its audiences" (BBC Management 2007). Audience research indicates that people greatly appreciate the BBC's blogs, illustrated in this viewer comment:

> The Editors blog is a great way of developing a relationship between the BBC and viewers. It allows the editors to explain their decisions and viewers to give feedback, and thus allows a continuous dialogue between the BBC and its audience. (quoted in BBC Trust 2008)

The discourse on blogging at the BBC has been framed in terms of making the corporation more accountable to its audience. An internal BBC News report recommended that blogs be introduced, as they would "allow us to engage in a conversation with our audiences, increasing transparency, trust and responsiveness" (Anderson 2005: 1). This report reflected the debates within the BBC, and specifically with the news website, resulting in a news department's editor publicly pledging to create a blog to "explain some of our editorial decisions, our priorities, answer criticisms" (Clifton 2005). While the editorial blog initially focused on the BBC's online journalism, it was hoped it would "draw other parts of BBC News into the process as well" (Clifton 2005). This became The Editors blog, launched in May 2006 as a platform for news editors to explain editorial decisions, as explained in the first post:

> The BBC wants to be open and accountable, and so this site is a public space where you can engage with us as much as the medium allows. We're happy for you to criticise the BBC in your e-mails and comments, and to ask serious, probing questions of us — we'll do our best to respond to them. (BBC 2006)

Clifton described The Editors blog as "part of our drive to be more accountable" (Clifton 2008), while the editor of the BBC News website, Steve Herrmann, called it "a means to provide greater accountability and transparency and hopefully foster greater audience understanding and trust" (Herrmann 2008). By January 2008 The Editors blog featured posts by ninety-three editors from thirty-one BBC news and current affairs outlets.

The preoccupation with greater openness and transparency runs through many of the comments by people involved in the launch of blogging at the BBC. In his first post on the first official BBC blog, political editor Nick Robinson described it as a "conversation" that "can really change the relationship between author and reader" (Robinson 2005). An article in the BBC's internal magazine *Ariel* in 2005 said the primary aim of the blogging initiative was "to have a more direct relationship with our audiences and have different kinds of conversations with them, wherever they are generated" (Hooberman 2005). Other remarks by senior news executives suggest that a concern within the BBC to rebuild trust in its journalism drove this shift towards greater openness:

> We run an Editors blog and host discussions about that — an essential part of a push towards greater accountability and openness and a way of enhancing and repairing the damaged trust in the BBC. Sometimes it can be pretty uncomfortable to own up to mistakes in real time, but we have found that making redress quickly, whatever the fallout in adverse press coverage, is better than trying to hide from audience criticism. (Horrocks 2008)

The adoption of the informal, more personal and conversational tone of blogs has affected how the BBC communicates with audiences. Senior editors contend that blogs allow reporters "greater flexibility in format, tone and length than traditional text or broadcast", helping to "convey not just the stories, but what we think of them and how we get them" (Herrmann 2008). Blogging "allows us a different tone of voice which, being less formal, can convey more of an insight into the perspectives, predicaments and personalities of our reporters (and editors)" (Nixon 2006). It is "effective at giving that individual [correspondent] a voice in a particularly direct and transparent way" (Wilson 2008).

THE LIMITS OF BLOGGING

However, there are limitations on how far the corporation is engaging with its audience through blogging. One key aspect of blogs is the ability of users to comment, with bloggers responding and creating a conversation online. An internal BBC report said that "commitment from the author to engage and respond to the audience" should be a vital feature of BBC News blogs (Anderson 2005: 1). But the BBC acknowledges that it has not lived up to expectations of the blog format. BBC News website editor Steve Herrmann has recognized that "responding to comments consistently across the blogs continues to be one of the biggest challenges for all concerned" (Herrmann 2007), while blogs producer Robin Hamman recognizes that "we haven't quite got the knack of responding to comments, and indeed criticisms, we receive on our posts as well as we should. But we're getting better" (Hamman 2008).

As other news organizations have found, the more popular a blog becomes, the more time and effort needs to be dedicated to its upkeep (Hermida and Thurman 2008). BBC blogs have found a steadily growing audience, with the number of monthly visits to all blogs rising from under 1 million in April 2006 to more than 7 million by October 2007 (Hamman 2007a). The experience of the BBC blog on technology, *dotlife*, provides a snapshot of the issue facing journalists. Technology correspondent Rory Cellan-Jones explained the dilemma, saying that the blog had "proved both successful — in terms of audience — and time-consuming. Eleven weeks in, we've posted 143 entries and received over 7,000 comments" (Cellan-Jones 2008).

Additionally, the BBC has faced technical challenges in coping with the response to blogs. These are common when news organizations seek to integrate new technology into their editorial processes (Thurman 2008; Hermida and Thurman 2008). In an assessment of the first eighteen months of blogs, Hamman wrote of the "increasingly unstable" nature of the infrastructure (Hamman 2007a), with editors frustrated "by pretty catastrophic technical problems here at the BBC which made publishing anything on the blogs — and on several other parts of the BBC website — impossible" (Barron 2007). The BBC has addressed these technical issues with an overhaul of its blogging infrastructure (Reynolds 2008).

The BBC's shortcomings in engaging with readers cannot be blamed solely on technology. Research commissioned by the BBC into its blogging initiatives criticized an approach to blogging rooted in broadcasting (Hamman 2007b). Senior news executives shared this assessment:

> They did not feel genuinely interactive. It was still too much of a one-way process of people at the BBC writing and various comments then being posted without further response from the blog writer. This is a fair criticism of some of the ones we do in News. It is very hard to get correspondents to write posts and then respond again to comments, but it is something we should strive for. (Clifton 2008)

The research criticized BBC blogs for failing to link to other websites, even though linking out is considered one of the key attributes of blogging. Only one in eight posts provided external links, and only a small number of BBC bloggers used tools such as Technorati to track and engage in conversations on related topics taking place in the wider blogosphere (Hamman 2007b).

Given these limitations, the impact of BBC News blogs on its relationship with the audience is "unclear", according to BBC News website editor Steve Herrmann. BBC News blogs editor Giles Wilson said that the impact on the BBC's relationship with audiences was "hard to say. I like to think a good one — that people see we are prepared to be honest and open, but I suspect that's slightly wishful thinking" (Wilson 2008). Even blogging advocates such as Robin Hamman admit that there is a risk of exaggerating the influence of blogs on the corporation's journalism. BBC News employs around 2,000 journalists and "most of our news and current affairs staff, and indeed programmes, continue to completely ignore blogs. They don't read them, they don't use them in their work and they don't author them" (Hamman 2008).

CONCLUSION

The adoption of blogging took place during one of the most turbulent periods in the BBC's history, when there were questions over its journalism, radical changes in its governance and scandals over its broadcast ethics (Lee-Wright 2008). The start of this millennium saw an acknowledgement by the BBC that it needed to change its twentieth-century, paternalistic approach towards the audience, encapsulated in this quote from Director-General Mark Thompson: "The BBC does not have the public's trust as of right; it has to earn and maintain it" (Thompson, quoted in BBC Press Office 2004). As Enli has argued, "participation, facilitated by digital technology, is a key strategy for the public broadcasters in an attempt to regain the position as a national arena" when faced with challenges from deregulation, digitization and convergence (Enli 2008: 117). These conditions provided fertile ground for the rapid adoption of a form of audience participation, accountability and transparency based on an emergent new media technology. Greater openness became a priority for the BBC as it sought to adapt the organization for the twenty-first century, thus creating an environment conducive for blogging to spread beyond a handful of early adopters within the corporation. It explains why the BBC as an organization was a late adopter of blogging despite being an innovator in the field of online journalism in the late 1990s with the launch of the BBC News website in 1997.

In the space of three years blogging at the BBC went from being an experimental activity involving a small number of staff to an undertaking cited in policy documents as evidence of the corporation's aspiration to be more accountable (BBC Trust 2008; BBC Management 2007), with senior executives citing The Editors blog as the prime example of the corporation's new willingness to be transparent and open:

> The News Editors' blog has already become something of a byword in the industry for what you might call proactive candour, with senior figures admitting to varying degrees of error or cock-up, usually before the outside world has even noticed. (Keating 2008)

Blogs offered the BBC a platform to address the public in a way that goes beyond the publication of press releases, reviews and policy statements. In BBC News, The Editors blog provides a medium to address editorial issues in a timely fashion. Editors have welcomed the ability to adopt the personal and informal tone associated with blogs, marking a significant shift away from the impersonal and institutional abstract voice of authority of the Reithian era. There is evidence to suggest that audiences value this, given that blogs have become a favoured way for the public to interact online with the BBC.

During the period covered by this research, blogging was recognized by the BBC as a new media technology that encourages participation with the potential to foster a closer and more personal relationship with the audience than possible in broadcast. However, there are limits on how far the BBC has incorporated the participatory nature of blogs within its institutional structures. This research indicates that the corporation has yet to embrace blogs fully as a platform for a conversation with the audience, suggesting it is still heavily influenced by its broadcast culture and has adopted blogs as a publishing, rather than participatory, platform. Despite a rhetoric of account-ability, editors and executives tend to consider blogs as a way to explain and justify decisions rather than to engage in a discussion. Nevertheless, some editors are aware of the limitations of current BBC blogging practices. Indeed some bloggers are experi-menting with ways of fostering greater dialogue — an endeavour more appropriate to the format's participatory promise.

References

Anderson, K. (2004) "Blogging the US Election – I", BBC News website. Retrieved 14 January 2008 from: http://news.bbc.co.uk/1/hi/world/americas/3726132.stm.

Anderson, K. (2005) "BBC Blogs: News as Conversation". Internal report for BBC News Interactive, August 2005.

Andrews, P. (2003) "Is Blogging Journalism?", *Nieman Reports*, 57 (3), pp. 63–4.

Barnett, S., and Curry, A. (1994) *The Battle for the BBC: A British Broadcasting Conspiracy.* London: Aurum Press.

Barnhurst, K., and Nerone, J. (2001) *The Form of News: A History.* New York: Guilford Press.

Barron, P. (2007) "Editors Blog — the First Year". BBC News: The Editors, 15 June 2007. Retrieved 14 March 2008 from: http://www.bbc.co.uk/blogs/theeditors/2007/06/editors_blog_the_first_year.html.

BBC (2001) "What is Newslog", BBC News website. Retrieved 16 January 2008 from: http://news.bbc.co.uk/1/hi/uk/1692330.stm.

BBC (2004) "Building Public Value", BBC. Retrieved 12 March 2008 from: http://www.bbc.co.uk/foi/docs/bbc_constitution/bbc_royal_charter_and_agreement/Building_Public_Value.pdf.

BBC (2005) "The Election Monitor: Our Campaign Weblog", BBC News website. Retrieved 21 January 2008 from: http://news.bbc.co.uk/1/hi/uk_politics/vote_2005/blog/default.stm.

BBC (2006) "Welcome to The Editors". BBC News: The Editors. Retrieved 14 January 2008 from: http://www.bbc.co.uk/blogs/theeditors/2006/05/welcome_to_the_editors.html.

BBC Press Office (2004) "Neil Report Recommends How to Strengthen BBC Journalism", BBC. Retrieved 12 March 2008 from: http://www.bbc.co.uk/pressoffice/pressreleases/stories/2004/06_june/23/neil.shtml.

BBC Management (2007) "Review of bbc.co.uk: BBC Management's Submission to the BBC Trust's Review", BBC Trust. Retrieved 29 May 2008 from: http://www.bbc.co.uk/bbctrust/assets/files/pdf/regulatory_framework/service_licences/service_reviews/management_submission.pdf.

BBC Trust (2008) "Service Review: bbc.co.uk". BBC Trust, May. Retrieved 29 May 2008 from: http://www.bbc.co.uk/bbctrust/assets/files/pdf/regulatory_framework/service_licences/service_reviews/report_bbc.co.uk_review.pdf.

Birt, J. (2002) Quoted in "An Outsider at the BBC", *The Times*, 14 October. Retrieved 16 January 2008 from: http://entertainment.timesonline.co.uk/tol/arts_and_entertainment/books/article1170807.ece.

Blumler, J. G. (ed.) (1992) *Television and the Public Interest: Vulnerable Values in West European Broadcasting.* Newbury Park: Sage.

Born, G. (2002) "Reflexivity and Ambivalence: Culture, Creativity and Government in the BBC", *Journal for Cultural Research*, 6 (1), pp. 65–90.

Born, G. (2004) *Uncertain Vision: Birt, Dyke and the Reinvention of the BBC*. London: Secker & Warburg.

Bridcut, J. (2007) "From Seesaw to Wagon Wheel: Safeguarding Impartiality in the 21st Century", BBC Trust. Retrieved 21 January 2008 from: http://news.bbc.co.uk/1/shared/bsp/hi/pdfs/18_06_07impartialitybbc.pdf.

Bruns, A. (2005) *Gatewatching: Collaborative Online News Production*. New York: Peter Lang.

Cellan-Jones, R. (2008) Personal communication, 18 March.

Clifton, P. (2005) "From the Editor's Desktop", BBC News website, 29 July 2005. Retrieved 22 January 2008 from: http://news.bbc.co.uk/1/hi/magazine/4727579.stm.

Clifton, P. (2008) Personal communication, 4 March.

Delwiche, A. (2005) "Agenda-Setting, Opinion Leadership, and the World of Web Logs", *First Monday*, 10 (12). Retrieved 30 June 2008 from: http://www.firstmonday.org/issues/issue10_12/delwiche/index.html.

Douglas, T. (2005) "Blogging and the BBC", BBC News website. Retrieved 17 January 2008 from: http://news.bbc.co.uk/newswatch/ukfs/hi/newsid_4280000/newsid_4286400/4286490.stm.

Duran, M. (2007) "Study Shows Video Playing Big Role for Newspaper Sites", *Newspapers & Technology*. Retrieved 16 March 2008 from: http://www.newsandtech.com/issues/2007/09-07/ot/09-07_video-study.htm.

Enli, G. (2008) "Redefining Public Service Broadcasting", *Convergence*, 14 (1), pp. 105–20.

Gallo, J. (2004) "Weblog Journalism: Between Infiltration and Integration". In L. Gurak, S. Antonijevic, L. Johnson, C. Ratliff, and J. Reyman (2004) (eds), *Into the Blogosphere: Rhetoric, Community and the Culture of Weblogs*. Retrieved 30 June 2008 from: http://blog.lib.umn.edu/blogosphere/weblog_journalism.html.

Gillmor, D. (2004) *We the Media: Grassroots Journalism by the People, for the People*. Sebastopol, CA: O'Reilly.

Glaser, M. (2004) "Papers' Online Units Allow Editorial Boards to Lift Veil with Video, Blog", *Online Journalism Review*, 9 March 2004. Retrieved from: http://www.ojr.org/ojr/glaser/1078877295.php.

Hamman, R. (2006) "What's the Purpose of TV and Radio Blogs?", *BBC Pods & Blogs*, 15 November. Retrieved 17 January 2008 from: http://www.bbc.co.uk/blogs/podsandblogs/2006/11/whats_the_purpose_of_t_and_ra.shtml.

Hamman, R. (2007a) "18 Months of Blogs (Part 1)", BBC Internet Blog. Retrieved 17 January 2008 from: http://www.bbc.co.uk/blogs/bbcinternet/2007/11/robin_post_part_i_1.html.

Hamman, R. (2007b) "18 Months of Blogs (Part 2)", BBC Internet Blog. Retrieved 17 January 2008 from: http://www.bbc.co.uk/blogs/bbcinternet/2007/11/18_months_of_blogs_part_2_1.html.

Hamman, R. (2008) Personal communication, 16 April.

Haas, T. (2005) "Public Journalism as a Journalism of Publics: Implications of the Habermas–Fraser Debate for Public Journalism", *Journalism Studies*, 6 (3), pp. 387–96.

Hermida, A. (2008) "The BBC Goes Blogging: Is 'Auntie' Finally Listening?" Paper presented to the 9th International Online Journalism Symposium, 4 April 2008, University of Texas, Austin.

Hermida, A., and Thurman, N. (2008) "A Clash of Cultures: The Integration of User-Generated Content within Professional Journalistic Frameworks at British Newspaper Websites", *Journalism Practice*, 2 (3).

Herrmann, S. (2007) "Taking Stock", BBC News: The Editors. Retrieved 17 January 2008 from: http://www.bbc.co.uk/blogs/theeditors/2007/11/taking_stock.html.

Herrmann, S. (2008) Personal communication, 18 March.

Hooberman, L. (2005) "Join the Brave New World of BBC Blogging", *Ariel*, 13 December 2005.

Horrocks, P. (2008) "Value of Citizen Journalism", BBC News: The Editors, 7 January 2008. Retrieved 12 March 2008 from: http://www.bbc.co.uk/blogs/theeditors/2008/01/value_of_citizen_journalism.html.

Keating, R. (2008) "The BBC's Digital Strategy in a World beyond Boundaries", BBC Press Office, 17 June. Retrieved 28 June 2008, from: http://www.bbc.co.uk/pressoffice/speeches/stories/keating_tardis.shtml.

Kung-Shankleman, L. (2000) *Inside the BBC and CNN*. London: Routledge.

Kung-Shankleman, L. (2003) "When Old Dogs Learn New Tricks: The Launch of BBC News Online", *European Case Clearing House*, England, 303-119-1.

Landow, G. P. (1997) *Hypertext 2.0: The Convergence of Contemporary Critical Theory and Technology*. Baltimore, MD: The John Hopkins University Press.

Lee-Wright, P. (2008) "Virtual News: BBC News at a 'Future Media and Technology' Crossroads", *Convergence*, 14 (3), pp. 249–60.

Lowrey, W. (2006) "Mapping the Journalism–Blogging Relationship", *Journalism*, 7 (4), pp. 477–500.

Matheson, D. (2004) "Weblogs and the Epistemology of the News: Some Trends in Online Journalism", *New Media and Society*, 6 (4), pp. 443–68.

Murray, J. (1997) *Hamlet on the Holodeck: The Future of Narrative in Cyberspace*. New York: The Free Press.

Nixon, R. (2006) "US Mid-Terms Blog". Internal report for BBC News Interactive, 4 September 2006.

Nixon, R. (2008) Personal communication, 28 March.

Reynolds, N. (2008) Personal communication, 13 March.

Roberts, L. D., Smith, L. M., and Pollock, C. (1997) "U r a Lot Bolder on the Net: The Social Use of Text-Based Virtual Environments by Shy Individuals". Paper presented to First International Conference on Shyness and Self-Consciousness, Cardiff University, July 1997.

Robinson, N. (2005) "The Beauty of Blogging", Newslog, BBC News. Retrieved 21 January 2008 from: http://www.bbc.co.uk/blogs/nickrobinson/2005/12/the_beauty_of_b.html.

Singer, J. (2001) "The Metro Wide Web: Changes in Newspapers' Gatekeeping Role Online", *Journalism and Mass Communication Quarterly*, 78 (1), pp. 65–80.

Singer, J. (2003) "Campaign Contributions: Online Newspaper Coverage of Election 2000", *Journalism and Mass Communication Quarterly*, 80 (1), pp. 39–56.

Singer, J. (2005) "The Political J-Blogger: 'Normalising' a New Media Form to Fit Old Norms and Practices", *Journalism: Theory, Practice and Criticism*, 6 (2), pp. 173–98.

Spender, D. (1995) *Nattering on the Net: Women, Power and Cyberspace*. Melbourne: Spinifex Press.

Sullivan, C. (2004) "Blogging's Power to Change Journalism", *Editor & Publisher*. Retrieved 30 June 2008 from: http://www.editorandpublisher.com/eandp/article_brief/eandp/1/1000480726.

Thach, E. (1995) "Using Electronic Mail to Conduct Survey Research", *Educational Technology*, 35 (2), pp. 27–31.

Thurman, N. (2008) "Forums for Citizen Journalists? Adoption of User Generated Content Initiatives by Online News Media", *New Media & Society*, 10 (1), pp. 139–57.

Wall, M. (2005) "Blogs of War: Weblogs as News", *Journalism: Theory, Practice & Criticism*, 6 (2), pp. 153–72.

Wilson, G. (2008) Personal communication, 12 April.

{{ **CHAPTER** }}
21

Online Television: A Threat to Balanced Political Reporting

NICHOLAS JONES

This chapter will make the argument that online television poses a significant threat to balanced political reporting. In the UK objective political broadcast news coverage has been governed by a regulatory framework, which has developed historically and now appears under challenge.

In a very short space of time the availability of cheap or free Web publishing tools has made it possible for individual blogs to shift from being crude text and image sites to becoming sophisticated televisual locations. Many of these are political in nature and offer programmes that appear similar to broadcast news transmissions. This has disrupted the delivery of news by traditional media on two counts. First, audiences now have a greater number of choices about how and where they obtain news. Second, the ability of the audience to create their own news agenda has challenged the traditional gatekeeping role of the professional media. A potential confirmation of the power of these new lines of communication has been the adoption of this form not just by individual political activists but also by organized political parties (Stanyer 2003; 2006). Indeed, the British government's Media Monitoring Unit, which tracks and summarizes domestic and international news coverage twenty-four hours a day, became part of the remit of the administration's Central Office of Information in 2006 and expanded its horizon to include political blogs.

Alongside the increasing sophistication of blogging tools, the move online by the UK press has also proved a valuable mechanism for drawing in significant audiences in the battle to maintain numbers. Once websites started streaming audio-visual material, the newspapers did all they could to attract new users in the UK. Such was the versatility of their newsgathering operations that they found that, via the Internet, they could compete directly with established broadcasters and hoped in the process to gain a share of both the television audience and advertising revenue. Unique users of Mail Online doubled within a year, hitting 18.7 million in May 2008, overtaking the *Telegraph* (18.6 million) and *Guardian* (18.3 million) sites, which were both well ahead of Times Online (15.8 million). Tabloid newspapers have been equally inventive in trying to increase their share of digital traffic: videos featuring exclusive political interviews began to appear on the website of the *Mail on Sunday* (www.mailonsunday.co.uk) and in an attempt to increase traffic to their sites, the *Sun* and the *News of the World* have offered a range of sensational videos, often featuring unauthorized and sometimes intrusive footage of celebrities misbehaving. In May 2008 the *Sun* online network recorded 14.9 million unique users of which 4.5 million were for the *News of the World*.

A number of important questions emerge from this convergence of traditional media platforms. Some debates centre on whether or not private voices have an impact on journalistic practice and whether bloggers should have any restrictions requiring fair and objective practice. Britain has what is regarded as a free press, which, with only a few restraints, can campaign for whichever political party or persuasion a newspaper prefers. Balancing the editorial freedom of the press has been the equally strong tradition of upholding the political impartiality of broadcasting. Under long-standing regulations and conventions, radio and television services have been required to give a fair allocation of airtime to the policies of competing political parties, a safeguard that has been rigidly observed during successive election campaigns, when the candidates and manifestos of even minority parties cannot be entirely ignored.

There is a powerful, if strongly contested, orthodoxy that dates back the emergence of a "free" press in the nineteenth century (Curran 2002). The British press can be understood to be "free" in two senses; first, in that it can be privately owned and free from government regulation. Second, it is also "free" to mount campaigns and argue an editorial case. However partisan, it has been generally understood that the press should inform the public about the affairs of the state and make the opinions and needs of the public known to politicians, who manage state business. In doing this, the press has been a conduit for political decision-making, facilitating citizens in making their choices (McQuail 1977; Blumler and Gurevitch 1995).

Broadcast news, on the other hand, developed within a public corporation, the BBC, funded by a tax on the ownership of, first, radio and later, television sets, the licence fee. As a publicly funded monopoly, the BBC was required to be politically impartial, and this requirement was extended to the commercial companies when BBC television was joined by Independent Television (ITV) in 1955. However, it could be argued that control over the news about important issues or, indeed, establishing the agenda for what was considered important remained under the control of a small number of players who controlled the means of production. Given the expense and complexity of operating a broadcast company, even the emergence of independent radio and TV did little to change this. Today's vast television empires are in the hands of a small number of people, and public service broadcasters compete to obtain a share of the audience.

To some extent, the freedom of the press is facilitated by the lack of legislative power imposed upon it, with the state relying instead on self-regulation agreements. In 1991 the UK Press Complaints Commission (PCC) was created and financed by the newspaper industry to replace the Press Council as an alternative to state regulation of the press (O'Malley and Soley 2000: 89). Having been given the opportunity to "plant the standard of self-regulation",[1] the PCC widened its brief in 1999 to take in complaints about the editorial content of newspaper websites.[2] The commission justified this because it regarded the adjudication of disputes affecting the online publication of text and photographs as a logical progression of its work.

The PCC moved swiftly to build up its expertise in video journalism and within a year claimed it had "the greatest internet penetration of any UK media regulator".[3] Complaints about online journalism were small in comparison with the printed media and those which had been received involved concerns about invasions of privacy through the reuse by newspaper websites of personal videos posted on video-sharing sharing sites such as YouTube.

British newspapers began to compete head-on with established broadcasters such as the BBC, ITV and Sky News, first with audio podcasts and then with video news reports. As this developed, the press companies realized that, in a digital age, they could exploit what for them had always been a distinct selling point for the printed news media in the UK. They could offer comment and opinion of an often highly partisan nature. Allied with this, the newspapers criticized the BBC for its increased spending on online activities, which the companies claimed was unfair competition because it was funded by the licence-payer.

Andy Burnham, the former UK Secretary of State for Culture, Media and Sport, has argued that if a video on YouTube attracts a million hits, it is "akin to broadcasting".[4] Although the Web traffic of newspapers has yet to match that of the video-sharing sites, the market leaders have achieved spectacular growth; nevertheless, from the point of view of regulation they are not dealt with as broadcasters.

Since 2003 the regulation of broadcasting in the UK has been governed by rules laid down by the Office of Communications (Ofcom). These rules dictate standards of professionalism, objectivity and impartiality for news broadcasting — to ensure that news, in whatever form, is reported with due accuracy and presented with due impartiality. The rules also stipulate that presenters and reporters of news programmes may not express their own views on matters of political or industrial controversy or matters relating to current public policy. A similar set of rules are embedded in the BBC's Charter.[5]

As Ofcom itself states, "due impartiality" does not mean an equal division of time has to be given to every view, or that every argument and every facet of every argument has to be represented. The approach to due impartiality may vary according to the nature of the subject, the type of programme and channel. Some have argued that one consequence of this is that minority voices get no say. This argument has become a tool that net TV producers use to defend the need for the freedom to expound views in an unregulated or self-regulating environment.[6]

This legislative requirement is not replicated in the press. The freedom to make partisan cases around political issues is very much a part of a British sense of press freedom. Even politicians may author articles, and newspapers are well known for their partisan support (Jones 1999; 2002; 2006).

TIPPING THE BALANCE

A critical series of elections in May 2008 provided the first real showcase for the digital diversification of the press and a powerful demonstration of the wider political impact of newspaper websites. In March 2007, in the run-up to the London mayoral elections, the kind of television advertising that had become infamous in US presidential elections started to appear on political blogs such as the now defunct 18doughtystreet. This was one of the early UK political websites, with a right-of-centre message. Its owner, Stephan Shakespeare, broke new ground during 2007 when he broadcast *Vox Politix*, a nightly televised discussion hosted by the Conservative blogger Iain Dale, a Tory candidate in the 2005 general election. MPs and journalists from the across the political spectrum were interviewed, and the debates were wide-ranging. Nonetheless, the two-hour programme did not seek to present itself as a balanced platform or suggest it was offering an equal share of time to Labour and the Liberal Democrats.

Perhaps the most controversial slot on 18doughtystreet was a two-minute attack-style advertisement that sought to demolish the record of Ken Livingstone, then Labour mayor of London, who was defeated when he stood for re-election in May 2008. Well-edited video footage and hard-hitting lines hammered home the message: London was "less safe than New York"; how "as London's problems mount Ken Livingstone is enjoying himself and found time to visit Cuba"; and how Livingstone had the support of the rail union leader, Bob Crow, known as "Bob the striker".[7]

Also in September 2007 came the clearest illustration of the changing landscape, with the launch of Telegraph TV News Now (www.telegraph.co.uk). Within a matter of weeks the *Daily Telegraph*'s website had progressed from supplying "on-demand video news" to the transmission of twelve separate television programmes, in addition to a daily news bulletin. Its weekly political offering, hosted by the Conservative MP Ann Widdecombe and the paper's columnist Simon Heffer, made a virtue of being free of the constraints that applied to mainstream political programming. *Right On* was promoted by the *Daily Telegraph* as being the "show that's politically right, not politically correct".[8]

Equally, press proprietors have found that advertisements placed at the start of podcasts and news videos have the potential to become a reliable source of income. As a result, website executives from the *Daily Telegraph* and *The Guardian* are upbeat about the future of their audio-visual output. For example, Ian Douglas, the *Telegraph*'s head of digital production, describes how advertisers are prepared to pay a premium for fifteen-second commercials appearing at the front of video news and political programmes. "What attracts advertisers is they know that a user has requested to view the item and as we are now hitting nearly four million downloads a month, these ads are becoming a healthy source of income."[9] At *The Guardian*'s website (www.guardian.co.uk) there has been a greater emphasis on the production of podcasts by correspondents and columnists, and according to the paper's head of audio, Matt Wells, an advertisement at the front proves an equally attractive proposition.[10]

Crucially, Douglas and Wells both believe that exemption from Ofcom's rules on political impartiality could become a key factor in their future success, because, as

Wells explains, it is the "confrontational and provocative" nature of their podcasts and videos that enabled newspapers to start competing with public service broadcasters.

The *Mail on Sunday* also chose the eve of the mayoral and wider local authority elections to start serializing the autobiography of Lord Levy, formerly Labour's chief fundraiser, when Tony Blair was leader of the Labour Party and prime minister. Levy's most sensational claim was that Blair believed that his successor as prime minister, Gordon Brown, "could never beat" the Conservative Party leader, David Cameron, in a general election. There could hardly have been a more damaging assault on a new prime minister and Labour leader facing his first significant electoral test against a background of dire opinion polls. Seven pages of the *Mail on Sunday* were devoted to what was billed a "world exclusive", and, on its website, the paper broadcast an interview with Lord Levy conducted by the paper's political editor, Simon Walters. An extract from the video was released for use in radio and television news bulletins on the previous Saturday evening. And the clip of Lord Levy, with the *Mail* logo burned into the corner of the shot, dominated television news coverage that weekend. Through its purchase of the serialization rights and an astute sense of timing the *Mail on Sunday* had not only dictated the news agenda that weekend; it had also forced established broadcasters, which were denied access to Lord Levy, to give air-time to its exclusive video and to encourage viewers to watch the full interview at Mail Online.

After the defeat later that week of Ken Livingstone and the election of the first Conservative mayor of London, the loss of over 300 council seats and the lowest-ever share of the vote for a UK governing party, Prime Minister Brown had to brace himself for the party's imminent defeat in the Labour-held constituency of Crewe and Nantwich. Coverage of the by-election became a trial of strength for the rival arms of the electronic news media. This was because television and radio correspondents, who were required to provide "balanced" reporting, were competing head-to-head with video journalists from newspapers and other websites, who faced no such constraints.

In the two days preceding polling day, Telegraph TV also offered lengthy interviews conducted by Conservative blogger Iain Dale, first with the shadow Foreign Secretary, William Hague, and then, on the eve of the by-election, with the Conservative candidate Edward Timpson, who went on to win the seat on a 17 percent swing. Telegraph TV did not offer interviews with Timpson's opponents, nor was there a list of the other candidates or a link to their names, as would be expected under UK broadcast regulations.

Polling day coverage of television and radio news bulletins and BBC News Online (www.bbc.co.uk) was strictly limited to non-contentious information about the weather, the likelihood of a high turn-out and a list of candidates. Yet online newspaper sites were not bound by the same rules. Two reports were available on Telegraph TV alongside a news video entitled "Crewe By-Election: How Not to Campaign" and a separate piece to camera by the paper's public policy editor, Toby Helm, who described it as a crucial test for all three party leaders and said that, if they failed to take the seat, the Conservatives would be "massively disappointed".

On the other side of the political coin, "Whatever Happened to the Labour Vote?" was streamed from the *Times* site on the day of the election. Reporter Nico Hines said

321

the Conservatives were poised to make their first by-election gain against Labour since 1978 because "people who have voted Labour all their lives are deserting the party". His report included a clip from an interview with the Labour candidate, Tamsin Dunwoody, and a response from a visiting Labour MP, Robert Flello, but did not feature the reaction of either the Conservative or the Liberal Democrat candidate.

Much of the opinionated audio-visual reporting of the by-election was re-broadcast on a newly established site, www.politicshome.com, which offered what it claimed was an "intelligent filter" of the varied output of television, radio, newspaper websites and political blogs. Stephan Shakespeare had launched PoliticsHome as the successor to 18doughtystreet and, with an eye firmly on the impact of convergence and a hoped-for easing of the rules on impartiality, he declared it was the first political website properly to reflect "the crumbling distinction between the different types of media".[11]

Staff at talkSPORT radio, a commercial radio station and part of the "old" broadcast media, did not share Shakespeare's optimism about a blurring of the output of broadcasters and newspaper websites. The politically loaded, online broadcasting of the press had apparently passed off without comment or complaint during the elections in May. However, a talkSPORT presenter, James Whale, was sacked for a breach of the broadcasting code after telling listeners to his phone-in show to "vote Boris, vote Boris" during the campaign for mayor of London. A warning was issued to another presenter George Lamb, of BBC6Music, who told listeners on polling day that he was going to vote for the candidate with "blond hair". Although Lamb's remark had not broken the Ofcom code, he had breached the BBC's editorial guidelines. A third radio presenter, Jason Donovan, of Invicta FM, was not so fortunate. After an Ofcom investigation he was criticized for a "very serious breach" of the code on due impartiality. A listener complained about Donovan's Sunday evening entertainment programme after he welcomed the prospect of the mayoral election because "it's definitely time for a change . . . Boris Johnson". However, Ofcom felt that because Donovan was "relatively new to his role" and it was an "isolated" comment, no regulatory action needed to be taken (Ofcom Broadcast Bulletin 2008). Within the broadcasting industry there was considerable sympathy for the three presenters and renewed demands for commercial radio stations to be freed from the impartiality requirement, in view of the expansion in the audio-visual output of newspaper websites.

A Lighter Touch

The technological evolution of the Web, faster broadband and increasing levels of access have rapidly shifted private and corporate blogs from ones that primarily deliver words and images to ones that can deliver audio-visual content of a kind that is identical to television programming. It could be argued that the kind of legislation required to protect impartiality has not caught up with the new technological developments of the Internet. However, it seems more likely that this situation is indicative of a trend towards deregulation that is, to some extent, a reflection of a particular relationship between UK politics and media business interests. As the head of Sky News, John

Ryley, predicted in 2006, the growth in digital channels and the increased delivery of news and information by the Internet is calling into question the British government's ability to sustain different regulatory regimes for newspaper websites and television stations. As the *Daily Telegraph*'s, editor, Will Lewis has readily acknowledged, the British government's decision to opt for a "light touch" regulatory regime has allowed them to extend their lobby from print to the televisual.[12]

The definitions of broadcasting that identify the simultaneous one-to-many flow are not applied to the Web. This is conceived of as a medium that has more in common with the on-demand consumer structures that reflect the process of buying a newspaper. There is an assumption in this thinking that the instantaneous nature of reaching a lot of people at the same moment in time has more capacity for influencing public opinion.

Perhaps the pivotal moment in the threat to balanced reporting by television journalists was the confirmation in the autumn of 2006 that Ofcom, the state-funded regulator for the communications industry, had no intention of seeking to regulate the audio-visual content of newspaper websites. By voluntarily relinquishing the chance to have a say in monitoring how the newspaper industry exploited online television, Ofcom had, in effect, handed over responsibility to the Press Complaints Commission. Needless to say, a further extension of the PCC remit to take in the rapidly expanding output of audio and video material was of far greater significance. It meant that the online operations of the press proprietors had escaped being subjected to Ofcom's stringent regulatory regime, which had resulted in multi-million pound fines for television programmes that had breached the broadcasting code. Sir Christopher Meyer, chairman of the PCC, announced at the annual conference of the Society of Editors in November 2006 that his organization had been given a vote of confidence and was being afforded the opportunity to "plant the standard of self-regulation in the new and virgin field of the video and audio content" of newspaper websites. Sir Christopher assured the assembled editors that he was confident the PCC's adjudications would be accepted by the public: "I hope the knowledge that the product you are reading and now viewing comes under the codes of the Press Complaints Commission will be seen as a kind of kite mark."[13]

The Ofcom report *New News, Future News* (Ofcom 2007) was part of a wider review of public service broadcasting (PSB) in the UK, considering the future of public service commitments in the all-digital environment that will follow the switch off of the analogue broadcasting signals in 2012. *New News, Future News* focused on four areas of change in the news environment and its importance "for all citizens of an informed modern democracy". The four issues were:

- plurality and diversity in UK national and international news
- the prospects for television news in the UK nations and regions
- issues of engagement and disengagement with news — particularly for the young and members of some ethnic communities
- the relevance and practicality of requirements for due impartiality in digital news.

The report set out not to make policy recommendations but to open up areas of debate, although the report concluded that political impartiality "will become less enforceable in the future", and it suggested that the rules on due impartiality should be relaxed initially for "small niche channels". Summarizing some aspects of the consultation, Peter Phillips, who has responsibility for Ofcom's strategy, policy development and consumer policy, said:

> One possibility — no more than that — post-2014 might be relaxation of the statutory rules on impartiality. We believe these will remain absolutely essential for maintaining overall trust in key PSB providers, such as the BBC and Channel 4. But might a degree of relaxation for other services enable a wider range of voices to be heard, and for minority groups to feel more engaged? Minority ethnic groups don't see mainstream media [BBC, ITV, broadsheets] as being as impartial as do the rest of the population. C4 performs better among minority ethnic groups than white people for impartiality. Such relaxation could also reflect that, by 2014, convergence may have reached the point where similar-seeming services may reach the same screen in the same way, but from an entirely different regulatory background — regulated "TV" alongside unregulated press or internet. (Ofcom 2007)

At a time when many have claimed that newspapers are dying, the industry has welcomed these signals. Alan Rusbridger, editor of *The Guardian*, had said that this greater editorial freedom would help newspapers to compete with established broadcasters. Although the BBC's video output would continue to be far superior, he was convinced the 600 journalists employed by the Guardian group would benefit from self-regulation. "We don't have to be fair, impartial and balanced — and all that stuff — and that will give us some kind of advantage." As Jeff Randall, editor-at-large at the *Daily Telegraph* and a regular contributor to Telegraph TV, has pointed out, "people like biased television".[14] Indeed, such an approach is in line with the broadcasting rationale of the UK's leading press proprietor. Rupert Murdoch argued to a British House of Lords Select Committee on Communications in 2008 that Sky News should have the same political freedom as his American channel Fox News so that Sky could become "a proper alternative to the BBC".[15]

What gives this *laissez-faire* approach a more politically partisan edge was the publication in March 2008 of a Conservative Party discussion document that suggested that the requirement for political impartiality should be relaxed for those broadcasting organizations that were not in receipt of public funds or subsidies. Although the party agreed that impartiality should remain a central obligation of public service broadcasters, the Conservatives thought the regulators should be asked to consider whether such an obligation stifled creativity and diversity.

> Why should Telegraph TV — or for that matter Guardian TV — be prevented from following the editorial lines pursued by their newspapers if they were to become digital channels and not simply broadcast on the Internet? Providing broadcasters stay within the law, such provisions are unnecessary and restrict the development of a diverse broadcasting sector.[16]

Such was the force of the Conservatives' broadside against the concept of impartiality in broadcasting that it created a dilemma for the British government. Andy Burnham, the Secretary of State for Culture, Media and Sport, declared that he was determined to resist the advent of politically biased news on radio and television. But at the same time it was clear that ministers were anxious to allow the press proprietors the freedom they needed to innovate. In a speech in June 2008 to his department's convergence think-tank Burnham acknowledged that the "distinction between online newspaper sites and television news is blurring" and that there was an argument for allowing that process of levelling out to "proceed with more pace". While he conceded that "attitudes and perspectives" were changing very fast, he was concerned that the "online world will simply wash away all of the standards that have built up over time". Therefore his department would not permit the removal of the existing impartiality requirement because a Fox News-style service would apply creeping pressure to other-broadcasters. "With so much of the online world un-trusted, I feel we should preserve standards of accuracy, impartiality and trustworthiness, rather than dismantle them. People still use the Internet and television for different reasons and with different expectations and we must not forget that."[17]

The House of Lords Select Committee on Communications has also mounted a strong defence of the requirement that all UK radio and television stations should continue to be impartial in its report *The Ownership of the News* (2008). It said Ofcom's proposal that additional channels should be allowed to offer the kind of partial news available on newspaper websites would have "a negative impact on the quality and trustworthiness" of news services. The only beneficiaries would be Sky News and News International, which currently controls 35 percent of the national newspaper market. Online newspapers could have a "significant political impact", and the committee feared it was still possible for "one voice to become too powerful to be acceptable in a healthy democracy". Much of the news available on the Internet through the "high-profile Web presence" of the press had been "repackaged" and had not been matched by a corresponding expansion in "professional and investigative journalism" (a claim also born out by Hudson and Temple in Chapter 3 of this book).

In an earlier judgement in March 2008 the House of Lords had underlined the unique position of broadcasting on the Web, when five law lords ruled that there was a "pressing social need" to continue the blanket prohibition on political advertising on television and radio because of its "greater immediacy and impact" when compared with the press, cinema and other media. In his judgement Lord Bingham said it was highly desirable in the democratic process that there was a level playing field of debate and it was the "duty of broadcasters to achieve that impartiality by presenting balanced programmes in which all lawful views might be ventilated".[18] Yet again there had been no mention of the potential influence of political broadcasting via the Internet, which was perhaps hardly surprising given the hands-off approach adopted by both ministers and regulators.

CONCLUSION

Evidently, television and radio editors will be at a significant disadvantage if broadcasting continues to be controlled by a regulatory regime that bans the kind of opinionated audio-visual journalism that newspapers are able to offer on their websites. Politicians have long complained of bias in the press. Now digital convergence and light-touch regulation of online newspapers has opened the door to politically motivated broadcasting.

Having effectively given a green light to the continued and unhindered development of online newspapers, the government has turned a blind eye to what the press proprietors have already achieved. Politically motivated programming has become well established, and a new generation of video journalists, freed from the responsibility of "not favouring one side over another", is busily rewriting the broadcasters' rule book on the impartial reporting of election campaigns. Restrictions that have been observed for decades are being bypassed or ignored. Likewise, on websites, television-style attack advertising does not have to fit within the rigid restrictions that are applied to the timing and format of party election broadcasts.

Out in the blogosphere the general opinion is, the more the competition the better. With limitless opportunities and the freedom for all-comers to participate it does not matter if there is a lack of fairness towards one political party or a hostile advertising campaign against another, because over time the competing output will balance itself out.

Within the space of a couple of years opinionated journalism in podcasts and videos has secured a firm foothold in the hitherto politically neutral world of broadcasting. A new generation of video journalists has demonstrated that elections can be reported on the Internet without having to defer to Ofcom's rules on due impartiality. Years of declining sales for newspapers have forced the owners to diversify and, after investing so much in developing online production, they are demonstrating that audio-visual output is one way to make it pay.

Given the power of the national press and its ability to command the news agenda, broadcasters realize they have a fight on their hands trying to defend their well-established customs and practices when reporting politics. The Internet has given newspapers a chance to offer an alternative. It seems likely that newspaper proprietors will probably go on strengthening their digital output in the run-up to the UK 2010 general election. If so, they will be getting ready for the moment when they will be able to show whether or not the political patronage that they have exercised for so long through the printed media can be wielded to the same extent on the Web.

Notes

1   Quoted from a speech by Sir Christopher Meyer, chairman Press Complaints Commission, annual conference, Society of Editors, November 2006.
2   Quoted from a speech by Sir Christopher Meyer, chairman Press Complaints Commission, annual conference, Society of Editors, November 2006.
3   Quote from an article by Sir Christopher Meyer, chairman, Press Complaints Commission,

The Review 2007, published by PCC June 2008.

4 Speech by Andy Burnham, Secretary of State for Culture, Media and Sport, Convergence Think-Tank, 11 June 2008.

5 Retrieved from: www.bbc.co.uk/bbctrust/framework/charter.html.

6 Interview by Roy Greenslade with Jeff Randall, editor-at-large, *Daily Telegraph*, published in the *Evening Standard*, London, 7 May 2008.

7 "Bob the striker", Ken Livingstone attack advertisement, first broadcast in March 2007 on www.18doughtystreet.com.

8 Advertisement promoting Right On on www.telegraph.co.uk, first published in the *Daily Telegraph*, 4 February 2008.

9 Print Online, "Making it Pay", debate at Frontline Club, London, 26 June 2008.

10 Print Online, "Making it Pay", debate at Frontline Club, London, 26 June 2008.

11 "Statement of Aims: About Us". www.politicshome.com.

12 Will Lewis, lecture given at City University, London, 24 April, 2008.

13 Speech by Sir Christopher Meyer, chairman, Press Complaints Commission, annual conference, Society of Editors, November 2006.

14 Interview by Roy Greenslade with Jeff Randall, editor-at-large, *Daily Telegraph*, published in the *Evening Standard*, London, 7 May 2008.

15 Evidence given by Rupert Murdoch, to the House of Lords Select Committee on Communications. The Ownership of the News, House of Lords Select Committee on Communications, June 2008).

16 The Future of Public Service Broadcasting, Conservative Research Department, March 2008.

17 Speech by Andy Burnham, Secretary of State for Culture, Media and Sport, Convergence Think-Tank, 11 June 2008.

18 "House of Lords: Regina (Animal Defenders International) v. Secretary of State for Culture, Media and Sport", law report, The Times, 17 March 2008.

References

Blumler, J. G., and Gurevitch, M. (1995) *The Crisis of Public Communication*. London: Routledge.

Conservative Research Department (March 2008) *The Future of Public Service Broadcasting*.

Curran, J. (2002) *Media and Power*. London: Routledge.

Curran, J., and Seaton, J. (2003) *Power without Responsibility: The Press, Broadcasting, and New Media in Britain*. 6th edn. London: Routledge.

House of Lords Select Committee on Communications (2008) *The Ownership of the News*.

Jones, N. (1999) *Sultans of Spin*. London: Gollancz.

Jones, N. (2002) *The Control Freaks: How New Labour Gets Its Own Way*. London: Politicos.

Jones, N. (2006) *Trading Information: Leaks, Lies and Tip-Offs*. London: Politicos.

McQuail, D. (1977) "The Influence and Effects of Mass Media". In J. Curran, M. Gurevitch, and J. Woollacott (eds), *Mass Communication and Society*. London: Edward Arnold, pp. 70–94.

Ofcom (2007) *New News, Future News*.

Ofcom Broadcast Bulletin (2008) "Broadcast Bulletin", 113, 7 July 2008. Retrieved 14 September 2008 from: http://www.ofcom.org.uk/tv/obb/prog_cb/obb113.

O'Malley, T., and Soley, C. (2000) *Regulating the Press*. London: Pluto.

Stanyer, J. (2003) "Intraparty Conflict and the Struggle to Shape News Agendas: Television News and the Coverage of the Annual British Party Conferences", *Harvard International Journal of Press and Politics*, 8 (2), pp. 71–89.

Nicholas Jones

Stanyer, J. (2006) "Online Campaign Communication and the Phenomenon of Blogging: An Analysis of Web Logs during the 2005 British General Election Campaign", *Aslib Proceedings*, 58 (5), pp. 404–15.

The Times (2008) "House of Lords: Regina (Animal Defenders International) v. Secretary of State for Culture, Media and Sport", law report, 17 March.

⟨⟨ *The Contributors* ⟩⟩

Stuart Allan is Professor of Journalism in the Media School, Bournemouth University, UK. He is the author of *News Culture* (1999; 2nd edn 2004), *Media, Risk and Science* (2002) and *Online News: Journalism and the Internet* (2006) and co-author, with Donald Matheson, of *Digital War Reporting* (2009). Recent edited collections include: *Journalism after September 11* (2002; with Barbie Zelizer), *Reporting War: Journalism in Wartime* (2004; with Barbie Zelizer) and *Journalism: Critical Issues* (2005). He is a book series editor for Open University Press and serves on the editorial boards of several peer-reviewed journals.

Aaron Barlow is Assistant Professor of English at New York City College of Technology of the City University of New York, US. He is author of *Blogging America: The New Public Sphere* and *The Rise of the Blogosphere*.

Rena Kim Bivens lectures in Digital Media and Mass Communications at the University of Nottingham Ningbo, China. Rena completed her Ph.D. in New Media and Journalism at the University of Glasgow and her master's thesis, *The Road to War: Manufacturing Public Opinion in Support of U.S. Foreign Policy* (University of Western Ontario), was published by GRIN Publishing. She has published in *Variant* and *Journalism Practice*.

Ryan Bowman is a partner in Shakeup Media. The company provides consultancy for large media brands navigating the transition from traditional to online publishing. Its clients include the *Financial Times*, Nation Media Group in East Africa and the *Gulf Times* in Qatar. Ryan studied at University College London, University of California at Berkeley, the Academy of Art College, San Francisco, and Haverford College, Pennsylvania, where he was a Mellon fellow.

Paul Bradshaw is Degree Leader for Web & New Media at Birmingham City University, UK. Paul has variously been described as "one of the UK's most influential journalism bloggers" (*Press Gazette*) and "a very shrewd commentator" (Peter Horrocks, Head of BBC Newsroom). His Online Journalism blog is one of the leading spaces for discussion of developments in journalism and new media and his "Model for a 21st Century Newsroom" has formed part of many news organizations' strategy as they move to multi-platform publishing. He has been invited to speak about the model with news organizations including Trinity Mirror and the BBC, as well as at a number of international journalism events. Former Editor of *Internet Monthly* and Managing Editor of the Education-Quest family of websites, Paul has also written for the *Daily Telegraph*, *Press Gazette* and Journalism.co.uk, and has contributed to a number of books, including *Citizen Journalism: Global Perspectives*, *How to do Just About Anything on the Internet*, *The Rough Guide to Cult Fiction* and the second edition of *Investigative Journalism*. He is currently working on a book on online journalism.

Vincent Campbell is a lecturer in the Department of Media and Communication at the University of Leicester, UK, whose research interests include political communication and journalism studies.

Serena Carpenter is an assistant professor who teaches social media and newer media at Arizona State University, US. Carpenter uses her Online Journalism blog, http://serenacarpenter.com, to share information with others on the teaching and research of newer media with an emphasis on journalism. Before entering academia, she was a broadcast journalist. Her research interests include: media sociology, newer media and alternative journalism. Her research has been published in the *Journalism & Mass Communication Educator*, *Journal of Broadcasting & Electronic Media*, *Journalism and Mass Communication Quarterly*, *Mass Communication and Society* and *Telecommunications Policy*. Carpenter has won several research paper awards from the National Communication Association, Association for Education in Journalism and Mass Communication and Southwest Education Council for Journalism and Mass Communication.

Cynthia Carter is Senior Lecturer at the Cardiff School of Journalism, Media and Cultural Studies, Cardiff University, UK. She is the co-author of *Violence and the Media* (2003; with Kay Weaver) and co-editor of *Critical Readings: Violence and the Media* (2006; with Kay Weaver), *Critical Readings: Media and Gender* (2004; with Linda Steiner), *Environmental Risks and the Media* (2000; with Stuart Allan and Barbara Adam) and *News, Gender and Power* (1998; with Gill Branston and Stuart Allan). She is a founding co-editor of the journal *Feminist Media Studies* and serves on the editorial boards of several peer-reviewed journals.

Saayan Chattopadhyay is a lecturer in Media and Film Studies at Pailan School of International Studies at the West Bengal University of Technology, Kolkata, India. He worked previously as a professional journalist in Indian print, television and Web media. He has published his works in various journals. Saayan also works as a freelance writer and reviewer for online publications. His research interests include new media, performative theory, gender representations and post-colonial media studies.

Dmitry Epstein is a doctoral candidate in the Department of Communication at Cornell University, US. His research interests focus on media, information and communication technology and society. He is primarily interested in how the social meanings of technology and communication are negotiated in international policy debates. He is also interested in how technological platforms mediate the discourse, particularly when it comes to contested topics such as conflict and politics.

Rachel Gibson is Professor of Political Science at the Institute for Social Change, University of Manchester, UK. She has published extensively on the topic of election campaigning and new media in a range of contexts including the UK, Australia and Germany. Along with her co-authors she has been engaged in a Nuffield Foundation-funded study of the role of blogs in setting the news agenda.

Qian Gong is currently a research assistant on the "Political Communication in New Democracies" project at the University of Leeds, UK. She has studied at the Nanhua University, China, and the University of Leeds, Institute of Communications Studies, where she recently completed a Ph.D. on the Extended Media Public Sphere in China. She has taught at the Sichuan Normal University, Chengdu, China. Her research interests also include Internet regulation in China and its social impact.

Barrie Gunter has been Professor of Mass Communications and Head of the Department of Media and Communication, University of Leicester, UK, since 2005. He is also current Director of the Centre of Mass Communication Research, Leicester, and an Honorary Visiting Fellow at the School of Library, Archive and Information Studies, University College, London. He has written 44 books and more than 250 journal papers, book chapters and technical reports on communication, media, marketing and management topics. His current research interests centre on the use and usability of the Internet for information as well as for consumer and social purposes, the role of mass media in social marketing in areas such as alcohol, food and tobacco consumption, and the future of television in the digital era.

Alfred Hermida is an assistant professor at the Graduate School of Journalism at the University of British Columbia, Canada. He is an award-winning online news pioneer, having been a founding news editor of the BBC News website. During his sixteen years as a journalist at the BBC he worked in television, radio and online, covering regional, national and international news. His work has also appeared in the *Wall Street Journal*, *The Times* and *The Guardian*. His research interests include participatory journalism, emerging genres of digital journalism and new integrated models of journalism education. His research has appeared in *Journalism Practice* and he comments on developments in digital journalism at Reportr.net.

Gary Hudson teaches broadcast journalism and sports journalism. Formerly BBC TV's Chief News Reporter in the Midlands, he has reported from around the world — including the first Gulf War. His other work includes football commentary on radio and sports reporting for ITV and Sky. He has also worked for the US network programme *Inside Edition* and produced live television debates. He is the co-author of

The Broadcast Journalism Handbook (Pearson 2007) and author of a chapter on sports broadcast journalism in *Broadcast Journalism: A Critical Introduction* (Routledge 2008).

Janet Jones is Principal Lecturer in Journalism and Deputy Head of Department at the University of the West of England, UK. Previously she has been a television producer and journalist at the BBC, where she was series editor for *BBC for Business* and worked across a range of financial and political programmes, including *The Money Programme*, *The Financial World Tonight*, *In Business* and *Panorama*. She has written several academic articles and books on the subject of journalism and democracy, the study of the Internet and the public sphere, the future of public service broadcasting in Europe and public participation in multi-platform media.

Nicholas Jones was a BBC industrial and political correspondent for thirty years. He has written extensively on the relationship between the news media and figures in public life such as politicians and trade union leaders. He has examined the attempts of successive governments to manipulate the media and also the various ways in which newspapers, television and radio have sought to command the news agenda — a degree of influence that he believes media companies are determined to maintain online as they expand the content and audio-visual output of their websites. Jones was a local newspaper reporter (*The News*, Portsmouth, and *Oxford Mail*) before moving to *The Times* in 1968 as a parliamentary reporter. He joined the BBC in 1972 as a producer for Radio Leicester and was promoted to BBC Radio 4 the following year. His books include *Strikes and the Media* (1986), *Campaign* (1997), *Soundbites and Spin Doctors* (1995), *Sultans of Spin* (1999) and *Trading Information: Leaks, Lies and Tip-offs* (2006). Jones is currently a freelance journalist (www.nicholasjones.org.uk).

Chen Li is a doctoral candidate studying with the Glasgow University Media Group, UK. Her research interests focus on trends in the production of citizen journalism in China and how this interacts with traditional media.

Tim Markham is Lecturer in Media (Journalism) at Birkbeck, University of London, UK. His recent research focuses on the political phenomenology of journalism and the practice of war reporting, and ongoing work explores the constitution of authenticity and moral authority in new media. His is co-author (with Nick Couldry and Sonia Livingstone) of *Media Consumption and Public Engagement: Beyond the Presumption of Attention* (Palgrave 2007).

Kevin Marsh became editor of the BBC College of Journalism in April 2006. Before that, he was editor of BBC Radio 4's *Today* from November 2002 to March 2006 — *Today* broadcasts to over 6 million listeners each morning. He joined the BBC as a news trainee in 1978 and worked in Belfast and Birmingham before joining *The World at One* in 1980. He became editor of *PM* in August 1989, *The World at One* in 1993 and then both programmes together in 1996. In 1998 he developed and launched *Broadcasting House* — the first new news programme on Radio 4 for a decade. His programmes have won seven Sony awards and an Amnesty International award. He is a Visiting Fellow at Bournemouth University Media School, a Fellow of the Royal Society for the Arts and Commerce, an alumnus of the Cambridge Programme for Business and the Environment, a member of Chatham House and a patron of St George's House, Windsor. He has been a participant and panellist at four World Economic Forums in Davos and lectures regularly on the media to international audiences.

Andy Price is the Assistant Director in the Institute of Digital Innovation at The University of Teesside in Middlesbrough, UK. His main responsibilities are in curriculum development in digital media and external liaison with the media industry. He was previously Principal Lecturer in New Media at the university and programme leader of the BA (Hons.) Multimedia Journalism Professional Practice Programme. His academic interests include online journalism, the newspaper industry and new media, large website design and usability and media production pedagogy.

Dor Reich is a master's student at the University of Toronto, Canada. His research focuses on the social contexts of information and communication technologies — in particular new-media literacy, open education and inclusive design.

Simon Gwyn Roberts is currently Senior Lecturer in Journalism at the University of Chester, UK. His research centres on the role of the media in the process of political devolution across the EU: in particular, it examines the relationship between the wider media and questions of political engagement and cultural identity. Before re-entering academia, Simon was a practising journalist for ten years, writing about current affairs and a range of other subjects before going on to edit several London-based business publications. He is a graduate of the University of Manchester and a postgraduate of the University of Liverpool.

Annie Seaton is Associate Dean of Students, Director of Multicultural Affairs and Visiting Assistant Professor of Humanities at Bard College, US. She has taught at Harvard University, Stanford University and Skidmore College, and has been a Mellon fellow and a Pembroke postdoctoral fellow at Brown University. She earned her doctorate at Harvard University, where she wrote her dissertation on race, aesthetics and politics. She is currently at work on a book-length project: *Reading Lacan and Freud in Black and White: The American Scene.*

Mick Temple is Professor in Journalism & Politics at Staffordshire University, UK. He specializes in political journalism. He has published extensively on many areas of British politics, the media and political theory in academic journals, newspapers and magazines. His books include *The British Press* (Open University Press 2008), *Blair* (Haus 2006) and *How Britain Works: From Ideology to Output Politics* (Macmillan 2000). He also broadcasts regularly on current affairs and was BBC television's election night analyst for the West Midlands at the 2005 general election. He is the elected chair of the Association for Journalism Education, which represents the interests of university journalism departments.

Einar Thorsen is Senior Lecturer in Multimedia Journalism at the University of Teesside, UK, and a Ph.D. candidate in Journalism Studies at Bournemouth University, UK. His thesis, funded by the Arts and Humanities Research Council, focuses on civic engagement and citizen voices on the BBC News website during the 2005 UK General Election. He has co-edited (with Stuart Allan) *Citizen Journalism: Global Perspectives* (2009), for which he also contributed a chapter on the reporting of climate change. Other research includes articles on the history of BBC News Online and the development of public service policies in an online environment.

Neil Thurman is Senior Lecturer in the Graduate School of Journalism at City University London. He directed their successful master's in Electronic Publishing from 1999 to 2004 and continues to teach on that programme, as well as leading a new Erasmus Mundus master's in Journalism and Media within Globalization. Neil's other work on online journalism has appeared in: *Convergence*, *Journalism: Theory, Practice & Criticism*, *Journalism Practice*, *Journalism Studies* and *New Media & Society*. He is a three times winner of "best paper" at the International Symposium on Online Journalism.

Maria Touri is a lecturer in the Department of Media and Communications, University of Leicester, UK. Her research concerns the potential effects of media logic and media framing on decision-making in international relations and situations of conflict, and the contribution that decision-making theories can have in the field of communications.

Igor Vobič is a teaching assistant at the Department for Journalism and research assistant at Social Communication Research Centre at the Faculty of Social Sciences of the University of Ljubljana, Slovenia. His research interests include the transformation of journalism in contemporary media eco-systems, online journalism, media and journalism ethics, and journalism education. From 2004 to 2006 he worked as an international news reporter for the news programme *24ur* at the Slovenian television station POP TV.

Lian Zhu is a lecturer in Journalism and Communication in the Media School in Bournemouth University, UK. Her main research interests are in the area of political economy, journalism, new media, globalization and, in particular, modern Chinese broadcasting. She worked as a programme director in television and as a freelance journalist and editor.

⦃ Index ⦄

Index

China *(continued)*
  Zola (Shuguang, Zhou), 279-280, n283
China Internet Information Center (CINIC),
    276, 277, 283
citizen-generated content
  see user-generated content
citizen journalism, vii, x, 8, 34, 47–8, 81, 157
  alternative to mainstream journalism, 226
  and anti-social online behaviour, 14
  in China, 279–80, 281
  collaboration with mainstream, 173
  and commercialization, 176–7
  in conflict situations, 226–7, 230–44
    building structural argument, 231–4
  definition, 48, 228–9
  editorial control, 175–6, 229
  and exploitation of public, 171
  formats for participation, 49–51, 54–6
  growth of use by mainstream publications,
    50–3
  independent citizen media, 171–2
  incorporation, 10, 11, 12, 173–7
  in India, 297–8, 299
  joined by mainstream media, 170–1
  and mainstream media, 229–30
  moderation and control, 56–7, 58
  need for traditional media, 176
  in nineteenth century, 171
  and online newspapers survey, 196–204
  and participatory journalism, 47–8
  popularity of, 172
  power of, 168–9
  publications, 192–3
  quality of, 53
  in regional television, 173–6
  and user-generated content (UGC), 174
  variations of provision, 57–8
  see also blogs/blogging
citizenship, viii, ix, 11, 16, 17, 18, 19, 21, 69,
    77, 78, 79, 89, 90–1, 107–9, 116–17,
    120–3, 124n, 154, 180–9, 261–72,
    275–6, 280–3, 323
  basis of democracy, 170
  in a border community, 126–35
  and commercialization, 176–7
  "contracted citizenship" in China, 263
  and free flow of information, 170
  passive and active, 16
  and race, 211–12, 220, 223

  and rights, 169–70
Clifton, P., 309, 310, 312
Clinton–Lewinsky scandal, 229
CNN, 48, 117, 171, 187, 216, 220–1, 230
  iReport, 170
Coleman, S., 30, 32, 66, 77, 122, 151
Coleman, S. and Gøtze, J., 261
Columbia Journalism Review, 48
commercialization
  and citizen journalism, 176–7
  of media, 69, 169, 170, 171, 176–7
CompuServe, 2,
computer technology: developments, 2–4
Conboy, M., 83, 85
conflict and peace journalism, 16-17, 230–44
  factors influencing (Blasi), 232
  study, 234–42
Conservative Party (UK), 127, 320, 321, 322,
    324, 325
Corrigan, Tracy, 53
Couldry, N., 86
Couldry, N. *et al.*, 77, 78, 182
Coupland, N. *et al.*, 128
Cozby, P.C., 195
credibility of news media, viii, 296–7
Croen and Mapes, 17
crowdsourcing and open-source news, 10, 12,
    101, 150, 151, 158, 159, 160, 161, 163,
    164
Culf, A., 110–11
cultural value
  see symbolic capital
Curran, J., 5, 152, 169, 318
Curran, J. and Seaton, J., 71
Cyberjournalist.net, 197

Dahlgren, P.
  blogs and agenda-setting, 7
  democracy and participatory journalism,
    261
  journalism and gatekeeping, 8, 12, 182
  mediated public sphere, 68, 69
  new technology as effective means of
    communication, 277
  participatory journalism, 181, 263
Dahlgren, P. and Sparks, C., 5, 131, 277
Daily Express, 112
Daily Kos, 216
Daily Mail, 3, 109, 112

Index

Index